Smirk, Sneer and Scream

Smirk, Sneer and Scream

Great Acting in Horror Cinema

MARK CLARK

McFarland & Company, Inc., Publishers
Jefferson, North Carolina, and London

ALSO BY MARK CLARK

Sixties Shockers: A Critical Filmography of Horror Cinema, 1960–1969 (McFarland, 2011)

Frontispiece: Monster's Ball: Kathy Bates, who won an Oscar for *Misery*, presents Anthony Hopkins with the 1991 Best Actor Academy Award for his performance in *The Silence of the Lambs*. This marked the only such exchange in history between two horror film actors.

The present work is a reprint of the illustrated case bound edition of Smirk, Sneer and Scream: Great Acting in Horror Cinema, *first published in 2004 by McFarland.*

LIBRARY OF CONGRESS CATALOGUING-IN-PUBLICATION DATA

Clark, Mark, 1966–
Smirk, sneer and scream : great acting in horror cinema / Mark Clark.
p.   cm.
Includes bibliographical references and index.

ISBN 978-0-7864-6419-7
softcover : 50# alkaline paper ∞

1. Horror films—History and criticism. I. Title.
PN1995.9.H6C515   2011   791.43'6164—dc22   2004006354

BRITISH LIBRARY CATALOGUING DATA ARE AVAILABLE

© 2004 Mark Clark. All rights reserved

No part of this book may be reproduced or transmitted in any form or by any means, electronic or mechanical, including photocopying or recording, or by any information storage and retrieval system, without permission in writing from the publisher.

On the cover: Boris Karloff as Cabman John Gray in the 1945 film *The Body Snatcher*

Manufactured in the United States of America

*McFarland & Company, Inc., Publishers
Box 611, Jefferson, North Carolina 28640
www.mcfarlandpub.com*

To my uncle Marty, who kept me up late watching
Fright Night movie reruns on television,
and to my parents,
who let him get away with it

Acknowledgments

Writing this book was a labor of love, or, during its most trying moments, at least a labor of like. But it was not my labor alone. I received the generous assistance of many people whom I would like to recognize. Thanks, salutations and kudos to:

Bryan Senn, for proof-reading, fact-checking and making smart aleck comments about this manuscript throughout its various revisions, and for the loan of several photographs.

Ron Adams, David Harnack, Mark Miller, Ted Okuda, Robert Tinnell and Leonard Kohl, who provided insights and, in some cases, loaned photographs, videotapes or other materials.

The following friends and colleagues inspired, encouraged and, when I needed it, harassed me: Tom Amarosi, Anthony Ambrogio, Ron Borst, Ken Hanke, David Hogan, James Janis, Paul Jensen, Dick Klemensen, Jonathan Lampley, Tim Lucas, Arthur Lundquist, Bob Madison, Lynn Naron, Gary Don Rhodes, Bob Sargent, Jayne Schneider, David Skal, Brian Smith, Cindy Collins Smith, Gary and Susan Svehla, Steven Thornton, Richard Valley, Neil Vokes and Tom Weaver. Special thanks to my longtime friends Ken Hardin, Joe Hans and Gregory Harris, who saw much less of me on account of this project.

And, finally, love to my wife and too frequent "book widow," Vanessa, for her abiding belief in me and for supplying a badly needed "real world" perspective on this manuscript.

Table of Contents

Preface 1

Part One: Horror Stars 5

Lon Chaney 7

Boris Karloff 13

Bela Lugosi 37

Lionel Atwill 54

Dwight Frye 61

Peter Lorre 66

John Carradine 73

George Zucco 79

Lon Chaney, Jr. 84

Vincent Price 90

Peter Cushing 104

Christopher Lee 119

Other Horror Stars 128

Part Two: Mainstream Actors 139

Fredric March in *Dr. Jekyll and Mr. Hyde* 141 • Charles Laughton in *Island of Lost Souls* 145 • Claude Rains in *The Invisible Man* 148 • Laird Cregar in *The Lodger* 152 • Anthony Perkins in *Psycho* 156 • Duane Jones in *Night of the Living Dead* 160 • Michael Rooker in *Henry, Portrait of a Serial Killer* 164 • Anthony Hopkins in *The Silence of the Lambs* 169 • Haley Joel Osment in *The Sixth Sense* 172 • Other Mainstream Actors 176

Part Three: Leading Ladies 181

Gloria Holden in *Dracula's Daughter* 184 • Simone Simon in *Cat People* 189 • Bette Davis in *What Ever Happened to Baby Jane?* 193 • Mia Farrow in *Rosemary's Baby* 198 • Ellen Burstyn and Linda Blair in *The Exorcist* 203 • Sissy Spacek in *Carrie* 209 • Jamie Lee Curtis in *Halloween* 213 • Kathy Bates in *Misery* 218 • Jodie Foster in *The Silence of the Lambs* 222 • Other Leading Ladies 227

Appendix: Horror Cinema and the Academy Awards   235

Bibliography   243

Index   249

Preface

I spent much of the last six years, working in fits and starts, researching and writing this manuscript. During that time, I fielded many questions about this project. I have decided to respond to the most common of these — or, rather *some* of the most common — here.

The most frequent of all ("How's the book coming?" and "Are you ever going to finish that thing?") I trust I have finally answered.

Why write a book about great acting in horror movies?

I discovered horror cinema as a boy, through late night television showings of the classic Universal, Hammer and American International chillers. Every Friday night I sat cross-legged on the floor in front of our big console television, our living room illuminated only by the spooky, flickering light from the screen, and soaked up the *Fright Night* late show from WDRB in Louisville, Kentucky.

After a few Fridays, images of the monsters, and of the men who played the monsters, became burned into my memory: Boris Karloff's sad, heavy-lidded eyes as the Frankenstein Monster; Bela Lugosi, a vision of otherworldly grace in his Dracula cape; Vincent Price's devilish grin as Prince Prospero; and Peter Cushing, a blur of motion in *everything*. It seemed like magic to me then, the way these men could conjure up characters that seemed so alive, usually out of nothing more than greasepaint and imagination.

While researching this book, I revisited many of the performances that had bewitched me as a boy. This time, however, I watched with pen in hand, observing the actors' work in minute detail and jotting down notes about posture, gait, vocal inflection, even the way the actor listened to his fellow performers. I wanted to understand how Karloff and his fellow sorcerers had brought these characters to life. After a while, I began to feel as if I had drawn back the curtain and discovered how the magician performed his tricks. But I did not grow disenchanted. This experience only strengthened my admiration for these performers. It also made me more keenly aware of how under-appreciated the great horror stars were in their lifetimes, and of how even today actors who perform in horror films do so with little hope of recognition, even for outstanding work.

Ever since French critics first applied the word "auteur" to cinema, film comment has focused almost exclusively on the director. Yet cinema has always been a collaborative art form, and the significance of the performers who appear in front of the camera should not be underestimated. After all, filmgoers during horror cinema's Golden Age didn't pay to see the latest James Whale or Tod Browning picture. Most paid no attention at all to the director's credit. Audiences paid to see Boris Karloff or Bela Lugosi or, on a few happy occasions, both.

"The first-class actor gets scanty attention unless he or she is in a first-class film, and even then not always." Stanley Kaufman, film critic for *The New Republic*, wrote those words for his July 1, 2002, column, and he is correct. He wasn't speaking specifically about horror films, but he may as well have been. There have been hundreds of magnificent portrayals delivered in horror movies over the decades, almost none of which have received the full measure of critical respect they are due.

Explain your "Horror Stars," "Mainstream Actors" and "Leading Ladies" categories.

The book is divided into three parts. The first, "Horror Stars," honors landmark portrayals by actors whose names are virtually synonymous with screen terror. The second, "Mainstream Actors," celebrates great performances by male performers not necessarily associated with horror films. The third, "Leading Ladies," exalts outstanding performances by women, which I elected to address separately for reasons outlined in that section. The horror stars are presented in chronological order, according to the date of their first screen appearance. This is intended to lend the "Horror Stars" discussion a kind of historical arc, demonstrating how the genre grew with the emergence of its best-known stars. Other entries are presented in chronological order by release date, also to provide a type of historical narrative.

Why didn't you include a plot synopsis for every film? Why did you give away the ending to some of the films? Why didn't you include complete biographies of the actors?

In preparing this manuscript, I assumed that my readers would be reasonably familiar with most of the featured films and performers and I elected not to include detailed plot summaries. Partial synopses are included when this information is essential for detailed analysis of the performance. Unfortunately, in some instances, that means revealing the end of the story. For similar reasons, I did not include an in-depth biography of each performer. In some cases I have written brief biographical sketches, which serve as gateways for in-depth examination of the performers' techniques, abilities and limitations. There are plenty of other resources available if you want plot summaries or biographies. Besides, if you need a plot synopsis for the Lugosi *Dracula*, you're reading the wrong book.

So what, in your opinion, constitutes a great performance?

Naturally, this remains subjective. One man's velvet Elvis is another man's Mona Lisa. I employed the following elastic definition: A great performance is one in which the actor is so convincing and realistic that his or her character seems to take on a life of its own, possessing a fully realized personality separate from that of its creator. Or it can be one where the actor is so splendidly, spellbindingly stylized that you simply can't take your eyes off him. Damn the Method, full speed ahead! Impressionism and photo-realism are equally valid visual art styles, because strict naturalism is not always the best way to convey the inner truth of a subject. The same is true, I believe, of acting.

While weighing the craftsmanship and aesthetic success of the performances under consideration for inclusion in this book, I decided to exclude any performance — no matter how good — that was not integral to the success of the picture. This was a choice born of my desire to keep this book relatively short and, hopefully, readable. I further deemed that I should pay tribute to performances of historical significance (those pivotal, or at least notable, in the development of the genre), but I revered no sacred cows and I fully anticipate that a few of my choices may raise the ire of some readers.

Why did you write about so many old movies and so few recent ones?

One night at a party, a young woman asked me what my book was about (yet another common question). Looking for a simple, quick response, I said, "Mostly, it's about really old horror movies."

"You mean like *Halloween*?" she replied, proving again that all things are relative.

I freely admit that this project reflects the prejudices of its author. Readers will quickly detect my affinity for films from the classic era of horror cinema, which I date from *The Cabinet of Dr. Caligari* in 1919 through the early 1960s. The majority of the performances covered in this book date from this period. However, my rationale goes beyond personal preference for those movies.

The genre underwent a sea change in the mid–1960s. Most horror films made since then have relied heavily on inventive direction, judicious editing and gory special effects to generate chills. Horrors from the classic era did it differently. "In those days ... we relied on performance and style," says Christopher Lee in the *Scars of Dracula* DVD audio commentary.

It's not that actors no longer give good performances in horror films (they still do), and it's not as if direction, editing and special effects weren't important in the classic horror film era. But in most modern horrors, concept is more important than cast. Horror has become a director's genre more than an actor's genre. During the classic era, the genre's biggest stars were Boris Karloff, Bela Lugosi, Vincent Price and Peter Cushing. In the years since, its brightest luminaries have been Mario Bava, George Romero, Wes Craven and M. Night Shyamalan.

What do you mean by "horror film," anyway?

This issue raised its head many times in the writing of this book and I have given it more thought than is probably healthy. Some fans contend that true horror films must contain some supernatural element. However, such a restrictive definition would exclude hundreds of pictures traditionally considered part of the genre (everything from *The Phantom of the Opera* to *The Texas Chain Saw Massacre*) and delegate many watershed films (everything from *Frankenstein* to *Night of the Living Dead*) to the realm of science fiction.

I stand by the following simple, inclusive (although perhaps circular) statement: A horror film is a film that sets out to horrify. Not merely to thrill or even to frighten, mind you, but to horrify. To paraphrase Steven Schneider's essay from *The Horror Film Reader*, lightning may terrify you but it cannot horrify you. Horror films are, almost invariably, stories about monsters. It doesn't matter what form that monster takes—a vampire, a giant radioactive lizard, a serial killer, whatever—so long as it is portrayed as a monster, the physical embodiment of something monstrous, something horrific, in the mind of the audience.

I also elected to include horror spoofs and parodies, although few of those proved worthy of note. To keep from introducing further confusion, I excluded science fiction films, even though many sci-fi classics contain significant horror elements.

Why didn't you include fill-in-the-blank actor/role?

Once I hit upon this definition, of horror, I tried to apply it stringently. As a result, for every performance mentioned here, a dozen other superb portrayals were omitted for being out of scope. As badly as I wanted to write about Robert Mitchum's chilling performance in *The Night of the Hunter* or Robert DeNiro's blood-curdling work in *Taxi Driver*, I could not comfortably label either picture as horror.

Further, the number of excellent horror film performances is far greater than can be covered in a single book. Any overview of this type must be highly selective. After giving the matter great consideration, I decided the best course was to restrict this volume to the very pinnacle of horror film acting, to only the most brilliant and influential portrayals. This book was never meant to be comprehensive. It is intended to serve as a fire-starter for further critical assessment and debate.

And for the record, no, I did not attempt to see every horror film ever made in order to write this book. I did, however, screen many hundreds of horror movies during my research, supplementing the thousands I had already seen in my lifetime. Naturally, I also watched the films included in this book again before writing about them. Some of them I watched several times. All of which helps to account for why it took so long to finish this manuscript. All this time spent watching horror movies also explains the origin of another question I'm surprised I wasn't asked more often: "What are you, some kind of weirdo?" (My answer to that one remains, "Well, maybe.")

Be certain of this: There was no shortage of excellent performances to choose from. As Kaufman writes later in the same column quoted previously, the "persistence of good acting is a blessing." Amen to that.

Here, then, is a survey of the finest acting horror films have to offer. I submit that these performances rank among the best to be found anywhere.

Mark Clark
Columbus, Ohio
March 2004

PART ONE
Horror Stars

LON CHANEY

Studio publicity billed Lon Chaney as "The Man of a Thousand Faces," but that title told only half the story. From role to role, it wasn't only Chaney's face that changed, it was—or, at least, it appeared to be—his entire body. Chaney walked, crawled, hobbled, crouched, stood and leaned (or *didn't* lean) differently in every film. From movie to movie, he seemed to grow taller, then shorter, then thicker, then leaner. Only one thing remained constant: Whatever his character's age, race, disability or deformity, Chaney found a way to connect with viewers. More often than not, he made that connection by scaring the hell out of them.

Chaney's consummate mastery of craft and legendary dedication to his characters established a lofty standard for performers who followed. "Lon Chaney was an actor of great power and enormous eloquence," Orson Welles told BBC interviewers. "Certainly I've never heard a tribute to Chaney of anything like the dimensions he deserves."

Christopher Lee, in an afterword for a book of horror stories titled *The Ghouls*, wrote that, of "the actors who have played ghouls ... I consider Lon Chaney the greatest of them all, a genius in fact."

Some film historians theorize that, had throat cancer not claimed Chaney's life in 1930, he would have starred in Universal's *Dracula* and claimed the role of the Monster in *Frankenstein*. If so, the history of horror cinema would have unfolded quite differently. What would Chaney's version of the Frankenstein Monster have looked like? It's a fascinating riddle, but entirely academic. In fact, it's unlikely that Chaney would have played either of those parts, considering that he had recently signed a lucrative contract with MGM. The studio was not predisposed to loan out its high-priced star to a second-stringer like Universal.

If the vision of Chaney as Dracula remains tantalizing, perhaps this is because—despite his reputation as a master of terror—Chaney actually made very few films that can be firmly placed in the horror genre. Horror cinema didn't exist as a recognizable genre until movies learned to talk. While a few films dealing with the fantastic and supernatural emerged during the silent era (notably, *The Cabinet of Dr. Caligari, Nosferatu, The Phantom of the Opera, Der Golem* and *Haxan*, aka *Witchcraft Through the Ages*), the silent cinema produced far more gruesome crime stories and bizarre melodramas than full-blooded horror pictures. Not until 1931, when movie audiences made *Dracula, Frankenstein* and Paramount's *Dr. Jekyll and Mr. Hyde* smash hits, did filmmakers and studios first glimpse the full artistic and commercial potential of screen terror.

Chaney's most important role in the development of the genre was as a pathfinder. He proved that the public would embrace a performer who specialized in the macabre, blazing a trail that Karloff, Bela Lugosi and others would follow. In the process, he created some of the most hallowed portrayals in screen history, along with a great many other sublime, yet less known, performances. Almost invariably, Chaney's work was astonishingly good.

Lon Chaney applies one of his "thousand faces."

His life is the stuff of Hollywood legend, and many myths surround Chaney's rise to stardom. This much is clear: Leonidas Frank Chaney was the second of four children born to deaf-mute parents. He developed his gift for pantomime in order to communicate with his mother and father. All the Chaney children could hear and speak, and one of them, Lon's brother John, was involved in the theater. The two of them launched a moneymaking amateur production, beginning Lon's lifelong association with acting.

During his poverty-ridden days with traveling theater troupes, Chaney met and married singer Cleva Creighton, who in 1905 bore him a son named Creighton Tull Chaney (later Lon Chaney, Jr.). The marriage did not last. According to some accounts, the Chaneys split because Cleva at the time enjoyed more professional success than Lon. Lon wanted Cleva to devote more energy to her duties as a wife and mother at the expense of her career. Dejected, Cleva attempted suicide. Shortly afterward, in 1914, Chaney divorced Cleva and married his second wife, Hazel Hastings.

Chaney made his first film in 1913, but didn't gain popular attention until 1919, when he won a flashy bit part as a crippled man cured by a faith healer in *The Miracle*

Man (a film that, lamentably, is now lost). This success led to larger and better roles, most of which capitalized on Chaney's self-taught skill with makeup and his affinity for playing grotesque villains. His first horror film was *While Paris Sleeps*, which was filmed in 1920 but not released until 1923. In this forerunner of *Mystery of the Wax Museum* (1933), Chaney starred as a crazed sculptor.

The actor moved up from character player to superstar with his towering performance in *The Hunchback of Notre Dame* in 1923 and delivered his crowning achievement, *The Phantom of the Opera*, in 1925. Later, he appeared in several thrillers directed by the controversial Tod Browning, including near-horrors *The Unknown* and *London After Midnight* (both 1927), as well as *West of Zanzibar* (1928). He and Browning filmed *The Unholy Three* in 1925; in the 1930 Jack Conway–directed remake, Chaney made a smooth transition to talking pictures. After providing five distinct voices for the production, he was billed as "the Man of a Thousand Voices." Unfortunately, audiences never heard the other 995 voices. Chaney died shortly after the release of the sound *Unholy Three*.

Here's a closer look at Chaney's greatest portrayal:

The Phantom of the Opera (1925)

— Although preceded by memorable performances from Conrad Veidt in *The Cabinet of Dr. Caligari* (1919), John Barrymore in *Dr. Jekyll and Mr. Hyde* (1920) and Max Schreck in *Nosferatu* (1921), Chaney's *Phantom of the Opera* marked horror cinema's first watershed portrayal. With this role, Chaney charted new terrain and established signposts that would guide performers for decades.

Erik, the Phantom, was a wholly new type of screen character, one who generated equal parts pathos and terror. Audiences cringed at the sight of the Phantom, yet empathized with him. Previously, the villains of horror cinema were either diabolical sadists (such as Barrymore's Hyde), soulless monsters (Schreck's Count Orlok) or mindless automatons (Veidt's somnambulist). Chaney's Quasimodo had been a hideous yet pathetic character, but he was the hero of *The Hunchback of Notre Dame*; Jehan (Brandon Hurst) was the story's heavy.

As the Phantom, Chaney proved audiences would embrace even a hideously ugly and thoroughly ruthless villain, as long the character's motivation remained romantic. Erik's unrequited love for the singer Christine (Mary Philbin) taps into the deep wellspring of courtly romance. This blend of menace and nobility presaged Karloff's Frankenstein Monster and scores of other cinema creepers that would follow.

Chaney's makeup also proved influential. Erik's death's-head visage, at once repellent and strangely dignified, ranks among the most enduring creations in all of horror cinema. Over the decades, filmmakers have copied Chaney's skull-faced Phantom (with minor alterations) ad infinitum, in movies such as *Mystery of the Wax Museum* (1933), *House of Wax* (1953), *The Abominable Dr. Phibes* (1971) and *Darkman* (1990).

Erik's face remains hidden for the first half of *Phantom*, building suspense toward the story's unmasking scene. During the film's opening reels, the Phantom is glimpsed only in shadow. Yet, working exclusively in silhouette, communicating with body

Christine (Mary Philbin) pleads with Erik (Chaney) for her freedom in *The Phantom of the Opera* (1925). Chaney's menacing yet sympathetic performance set the template for many later classic monsters.

language alone, Chaney brings tremendous vitality and power to these early sequences, particularly the famous chandelier-dropping scene.

When the camera finally fixes on the Phantom, his face is covered with a mask. Chaney overcomes the handicap of his expressionless mask with an array of articulate hand gestures that enliven Erik's "dialogue." When Christine meets Erik in a secret chamber adjoining the singer's dressing room, he approaches her tentatively.

Chaney's fingers reach out, hesitate and then gingerly tap her on the shoulder. "Christine, it is I, your master," reads the title card. But as Christine's "master," Chaney genuflects before her, dropping to one knee. "Look not upon my mask—think of my devotion which has brought you the gift of song," Erik pleads. He lifts her and gingerly places her on horseback, leads her through the catacombs beneath the Opera House, then rows her in a gondola through the building's flooded cellars.

Erik's tenderness persists once they reach his secret lair. He kisses the hem of her gown and, with a hand on his heart, pronounces: "I have brought you here, five cellars underground—because I love you! For long weary months, I have awaited this hour, so that which is good in me, aroused by your purity, might plead for your love." He entreats her with worshipful hand movements.

Erik recoils, withdrawing physically — as if too close to a hot oven — when Christine identifies him as the Phantom. "If I am the Phantom, it is because man's hatred has made me so," he declares. "If I shall be saved, it shall be because your love redeems me." When Christine faints, Erik rushes her to a boudoir he has obviously prepared for her — elaborately frilled and stocked with shoes, dresses and even a monogrammed hand mirror.

If Erik can win Christine's love, then his "good side" will have won out; he no longer will be ruled by his ruthless, murderous side (which, ironically, is responsible for Christine's rapid ascendancy within the Paris Opera). Chaney makes us believe Erik truly wants to overcome his darker impulses. Erik seems nervously happy, playing a romantic theme ("Don Juan Triumphant") just before the pivotal unmasking scene.

This sequence can be counted among the most celebrated and best-known in movie history, and it certainly represents one of the highlights of horror cinema. It begins as Christine nervously approaches Erik from behind as he sits at the keyboard. Her tentative gestures, as she warily reaches out to pluck the mask from his face, echo Erik's delicate movements during his first meeting with Christine. Then, suddenly, the mask is gone and Erik's hideous, skeletal features fill the screen. This sight never fails to jolt audiences, but the most impressive aspect of the sequence is that Erik appears as shocked as the audiences watching the film. Chaney's eyes bulge and his smile becomes a horrified grimace. He thrusts his fists in the air in anger and anguish.

Visibly, the Phantom's dark side takes hold. He begins to laugh, a full-bellied, maniacal cackle, then turns and pulls Christine's face close to his own. "Feast your eyes—glut your soul on my accursed ugliness!" he dares her before suddenly recoiling. Erik covers his face with his hands, devastated by heartache, shame and desperation. Like all great sequences in silent films, this scene plays just as well without title cards.

Christine returns to the opera after promising never again to see her lover, Raoul (Norman Kerry). However, she plots to secretly meet with Raoul at the opera's masked ball. Erik, costumed as The Red Death, tails her and discovers her rendezvous with Raoul. Enraged, Erik recaptures the girl and warns her: "Now you shall see the evil spirit that makes my evil face!"

From this point forward, Chaney reverts to cartoonish villainy, but it's expertly executed cartoonish villainy, stylish and exciting.

Chaney crafted this exemplary performance amid a whirlwind of difficulties that vexed the film. After director Rupert Julian was fired midway through production, Chaney directed some scenes himself. Devising a satisfactory conclusion to the story proved another major problem. After shooting several different versions, producer Carl Laemmle opted for a climax built around an improvisation of Chaney's.

Flushed from his subterranean sanctuary by torch-bearing Parisians, the Phantom flees in a stolen carriage. When the carriage overturns, the townspeople converge on Erik. The crafty villain briefly holds them at bay by feigning possession of an explosive in his fist, held high over his head. But he can't resist revealing his deception to the crowd and opens his empty hand. Erik enjoys a crazed last laugh as the mob closes in around him. They pummel him to death and toss his body into the Seine.

In its day, *The Phantom of the Opera* was a box office blockbuster and a critical triumph, especially for Chaney. Even conservative critics like *The New York Times'* squeamish Mordaunt Hall praised Chaney's performance: "It is a role suited to [Chaney's] liking, and one which he handles with a certain skill, a little exaggerated at times, but none the less compelling."

Since then, the film's critical reputation has declined, although most observers still consider it the finest screen adaptation of Gaston Leroux's oft-filmed novel. Chaney's brilliant performance, meanwhile, has endured the decades without assault. In his book *Classics of the Horror Film*, historian William K. Everson praises "the eloquent pantomime of Chaney" and called the unmasking scene "one of the screen's peak moments of terror." Calvin Thomas Beck, in his *Heroes of the Horrors*, writes, "*The Phantom of the Opera* owes all its power to Chaney's inspired performance and makeup ingenuity, which manages superbly to draw attention away from acute production problems and flaws."

When the U.S. Postal Service issued five commemorative stamps honoring horror cinema greats in 1998, Chaney's Phantom was the only silent horror character represented. Producing such a set without the character would have been unthinkable. Chaney's Phantom can be counted among the handful of the greatest performances in the history of horror cinema.

Other Notable Performances

Nearly every surviving Chaney performance is notable for one reason or another, perhaps none more so than *The Hunchback of Notre Dame*. In retrospect, Chaney seemed destined for this role. The part provided the greatest test yet for his makeup artistry and pantomimic prowess. Moreover, it enabled him to play a deaf character, which must have been especially inspirational for the son of deaf parents. Chaney's triumph in this film was complete. This book won't examine his Quasimodo in greater detail only because categorizing *Hunchback* as a horror film remains, at best, a debatable proposition.

The Unknown, wherein Chaney plays a killer masquerading as an armless circus performer, ranks second only to *The Phantom* as the actor's smoothest blend of menace and pathos. Chaney also contributed superb performances to Browning's gangster opus *Outside the Law* (1921) and to the acclaimed military drama *Tell It to the Marines* (1926). Chaney offered a delightful, tongue-in-cheek turn as a mad scientist in the horror spoof *The Monster* (1925).

Unless either film is someday recovered, we'll never know how effective Chaney may or may not have been in 1927's *London After Midnight* (the first American film to deal with vampirism) or another lost horror, 1922's *A Blind Bargain* (featuring Chaney in dual roles as a mad scientist and his ape-man creation). Alas, the chance of either film resurfacing remains remote. The loss of those two pictures (along with more than a hundred other vanished Chaney films) should only make us cherish more deeply Chaney's surviving films. Nearly every extant Chaney performance is a treasure.

BORIS KARLOFF

The Frankenstein Monster. Imhotep, the living mummy. Satanist Hjalmar Poelzig. John Gray, the body snatcher. These characters are so vividly rendered, so believably realized, they seem to exist on a different plane from other silver screen bogeymen. They are 3-D creations in a two-dimensional world.

The actor who conjured up these rogues was, of course, Boris Karloff. In fact, Karloff breathed life into a greater number of fabled characters than any other player in horror cinema history. He remains the unparalleled standard-bearer for acting excellence in horror cinema.

During a career that spanned six decades, Karloff gave dozens of timeless performances and starred in more groundbreaking fright films than any other actor. Although monster movie fans often compare Karloff with Bela Lugosi, or Vincent Price or Peter Cushing, such comparisons understate Karloff's impact. He may more accurately be compared with John Wayne or Fred Astaire. Karloff's career shaped the development of horror cinema in much the same way Wayne and Astaire stamped their personalities on Western and musical pictures, respectively. As decades passed, Karloff, Wayne and Astaire became living symbols of their genres—despite efforts each made to prove themselves capable of more.

In at least one respect, Karloff surpassed even Wayne and Astaire. Those stars—like many of the great performers from Hollywood's golden age—carried a carefully crafted persona largely unchanged from film to film. With his willingness to take grotesque roles and to labor under heavy makeup, Karloff in his prime (like Chaney before him) blurred the traditional Hollywood demarcation between stars and character actors. He played leading roles and supporting parts, appeared as villain and hero in both drama and comedy. Whether headlining a top-notch, major studio production or slumming in a cheap, independent potboiler, Karloff remained impressive. As biographer Paul M. Jensen writes in *Boris Karloff and His Films*: "As an actor of considerable intuitive skill, he infused trite material with life and improved worthwhile writing with his presence."

Karloff, like any actor, had weaknesses. Sometimes, especially later in his career, his dissatisfaction with subpar material was all too visible. His tendency to underact served him poorly at times, making thinly scripted characters seem colorless. For instance, he delivered weak performances in lowly productions such as *Voodoo Island* (1957) and *Frankenstein 1970* (1958). Usually, however, Karloff masked his shortcomings masterfully.

The slender ribbon that ties together Karloff's best performances is the disarming sense of vulnerability he brought to the screen, a humanity that could not be hidden beneath any amount of greasepaint and collodion. Off-screen, he was famously un-frightening, good-humored and genteel. Perhaps from his fundamental kindness sprang Karloff's unique ability to make even the vilest villains somewhat sympathetic. How was such a quiet, affable gentleman able to immerse himself in characters so unlike himself?

Director Samuel Fuller once attributed the success of actress Barbara Stanwyck to "all those closeted thoughts to be selected at will." Karloff, an intensely private man, also possessed a wealth of closeted thoughts. Because of his secretiveness, little is known about the earliest days of his career. Since he refused to discuss his former marriages, even with his current wives, it's unclear whether he married five times or six! Karloff, who grew up in a family of diplomats, became an outcast in his own family when he turned his back on civil service to pursue acting as his profession. This may have helped him develop a deep well of empathy for his characters, which were more often misunderstood than truly monstrous.

Karloff, born William Henry Pratt, must have wondered for years if his family had been correct in warning him against a dramatic career. By the time *Frankenstein* made him a star in 1931, he was already 44 years old and had a quarter-century of bitter struggle behind him — living near starvation, working odd jobs between stints with traveling theater troupes and taking whatever bit parts motion pictures offered. Once fortune arrived, however, Karloff never struggled again.

He managed his finances expertly and, in most cases, chose his roles wisely. After *Frankenstein*, Karloff appeared as

Boris Karloff, the jovial English gentleman, as captured in this publicity still.

star or featured player in more than 80 films. But his achievements weren't limited to the screen. He triumphed on Broadway in *Arsenic and Old Lace* and as Captain Hook in *Peter Pan*. He hosted the popular television series *Thriller*. Off-stage, in the 1930s, he was a key figure in the establishment of the Screen Actors Guild. In the 1960s, the enterprising star turned his name and likeness into a cottage industry, appearing on the cover of short story anthologies, record albums and comic books. Yet throughout his lifetime, Karloff retained an abiding love of the craft of acting. He worked almost literally until his dying day, even though he could have retired in comfort decades earlier.

What follows is a review of the finest work from his storied career:

***Frankenstein* (1931)**—With his star-making turn as the Frankenstein Monster, Karloff sculpted a cinematic landmark. No one had ever attempted a role quite like it. And, despite numerous efforts, no one has yet surpassed it. One indicator of Karloff's success is that, shortly after the release of this film, a new phrase entered the American vernacular: "creating a Frankenstein." Karloff's Monster, like other fictional characters such as Superman and Tarzan, quickly became a cultural touchstone. *Frankenstein* remains not only the best and most important performance of Karloff's career, it ranks among the most striking portrayals in cinema history and stands, arguably, as the greatest ever offered in a horror film.

Christopher Lee, who studied Karloff's portrayal before essaying the role himself in Hammer Films' *The Curse of Frankenstein* (1957), offers perceptive commentary in Mark A. Miller's book *Christopher Lee and Peter Cushing and Horror Cinema*: "To create a character without really having anything to follow in terms of an interpretation and to make it sympathetic as it must be, to make it powerful and dangerous, murderous without knowing why—all these elements, if you take them together, result in an unforgettable performance which I think is unique in the history of cinema, not only in this particular kind of film but in any film."

Karloff's performance provided the linchpin for the phenomenal success of *Frankenstein*. The film's commercial triumph, coupled with Universal's other 1931 hit, *Dracula*, sired the Golden Age of horror cinema. In addition, Karloff's interpretation of the Monster as a sympathetic character provided a road map for legendary Universal monsters that would follow. Characters such as the Mummy, the Invisible Man, the Wolf Man and, later, the Creature from the Black Lagoon would inspire as much pathos as terror, endearing themselves to generations of moviegoers.

Colin Clive dominates *Frankenstein*'s early sequences and is particularly effective in the film's thrilling creation scene. But the moment the monster's hand begins its shaky, curious rise (which indicates that "it's *alive!*") all eyes are riveted on Karloff's creature. Director James Whale gives the Monster a dramatic entrance, as it backs out of its basement cell and slowly turns toward the camera. The Monster's face—with its heavy lidded, watery eyes, flat head and bolts protruding from its neck—jolted 1931 audiences and remains fascinating even today. Greasepaint guru Jack P. Pierce crafted this makeup masterpiece, carefully designed to afford Karloff a full range of facial expression.

Karloff totters, shuffling laboriously and leaning forward, like a cross-country skier entering a strong headwind. His arms hang heavily at his sides. Children and comedians sometimes parody the Monster with mechanical motions but as Lee points out, this was not at all Karloff's approach. His movements "were uncoordinated to a certain extent, but they weren't stiff and robotic at all," Lee says in Miller's book. "They were, at times, verging on the normal, but frequently they were quick, fast, uncoordinated, childlike, uncertain — all the things, in fact, they would be."

"Childlike" is the key adjective in Lee's analysis. At one point, Frankenstein cautions Dr. Waldman (Edward Van Sloan): "He's only a few days old, remember." The Monster lacks adult understanding of the world around him. When Frankenstein shows the Monster his first rays of sunlight, the creature reaches for the Sun the way a baby would grasp at a dangling bauble. When Frankenstein closes the skylight, the Monster turns to his creator, eyes full of yearning, and extends his open hands, plaintively. *Bring it back*, Karloff seems to beg.

The Monster cannot comprehend why Frankenstein's assistant, Fritz (Dwight Frye), torments him. Confused, it flails and backs away. After clumsily knocking over a chair, it sulks in the corner. When Fritz continues to poke at the Monster with a torch, it lashes out in anger but is subdued by Frankenstein and Waldman. Locked in the cellar, the creature is sadistically whipped by Fritz. Eyes wide with fear, the Monster howls mournfully.

Although he has no lines, Karloff invented for the Monster a surprisingly expressive "vocabulary" of growls and moans. Combined with his exquisite pantomime (cringing from the whip, throwing his arms up in terror), he beautifully evokes our sympathy. The Monster kills Fritz, and later Dr. Waldman (who is attempting to vivisect the creature), but in self-defense. Despite its crimes, the Monster remains, in the truest definition of the word, an innocent.

"This was a pathetic creature who, like us all, had neither wish nor say in his creation and certainly did not wish upon itself the hideous image which automatically terrified humans whom it tried to befriend," Karloff said in a 1965 interview. This mournful naiveté, touchingly effected by Karloff, lends power to the film's most emotionally charged scene — the Monster's fateful encounter with the little girl, Maria (Marilyn Harris).

The monster-child, who has endured abuse and abandonment, finally finds acceptance, a playmate. It looks awestruck when Maria tenderly offers daisies. Her tiny, soft hand disappears into the Monster's giant, rough one. Wearing a toothy grin, it follows her lead, tossing blossoms into the lake and watching them float away. When the flowers are all gone, it reaches out for Maria, still smiling, hands open, palms up (all gestures that indicate friendship, playfulness) and tosses her into the water. When the girl, unlike the flowers, quickly sinks, the Monster's arms flail in panic. It stumbles away through the bushes, its face twisted with confusion and horror. Karloff plays this heart-wrenching scene so believably that it can be difficult to watch. The 1991 restoration of the film, which reinstated the long lost conclusion of this sequence, enriched *Frankenstein* immeasurably. Ironically, Karloff himself lobbied Whale to edit this scene, which he considered too brutal.

Karloff's final shining moment comes at the film's climax. The Monster has over-

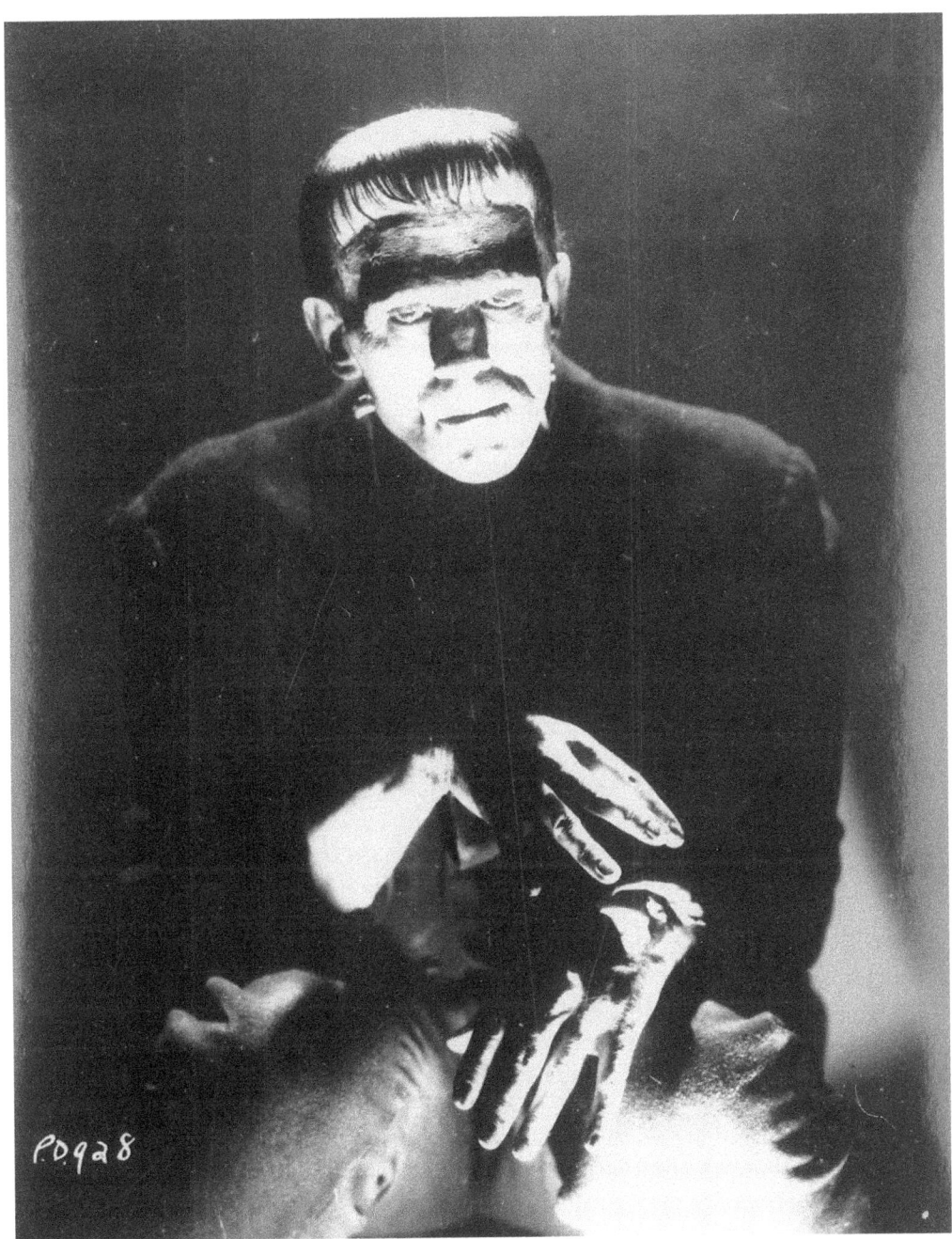

Karloff as the Monster in *Frankenstein* (1931), the role that made him a star. Could this be the single greatest performance in horror movie history?

powered Frankenstein and carried him to an isolated windmill, pursued by torch-bearing villagers. The generally accepted idea is that the Monster kidnaps its creator to exact revenge. More likely, the Monster did so simply to gain Frankenstein's attention, the way a child might commit some minor transgression to capture the interest of an inattentive parent. It doesn't turn against Frankenstein until the scientist attempts to flee. Enraged at being rejected once again, the Monster tosses his "father" off the roof.

This leaves the creature alone in the tower, however, and the villagers set fire to the windmill. Trapped inside, the Monster faces its greatest fear — fire — with no hope of escape (at least, not until the sequel). It beats on a wooden railing and runs about waving its arms, howling with fear, eyes popping with stark terror as flames engulf the tower. A heavy beam falls, trapping it. Our last glimpse of the Monster, helplessly wailing against certain doom, remains as sad as it is terrifying.

At the time of *Frankenstein*'s release, critics raved about Karloff. Many compared him with Chaney. "If Universal's production of *Frankenstein* does nothing else, it establishes Boris Karloff as the one important candidate who has arisen for the mantle of the late Lon Chaney as the delineator of weird roles," gushed a critic from *The Hollywood Reporter*. "Whether you like the picture or not, you won't deny his efficacy." *Variety* called Karloff's Monster "a fascinating acting bit of mesmerism." While other performances of the Golden Age have lost their luster, Karloff's Monster continues to sparkle. Historians and writers remain as unanimous in their praise for Karloff as their predecessors were decades ago. Critic Phil Hardy, in his *Encyclopedia of Horror Movies*, rightly calls Karloff's work "one of the great performances of all time."

Karloff reprised the role of the Monster memorably in *Bride of Frankenstein* (1935). Some critics and fans argue that he is even more impressive in *Bride* than in the original film. The Monster learns to speak in this sequel, enabling Karloff to better display his vocal talents. And Karloff enjoys several outstanding sequences, including the Monster's encounter with a blind hermit. However, everything Karloff does in this film stands on the shoulders of his work in the original. It is merely an elaboration, albeit a masterful and deeply moving elaboration, of his groundbreaking initial portrayal. In addition, factors for the most part beyond the actor's control conspire against Karloff in *Bride*. He had gained a noticeable amount of weight since the first picture and as a result the Monster lacks the eerie, cadaverous appearance it had in the first film. Secondly, since entire subplots were chopped out of the story (after it bombed at a preview, Universal slashed the film's running time by nearly a half-hour), some of the Monster's actions seem like unmotivated mayhem, undercutting the pathos central to the character.

Karloff played the Monster, rendered mute again, a third time in *Son of Frankenstein* (1939) but was given relatively little to do. As a result, Karloff found himself upstaged by supporting players Bela Lugosi (as Ygor) and Lionel Atwill (as Inspector Krogh). Karloff returned as a mad scientist in *House of Frankenstein* (1944), and appeared as a different mad doctor in the low-budget *Frankenstein 1970* (1958). He donned the Monster makeup a final time during a guest appearance on an episode of the TV series *Route 66*, where he co-starred with Lon Chaney, Jr., and Peter Lorre.

Throughout his career, Karloff always spoke fondly of *Frankenstein*, referring to the Monster as his "friend," even though the part irrevocably typecast him. Perhaps Karloff understood that whatever else he might accomplish, *Frankenstein* would endure. Chances are, even if you know nothing of Michelangelo's other works, you recognize the ceiling of the Sistine Chapel. Chances are, a hundred years from now, even if his other creations are forgotten, audiences will remember the Monster who made daisy-boats with little Maria.

The Mummy (1932)—Some argue that Karloff's second archetypal monster—Imhotep, the living mummy—surpasses even his Frankenstein Monster, since the role demonstrates his vocal prowess as well as his pantomimic skill. (The fact that fans argue over which performance is his best provides another testament to the stature of his body of work.) Without question, *The Mummy* remains the actor's most efficient performance. Though Karloff often underplayed, he never projected such emotional range with so little movement as he did in *The Mummy*.

The key to his portrayal is its very stillness. As Paul M. Jensen writes in his essay on *The Mummy* in Midnight Marquee Press' *Actors Series: Boris Karloff* volume, "By doing nothing, he manages to seem constantly in control, both of himself and of the situation."

Imhotep rises from the dead when an over-eager archaeologist (Bramwell Fletcher) unadvisedly reads the sacred Scroll of Thoth aloud. Though barely glimpsed, Karloff makes a powerful impression when his eyes, hazy as if clouded by a long sleep, slowly open.

The story flashes forward 11 years. Imhotep, in the guise of Ardeth Bey, tips off archaeologists to the location of the tomb of Princess Anck-es-en-amon. Imhotep-Bey is 3,700 years old and looks every day of it—not only because of Pierce's masterful makeup, but also because of the way Karloff speaks (slowly, in a carefully measured baritone) and carries himself (stiffly, almost perfectly vertical, with his shoulders back and arms held at his sides). His manner is delicate, brittle. When the archaeologists ask him why he volunteers such valuable information, Bey answers in his low, lilting voice, "We Egyptians are not permitted to dig up our ancient dead. Only *foreign* museums." The added emphasis on "foreign" is subtle, but it makes his distaste amply apparent.

Bey wants Anck-es-en-amon's mummy exhumed so that, using the Scroll, he can revive her from the dead. His attempt to raise Anck-es-en-amon fails when a museum guard intervenes. Imhotep promptly murders the interloper. In the confusion, however, he leaves the Scroll at the museum. Archaeologist Joseph Whemple (Arthur Byron) and occultist Dr. Muller (Edward Van Sloan) recover the Scroll; Bey arrives at Whemple's residence to claim it. There he meets lovely Helen Grosvenor (Zita Johann), whom he realizes is the reincarnation of Anck-es-en-amon. When Bey sees her, dozing on a couch, he instantly freezes. In close-up, Karloff appears baffled, dazed. When she awakes, Bey quickly regains his composure and asks simply, "Have we not met before, Miss Grosvenor?"

While his hosts prattle on, Bey remains deathly still, focusing his mesmeric gaze at Grosvenor, oblivious to all else around him. Only when she leaves does he address the matter of the Scroll. The change in tenor of Karloff's voice is barely perceptible, yet it conveys Bey's anger—and his power. In a series of brief, declarative sentences (contrasting with his usual stately dialogue), he warns them: "That Scroll is my property. I bought it from a dealer. It is here in this house.... You have studied our ancient

Karloff, in full Ardath Bey makeup, pretends to study his lines in this publicity photo for *The Mummy* (1932). Unlike *Frankenstein*, Karloff actually *had* lines in *The Mummy*, and delivered them expertly.

arts and you know you cannot harm me. You must also know that you must return that Scroll or die."

Karloff's single, marginally florid moment comes when Grosvenor visits Bey at his home. After hypnotizing her, Bey shows her (via images that appear on the surface of a magic pool of water) their past in ancient Egypt, where he had loved her—and dared steal the sacred Scroll to try and revive her after her death. He was discovered and for his sacrilege was buried alive. "Anck-es-en-amon, my love has lasted longer than the temples of our Gods," Bey declares. Karloff lifts his head very slightly and lets the words roll across his tongue like honey. As his speech continues, the pitch of Karloff's voice rises noticeably, revealing the passions stirred within Imhotep's ancient heart. Bey explains that he no longer wants to revive Anck-es-enamon's mummy, since her soul now resides in Grosvenor's body. "It was not only this body I loved, but thy soul." His hand passes over the female mummy but his head tilts toward Grosvenor.

It's a tiny, subtle gesture, but the brilliance of Karloff's performance lies in the accumulation of these minute touches. The closer you observe his work in this film, the more you appreciate how truly gifted an actor Karloff was.

Critics apparently weren't paying such close attention in 1932. The tide of criticism had turned against the burgeoning horror genre by that year, and both *The Mummy* and Karloff's performance were caught in this backlash. *The New York Times* offered the following dubious praise: "Mr. Karloff acts with the restraint natural to a man whose face is hidden behind synthetic wrinkles." Fortunately, later reviewers corrected the slights Karloff endured in 1932. "Karloff's excellent diction and controlled playing, backed by the outstanding makeup by Jack Pierce, creates one of his finest roles," Everson wrote in *Classics of the Horror Film*. "This film billed Boris Karloff as 'Karloff the Uncanny,' and his performance lives up to every adjective the Universal publicity department could dream up," Bryan Senn wrote in his book, *Golden Horrors*. Historians Tom Weaver and John and Michael Brunas, in their *Universal Horrors*, concur: "Quietly understated and free of theatrical affectation, *The Mummy* is among the handful of Karloff's finest performances."

The success of *The Mummy* spawned a long series of inferior sequels that bear only a tenuous kinship with the original. Karloff appeared in none of those pictures but did star in a British knock-off, *The Ghoul* (1933). In 1997, when the United States Postal Service issued a series of five stamps honoring classic movie monsters, Karloff was the only actor to be pictured on more than one stamp. One featured his Frankenstein Monster, naturally; the other immortalized *The Mummy*.

***The Black Cat* (1934)**—As an architect-turned-Satanist in *The Black Cat*, Karloff paints an astonishing portrait of evil. Hjalmar Poelzig provides the nexus for the film's catalogue of perversions, which includes devil worship, rape, incest, sadism and necrophilia. This is remarkable in and of itself since, despite his reputation as the King of Horror, Karloff seldom played truly diabolical characters. Here, however, he equals Bela Lugosi (who co-stars, in an uncharacteristically sympathetic role) as a purveyor of stylish malevolence.

Reportedly, Karloff was underwhelmed by the movie's script but accepted the role because he was fond of the wardrobe(!). Karloff indeed looks splendid in his snugly fitted, jet-black attire, which accentuates his lithe physique. With his hair combed to an exaggerated widow's peak, his enhanced eyebrows and obvious use of rouge and lipstick, Karloff never looked more striking—evil yet handsome in an odd, gender-ambivalent way.

More than 12 minutes unspool before Poelzig enters the story. The film's early moments introduce his nemesis, Dr. Vitus Werdegast (Lugosi), and Werdegast's traveling companions, newlyweds Peter (David Manners) and Joan Alison (Jacqueline Wells). Werdegast and the Alisons arrive at Poelzig's weird Eastern European home

Nice threads: Karloff, dressed as Hjalmar Poelzig, poses for this evocative publicity still for *The Black Cat* (1934). Reportedly, the actor wasn't too keen on the script, but loved the wardrobe. (Photograph courtesy Bryan Senn.)

(actually a weird Southern Californian home designed by Frank Lloyd Wright) after their bus crashes.

Karloff, dressed in form-fitting black silk pajamas, rises stiffly from his bed, keeping his back perfectly erect — like a vampire rising from its coffin. His posture remains rigid, all straight lines and right angles, yet he moves with unearthly grace, seeming to glide across the floor. At first Poelzig barely speaks, preferring to silently take stock of the situation.

Werdegast pulls him aside and subjects him to a litany of accusations, calling him "the murderer of 10,000 men." We learn that Poelzig turned traitor and sabotaged a World War I battle, killing thousands of soldiers and leading to the capture of many more — including Werdegast, who has languished in a prison camp for 15 years. After the war, Werdegast claims, Poelzig stole away with Werdegast's wife and daughter. Poelzig remains impassive, detached. Finally, when Werdegast's tirade ends, Poelzig responds matter-of-factly, in low, sonorous tones: "Vitus, you are *mad*." When Peter barges in on their exchange, Poelzig instantly affects a condescending grin, and the flavor of Karloff's voice sweetens: "Come in. We were just about to have something to drink. Perhaps you'll join us?"

Joan enters, tottering in a dreamy, narcotic haze from medication Werdegast administered to treat injuries she suffered in the bus crash. Poelzig's eyes seize her. Then Poelzig's black cat pads into the room and throws Werdegast into hysteria. Poelzig grins with delight, informing the Alisons that Werdegast "is the victim of one of the commoner phobias, but in an extreme form. He has an intense and all-consuming horror ... of *cats*." When Joan plants a lusty kiss on her husband, Poelzig vents his jealousy and desire by clutching a nude statuette placed in the foreground.

Later, Poelzig responds to Werdegast's accusations more fully — not with a denial, but with a plea for compassion. His speech beautifully evokes the psychological aftershock that plagued many World War I veterans, and ranks among Karloff's most satisfying monologues:

> *Come, Vitus — are we men or are we children?* [Karloff's intonation is warm, welcoming.] *You say your soul was killed, that you have been dead all these years. And what of me? Did we not* both *die here at Marmarus 15 years ago? Are we any less victims of the war than those whose bodies were torn asunder? Are we not both the living dead?*

The film's next sequence, when Poelzig shows Werdegast the preserved body of the doctor's dead wife, provides another high point. When he tells Werdegast, "I have cared for her tenderly and well.... I loved her too, Vitus," viewers can only cringe at Poelzig's warped understanding of tenderness and love. His statement may, in fact, be an attempt to torment Werdegast further, to inflict the grand sadism of stealing from his foe even Werdegast's grief for his wife. Werdegast's feelings are nothing special, after all, since Poelzig feels the same way. At best, his words indicate Poelzig has deluded himself. This appears to be the case later, when he refers to his current wife, Karin (Werdegast's daughter), as "the very core and meaning of my life" — then murders her in the next reel.

Poelzig, who reads *The Rites of Lucifer* in bed, intends to employ Joan in a Black Mass, where she will be raped and murdered. Werdegast challenges Poelzig to battle him *mano a mano* for the life of the girl and her husband. Poelzig suggests they play chess and Werdegast agrees, "provided if I win, they are free to go." Poelzig nods his head and responds, with an unexpectedly mournful note, "You won't win, Vitus."

Poelzig's prediction comes true. With victory in hand, he toys with his "guests," promising Peter he will allow the Alisons to use his car and his phone. Both prove inoperative. When Peter sourly notes, "The phone's dead," a saccharine smile spreads across Poelzig's face. "You hear that, Vitus?" Karloff's voice is syrupy with dark humor. "The phone is dead. Even the *phone* is dead."

The film's Black Mass is powerfully realized, with Karloff resplendent in his satanic robes, as he leads his followers from a pulpit resembling a mangled crucifix. As Poelzig recites Latin in Karloff's deep, frosty voice, a member of the cult shouts, then collapses. Werdegast and his manservant take advantage of the ensuing confusion to spirit Joan away.

This sets up the climactic battle between Poelzig and Werdegast. Forget *Frankenstein Meets the Wolf Man*. This is the true clash of titans: Karloff versus Lugosi. The two grapple, Lugosi gritting his teeth, Karloff wincing and snarling. Each star appears intent on throttling the other. They are literally at each other's throats until Werdegast's servant intervenes and helps subdue Poelzig, for whom Werdegast has devised a grisly fate.

The disdain reviewers held for *The Black Cat* undercut critical reception of Karloff's performance in the picture. Director Edgar G. Ulmer's dark fantasy ranks alongside *Freaks* and *Island of Lost Souls* as one of the most disturbing creations from screen horror's Golden Age. Many 1934 critics were aghast. *Variety* called *The Black Cat* "truly horrible and nauseating." No one, it seems, had a kind word for Karloff or Lugosi. Today, *The Black Cat* is widely accepted as a work of daring artistry, as is Karloff's performance. Weaver, Brunas and Brunas, in *Universal Horrors*, call Poelzig "one of the most fascinating of the pre–Code horror characters." Everson wrote in *Classics of the Horror Film*: "[H]is Hjalmar Poelzig is a marvelous incarnation of evil for its own sake."

The Black Cat features Karloff's most frightening portrayal.

***The Black Room* (1935)**—Karloff never enjoyed a better showcase for the full spectrum of his gifts than *The Black Room*. Essaying dual roles as twins Anton and Gregor Berghman, he is on screen almost constantly as one (or both) of the brothers. The twin portrayals call upon him to utilize the full range of his remarkably versatile voice and to supply a host of pantomimic embellishments.

At the time of its release, Karloff called *The Black Room* "my favorite picture so far." His enthusiasm is understandable. Although director Roy William Neill performs commendably and screenwriters Arthur Strawn and Henry Myers contribute a solid script, the project would have crumbled without Karloff. More than any other of his classic films from the 1930s, this is Karloff's movie.

He draws both characters with scrupulous precision, boldly marking the contrasts between kindly Anton and kinky Gregor. Anton is meticulously neat, even a little prissy, with his carefully combed hair and dignified, graceful posture. He smiles benevolently most of the time and speaks in soft, feathery tones. Anton's paralyzed right arm clutches to his breast like a lame claw. Brother Gregor is unkempt, his hair disheveled. He slouches and wears a perpetual scowl. Gregor barks at his underlings in a harsh, gravelly voice. It's as if Karloff were playing Felix Unger and Oscar Madison simultaneously. The greatest testament to his success is that the scenes in which both characters interact seem entirely natural. Each brother is etched so vividly that it's possible to forget that the same actor is playing both parts.

After more than a decade apart, Gregor calls his wandering brother back to the Hungarian province of their birth. Anton left home to flee a family curse that predicts he will someday kill Gregor. When he arrives, villagers mistake Anton for his brother, a despised tyrant, and nearly assassinate the innocent twin on his way to the family estate. After a short exchange between the two brothers, a peasant storms the Berghman manor and demands justice. He accuses Gregor of murdering the young women of the village. Anton's dog attacks the intruder. When the dog strikes, merciless Gregor grins and urges the animal on: "Kill him, Tor!" But tender Anton literally calls off the dogs, asking Gregor, "Do you want to *kill* him?" Gregor remains silent, but we know the answer.

Surprisingly, *The Black Room*'s finest scene isn't one of its remarkable double–Karloff sequences. The film reaches its dramatic zenith with an icy confrontation between Gregor and his jealous mistress, Mashka (Katherine DeMille). The brothers Berghman have returned from the home of Col. Hassel (Thurston Hall) and his lovely daughter, Thea (Marian Marsh), who sang a song for her guests. Mashka imitates Thea's ditty, but Gregor ignores her, concentrating instead on slicing and eating a pear. When she finishes singing, Mashka kisses Gregor on the forehead, but still he ignores her, continuing his snack.

> MASHKA: *Don't you want to kiss me?*
> GREGOR: *A pear's the best fruit.* (Karloff continues admiring the pear. He does not bother to look at Mashka.)
> MASHKA: *Every time you see her, you want to be rid of me.*
> GREGOR: *Lots of juice in a pear.* (Karloff does, indeed, seem to be enjoying the fruit.)
> MASHKA: *I won't be got rid of so easy. Do you hear what I say?*
> GREGOR (expansively): *Adam should have chosen a pear!* (This seemingly innocuous line swells with hidden menace, given the connotations of the Eden myth.)
> MASHKA: *You've got it all planned, don't you? You're going to marry her, make her your wife, your baroness.*
> GREGOR (adjusting his grip on the fruit): *I like the feel of a pear. When you're through with it....*

Gregor nonchalantly tosses the pear across the room. Suddenly it's apparent that she, not he, is the one who has been oblivious. She is the pear and will be cast aside just as easily when his appetite has been sated. Mashka threatens to blackmail him. Only then does Karloff turn and face her, and when he does his steely eyes reveal Mashka's impending doom. Gregor kills Mashka and tosses her down a pit in the Black Room, a chamber with onyx-lined walls.

Since Gregor is utterly despicable, Karloff can generate none of his usual pathos. Instead, he enlivens the character with despotic conceit. Gregor carries himself as if he's quite accustomed to ruling, and viewers have to admire his supreme confidence. After Mashka's murder, villagers storm the castle to claim Gregor's head, but the baron remains unperturbed. He leans back in his chair, feet up, placidly smoking a pipe, looking more bored than frightened. When the mob converges on him, Gregor drops a bombshell: He renounces his title in favor of Anton.

"A pear's the best fruit." The sardonic exchange between Gregor Berghman (Karloff) and his mistress, Mashka (Katherine DeMille), provides some of the highlights of *The Black Room* (1935). (Photograph courtesy Bryan Senn.)

Before leaving to begin his exile, however, Gregor lures gullible Anton into the Black Room. There, Anton discovers a pit filled with the bodies of Gregor's victims, including Mashka. "The horrible things they say about you are true!" Anton exclaims. "Yes," Gregor casually concurs, then tosses his brother into the pit to die. (Perhaps Anton would have made as poor a baron as Gregor. How much trust could villagers place in a ruler dopey enough to fall for this gag?) With his dying breath Anton vows to return and kill his traitorous brother, "even from the dead."

Gregor assumes his brother's identity so he may continue to rule, disguised as Anton. Karloff begins playing what amounts to a third character, Gregor-as-Anton. This transformation takes place before our very eyes, when Gregor looks at his reflection in the onyx walls of the Black Room, adjusting his hair and mimicking his brother's effete mannerisms. Karloff excels again, letting just enough of Gregor's gruffness seep through Anton's prissiness. He even gets in a wry joke later, when "Anton" assures Col. Hassel, "No one knows Gregor better than I."

Many 1935 reviewers lauded Karloff's performance in *The Black Room*, including esteemed critic and novelist Graham Greene. Writing for Britain's *The Spectator*, he opined that Karloff "carries the whole film, so far as acting is concerned, on his own shoulders." Modern critics have been similarly generous. Hardy (in his *Encyclopedia*) calls Karloff's work "outstanding throughout," Everson (in *Classics*) labels it "excellent," and Senn (in *Golden Horrors*) praises it as "a joy for Karloff admirers ... arguably his finest vehicle."

The Black Room offered Karloff the kind of role(s) actors dream about, and he responded with the kind of performance movie lovers dream about.

The Walking Dead (1936)

—Saintly John Elman, the most benign of Karloff's great characterizations, represents the opposite end of the spectrum from Hjalmar Poelzig and Gregor Berghman. Elman begins as a mild-mannered musician and becomes an instrument of Divine justice in director Michael Curtiz's *The Walking Dead*.

With this performance Karloff scales the pinnacle of pathos. From the second he appears, our hearts go out to poor Elman, who wanders meekly into this story like a lost kitten and becomes tangled in a web of deceit beyond his comprehension. A gang of racketeers—including Nolan (Ricardo Cortez), Merritt (Robert Strange), Blackstone (Paul Harvey) and their hit man, Trigger (Joseph Sawyer)—plan to murder a prominent judge who recently sentenced one of their cohorts to prison. Their scheme is to pin the crime on ex-con Elman, who was once sentenced to ten years on a manslaughter conviction by the same judge. (Elman, while defending his wife, accidentally killed her assailant.)

The scheme works nearly flawlessly. Police discover the judge's corpse in Elman's car. The ex-con protests his innocence, but has no alibi. A young couple, Jimmy (Warren Hull) and Nancy (Marguerite Churchill), spot the real killers, but racketeers intimidate the couple into silence. Elman is convicted and sentenced to die in the electric chair.

Karloff plays what amounts to two roles, as the living Elman and the resurrected Elman. Early in the film he is intentionally melodramatic, offering line readings among his hammiest this side of *The Lost Patrol* (1934). During a particularly bombastic scene with the prison warden, Karloff milks every word of Elman's tormented plea: "But you can't kill me for something I didn't do! You can't, I tell you, you *can't*!" Then there's his theatrical last request. "Anything I want? I'll give you something easy, Warden. I'd like music." So Elman makes his long walk accompanied by a somber cello solo. Along the way, Elman pauses, looks upward into the light, and proclaims, "He'll believe me."

Jimmy and Nancy eventually come forward, but do so too late to save Elman. To salve their consciences, they arrange to have Elman used in a bizarre experiment launched by their employer, scientist Dr. Beaumont (Edmund Gwenn). Beaumont, to the amazement of Jimmy, Nancy and the rest of the world, succeeds in reviving Elman from the dead (using a process curiously similar to the creation scene from *Frankenstein*). The reborn Elman is far different from the original version. Outwardly, the only change is a shock of gray hair. The rest is pure Karloff.

After carrying on so audaciously during the film's early reels, Karloff suddenly begins to underplay. His movements are slow, his line readings hushed, reserved. Elman's once-ebullient demeanor becomes cadaverous. The contrast with his earlier,

Executed for a crime he didn't commit, John Elman (Karloff, center) is resurrected by Dr. Beaumont (Edmund Gwenn) and his assistant Nancy (Marguerite Churchill) in *The Walking Dead* (1936). Karloff's haunting portrayal ranks among his most underrated. (Photograph courtesy Ted Okuda.)

livelier self makes Elman appear even deader. Beaumont presses Elman for information about death and the afterlife, but Elman has no interest in the topic — or in much of anything other than playing the piano.

Mysteriously, however, Elman now knows the identities of those who plotted against him. In the film's most memorable scene, the scientist arranges a concert by Elman — with the gangsters among those in attendance. Elman plays robotically, without looking at the keys. Instead, he faces the crowd, selecting his enemies one by one and glaring at them in silent, knowing condemnation. His stare bores into his persecutors' very souls. (Photographer Hal Mohr nicely enhances Karloff's performance by illuminating his eyes with pinlights.) The mobsters flee the auditorium. "I can't stand that man's eyes!" Merritt whimpers.

Elman confronts his enemies, but does so in search of understanding, not vengeance. In the process, the Almighty metes out His own justice. First, Elman confronts Trigger. "Why did you kill Judge Shaw?" Elman asks, blandly. When Trigger pulls a pistol, Elman warns, "You can't escape what you've done." Trigger tumbles backward over a chair and accidentally shoots himself. Blackstone, fleeing Elman, runs in front of an oncoming train. Merritt, at the sight of Elman, has a heart attack and falls out a window. Through it all, Karloff maintains a baleful passivity.

Finally, the remaining racketeers corral Elman in a rainswept cemetery and kill him again, this time riddling his body with bullets. (The killers flee, but their car skids off the road and collides with a telephone pole.) Nancy, Jimmy and Beaumont converge on Elman, who does not wish to be revived again. "I belong here," he says, echoing Karloff's final line from *Bride of Frankenstein* ("We belong dead"). Karloff then briefly reprises the theatrical delivery of the living Elman, as the character passes (for good) in the great beyond. "Leave the dead to their maker," he says. "The Lord our God is a jealous God."

By and large, *The Walking Dead* baffled critics, with its complex layering of spirituality, horror and crime drama, but a few found praise for Karloff. *The New York Times* reported: "There is no denying that he certainly makes an impressive zombie.... Karloff is something to haunt your sleep at nights." Modern scholars such as Everson, Jensen, Mank and Senn have praised both the film and Karloff. "Karloff has little dialogue or action to perform, and his only unusual makeup is a streak of white in his hair, but still he dominates the film with unassertive authority," Jensen writes in his biography.

Owing to the film's longstanding unavailability on home video, *The Walking Dead* remains the best Karloff performance many of the actor's fans have never seen. Although it was released on laserdisc in 2000, it still had not been released on VHS or DVD at the time this book was sent to press. If and when *The Walking Dead* finally reaches home video, a wider audience may at last discover one of Karloff's most skillful and resonant portrayals.

The Body Snatcher (1945)—Karloff once called producer Val Lewton "the man who rescued me from the living dead and restored my soul." Lewton facilitated this resurrection by casting Karloff in a trio of exquisite thrillers, none finer than *The Body Snatcher*. After spending much of the past few years in a succession of assembly-line mad doctor vehicles, and with the general quality of horror films rapidly fading, Karloff was overjoyed to be cast as John Gray, the title character in Lewton's masterpiece of psychological terror. Karloff's zeal is palpable throughout the film, as he tackles his role with verve unseen since his mid–1930s heyday.

Screenwriters Philip McDonald and Lewton, who wrote under his pseudonym Carlos Keith, draw Gray superbly. Gray, as his name suggests, is no simple black-and-white bogeyman but a complicated human being rife with inner turmoil. At least in his own mind, he is as much victim as victimizer. Karloff mines this emotional complexity for all it will bear.

When audiences first see Gray, he looks anything but villainous. He delivers a crippled girl to a clinic run by Dr. McFarlane (Henry Daniell), hoisting the child into his arms to carry her through the door. "Come, little miss, cabman Gray will carry you safe enough." Karloff speaks in the same warm tone he probably used with his real-life daughter, Sara Jane. Gray even pauses to allow the girl to pet the white horse that draws his cab.

Later, Gray makes a more ghoulish delivery — a body unearthed from a nearby

Cabman John Gray (Karloff) cackles over a body in *The Body Snatcher* (1945). Many fans consider this Karloff's finest work, and with good reason.

cemetery — to McFarlane's young assistant, Fettes (Russell Wade). "I've had some dealings with McFarlane in the past, and I've always gotten along with his assistants," Gray chimes, jovially tapping Fettes on the chest. Throughout the picture, Gray retains a beguiling cheerfulness that masks his darker motives.

McFarlane and Fettes encounter Gray again at the local pub. Gray insists on calling McFarlane "Toddy," even though (or because) the nickname galls the doctor. Gray is calm and confident as he incessantly needles McFarlane, leaning back in his chair with his head held high, ever smiling. McFarlane lowers his eyes and grimaces, bullied into silence.

Fettes pleads with McFarlane to operate on the crippled girl. At first, McFarlane refuses. Then Gray assures him: "You'll do it to oblige Mr. Fettes and meself. Maybe there's some private reasons between you and me that'll make ya. Some long-lost friends, eh, Toddy?" When McFarlane relents, Gray patronizes the doctor: "That's a good boy." McFarlane, with impotent rage, bitterly protests: "You only want me to do it because I don't want to. That's it, isn't it, Gray?" Gray doesn't bother to look at McFarlane. Instead, he turns to Fettes and, wearing his frozen smile, cheerfully notes, "Toddy hates me." This brand of amiable avarice is uniquely Karloffian. It's difficult to imagine anyone else succeeding as well with such a scene.

We soon learn that Gray is a former accomplice of notorious grave robbers Burke and Hare (whose exploits inspired the Robert Louis Stevenson story on which the film is based). McFarlane was an assistant under Burke and Hare's employer, Dr. Knox. Burke and Hare murdered 18 people to provide "specimens" for Knox's anatomy lab. Now Gray takes the same approach in his efforts for McFarlane. When McFarlane learns Gray has begun murdering specimens, not merely stealing them from graves, he immediately discharges the "cabman"—but Gray will not release McFarlane so easily. "Well, that's the end of business between us," Karloff says, his voice swells with mock sadness. "But we'll still be *friends*, Toddy."

When McFarlane's operation on the girl proves unsuccessful, the doctor laments his failure to Gray at the pub. He demonstrates the operation he performed by stacking two goblets, but Gray sends the glasses crashing to the floor.

> GRAY: *You can't build life the way you put blocks together, Toddy.*
> MCFARLANE: *I know the body. I know how it works.*
> GRAY: *You're a fool, Toddy, and no doctor. It's only the dead ones you know.* (He forces the physician to look in a mirror.) *Look at yourself. Could you be a doctor, a healing man, with the things those eyes have seen? A lotta knowledge in those eyes—but no understanding.*

Karloff underscores the disparate personality traits of his character, illuminating Gray with battling flashes of contempt and compassion. Gray revels in McFarlane's suffering, but his analysis of the doctor's character remains on-target. His futile attempt to correct McFarlane shows Gray has some degree of sympathy even for his nemesis. There's also some measure of altruism in Gray's desire for McFarlane to heal the crippled girl.

Gray "Burkes" McFarlane's janitor, Joseph (Bela Lugosi, in a thankless role) after Joseph attempts to blackmail the body snatcher. With his left hand still on the face of his smothered victim, Gray's right hand absently strokes his pet cat—again combining cruelty with kindness. Finally, McFarlane confronts Gray. He waits for the body snatcher in Gray's tiny, shabby room. "I must be rid of you," McFarlane explains. "You've become a cancer, a malignant evil cancer rotting my mind." McFarlane attempts to bribe Gray. Gray's rebuff provides Karloff with this extraordinary monologue:

It would be a hurt to me to see you no more, Toddy. You're a pleasure to me ... a pride to know I can force you to my will. I am a small man, a humble man, and being poor I have had to do much I did not want to do. So long as the great Dr. McFarlane jumps to my whistle, that long am I a man. And if I have not that, then I have nothing. I am only a cabman and a grave robber.

Throughout this mesmerizing speech, Karloff radiates the icy power that has held McFarlane helpless for so long. Yet his voice also reveals sorrow and regret, particularly in the phrase "I have had to do much I did not want to do." It's as impressive a soliloquy as Karloff would ever deliver.

Contemporary reviewers reacted coolly toward *The Body Snatcher*, as well as Karloff's performance. Despite the laurels heaped on Lewton's films today, critics of the 1940s considered these pictures beneath notice. Decades later, in *Classics of the Horror Film*, Everson wrote: "Karloff is superb. How sadly he was wasted in routine horror roles. His dialogue is beautifully written to begin with and equally well delivered." In *Boris Karloff and His Films*, Jensen writes: "Karloff inseparably combines the more superficial techniques of menace with a rounded personality."

John Gray ranks as Karloff's most naturalistic portrayal. Like the very finest performances by any actor, the character seems to take on a life of its own and exist wholly apart from the actor behind it. Many consider this Karloff's very finest portrayal, and it proves difficult to argue otherwise.

***Targets* (1968)**—Director Peter Bogdanovich may not have rescued Karloff from "the living dead" or "restored his soul" but, like Lewton, he surprised the actor with a plum role at a time when Karloff had come to expect far less. *Targets* gave Karloff the kind of project all great actors hope for but few actually receive. Like John Wayne had with *The Shootist* and Henry Fonda and Katharine Hepburn had with *On Golden Pond*, *Targets* enabled Karloff to put an evocative coda on his legendary career. Although not actually his last film (he would yet make the forgettable chillers *The Crimson Altar* and *Cauldron of Blood* and four Grade-Z Mexican chillers), *Targets* would be his last outstanding project.

Many critics have written that Karloff "plays himself" in *Targets* but that is, at best, a gross oversimplification.

True, there is a great deal of Karloff in Byron Orlok, the aging horror star whom he portrays. That's to be expected, since Bogdanovich tailored the part for Karloff. But Orlok and Karloff are not one in the same. Orlok is an irascible, salty-tongued curmudgeon—nothing like the ever-polite, unflappably likable Karloff. Orlok is burned out. He questions the value of his own work and longs to retire. Karloff was justifiably proud of his career, although (also justifiably) unhappy with some specific pictures. He never seriously entertained retirement. Even in his eighty-first year, slowed by emphysema, arthritis and chronic back problems, Karloff continued to work, spending his time off-camera in a wheelchair, breathing from an oxygen tank—all this simply because he loved to act. And acting is exactly what he's doing in *Targets*, not simply "playing himself."

The picture opens with the film's principals—Orlok, director Sammy Michaels (Bogdanovich), producer Marshall Smith (Monty Landis) and Orlok's aide Jenny

(Nancy Hsueh)—gathered for a screening of their latest schlock thriller (actually, clips from Roger Corman's *The Terror*). The film stops, the lights come up. Orlok looks disgusted. His head is bowed, his lips pursed. When Sammy and Smith begin discussing their next project with Orlok, he stuns them by announcing: "I'm not making any more films, Marshall. I'm retiring." Smith assures him that "this [next picture] is a real, new change of pace for you," but Orlok only smirks. He's heard it all before. When Smith pleads for a private conference with the star, Orlok sighs and rolls his eyes.

Orlok detests his own work (or, at least, his recent work), along with nearly everything else he sees around him in modern Los Angeles. "You're a sweet boy, Sammy, but you can't possibly understand what it feels like to be me. I'm an antique, out of date," he explains to the young director. Then his tone turns even more sour: "The world belongs to the young. Make way for them. They can have it." He tells Jenny, "I'm too old for play-acting. It's no fun any more."

Orlok swills martinis nonstop and relishes tormenting everyone around him. Back at his hotel room, he tries to cajole Jenny into resigning. She admonishes him: "You'd love it if you could somehow convince yourself you've been betrayed by everyone. Then you'd really be happy, no guilt and full of self-pity." Orlok does seem steeped in self-pity, especially after Jenny leaves and he sits alone in his empty room, staring at a room service dinner and yet another martini. Throughout these early scenes Karloff keeps his head bowed, as if he cannot bear to face the world around him.

Perhaps in his dark hours Karloff could relate to Orlok's woes. Chances are, however, that more of the real Karloff shines through in his next sequence, a lengthy dialogue with Bogdanovich that sounds as if it might have been transcribed from a story conference. It begins with Orlok watching himself on TV—a late-night rerun of Karloff's 1931 *The Criminal Code*. He grins, obviously delighted with the movie. It's *Targets*' warmest moment, and the one that seems the most authentic.

Good humor quickly deserts Orlok, however, as he complains to Sammy:

> *Everyone's dead, I feel like a dinosaur. And once I thought I'd be an actor. It's not that the films are bad, I've gone bad. I couldn't even play a straight part anymore, I've been doing the other thing too long.... My kind of horror isn't horror anymore. Look at that.* (Orlok points to a newspaper headline that reads, "Youth Kills Six in Supermarket.") *No one's afraid of a painted monster any more.*

Orlok does not know that, in a parallel story, Bobby Thompson (Tim O'Kelly) is preparing to launch an even more terrible killing spree.

In the film's most renowned scene, Orlok recites a short ghost story, "Appointment in Samarra," while preparing for a public appearance at a drive-in. Karloff tells the story from memory, with only the lilting tenor of his voice to carry the narrative. Throughout a long (two minute, 15 second) continuous take, the camera slowly dollies in, ever closer to Karloff's face. Reportedly, cast and crew broke into spontaneous applause at scene's end. Bogdanovich printed the first and only take. If, like Orlok, Karloff harbored any doubts as to his own abilities, this scene must have squelched them. He is sensational.

Horror star Byron Orlok (Boris Karloff) frightens even himself in this amusing moment from *Targets* (1968). That's Sammy (actor-director Peter Bogdanovich) sleeping in the background of the mirror-image. (Photograph courtesy Mark A. Miller.)

The film's two storylines converge during Orlok's appearance at the drive-in. While the picture rolls, Thompson shoots members of the audience with a high-powered rifle poked through a hole in the screen. When patrons begin fleeing the theater in droves, Orlok — not yet aware of the sniper — deadpans, "They seem to be loving it, don't they?" Thompson finally emerges from behind the screen, and Orlok spots him. "That man has a rifle!" he exclaims, incredulous. When Thompson wounds Jenny, Orlok becomes enraged and begins marching toward the sniper. Karloff frowns and clinches his teeth in moral indignation. His gait betrays age and infirmity, but he steps vigorously. Now — unlike earlier — Karloff holds his head high, not even bowing when a bullet grazes his temple.

Thompson becomes confused, seeing Orlok on screen and in the audience, and fires at both Orloks (revealing the young man's loss of touch with reality). Orlok knocks the gun from Thompson's hand with his cane and slaps the killer across the face three times. Karloff's facial expression looks as if a foul odor has drifted by. Thompson collapses in the corner with his head bowed, his arms and legs pulled together into an almost fetal position. Orlok looks at the pathetic creature and mutters to himself: "Is *that* what I was afraid of?"

Orlok, like Karloff himself, is triumphant.

Targets never reached the wide audience it deserved, perhaps because of the 1968 picture's eerie parallels to the assassinations of Martin Luther King and Robert Kennedy. Since its initial release, however, critics have elevated the film — and Karloff's performance — to classic status. In *Boris Karloff and His Films*, Jensen praises it as "the aesthetic climax of Karloff's career." Calvin Thomas Beck, in his book *Heroes of the Horrors*, writes, "Karloff attained perhaps the most important milestone of his career by appearing in *Targets*.... It is Karloff's legacy."

This author can only confess that *Targets* remains his sentimental favorite Karloff performance.

Other Notable Performances

Before establishing himself as a "horror star" (a term he loathed), Karloff gave memorable performances in several first-rate crime dramas, including director Howard Hawks' *The Criminal Code* (1931) and *Scarface* (1932). Despite his reputation as the King of Horror, Karloff continued to land supporting roles outside the genre throughout his career. He proved himself adept at comedy in the underrated *West of Shanghai* (1937).

Karloff's performance in the title role of *The Mask of Fu Manchu* (1932) stands not only as one of the most important portrayals of the actor's career, but also among the most enjoyable.

In *Classics of the Horror Film*, author William K. Everson grouped Karloff's work into three categories: dreary, low-budget pictures he merely "walked through"; top-drawer productions in which he "gave his best"; and those like "*The Mask of Fu Manchu*, where he realized that the roles could never be taken seriously and approached them in bravura, tongue-in-cheek style." *Fu Manchu* presents Karloff at his most flamboyant.

The actor wanted to make a splash with *Fu Manchu*, the first starring role in which he would speak. His previous speaking roles were merely supporting parts; and he appeared mute in both *Frankenstein* and *The Old Dark House* (1932), despite enjoying top billing in the latter. Rather than struggling against a script that is, to be polite, whimsical, Karloff embraced *Fu Manuchu*'s absurdity and turned the title character into a zesty, scenery-chewing *tour de force* unlike anything he had offered so far. Fu is impossibly diabolical, gleefully sadistic and possessed of a twisted sense of humor that reflected Karloff's own sardonic wit. Karloff approaches his role as he might the telling of a particularly ribald joke. His performance is a dark comic delight.

Karloff contributed another enjoyably arch performance in Universal's *The Invisible Ray* (1936) and a surprisingly sober one in Columbia's *The Devil Commands* (1941). His ferocious portrayal of the sadistic Master Sims in *Bedlam* (1946) — the last of his three collaborations with producer Val Lewton — is not to be missed.

Memorable performances from the later stages of Karloff's career include the actor's appearances in *The Haunted Strangler* (1958), playing a Jekyll-and-Hyde type of role; *Corridors of Blood* (1962), cast as a self-destructive physician bent on inventing anesthetia; *The Raven* (1963), a comedic turn as an underhanded sorcerer; and *Black Sabbath* (1964), in which—for the only time in his career—he played a vampire. *Black Sabbath* proved this kindly old man could still scare audiences out of their wits.

Finally, although it's neither horror nor cinema, placing detailed analysis beyond the scope of this book, no list of Karloff's greatest performances is complete without *How the Grinch Stole Christmas* (1966). By narrating and providing the Grinch's voice for this cherished holiday classic, Karloff co-created (along with author Ted Geisel and animator Chuck Jones) another cultural touchstone.

Karloff's reading of Seuss' playful verse is theatrical yet intimate, as inventive as the script itself. Once again, Karloff creates two characters: The Grinch and the story's narrator, and gives each a distinct voice. The Grinch's voice is deeper, raspier. He speaks quickly and forcefully. The narrator's voice is velvety. His delivery sounds soothing and warm. Karloff's gifts as a storyteller were honed through one of his treasured pastimes, reading to his children and grandchildren. He had also recorded hundreds of hours of children's stories for radio broadcasts. The Grinch's horrific elements (in the tradition of the Brothers Grimm) could only have made Karloff feel more at ease.

Karloff, made up the title role in *The Mask of Fu Manchu* (1932). His highly stylized performance perfectly suits the film's loopy scenario.

In his jagged Grinch voice, he seethes, "For 53 years I've put up with it now. I must stop Christmas from coming—but how?" By playing such lines straight, even a little snide as opposed to "cute," Karloff makes sure the Grinch lives up to his reputation for being "as cuddly as a cactus ... as charming as an eel." By contrast, as narrator, Karloff contributes a marvelous reading of the Grinch's epiphany. His resonates with wonder that Christmas "came without ribbons, it came without tags, it came without packages, boxes or bags," when the Whos begin their Christmas song despite the absence of the holiday trimmings.

Of all Karloff's roles, none are more beloved than this one, and few were more influential. *The Grinch*, with its revolutionary blend of holiday spirit and spookshow atmosphere, still reverberates through popular culture. Since its debut, all manner of kid-friendly horrors have emerged, everything from Frankenberry cereal to R.L. Stine's wildly successful Goosebumps books, not to mention the blockbuster big-screen remake of *The Grinch* starring Jim Carrey. *The Grinch* also impressed future filmmakers such as Tim Burton, whose *Nightmare Before Christmas* plays like a virtual love letter to Seuss and Karloff.

Finally, *The Grinch* provides a poetic symmetry to Karloff's career. While creating his first cultural icon, the Frankenstein Monster, Karloff was seen but did not speak; while creating his final one, he was heard but not seen.

BELA LUGOSI

All Mr. Lugosi has to do is look at people and they get either hypnosis or cramps from laughing.

That analysis comes from a 1939 *New York Times* review of the film *The Human Monster* (a.k.a. *Dark Eyes of London*). Sixty-plus years later those words remain true. The appeal of Bela Lugosi, perhaps the most divisive performer to star in horror films, remains a love-it or laugh-at-it proposition.

Although famous (or infamous) for his bombastic overacting, Lugosi could deliver a finely shaded, almost naturalistic portrayal when enticed by a savory role. Unfortunately, he was rarely so enticed, especially later in his career when the actor was forced

Bela Lugosi, the dashing young would-be leading man, poses for a publicity still. (Photograph courtesy Bryan Senn.)

to subsist on a meager diet of mad doctor and red herring assignments. During those bleak years, Lugosi fell back on his tried-and-true assortment of piercing stares and portentous grins. This made his portrayals repetitive and often unintentionally hilarious. But could anyone else have accomplished more with dreck like *Murder by Television*? Time and again, Lugosi faced incoherent dialogue delivered by delirious characters in ludicrous situations.

Even at his worst, Lugosi remained entertaining. As critic Tom Weaver writes in his book *Poverty Row Horrors!*, "Lugosi was almost never a great actor, but he was also almost never an uninteresting one." Lugosi poured everything he had into every role he ever played, no matter how inane the project — and nobody was ever saddled with more asinine parts than "Poor Bela" (as Boris Karloff patronizingly referred to him). Lugosi's unflagging, feverish intensity, more than any other asset, endeared him to a legion of cultish fans.

A long series of managerial blunders, not lack of talent, led Lugosi into professional purgatory. Lugosi, born Bela Blasko in Lugos, Hungary, was a classically trained actor with an impressive list of stage credits from his native country (where he played Romeo Montague and Jesus Christ, among other roles). He played an impressive variety of parts on stage and in silent films before making his auspicious appearance in *Dracula* (1931). In the film he reprised his equally impressive turn in the role on Broadway.

Almost immediately following that triumph, however, Lugosi committed the pivotal gaffe of his career. By declining to play the Monster in *Frankenstein* (also 1931), he not only lost a starring part in another blockbuster but also opened the door for newcomer Karloff, who immediately became a bigger critical success and box-office draw than Lugosi. This created a stunning one-two punch from which Lugosi's career never recovered: After *Dracula*, Lugosi was eternally typecast as a monster. Simultaneously, placed in competition with Karloff— and later with Lon Chaney, Jr.— Lugosi was categorized unfairly as a second-tier player.

The specter of Karloff looms over any discussion of Lugosi. Both stars, in their lifetimes, denied there was any sort of rivalry between the two actors. In fact, they claimed to be friends. And, while the two may have been competitors for some of the same roles, there's little evidence of any real acrimony between the two. The myth of a bitter relationship reached its greatest audience in director Tim Burton's film *Ed Wood*, in which Lugosi (played by Martin Landau) goes on a profanity-laced tirade against Karloff.

Along with the rivalry myth, fans have also propagated the following misconception: Karloff was technically proficient but he had little "pizzazz"; Lugosi possessed only marginal talent but was powerfully charismatic. In a nutshell: Karloff was good but dull, Lugosi was bad but fun. This popular supposition is dead wrong on all counts.

For one thing, Lugosiphiles tend unilaterally to categorize egregious overacting as "charismatic." Karloff brought a great deal of style to most of his projects and was capable of gnawing the scenery if that's what the role called for (and sometimes when it wasn't). Karloff fans, on the other hand, are too quick to dismiss Lugosi's best work, which includes performances as memorable as any in the Karloff canon.

Nevertheless, a fleeting early–1940s revival of his prospects notwithstanding, Lugosi's post–*Dracula* career became a 25-year tailspin. Lugosi scrambled for whatever work he could find, no matter how lowly the project, his desperation fueled in part by morphine addiction. In many of these shoestring productions, he provided a lightning bolt of screen presence that charges the whole production with an undeniable energy. In the process, and despite all odds, Lugosi sometimes managed to cobble together truly magical characters, even from woefully shoddy material.

The following films feature some of Lugosi's most enjoyable creations:

Dracula (1931)—"Because many people regard the story of *Dracula* as glorified superstition, the actor who plays the role is ... constantly striving to make the character so real that the audience will believe it."—Bela Lugosi, in a 1931 radio broadcast, as quoted in the MagicImage Filmbooks series volume *Dracula*.

Perhaps that explains why several cast and crew members related the same story over the years—that during shooting, between scenes, Lugosi, in full costume, would stand in front of a mirror, stare at his reflection and bellow, "I *am* Dracula!"

Cinema history has proven Lugosi correct. For millions of fans, forever after, Lugosi simply *was* Dracula. He wrote the definition of the classic movie vampire. Even today, anyone essaying the part of Count Dracula must respond to Lugosi's towering portrayal with either imitation or innovation. Like much of Lugosi's best work, it is not at all naturalistic, yet it remains endlessly compelling.

In recent years *Dracula* has gone from sacred cow to ground round. Granted, some reassessment was due. As Phil Hardy writes in his *Encyclopedia of Horror Films*: "For a film by a major director which became Universal's biggest box office hit of the year and which provided the impetus for a whole generation of horror movies, *Dracula* really isn't terribly good." However, most of the film's deficiencies are not due to Lugosi's acting but rather to uninspired direction by Tod Browning. After a breathtaking start, Browning allows the picture to plod miserably.

Unfortunately, revisionists have tarred Lugosi with the same brush as his director. *Dracula* may not represent Lugosi's artistic zenith, but writers like Tom Weaver and John and Michael Brunas, in *Universal Horrors*, greatly overstate the case by asserting that *Dracula* was "far from the best work Lugosi did in films." How could any performance, played by any actor, which had the enduring impact of Lugosi's Dracula, not rank among the finest work of that actor's career?

To fairly consider Lugosi's Count Dracula, viewers must set aside the endless parodies directed against the character (perpetrated by everyone from acerbic comedian Lenny Bruce to affable puppeteer Jim Hensen). Dismissing Lugosi's portrayal because of the humor now derived from it is equivalent to knocking Shakespeare because his plays are "full of clichés."

Lugosi's languid, stop-start delivery, paired with his thick accent, provide precisely the correct blend of the macabre and the exotic demanded by the role. Lugosi's reading of the famous "Children of the Night" speech is a fine example. As wolves bay outside his Transylvanian castle window, Dracula tells the visibly shaken Renfield (Dwight Frye), "Leesen to them—cheeldren of the night. What music *they* make."

The Immortal Count: Lugosi as *Dracula* (1931), the role that created — and perhaps destroyed — his movie career. (Photograph courtesy Ted Okuda.)

Lugosi's curious delivery, placing the emphasis on the most benign word in the line ("they"), only makes the dialogue creepier.

As Renfield's visit to Castle Dracula unfolds, more moments of sublime otherworldliness arise, as when Dracula casually explains, "I never drink ... wine." But Lugosi's eerie delivery of that menace-laced line is juxtaposed with his absurdly portentous reading of a completely innocent one: "We will be leavink ... to-morrow ... e-ven-ink." Tellingly, when Lugosi errs in *Dracula*, it's by simply trying too hard, attempting to milk chills from even the most banal dialogue. Eventually, this tendency became a hallmark of the vaunted "Lugosi style."

Another terrific moment arrives when Dracula meets his arch-nemesis, played by Edward Van Sloan: "Prof. Van Helsing, a most distinguished scientist ... whose name we know ... even in the wilds of Transylvania," says the smirking vampire when introduced. Lugosi seems delightfully smug, his voice dripping with sarcasm as he grins and bows to his would-be destroyer.

Some of Lugosi's most powerful scenes in *Dracula* contain no dialogue at all: Dracula, eyes ablaze with mesmeric power, rising from his coffin in the basement of his rat- (and armadillo-) infested castle; his attack on Mina, with Lugosi's face twisted into a horrific scowl as it lowers toward the camera lens (in a subjective shot from the point of view of the sleeping victim). Browning would recall how effective Lugosi was in these silent sequences when he worked with the actor again, four years later, on *Mark of the Vampire* (1935). In that film, Browning gave Lugosi only one line but used the actor to generate many of the movie's chills.

Lugosi's performance, considered creaky in the hindsight of many historians, possessed far greater power back in 1931. Many critics of the era, although lukewarm toward the picture as a whole, were lavish in their praise of Lugosi. "It's difficult to think of anybody who could quite match the performance in the vampire part of Bela Lugosi," reported *Variety*. Too bad Universal didn't share that opinion. Lugosi—who had to lobby for his role in *Dracula*—would be written out of *Dracula's Daughter* (1936) and passed over in favor of Chaney, Jr., for *Son of Dracula* (1943) and John Carradine for *House of Frankenstein* (1944) and *House of Dracula* (1945). Lugosi played an ersatz Dracula in Columbia's *The Return of the Vampire* (1943) before finally, and memorably, reprising the role in *Abbott & Costello Meet Frankenstein* (1948). But that's another entry.

Murders in the Rue Morgue (1932)

—After Lugosi spurned Frankenstein, Universal assigned its temperamental star to do penance in this unheralded programmer. But Lugosi's spirits were hardly dampened. He appears supremely confident here, still basking in his *Dracula* triumph. Essaying the first of his countless mad doctor roles, Lugosi is marvelous—marvelously fun to watch, anyway—wonderfully, shamelessly theatrical. He fires off every weapon in his arsenal and gnaws the scenery with voracious abandon. Lugosi even looks terrific, resplendent in period costume that includes a topcoat, tails and a cane. His wild mane of curly locks and extra-furry eyebrows dovetail nicely with his florid performance.

Critics and fans alike haggle over whether or not *Rue Morgue* qualifies as a good movie. Unquestionably, Universal's Poe-in-a-blender version of the story, featuring a beautiful girl, an obsessed scientist and a lovelorn gorilla, has its flaws. But just as certainly, Lugosi's performance is unforgettable. For starters, *Rue Morgue* affords Lugosi the most sensational entrance of his career. In the film's first sequence, he boldly addresses a tent full of carnival goers:

> *Silence! I am Dr. Mirakle, messieurs and Madames, and I am not a sideshow charlatan. If you expect to witness the usual carnival hocus-pocus, just go to the box office and get your money back!*

Lugosi delivers this introduction with his back to the camera, which shoots over his shoulders so we can see the startled looks on the faces in the crowd. From this perspective, Mirakle looms over the audience like a giant. Then the point of view shifts and suddenly we are in the crowd, looking up at Mirakle as he continues his speech. Mirakle displays a gorilla named Erik, whom he refers to as "the first man," then proceeds to forward evolutionary theory — most impressive, considering that the setting (Paris, 1845) predates Darwin by more than a decade! Lugosi smirks, preens, bellows, wiggles his eyebrows and punctuates sentences by stomping his cane.

In a bit of sublime nonsense, he even "translates" Erik's gorilla-speak for the crowd. "I am in the prime of my strength, and I am lonely," Mirakle relays on behalf of the ape. He practically sings the word "lonely." When someone cries "Heresy!" Mirakle becomes enraged — and Lugosi kicks in the afterburners, leaving even his most bombastic peers in the dust:

> *Heresy? Heresy? Do they still burn men for heresy? Then burn me, monsieur! Light the fire! Do you think your little candle will outshine the flame of truth? Do you think these boards and curtains are my whole life? They are merely a trap to catch the pennies of fools! My life is consecrated in a great experiment. I will prove your kinship with the ape. Erik's blood shall be mixed with the blood of man!*

The camera dollies slowly, steadily inward until Lugosi's face, all furrowed brow and blazing eyes, fills the screen. Throughout this sequence, Lugosi seems like a different actor than the one who starred in *Dracula*. His delivery is quick, forceful, brimming with feverish zeal. It would seem perfectly in character if Mirakle suddenly began bounding around the room, dancing a jig or rapping members of the audience on their heads with his cane.

The film's most famous sequence follows. Mirakle picks up a prostitute (Arlene Francis) and continues his attempts to "mix Erik's blood with the blood of man." The poor waif is strapped to a giant x-shaped structure, wailing and writhing against her bonds while Mirakle attempts to extract a blood sample. "Hush!" he repeatedly chastises her. "It will only last one minute more, then we shall see. We shall know if you are to be the bride of science!" Lugosi roars while continuing to struggle with the girl.

At last Mirakle gets the sample, places it on a slide and examines it under a microscope. The girl continues weeping in the background. Mirakle again admonishes her, "Hush! Hush!" He looks through the microscope, then pauses. Emotions roll across Lugosi's face. He is first despondent, then aghast and finally enraged. "Rotten blood!" He shouts, lashing out with one hand, knocking over the microscope and some test tubes. "Your blood is rotten, black as your sins!" he rants, shaking his fist in the girl's face. "You cheated me! Your beauty was a lie!"

Then, suddenly, he realizes: "Dead! You're ... dead." Again reactions race across Lugosi's face. He is confused, chagrined and (briefly) repentant, clasping his hands together as if to pray and dropping to his knees in front of the girl. But then he rises, collects himself and coolly instructs his assist Janos (Noble Johnson, appearing in whiteface) to "get rid of it." Janos cuts the corpse free from its bonds, and the girl drops through a trap door into the river. Mirakle once again thinks only of himself, moaning, "Will my search ... never end?"

Lugosi continues to mug shamelessly. After a brief encounter with the story's nominal hero (Leon Ames), Lugosi slowly turns and scowls directly into the camera. Mirakle next sets his sights on a lovely young Parisian named Camille (Sidney Fox), introduced amid the bluster of Lugosi's carnival scene. He raps at her door in the middle of the night with a message "from Erik." "He thinks only of you. There is something he must know," Mirakle says, leering at Camille obscenely. She immediately slams the door in Mirakle's face, so the doctor sends Erik to kidnap her.

Lugosi poses as the devious Dr. Mirakle in this publicity still for *Murders in the Rue Morgue* (1932), the most delightfully over-the-top portrayal of his entire career.

Back at the lab, Mirakle is overjoyed after examining Camille's blood. "Her blood is perfect!" Lugosi beams and pumps his fist in the air like a quarterback who has just thrown a touchdown pass. Mirakle's happiness proves short-lived. Gendarmes arrive and attempt to knock in the door. Then, inexplicably, Erik turns on his master and chokes him to death! Erik grabs the girl and a jolly rooftop chase scene ensues—a plot point predating *King Kong* by more than a year. But, for Lugosi fans, the show is over.

Few 1932 critics found kind words for *Rue Morgue* or Lugosi. *The New York Times*' reviewer carped that "the cast, inspired by the general hysteria, succumbs to the temptation to overact." Well, yes, but that's exactly the point. As historian Gregory W. Mank writes in his essay on this film in the Midnight Marquee *Actors Series: Bela Lugosi* volume: "No performance quite captures the theatricality, the passion, and the flamboyance of Bela Lugosi as does Dr. Mirakle."

Lugosi never looked as if he were having more fun.

***White Zombie* (1932)**—Arguably, this picture can be counted among the greatest films of horror's Golden Age. But without Lugosi, *White Zombie* would be useless—except as a potent sedative.

Lugosi's Murder Legendre remains endlessly fascinating, one of those rare performances viewers can revisit time and again, gaining a fresh insight, a previously unnoticed bit of business, each time. It may be the most intricate portrayal Lugosi ever gave, laden with meaningful body language as well as creepy line readings. No film gave more screen time to Lugosi's long, expressive hands. Much of the actor's best work in *White Zombie* is done not with his mouth, but with his wrists and fingers.

When we meet Legendre, the camera provides a lingering close-up of his hands as he swipes a scarf from around the neck of young Madeline (Madge Bellamy), who has come to Haiti to join her fiancé Neil (John Harron). The unfolding plot involves a triangle between the two lovers and their island host, the craven Beaumont (Robert Frazer).

Nothing of great interest happens until Beaumont visits Legendre at his sugar mill, where (in the film's best scene) a legion of zombies silently go about their chores, not even taking notice when one of the crew falls into a grinder! After witnessing this grisly spectacle, Beaumont meets with Legendre. Again the camera focuses on Lugosi's hand, extended to his guest in friendship. "Delighted to see you again, Mr. Beaumont," Lugosi chimes jovially. When Beaumont fails to offer his hand in return, Legendre curls his fingers in resentment, slowly forming an angry fist. Only then does the camera pan back to reveal Lugosi's seething visage, jaw set and eyes narrowing to slits. Then, suddenly, he bows his head and affects a pleasant grin. His voice remains soft, unthreatening.

Beaumont wants Legendre to kidnap Madeline and hold her captive for a month, in which time Beaumont intends to woo her away from her beloved. Legendre is (justifiably) dubious. "Do you think she will forget her lover in a month? Not in a month, or even a year. She is deep in love ... but not with you." Lugosi's tone is imperious.

"There must be a way," Beaumont whines.

Lugosi slowly rises until he looms over Beaumont. Then he intones: "There is ... a way." His voice resonates like thunder rolling over distant hills. Legendre's plan is to turn Madeline into the "white zombie" of the movie's title. He whispers this in Beaumont's ear, his hand resting on his guest's shoulder. Then, with a flourish of his hand, he produces a tiny vial of zombie powder. "Only a pinpoint (Lugosi underscores the word "pinpoint" by bringing his index and forefinger together as if to grasp a pin) in a glass of wine, or perhaps a flower," Legendre explains in a cheery-sounding voice.

After some broadly played mumbo-jumbo involving the zombie powder, a vulture and a candle carved into a crude voodoo figure (another bit of business focusing on Lugosi's hands), Madeline appears to drop dead. After the funeral, Legendre and Beaumont remove her body from her crypt with the aid of Legendre's zombies. In the film's strangest bit of hand business, Lugosi commands his minions by closing his eyes and interlocking his fingers in a sort of inverted cat's cradle. In short order Madeline is zombie-ized—and so is Beaumont! Legendre palms a zombie

Hand jive: Murder Legendre (Lugosi) carves a voodoo likeness as Beaumont (Robert Frazer) looks on in this scene from *White Zombie* (1932). No film used Lugosi's long, expressive hands more eloquently.

powder and sneaks it into Beaumont's wine glass. When Beaumont realizes he has been duped, Legendre taunts: "Only a pinpoint, Monsieur, in a flower ... or perhaps a glass of wine?" Lugosi grins venomously.

The sadistic Legendre further mocks Beaumont in the following scene, patting his victim's hand condescendingly and reminding him, "You refused to shake hands once.... We understand each other better now." Then, purely for his own amusement, Legendre commands Madeline to murder her fiancé. She fails. Neil awakens and gasps at the zombies surrounding him and asks, "Who are they?"

Legendre's reply provides Lugosi a moment nearly as powerful as his "I never drink ... wine": "For you, my friend," Lugosi reads with a surprising note of sympathy, "they are the angels of death." The line is, of course, accompanied by a flourish of the hand. Scant minutes later, Legendre topples from his castle balcony a watery grave, but Lugosi has long since cemented the character among his pantheon of brilliant bogeymen.

Critics in 1932 were surprisingly kind to *White Zombie*, but several faulted Lugosi's performance as heavy-handed—even though many of the same reviewers praised his remarkably similar work in *Dracula*. Everson, in *Classics of the Horror Film*, observes: "There is no comedy relief to upset the rhythm of his performance, and his own sardonic sense of humor comes through occasionally in lines which he delivers with wit and menace." Biographer Gary Don Rhodes, in his book *Lugosi: His Life in Films, on Stage, and in the Hearts of Horror Lovers*, writes, "Lugosi's performance remains quite melodramatic, yet for this film his style fits perfectly, turning Murder into one of the most dark, evil villains in cinema history."

In *Golden Horrors*, author Bryan Senn quotes two sources that insist Lugosi rewrote and blocked out some of the film's sequences and even directed a few scenes. If true, this could be one reason why *White Zombie* remains so enjoyable, while director Victor Halperin's other horror films (*Supernatural, Revolt of the Zombies*) are so disappointing. If the *Golden Horrors* accounts are true, Lugosi's triumph in *White Zombie* is even greater, since it demonstrates abilities beyond anything generally credited to him. Given the opportunity to develop these skills, perhaps Lugosi could have enjoyed a successful career behind the camera once roles began to dry up. Unfortunately, whatever gifts Lugosi may or may not have possessed for writing and directing remained unexplored.

The Black Cat (1934) — If *The Black Cat* gave Karloff a rare chance to play pure evil, it afforded Lugosi an even more precious opportunity — that of playing the hero, or the nearest thing to a hero found in director Edgar G. Ulmer's perverse tale.

Lugosi was the primary beneficiary of extensive recutting and additional filming ordered by Universal executives, who were repulsed by Ulmer's rough cut of *The Black Cat*. The director's original vision was to portray Peter and Joan Alison (David Manners and Jacqueline Wells) as helpless bystanders trapped in a crossfire between two warring madmen, Dr. Vitus Werdegast (Lugosi) and Hjalmar Poelzig (Karloff). The studio-mandated revisions softened Werdegast from revenge-crazed to merely neurotic. Enough of the original footage survives, however, to make it seem Werdegast is battling his own dark side as well as Poelzig. This inner turmoil makes Werdegast as compelling a figure as the demonic Poelzig.

In an early sequence aboard a train, Werdegast strokes Joan's hair as she sleeps, his eyes filled with mute lust. Quickly, he pulls back and apologizes to her husband, begging Peter's sympathy and explaining that Joan reminds him of his dead wife. Later, when Werdegast informs Joan she will be sacrificed in Poelzig's satanic rite, she throws herself into his arms, burying her head in his shoulder. Werdegast's hands hesitate tantalizingly over Joan's body as he bites back his desires, settling for a tender hug and a few words of encouragement ("Be brave!").

Werdegast reveals that he spent 15 years in a World War I prison camp, "where the soul is rotted, slowly." This offers a reasonable explanation for Lugosi's spacey demeanor and helps audiences sympathize with Werdegast as he struggles to do the right thing. He tends to wounds Joan suffers in a bus accident compassionately. He attempts (unsuccessfully) to win the Alisons' freedom in his grim chess match with Poelzig. Eventually, he and his servant rescue Joan from Poelzig's clutches. He even leaps to his feet to prevent a heavy suitcase from landing on Joan's head during that early scene on the train.

Battle of the Century: Vitus Werdegast (Lugosi) and Hjalmar Poelzig (Karloff) face off in *The Black Cat* (1934). (Photograph courtesy of Bryan Senn.)

Lugosi's crowning moment comes when Poelzig shows him the preserved body of his dead wife. She has been embalmed and now stands upright in a plastic tube, like some macabre waxwork. As Werdegast looks at her, his eyes water and his lips tremble. "Why is she ... why is she ... like this?" he finally asks, his voice torn by confusion and disgust. It's a heart-wrenching spectacle, easily the most tender, most human scene Lugosi ever played, and he plays it perfectly.

He is equally brilliant later, when Werdegast learns that his presumably dead daughter has survived. First, his eyes widen with joy. But his hopes are dashed just moments later when Poelzig slays the girl to deny Werdergast a happy reunion. At the sight of her corpse, Lugosi closes his eyes, clenches his fists and howls with primal anguish. By the time Werdegast sets about filleting Poelzig on the fiend's own embalming rack, the audience is practically rooting him on. "Did you ever see an animal skinned?" Lugosi grins maniacally at his now-helpless prey. "That's what I'm going to do. Flay the skin from your body, slowly, bit by bit!" Here Lugosi returns to his trademark, off-the-deep-end histrionics, but after such a calculated build-up, the act works.

The heroic flourishes of Lugosi's character add a poignant note of irony to the film's climax. Peter shoots Werdegast because he mistakenly thinks he is attacking Joan. "You fool," Lugosi seethes, "I was only trying to help you!"

Modern critics have praised *The Black Cat* and Lugosi's performance in it, even though contemporary reviewers did not. "Lugosi rises to the challenge and delivers one of the best performances of his career," Senn writes in *Golden Horrors*. "Lugosi uses subtleties of language and gesture often lacking in his later work," Rhodes observes in *Lugosi*.

Perhaps the most striking thing about Lugosi's performance in *The Black Cat* is its dearth of Lugosi-isms. He completed the film's 66 minutes with no mesmeric stares and without a single bombastic reading of an innocuous line. Especially when compared with his more theatrical style in *Dracula* and *White Zombie*, Lugosi appears loose, relaxed. He didn't conquer Karloff in this picture, but he held his own against one of his rival's greatest performances.

Son of Frankenstein (1939)

—This is Lugosi's finest hour (and 39 minutes).

His performance as the broken-necked Ygor marked the only time in their nine collaborations that Lugosi bested Karloff, whose Monster is reduced to little better than a walking prop. While stealing the show from Karloff and fellow luminaries Basil Rathbone and Lionel Atwill, Lugosi ascended to a singular place of honor—having starred in the films that launched both great horror cycles of the Golden Age (*Dracula* in 1931 and *Son of Frankenstein* in 1939). Plus, the success of *Son* helped bring monster movies back from the dead, creating greater demand for Lugosi's services.

Son remains one of the very few Lugosi movies it's possible to view and not think of the Lugosi character as, well, Lugosi. That's partially because this was one of Lugosi's rare appearances in disfiguring makeup. The short list of other such performances includes Paramount's *Island of Lost Souls* (1933), where he appeared as the half-man, half-ape Sayer of the Law, and *Frankenstein Meets the Wolf Man* (1943), where he finally played the Frankenstein Monster. Shaggy, scarred, bearded, hunchbacked and cursed with a mouth full of teeth only an impoverished orthodontist could love, Ygor ranks among makeup maestro Jack P. Pierce's greatest creations. It's more than makeup, however, that makes Lugosi unrecognizable. He submerges himself in the character, even altering his trademark delivery. His pidgin-German accent ("FRANK'n-shtine") isn't convincing, but he doesn't reduce the English language to his usual Hungarian goulash.

Appropriately enough, Ygor is the first character viewers meet as *Son* opens. In a long dolly shot, the camera pans from the gates of decrepit Castle Frankenstein up to a broken window. Behind panes of jagged glass lurks Ygor, leering at children playing on the street below. After creeping around in the background for a reel or so, Ygor announces his presence to Wolf von Frankenstein (Basil Rathbone) by attempting to drop a boulder on the young doctor's head. Ygor introduces himself and explains that he once was hanged, yet lived to tell the tale. "Why did they hang you?" Wolf asks. "Because I stole bodies ... *they said*." Lugosi's timing is flawless, making it clear that Ygor's half-hearted denial ("*they said*") is a mere afterthought.

Next, Ygor gives the new master of the castle a tour which concludes in the family crypt. There, Wolf is aghast to discover the Monster (Karloff) lying comatose on a concrete slab. One of the cleverest exchanges of Universal's entire *Frankenstein* series ensues:

YGOR: *Heinrich Frankenstein vas your father, too.*
WOLF (sneering at the monster): *You mean to imply, then, that is my brother?*
YGOR: *But his mother vas the lightning.*

Ygor tempts Wolf into reviving the Monster and then, without the doctor's knowledge, sends the creature out to kill the surviving members of the jury that sentenced him to hang. Wolf wants to replace the Monster's criminal brain with a new one, but Ygor won't let the doctor near the creature after its revival. "You not touch him again!" Ygor barks, his jealousy betraying a warm relationship between himself and the Monster.

Lugosi sketches Ygor so vividly and passionately, it becomes impossible not to care for him, even though the character's actions are as detestable as those of any Universal villain. There's tremen-

"Old Ygor": Lugosi wore elaborate makeup for *Son of Frankenstein* (1939) and delivered his best performance.

dous authenticity to Lugosi's portrayal. At this stage of his career, Lugosi certainly understood what Ygor must have suffered when left for dead. Perhaps he imagined the town elders were studio executives! While usually assigned purely malevolent roles, here Lugosi clearly demonstrates that, like Karloff, he could create a sympathetic monster.

Ygor doesn't survive for the film's finale — he takes four bullets in the chest from Frankenstein after staging a second attempt on the doctor's life. Yet, inexplicably, he returns unharmed in *The Ghost of Frankenstein* (1942). *Ghost*, lamentably, would mark the final appearance of Ygor. Though not up to the level of the first three Universal *Frankenstein* installments, *Ghost* remains an enjoyable romp, and it gave Lugosi a chance to act circles around his other major rival, Chaney, Jr., who played the Monster.

While *Son of Frankenstein* earned favorable notices from many 1939 critics, few singled out Lugosi for praise. Recent film scholarship has served him better. "The director left Lugosi on his own to develop the character, which turned out to be a prime example of Lugosi's versatility," historian Rhodes writes in *Lugosi*. Weaver, Brunas and Brunas, in *Universal Horrors*, write that Lugosi "gave the performance of his career."

It may not be entirely fair to say that Lugosi stole *Son of Frankenstein* from Karloff. The script, starting a trend that would continue throughout the rest of the series, focused more on Frankenstein (the scientist) and less on the Monster. Karloff had no lines (odd, since the monster had learned to speak in *Bride of Frankenstein*) and little to do except lurch about and strangle villagers. Nevertheless, Lugosi must have relished his triumph.

Abbott & Costello Meet Frankenstein (1948)

—This is where Universal's "monster rallies," which began with *Frankenstein Meets the Wolf Man* (1943) and grew sillier as they progressed, reached their logical endpoint. *Meet Frankenstein* remains the most enjoyable monster rally of all, with its horror played straight and its comedy genuinely funny. Best of all, it allowed Lugosi—after an agonizing wait of nearly two decades—to reprise his most famous role on film.

Meet Frankenstein showcases Lugosi's underrated comic timing. He appeared in more than a dozen comedies in his career, but usually with funny men of dubious caliber, such as the irritating East Side Kids (*Spooks Run Wild* [1941] and *Ghosts on the Loose* [1943]), the even more annoying Ritz Brothers (*The Gorilla*, 1939), and the unspeakably irksome Duke Mitchell and Sammy Petrillo (*Bela Lugosi Meets a Brooklyn Gorilla*, 1952). Playing opposite Abbott and Costello, one of Hollywood's greatest comedy teams, Lugosi flourished.

Lugosi erases many of the flaws from his first turn as Count Dracula and appears more at ease and in control here than in any outing since *Son of Frankenstein*. At age 66, Lugosi did not cut the suave figure he once had, but his delivery was smoother and more natural. This was essential because an unintentionally humorous performance (like the kind he gave repeatedly during his tenure at Monogram Pictures) would have sunk *Meet Frankenstein*. The movie's magic comes from the way its horror and humor play off one another, each strengthening the other by contrast. It works because Lugosi and co-stars Chaney, Jr. (the Wolf Man), and Glenn Strange (the Frankenstein Monster) proceed as if nobody told them this was a comedy.

His billing doesn't indicate it, but Lugosi landed the film's pivotal role. While clearly subordinate to Abbott and Costello, Lugosi's Dracula provides the catalyst for nearly all the action in the film, which more accurately might have been titled *Abbott and Costello Meet Dracula*. Bud Abbott and Lou Costello play Chick and Wilbur, bumbling baggage handlers who "meet" the Frankenstein Monster and Dracula when they deliver two new exhibits to Mr. McDougal's House of Horrors.

Using his hypnotic powers, the Count has made a servant of the Monster and plans to bring the creature back to full strength with the aid of an unscrupulous scientist, Sandra (Lenore Aubert), and her unwitting assistant, Prof. Stevens (Charles Bradstreet). (This film's rendition of Dracula is equal parts vampire and mad doctor.) "I do not want to repeat Frankenstein's error," Dracula warns. "This time the Monster must have no will of his own, no fiendish intellect to oppose his master." Sandra assures the count she has found the perfect brain—Wilbur's.

Meanwhile, Joan (Jane Randolph), an attractive insurance investigator, cozies up to Wilbur to learn the whereabouts of McDougal's missing exhibits. Things get more complicated when Larry (Wolf Man) Talbot shows up and promptly asks

"Young blood and brains." Dr. Lejos, a.k.a. Dracula (Lugosi), pays his compliments to Wilbur (Lou Costello) in *Abbott & Costello Meet Frankenstein* (1948). The film showcased Lugosi's under-appreciated comedic timing.

Wilbur to lock him away before the moon rises. Dracula reenters the picture the next day when Chick, Wilbur, Sandra and Joan attend a costume ball. Chick and Wilbur collect Sandra from the island castle where she and Prof. Stevens work, along with "Dr. Lejos" (Dracula incognito). "Lejos" jovially pats Wilbur on the head and tells him, "What we need today is young blood—and brains." Lugosi grins. For once, he is in on the joke. We laugh with Lugosi instead of at him.

Moments later, Sandra grows nervous and balks at going through with the plan. "I warn you, Sandra, I am accustomed to having my orders obeyed," he warns, convincingly. When threats don't work, Dracula mesmerizes the woman and turns her into a vampire "bride." Lugosi's stock hypnotic stare, replete with bulging eyes and wickedly posed fingers, hadn't looked this menacing since 1931.

At the party, Talbot changes into the Wolf Man and attacks McDougal, an offense for which Chick gets the blame. In the confusion, Dracula corrals Wilbur and entrances Joan, just for good measure. The next day, Chick and Talbot join forces and attempt to free Wilbur and Joan, foil Dracula and prove Chick's innocence. A melee ensues, with Dracula battling the Wolf Man (at one point tossing a potted plant at the lycanthrope) while the now-revived monster terrorizes Chick and Wilbur. Throughout this physically demanding comic climax, Lugosi displays vigor unseen in years.

Lugosi's standout performance contributed significantly to the success of the film, which proved a tremendous hit. It revived the flagging star status of Abbott and Costello and spawned a (too) long series of sequels. Lugosiphiles can revel in the knowledge that Karloff's two later appearances with Abbott and Costello, in *Abbott & Costello Meet the Killer, Boris Karloff* and *Abbott & Costello Meet Dr. Jekyll and Mr. Hyde*, combined aren't half as entertaining as *Meet Frankenstein*. Financial success didn't translate into favorable reviews, for the movie or for Lugosi. For years, *Meet Frankenstein* languished among the most underrated performances of Lugosi's career. That was corrected, to some degree, when in 2000 the American Film Institute named *Meet Frankenstein* one of 100 funniest American movies of all time.

This was Lugosi's final great performance. Despite the success of *Meet Frankenstein*, Lugosi's career quickly resumed its power dive into oblivion. The former star neared destitution and continued his battle with morphine addiction. Lugosi took his pathetic final bows in a series of atrocious productions by hapless would-be auteur Edward D. Wood, Jr. Just eight years after removing his Dracula cape when *Meet Frankenstein* wrapped, he would wear it one final time — for his burial in 1956.

Other Notable Performances

In *The Wolf Man* (1941), Lugosi plays the gypsy who passes the curse of the werewolf on to Larry Talbot (Chaney, Jr.). Though he appears in just one scene, he manages to elicit tremendous sympathy for his lycanthropic plight. Significantly to the success of the film, that sympathy transfers immediately to Talbot. Unfortunately, his role in *The Wolf Man* — like his outstanding supporting performances in *Island of Lost Souls* (1933) and *Mark of the Vampire* (1935) — are simply too brief to rank among his most significant work.

The Raven (1935) runs on a high-octane performance by Lugosi as Dr. Vollin, a crazed physician obsessed with Edgar Allan Poe. As in *Rue Morgue*, Lugosi hams with remorseless abandon. The actor is especially fun to watch as the movie nears its climax and Dr. Vollin exacts revenge on his perceived enemies with Poe-inspired torture devices. "Poe, you are avenged!" he froths.

Lugosi contributed unusually restrained performances to *Mystery of the Mary Celeste* (a.k.a. *The Phantom Ship*) (1936) and *Dark Eyes of London* (a.k.a. *The Human Monster*) (1939). The former picture contains perhaps the only Lugosi performance that can be categorized as subtle. His role is only a supporting one, but he is unusually convincing. The film was an early near-horror effort by future fright factory Hammer Films. Sadly, this marked the only time Lugosi worked with that studio's renowned artisans. It's probably not a coincidence that Lugosi gave an extraordinarily good performance in what ranks (for him) as an extraordinarily good production.

The actor returned to Great Britain three years later to make *The Human Monster*. Like *Mary Celeste*, *The Human Monster* offered a more plausible scenario and higher production values than most Lugosi vehicles. Once again, Lugosi responded with a quietly effective portrayal (an unfavorable notice from *The New York Times* notwithstanding). As Rhodes writes in *Lugosi*, the actor performs "in a very understated fashion, with the role becoming one of his best in the horror genre." Lugosi's successes in these films can only lead observers to wonder what the actor might have accomplished if he had been able to return to A-list productions instead of wasting away in no-budget grindhouse fodder.

Inexorably, however, that's where Lugosi was bound. Reserve then, a special place of honor in Lugosi's pantheon of prime performances for *The Devil Bat* (a.k.a. *Killer Bats*) (1940), since this film represents his finest effort for a Poverty Row studio (namely, Producers Releasing Corporation). For any other actor, that would be faint praise indeed, but Lugosi was the king of Poverty Row. He made ten films for lowly Monogram alone, and appeared in more than a dozen independent productions from the lower echelons. Many devotees find pictures such as *Invisible Ghost* (1941), *Voodoo Man* (1944) and even *The Ape Man* (1943) among Lugosi's most enjoyable vehicles, if only because these pictures afforded the star plenty of screen time to rifle through his reliable bag of tricks.

In *The Devil Bat*, Lugosi plays Dr. Carruthers, a dizzy scientist with a grudge against the owners of the perfume company that employs him. When he's not dreaming up new colognes, Carruthers uses "glandular stimulation through electrical process" to turn normal-sized bats into giant, bloodthirsty monsters. As he commands his winged minions, "You will strike ... to kill!" Lugosi gnashes his teeth in a lunatic grin, his eyes bulging with bloodlust.

The actor performs with unwarranted conviction throughout this preposterous production. The film's finest moment comes with a long exchange between Carruthers and Henry Morton (Guy Usher), his boss and nemesis. Scenario and dialogue have uncanny parallels to Lugosi's career. Carruthers' bitterness toward his rivals stems from a poor choice he made voluntarily, just as Lugosi's own misfortunes could be traced to his *Frankenstein* misstep. Fans gush with praise for Lugosi's "forsaken jungle hell" speech from *Bride of the Monster* (1955), which was recreated for and thus immortalized by director Tim Burton's *Ed Wood*. But Lugosi's work in this scene is just as emotionally charged.

Morton boasts that his company posted a $1 million annual profit: "Not bad, eh?, when you remember what we're built on — a mere $10,000 for your formula. You shouldn't have demanded all cash, Doc. You should have ridden along with us. Then you'd be rich, too. But then, you've had a lot of fun in your laboratory, with your experiments, dreaming up something new. You're a dreamer, Doc. Too much money's bad for dreamers."

Carruthers squirms and grimaces during Morton's patronizing babble, then lashes back: "So you try to pay me with flattery, saying I am a dreamer. Well, I *do* dream. Dreams that you could never guess!"

Repeatedly throughout his waning years, Lugosi was placed in one demeaning situation after another. It's fun to imagine that Carruthers' lines here speak for Lugosi himself—proud, still confident in his own ability to make the big comeback he felt was only that one, elusive good role away.

LIONEL ATWILL

Lionel Atwill deserves better.

Beyond the orbit of classic movie conventions, his films are seldom screened. Outside the hearts and minds of terror cinema buffs, Atwill is all but forgotten. Yet, in the 1930s and early '40s, Atwill ranked among Hollywood's supreme bogeymen. Off-screen, he was regarded as a gifted actor and a colorful personality. On screen, Atwill personified debonair villainy, whether headlining in gaudy horror shows such as *Mystery of the Wax Museum* or contributing supporting performances to mainstream features such as *Captain Blood*.

The British-born, stage-trained Atwill established himself as a respected leading man on the stages of both London and Broadway. Prophetically, he landed the starring role in a 1917 production of the Jack the Ripper play *The Lodger*. After alternating between film and theatrical projects for several years, Atwill turned his back on his thriving stage career to pursue film full-time in the early 1930s. Perhaps the star felt more at home in the freewheeling, anything-goes lifestyle of early Hollywood than in the stodgy drawing rooms of the theatrical circuit.

During the next decade, Atwill reinvented himself as one of cinema's foremost purveyors of elegant malevolence. While capable of finely shaded, naturalistic portrayals, Atwill was an unabashed ham who knew every scene-stealing trick in the book. His over-the-top histrionics in pictures like *Man Made Monster* prompted critics to label him "the Maddest Doctor of Them All."

According to author Gregory Mank's book *Hollywood's Maddest Doctors* (one of the few sources of credible biographical data on the star), Atwill's off-screen persona was nearly as crazy as his on-screen antics. The eccentric Atwill, inexplicably known to his friends as "Pinky," enjoyed being chauffeured in a Rolls-Royce mysteriously pockmarked with bullet holes. His appetite for wine, women and whatever was the stuff of legend. Atwill married four times, once to the ex-wife of Gen. Douglas MacArthur.

However, the star's reputation was ruined and his career derailed during a 1941 statutory rape trial, when testimony revealed that Atwill had hosted a 1940 Christmas orgy at his Pacific Palisades mansion. Atwill screened pornographic movies for his guests, then led revelers in acting out scenes from the film on the living room rug! Atwill denied the allegations under oath. It was not one of his most convincing performances. For his testimony he earned a perjury conviction. In the midst of the trial, Atwill received news that his son, John—a fighter pilot in the Royal Air Force battling the Nazis in Europe—had been killed.

After the trial, major studios stopped offering Atwill starring roles, although he continued to headline Poverty Row pictures and landed supporting parts at Universal.

In 1943, Atwill's perjury conviction was overturned. At age 59, Atwill remarried a final time — to 28-year-old radio singer Paula Printer — and his wife bore him another son. But there would be no happy ending. By the time he held his newborn son in his arms on Oct. 14, 1945, the actor knew he was terminally ill. Bronchial cancer took his life in 1946, when his son was only months old.

Lionel Atwill deserved better.

Lionel Atwill strikes a professorial pose for this publicity still.

Murders in the Zoo (1933)

—The opening credits of *Murders in the Zoo* introduce the film's cast in a unique way. A brief shot of an animal flashes on the screen, fades out, and then a slightly longer shot of one of the stars (in character) fades in. Each of the film's key performers and characters correlate with the pictured beast. Lionel Atwill, seen dragging on a cigarette as big game hunter Eric Gorman, is linked to a Bengal tiger. No other analogy could be more appropriate for Atwill's performance in this film. He prowls through *Murders in the Zoo* with the predatory grace of a jungle cat.

Gorman benefits from the most bloodthirsty introduction ever granted a Golden Age horror villain. We see two native guides holding a man to the ground, as Gorman meticulously works with needle and thread. We can't see precisely what he's doing. Calmly, in a distracted tone that makes clear he is focused on the mechanics of the task he's performing, Gorman says: "You'll never lie to a friend again. You'll never kiss another man's wife." When he's finished, Gorman sits back and mops his brow. After the hunter and his guides walk away, the camera finally reveals Gorman's handiwork — he has sewn shut the mouth of his victim and left the man defenseless, hands tied behind his back, in the jungle.

Atwill seems to have understood that, following this shocking opening scene, he didn't have to convince audiences that Gorman was a dangerous man. The hunter seems forever on the edge of some new, unspeakably cruel act. Although notorious for lapsing into arch theatrics, Atwill performs here with the quiet, coiled striking power of a beast tracking its prey. He glides effortlessly across the screen, speaking volumes with a barely perceptible change of tenor in his voice, unveiling his character's hidden passions with a simple, unguarded glance.

Gorman and his browbeaten wife, Evelyn (Kathleen Burke), return to America

Eric Gorman (Lionel Atwill) stares pop-eyed with jealousy alongside his wife Evelyn (Kathleen Burke) in *Murders in the Zoo* (1933). With looks like this one, it's no wonder critics dubbed him "The Maddest of Them All!" (Photograph courtesy Bryan Senn.)

by ocean liner. In port, Gorman grants an interview to a skittish newspaperman (Charlie Ruggles). Their conversation underscores Gorman's identification with the animals he hunts (not to kill, but to capture and sell to zoos). The hunter looks quite civilized, not to mention dashing, in a dark double-breasted suit and white hat. Underneath that dapper exterior lurks the heart of a beast. Gorman, seated in a cargo hold filled with crates of tigers, lions, snakes and the rest of the loot from his latest safari, explains, "I love [animals], their honesty, their simplicity, their primitive emotions. They love, they hate, they kill."

The reporter unwittingly reveals that Roger Hewitt (John Lodge) has taken an ill-advised fancy to Evelyn. Gorman pays a social call on his rival and interrupts a clandestine luncheon between Roger and Evelyn. She hides in the bedroom, but Gorman notices her lipstick on a teacup. This scene is rich in double entendres as the two men discuss their "mutual interest" in Gorman's "animals." Atwill's flair for this brand of dry humor ranks second only to the great George Sanders, and he displays that light, sardonic touch in this sequence. Gorman invites Hewitt to a fund-raising dinner at the zoo. "I can promise you a most unusual evening," he offers with a beaming grin.

When we see Gorman again, he poses in front of a caged tiger, waiting for guests to take their seats at the fund-raising dinner. During the meal, he stabs Hewitt with a snakehead device filled with deadly mamba venom. Afterward, Gorman brazenly lambastes zoologist Dr. Woodford (Randolph Scott), blaming him for Hewitt's death. Atwill's posture in this scene telegraphs the fact that Gorman is lying. Previously, Gorman's movements have been fluid and graceful. In this sequence he stands stiff and straight-backed. With nostrils flared, he bitterly accuses Woodford of "gross carelessness."

Later, when Evelyn accuses her husband of murdering Hewitt, Atwill resumes his starched "liar posture." Scoffing at the accusation, Gorman chuckles: "Why, you don't think I sat there all evening with an eight-foot mamba in my pocket, do you? Why, it would be an injustice to my tailor!" (An actor doesn't read lines like those every day.) Something other than a mamba begins to stir in Gorman's pocket. He runs his hand over Evelyn's shoulder, wraps his arms around her and tries to kiss her. "I've never wanted you more," he rasps lasciviously. Evelyn pulls away.

Throughout this sequence, Atwill appears to be on the verge of laughter. He never loses his lascivious grin. In his book *Classics of the Horror Film*, author William K. Everson wrote that Atwill, "apart from relishing every line and nuance, also managed to suggest general tendencies towards unspecified depravities which the scripts never intended." This sequence demonstrates precisely what Everson meant. It's easy to read this sort of thing into Atwill's performances, given his kinky offscreen habits. Nevertheless, it remains difficult to tell whether the twinkle in his eye during this scene comes from the mind of Gorman or Atwill.

Evelyn discovers the device her husband used to kill Hewitt and attempts to flee with it. Gorman intercepts her on a bridge overlooking the zoo's crocodile pit. Gorman pleads with his spouse: "Everything I've done, I've done because I love you. If I lacked the courage to kill for you, I couldn't expect you to go on loving me." Atwill delivers these lines with an unexpected note of sweetness, and with absolute conviction in their mad logic. Gorman tries to pull Evelyn close to him, and again she pulls away. Atwill's strangely touching work in this scene suggests that Gorman's egomaniacal possessiveness springs from deep-seated fears of inadequacy. He's overcompensating for his inner neediness with jungle bravado.

Gorman softly urges Evelyn, "Come along, let's go home." When she still refuses, Gorman's now-forced smile gives way to a pained, fearful expression. He must kill Evelyn now, not only because she knows about his murders but because she has seen his innermost self—his vulnerable, needy self—and has rejected him. With lips pursed in profound disappointment, he heaves his wife into the crocodile pit.

The only flaw in an otherwise masterful portrayal comes very late in the picture, and isn't entirely Atwill's fault. Gorman opens the zoo's cages to distract police who are attempting to apprehend him. He's seen fleeing the lions and tigers. Atwill's movements here—obviously running in place in front of a rear-projection screen—are awkward at best. He chugs along in a rapid waddle. This is especially noticeable because Atwill is so sleek in the film's preceding sequences. Viewers can only conclude that rugged Eric Gorman, macho big-game hunter and outdoorsman supreme, runs like a girl.

Despite its unusually brutal opening sequence and lurid storyline, *Murders in the Zoo* charmed many in 1933, including the *New York Times* reviewer who singled out Atwill for praise. "Lionel Atwill as the insanely jealous husband is almost too convincing for comfort," the *Times* opined. Latter day critics concur. Bryan Senn, in his *Golden Horrors*, writes that "the role of Eric Gorman was tailor-made for Lionel Atwill." Everson, again in *Classics of the Horror Film*, goes even further, venturing that the entire picture is primarily "a showcase for the bravura nastiness of Atwill."

Terrifying, funny and unexpectedly moving — Atwill's striking work in this picture makes *Murders in the Zoo* the quintessential Lionel Atwill film. His performance succinctly encapsulates everything special the actor brought to his many horror vehicles.

Son of Frankenstein (1939)

— In the minds of many horror aficionados, Atwill's greatest performance came in a supporting part — as the unforgettable, wooden-armed Inspector Krogh in *Son of Frankenstein*. Constructed with equal parts bottled rage and gallows humor, Krogh ranks as the most completely assembled supporting character of Universal's entire Frankenstein series (unless you count Bela Lugosi's Ygor, who became the de facto star of *Son* and *Ghost of Frankenstein*). Krogh also remains the only hero from the entire canon of Universal horror classics who's as much fun to watch as the studio's monsters and mad scientists.

Although fourth-billed, Atwill proved as integral to the success of *Son of Frankenstein* as the higher billed Boris Karloff (as the Monster), Basil Rathbone (in the title role) and Lugosi. Atwill's accomplishment becomes even more impressive if you factor in that he shares most of his screen time with notorious scene-stealer Rathbone, who radiates double espresso intensity, or with Lugosi, who gives a career-best performance.

The physicality of Atwill's performance alone is striking. He appears throughout the film in his dark gendarme uniform and moves with stiff military precision. He greets Frankenstein and his wife with a click of the heels and a curt bow of the head. Most impressively of all, he tosses in numerous tiny bits of business related to his prosthetic left arm, all of which convince us the inspector truly is missing a limb. This element of Atwill's performance was parodied hilariously by Kenneth Mars in *Young Frankenstein* (1974) and ripped off shamelessly by Peter Sellers in *Dr. Strangelove* (1964).

Atwill's role consists, primarily, of a series of verbal sparring matches with Rathbone. The first of these exchanges sets the tone for the rest of the film, insofar as the character of Inspector Krogh is concerned. Shortly after the baron's arrival in the village that bears his name, Krogh visits Castle Frankenstein to assure its new residents of protection. "As long as you continue to live in this place, you're in danger," Krogh cautions. But Frankenstein balks at the suggestion that his presence in the village inflames the residents' prejudices and superstitions.

Krogh bites back his own fear and suspicion, not to mention his irritation at Frankenstein's snobbery, because he has a sworn obligation to keep the peace. (This is lost on Frankenstein but, thanks to Atwill's resolute delivery, not on the audience.) The townsfolk, Krogh explains, remain convinced that the Monster created by

Inspector Krogh (Atwill) casts a suspicious, monocle-filled eye at Baron von Wolfe Frankenstein (Basil Rathbone) in this scene from *Son of Frankenstein* (1939).

Frankenstein's father remains at large. The creature is suspected in six unsolved murders. Again, Frankenstein scoffs. "Do you really know of one criminal act this poor creature committed?" he asks.

A grim pallor settles over Atwill's face. He slowly turns to face the camera, giving the lines added impact. It's a cheap trick, but effective. Atwill reads his lines with quiet understatement, but performs several fidgety "bits of business" that betray how powerful the recollection remains for Krogh, and how much pain lingers beneath the surface.

"The most vivid recollection of my life," Krogh begins. As Atwill speaks, he repositions his "wooden" arm, removes his monocle and places it between the wooden thumb and index finger. "I was but a child at the time, about the age of your own son, Herr Baron. The Monster had escaped and was ravaging the countryside — killing, maiming, terrorizing." He produces a handkerchief and cleans the monocle. "One night he burst into our house." He places the monocle back in his eye. "My father took a gun and fired at him, but the savage brute sent him crashing to the corner. He grabbed me by the arm...." He pushes his wooden arm back down to his side, and it strikes the wall behind him with a loud thump. "One doesn't easily forget, Herr Baron, an arm torn out by the roots."

For emphasis the camera dollies in, or Atwill steps closer to it. Krogh continues: "My lifelong ambition was to have been a soldier. If not for this [arm], I, who command seven gendarmes in a little mountain village, might have been a general."

Each of the first three Universal Frankenstein movies features a moment of sublime pathos. In *Frankenstein* it was the Monster's doomed encounter with the little girl, Maria. In *Bride of Frankenstein* it was the Monster's all-too-brief friendship with the blind hermit. In *Son of Frankenstein* it is this heartrending monologue by Krogh. The character never lapses into self-pity, however. In fact, he apologizes for any kind feelings he may have garnered ("I'm sorry if I have aroused sympathy") but this only makes Krogh more sympathetic.

Krogh enlists one of Frankenstein's servants as an informant. Over lunch, Krogh gingerly gathers incriminating testimony from Frankenstein's unwitting wife. He attends the autopsies of two more murdered villagers. He recovers crucial evidence (a watch) from the baron's son, Peter. (Peter reports that "a giant" gave the watch to him.) Throughout all this, Atwill infuses Krogh with a bruised dignity that seems to reinforce the character's professionalism and hold his anger in check. After finding the watch, however, long-suppressed fury begins to boil over.

Krogh (correctly) accuses Frankenstein of harboring the Monster, and announces that he plans to arrest the scientist for the murder of his missing butler (whose watch was given to Peter by the "giant"). At first Krogh remains stiff and professional, but when Frankenstein tries to blame the murder on Ygor, the inspector finally blows his cool. "By Heaven, I think you're a worse fiend than your father," he sneers. "I'll stay with you 'til you confess. And if you don't confess, I'll feed you to the villagers like the Romans fed Christians to the lions!"

All Krogh's closeted frustrations rush to the surface—his lifelong resentment over the loss of his arm, his bitterness over the death of his friends, his rage at Frankenstein's smug elitism. And Atwill manages to convey all this without resorting to a full-blown meltdown. In fact, Krogh recovers quickly and—ever the good sport—engages Frankenstein in a game of darts. Waiting for his turn to throw, in a small but unforgettable bit of dark comic business, he plants darts in his wooden forearm. Tiny moments like that one are what make Atwill's Krogh special.

Although *Son of Frankenstein* received, for the most part, favorable reviews during its initial release, few critics singled out Atwill for praise—probably due to his lower billing. Critical hindsight, however, provides effusive accolades for the actor. In their book *Universal Horrors*, authors Tom Weaver and John and Michael Brunas venture that "Lionel Atwill is peerless as Inspector Krogh.... He realized the potential for stylistic expression and milked the role for all it was worth." Senn, in *Golden Horrors*, writes, "With his forceful, formal bearing, clipped speech, and wide array of quirky mannerisms, Atwill creates a character wholly unique and unforgettable."

Atwill was so effective in *Son of Frankenstein*, and the picture was so successful, that Universal cast him in every subsequent Frankenstein film. Perhaps the studio used Atwill as a sort of good luck charm for their series. He won a juicy supporting role as—what else?—a mad doctor in the next Frankenstein opus, *The Ghost of Frankenstein* (1942). In *House of Frankenstein* (1944) and *House of Dracula* (1945) he again appeared as an inspector (but with two arms). While he's good in his other appearances in the series, there was no reproducing the magic of his performance in *Son of Frankenstein*. As Krogh, Atwill was lightning in a bottle.

Other Notable Performances

Like John Carradine and George Zucco, Atwill alternated between starring roles in horror films and supporting parts in mainstream movies, excelling in both arenas.

Working outside the horror genre, Atwill menaced Errol Flynn (and matched the star for sheer bravado and flair) in the sublime swashbuckler *Captain Blood* (1935). He enjoyed an unusually sympathetic role as a military officer led astray by Marlene Dietrich in *The Devil Is a Woman* (1935). With his cultured villainy as the nefarious Dr. Moriarity in *Sherlock Holmes and the Secret Weapon* (1942), however, Atwill scored his greatest non-horror triumph.

Despite his fine work outside the genre, Atwill remains linked to horror cinema by a long list of memorable fright flicks. The very best of that lot not already discussed at length includes *Mystery of the Wax Museum* (1933), one of Atwill's best-remembered and most effective performances. A pesky French accent, which he slips in and out throughout the film, blemishes an otherwise brilliant turn as a crazed sculptor. Atwill earned his "Maddest Doctor" nickname with delightful, rococo performances in movies such as *The Vampire Bat* (1933), *The Mad Doctor of Market Street* (1942) and especially *Man Made Monster* (1941). The latter film includes his most underrated performance. It's virtually impossible to take your eyes off Atwill in this. With giddy gusto he transforms Lon Chaney, Jr., from an amiable dimwit into a freak whose mere touch is deadly—and all the while virtually panting at Anne Nagel!

In roles like this, even the big screen was too small to contain Atwill's sadistic *joie de vivre*. He adored playing the villain, and this passion radiates from the screen. Audiences can only bask in that glow.

DWIGHT FRYE

Dwight Frye occupies a unique position in the firmament of horror cinema. He remains the only horror "star" never to have starred in a horror film. Frye earned the deathless devotion of monster movie mavens with a series of memorable supporting roles. After his striking performances in Universal's *Dracula* and *Frankenstein* (both 1931), Frye—to his never-ending dismay—found himself typecast in the role of the deformed henchman and/or crazed halfwit.

This provided a cruel fate for a gifted, versatile actor who had enjoyed a prosperous Broadway career, starring in all manner of productions. Typecasting within the horror genre warped the careers of performers such as Bela Lugosi and John Carradine, but it short-circuited Frye's career entirely.

Dwight Iliff Fry (he added the "e" later) was born in 1899 in rural Kansas. The Fry family moved to Denver a few years later, and there young Dwight displayed prodigious talent as a pianist and vocalist. His affection for performing blossomed into a love of acting, and he joined a barnstorming theatrical troupe as a teenager. By age 29, Frye (as he was now known) had amassed a trunk load of glowing reviews, a loyal following among the theater-going public of New York and a happy marriage.

In 1929, following the stock market crash, Frye set out for Hollywood, hoping to translate his triumphs on the stage to the screen. It didn't work out the way Frye envisioned.

He traveled from New York to Hollywood riding a crest of critical acclaim and popular appeal gained via his outstanding performances in hit plays, including the musical *Sitting Pretty* (1924), the melodrama *A Man's Man* (1925), the comedy *The Devil in the Cheese* (1926) and the drama *Mima* (1928). The sky seemed to be the limit for this gifted young performer. Even if he didn't emerge as a full-blown star (as he had on Broadway), his versatility and sheer talent seemed to assure him a long and prosperous career as a character player.

Flash-forward 12 years.

Frye's once stellar stage career was long since over. He was working full-time in a munitions factory, and taking whatever bit parts he could find on the side to help support his wife and son. He still delivered credible, professional performances. Yet, his roles and

Dwight Frye, made up as Renfield, feigns eating a fly for this publicity still from *Dracula* (1931).

billing continued to diminish. The parts he was able to land, usually in Grade Z productions, were demeaning rehashes of his early horror roles. Sometimes his roles were even worse. He sank to accepting speechless walk-ons and, at least according to Hollywood legend, even appeared in an early stag film — peeping through the hedges at frolicking female nudists. How could such a promising career have gone so wrong?

The answer is simple. Early in his career, in a couple of very memorable movies, Frye was too good for his own good.

Dracula **(1931)**—More than any other part, his role as Renfield in director Tod Browning's *Dracula* shaped audiences' (and producers') perception of Frye. His portrayal of the sniveling, giggling madman imprinted itself on the public consciousness almost as strongly as Lugosi's iconic performance in the title role. This performance continues to delight fans of classic horror films. Yet, the true measure of Frye's achievement in this film remains underappreciated.

Playing Renfield, the most complex of all *Dracula*'s characters, forced Frye to call upon nearly all the skills he had polished on Broadway — his comedic timing as well as his dramatic flair. Especially in the film's later sequences, Renfield provides comic relief, but his story remains essentially tragic.

Perhaps the greatest asset Frye brought to the role was a kind of internal logic that proved essential, since his character's tortured emotions vary radically from scene to scene, even from line to line within a scene. For instance: In a scene midway through the film, Renfield checks in with Drs. Seward and Van Helsing. At first, the patient seems sweet-tempered. ("Thanks, I'm feeling much better," he reports, smiling easily.) But when Van Helsing reaches out to touch Renfield, the patient bursts into fiery anger. ("Keep your filthy hands to yourself!" he snarls.) Then, moments later, Renfield turns scared and remorseful. ("Oh, Dr. Seward, send me away from this place. Send me far away," he pleads, weeping.) Against all odds, Frye makes this scene work.

As author David J. Skal points out in his book *Hollywood Gothic*, "the role of Renfield, with its shifting moods and explosive outbursts, would be an ideal showcase for Frye's versatility." An insightful producer could have looked at Frye's superb portrayal in this wide-ranging and colorful part and surmised that the actor could tackle almost any role. Instead, unimaginative producers afterward seemed incapable of envisioning Frye as anything other than a recycled Renfield.

Frye's Renfield serves as our point-of-view character during the most compelling sequences of Browning's film. In the opening two reels, Renfield arrives in Transylvania, makes his fateful carriage ride to Borgo Pass, is overtaken by Dracula and his wives and then makes his ocean voyage back to London. Throughout these events, audiences watch as Renfield disintegrates from an ambitious young professional to a gibbering, wide-eyed lunatic. Viewers grow more deeply engrossed in the film throughout Renfield's transformation. Once Dracula reaches London, and Renfield assumes a lesser role in the story, the film begins to drag.

In the early sequences at Castle Dracula, Frye provides an ideal foil for Lugosi. During Lugosi's famous "Children of the Night" speech, for instance, Frye affects an uneasy, puzzled expression perfect for that moment. He telegraphs Renfield's naïveté with subtle touches. For example, when the Count attempts to verify that Renfield has informed no one of his trip to Transylvania, Renfield responds with impish pride, "I followed your directions *im*-plicitly." The young realtor doesn't realize that this proud precision will cost him his life.

When he arrives at the castle, Renfield appears meticulously tidy and carefully coiffed. Frye musters a courteous smile. Twenty minutes later, when Dracula's ship reaches London, Frye is a pop-eyed, disheveled mess with a broad, toothy grin affixed to his face. As a brilliant finishing flourish, the actor adds the famous four-note Renfield Laugh: "Hnhh-hnhh-hnhh-hnhhh!" An off-screen character remarks, "Why, he's mad. Look at his eyes. The man's gone crazy!" The Renfield Laugh, by itself, makes that dialogue redundant.

Renfield is committed to Dr. Seward's asylum, where he and an exasperated attendant provide some comic relief. The attendant is particularly flummoxed by Renfield's fixation with eating insects. Although most of the sequences at the asylum are more comedic than dramatic, Frye does have one bravura monologue. In it, he betrays Dracula to Van Helsing:

"He came and stood beneath my window in the moonlight and he promised me things," Frye begins, almost whispering at this point. "Not in words but by *doing* them ... by making them happen. A red mist spread over the lawn, coming on like a flame of fire. And then he parted it." Frye's voice now swells with amazement. "And I could see that there were thousands of rats with their eyes blazing red. Like his, only smaller." Frye's delivery is almost giddy now. "And then he held up his hand and they all stopped." Frye leans in and places his hands on Van Sloan's lapels. "And I thought he seemed to be saying ... 'Rats, rats, rats. Thousands, millions of them. All red blood. All these I will give to your if you will obey me!'"

The emotional ebb and flow in this monologue encapsulates everything wonderful about Frye's portrayal — its maniacal intensity, its sardonic wit and its heartrending yearning. Funny, sad and creepy all at once, it's the quintessential Renfield moment.

To fully appreciate the brilliance of Frye's performance, simply compare his Renfield with the performances of any of the actors who have followed him in future adaptations of Bram Stoker's novel. Neither Pablo Alvarez Rubio, in the George Melford Spanish version produced concurrently with the Browning film, nor Jack Shepherd, in Phillip Saville's acclaimed 1977 television adaptation, nor Tony Hogarth, in John Badham's 1979 edition, nor Tom Waits, in Francis Ford Coppola's overhyped 1992 production, could match Frye's Renfield. His remains the definitive portrayal. No one else even comes close.

Tellingly, gifted screenwriters Jimmy Sangster (who wrote Hammer's watershed *Horror of Dracula* in 1957) and Richard Matheson (who wrote Dan Curtis' 1973 television version) both chose to eliminate the character entirely from their scripts. Perhaps they understood how difficult the part would be to cast. (Although it is fun to imagine Hammer stalwart Michael Ripper playing Renfield.)

Reviewers in 1931 might have written better notices for Frye had they been able to compare his performance with those of his successors. Those that mentioned Frye at all did so dismissively, with backhanded compliments. The *New York Times*' Mordaunt Hall was typical. He wrote only that, "Dwight Frye does fairly well as Renfield." With the benefit of hindsight, film historians have served Frye better. Author Bryan Senn, in his book *Golden Horrors*, opines that, "Frye's jittery Renfield ... seems animated by an explosive, unthinking energy.... Frye makes of his 'fly-eater' a veritable dynamo of insane lust and tormented guilt."

Frye's Renfield is a performance of extraordinary (and sadly underestimated) range and depth—blending bizarre mania with gallows humor and a surprising dash of pathos. Although Frye was asked to play this type of character many times afterward, his subsequent quasi–Renfields were never written as well as the original. As a result, Frye's Renfield remains a singular accomplishment—a unique and striking portrayal unlike anything else from horror cinema's Golden Age.

Other Notable Performances

Dracula marked Frye's fourth screen appearance. In its wake, the actor earned the role of gunman Wilmer Cook in the original 1931 production of *The Maltese Falcon*. (Elisha Cook, Jr., played Wilmer in the famous 1941 version, which starred Humphrey Bogart.) Frye also appeared (alongside Lugosi again) as Jessop, the butler, in the early Charlie Chan mystery *The Black Camel* (1931).

By far, however, Frye's finest and best-remembered subsequent role was as Fritz, the sadistic, grave-robbing hunchback from director James Whale's *Frankenstein* (1931). Like *Dracula*, *Frankenstein* proved both a blessing and a curse for Frye. On the one hand, Frye's Fritz remains one of his primary claims to fame. This performance has delighted generations of horror cinema buffs. Also, the part began a long and fruitful association between Frye and Whale, who gave the actor small roles in several later films. On the other hand, his colorful performance as Fritz, coming so quickly after his vivid portrayal of Renfield, virtually ensured that producers would thereafter think of Frye only as the freak assistant to monsters and madmen (if producers thought of him at all). Nearly all of Frye's roles of any size that followed *Frankenstein* would be thinly disguised copies of either Renfield or Fritz or, in the case of *Dead Men Walk* (1943), an amalgam of both.

Fritz is the closest thing to pure evil to be found in Whale's *Frankenstein*. Colin Clive paints his title character more as an overreaching explorer than as a truly malevolent figure. Karloff's Monster, of course, remains a childlike innocent. It's Fritz who bungles the theft of a brain, so that Frankenstein's creation is born with the mind of a degenerate criminal rather than a gifted intellectual. It's Fritz who taunts the creature with a torch, introducing the Monster to fear and hatred. All this Frye executes with great aplomb and comedic flourishes that endeared the actor to Whale. (Note how, while ascending the staircase in Frankenstein's tower laboratory, Frye pauses—to pull up his rumpled sock!) He snarls and snivels convincingly, but does so with tongue in cheek. However, there's a limit to what even an actor as gifted as Frye can accomplish with a thinly written part, and Fritz remains essentially a one-note character.

Nevertheless, Whale was so delighted with Frye's performance that he created a distinctly Fritz-like role for Frye, that of the grave-robber Karl in *Bride of Frankenstein* (1935). For Frye's benefit, Whale took an early draft of the screenplay and combined three parts into the lone character of Karl. Unfortunately, most of Frye's work in the role wound up on the editing room floor after Universal ordered the picture trimmed from 90 minutes to 75.

Frye enjoyed a showy, Renfield-like red herring role in the 1933 chiller *The Vampire Bat*. Co-starring alongside Lionel Atwill and Fay Wray, Frye plays Herman Gleib, the bat-loving town idiot who is accused of vampirism.

Frye's most satisfying part must have been as the noble Dr. Thomas in *The Crime of Dr. Crespi* (1935). Frye had the rare treat of playing the hero in this melodrama, which was based on an Edgar Allan Poe story and starred Erich von Stroheim as the maniacal title character. Although barely remembered today, the film remains notable for the commendable work of Frye and von Stroheim.

Even by the time he appeared in this film, however, Frye's already meager parts — he never scored a leading role in a Hollywood film — had begun to diminish rapidly. As roles grew smaller and less frequent, he took a job as a tool and die maker in a munitions factory to support his family.

Then, in 1943, Frye scored an unexpected coup, winning a straight (non-ghoulish) supporting role in director Henry King's prestigious, big-budget production, *Wilson*. This A-list picture went on to earn nine Academy Award nominations, including Best Picture. Frye hoped *Wilson* would revitalize his flagging screen career. But, alas, he never completed the film. On November 7, 1943, after taking his family to the movies, Frye suffered a massive heart attack and died. He was just 44 years old.

PETER LORRE

In retrospect, Peter Lorre seems the unlikeliest of screen bogeymen. How could a guy standing just five-foot-five, with a soft build and an even softer voice, intimidate anybody? The answer, surely, has something to do with his eyes — those round, watery, unforgettable eyes. Or perhaps the answer lies behind those eyes, which always seemed to mask a painful secret, something lonely and macabre.

Many historians invest great significance in the fact that before finding his niche as an actor, Lorre studied psychiatry. They contend that this gave him special insight into his mad characters. In and of itself, this assertion is probably an overstatement. But Lorre's interest in psychiatry, coupled with the charitable work on behalf of the mentally ill that he quietly performed throughout his life, demonstrates that the actor had profound empathy for people with troubled minds. This showed in his work. He presented his demented and disenfranchised characters with an uncommon note of compassion, and managed to craft characters audiences sympathized with, even though they found the characters' actions repulsive.

Lorre gave the keynote performance of his career in Fritz Lang's thriller *M* (1931),

Young Peter Lorre, recently arrived from Europe, poses for an early publicity still.

his first starring film role. Cast as the most gruesome and despicable of villains (a child-murdering pedophile), Lorre nevertheless skillfully elicits sympathy. The pathos Lorre engenders proves essential to the picture's key supposition: Even the sickest of mad reprobates should be reviled less than sane criminals. Captured and forced to defend himself in a kangaroo court of underworld thugs, Lorre's nameless character pleads: "You are all criminals because you choose to be. But I, I do what I do because I can't help it!" Lorre's unbalanced character, driven by impulses beyond his control, is as much victim as victimizer.

Lorre was born Laszlo Lowenstein in a village in the Carpathian Mountains but moved with his family to Vienna as a young boy. As a teenager he ran away from home to join the theater, only to discover that the theater didn't want him (or, presumably, any other gawky-looking youngsters with no experience). In desperation, Lorre formed his own improvisational theater group, which he funded by taking a day job at a bank. That endeavor folded, but Lorre went on to earn ever larger parts in ever more important theaters in Vienna, Zurich and Berlin. Lang made a star of the relatively unknown Lorre by casting him in *M*.

Lang, Lorre, and much of the rest of the German film industry fled the country when the Nazi party took power. Director Alfred Hitchcock gave Lorre one of his first English-speaking parts in his 1934 production of *The Man Who Knew Too Much*, a splashy supporting role as an anarchist saboteur. Soon after, Lorre made his way to the U.S. In America, Lorre enjoyed his longest tenure as a heroic lead in 20th Century–Fox's eight-picture Mr. Moto series (1937–39), playing an ersatz Charlie Chan. Lorre appeared alongside rotund Sydney Greenstreet in Warners' *The Maltese Falcon* (1941). The duo made such an impression that producers reunited Lorre and Greenstreet in eight more films. One testament to Lorre's popularity is that in the late 1940s and early 1950s he became one of the most-parodied personalities in Hollywood. Comics lampooned him incessantly, and caricatures of him sometimes menaced Bugs Bunny in Warner Brothers cartoons.

At the height of his success, illness forced Lorre to take a year off. While recovering, he gained a significant amount of weight and wasn't able to lose the extra pounds. He returned to the screen in 1956, but his career never recaptured its previous momentum. This was not necessarily due to diminished abilities. Rather, it seems that during his short hiatus from the screen, producers forgot how to cast the actor. As author Bill Warren points out in his book *Keep Watching the Skies!*: "Lorre was quite literally one of the greatest actors ever to appear in movies and, like all great actors he was unique and irreplaceable. He should have been cast with great and loving care, but people used him for his screen image, not his ability."

When he died of heart failure in March 1964, he was just 59 years old. Vincent Price provided the eulogy at his funeral. Lorre left behind a treasure trove of priceless performances. To the horror genre, he bequeathed one crown jewel.

Mad Love **(1935)**—Lorre had a great deal riding on *Mad Love*. It was the actor's first American motion picture. Still freelancing and, despite his successes in Europe, far from secure financially, Lorre badly wanted to provide American audiences—and producers—with a glimpse of what he could do. Lorre gave them an eyeful.

If ever a role and an actor were meant for one another, it was Dr. Gogol and Peter Lorre. So focused on the project was Lorre that he took the dramatic step of shaving his head for the role. *Mad Love* stands as a horror classic for a variety of reasons: Karl Freund's expressionistic, moody direction; P.J. Wolfson and John Balderson's clever screenplay; the story's solid literary foundation in Maurice Renard's novel *Les Mans d'Orlac*; convincing work from co-stars Frances Drake and especially Colin Clive. However, Lorre's *tour de force* performance towers above all the film's other strengths. His lovesick, lunatic Dr. Gogol remains one of the most memorable mad medicos in the history of horror cinema.

Throughout the film, Lorre demonstrates remarkable patience and an uncanny sense of timing. He heats his characterization of Gogol like a pot over a low flame, letting it simmer and bubble before boiling over in the final reel. Whether Freund led him to this approach or whether Freund and editor Hugh Wynn cut the film to capitalize on Lorre's excellent work remains open to conjecture. But *Mad Love* proceeds at the ever-quickening tempo of Gogol's descent into madness.

The film's opening scenes inform us that the wealthy and respected Dr. Gogol has attended 47 consecutive performances by actress Yvonne Orlac (Drake) at a Parisian Grand Guignol–like theater and sent her flowers after every show. Gogol greets the actress backstage after her final performance of the season. In

Peter Lorre's bald pate and piercing eyes are featured prominently in this theatrical poster for *Mad Love* (1935). Co-star Frances Drake is also pictured. (Photograph courtesy Ted Okuda.)

this early scene, Lorre's delivery is soft and soothing. "Every night I've watched and tonight, the last night, I felt I must come and thank you for what you've meant to me," he coos.

Gogol is shocked to learn that Yvonne is married and that she plans to retire from the theater to be a full-time wife to her pianist husband, Stephen (Clive). "But I must see you again, I *must*," Gogol demands. Lorre's tone grows noticeably sterner. He leans forward into the camera, and his bulbous, heavy-lidded eyes nearly fill the screen. During the cast party, the theater manager insists that Yvonne give Gogol a piece of cake and a kiss. Gogol seizes the opportunity—and Yvonne, clutching her in a romantic embrace.

Afterward, Gogol buys a wax figure of Yvonne that had stood in the theater lobby. He recounts the story of Pygmalion to the dubious seller. Gogol's wistful telling of the tale ("…then, she came to life!") betrays his weakening grasp on reality. Nevertheless, Gogol remains a solid citizen in the eyes of the public.

Whenever cast as a madman or a criminal, Lorre took every opportunity to underscore the redeeming, human qualities of his character. *Mad Love* grants him that chance with another early sequence, in which Gogol tends to a crippled young girl whose legs he will repair. He speaks to his assistant about the girl in his most delicate tone, and gingerly strokes the back of her hand as she sleeps. When a nurse interrupts, Gogol chastises her for disrupting his time with his patient. Clearly, Gogol remains a skilled and compassionate healer. Later, the doctor turns down a lucrative offer to write a series of articles for an American newspaper. Lorre strikes just the correct note of distaste in his refusal to convince us Gogol isn't motivated by greed or pride. Indeed, Gogol's single failing appears to be his romantic awkwardness, which gives rise to his monomaniacal fixation on Yvonne. This elevates Gogol's downfall to something like classical tragedy.

From this point, *Mad Love* begins to pick up speed. French police guillotine a knife-wielding circus performer–turned–murderer named Rollo. Shortly after, a train wreck crushes Stephen's hands. Yvonne brings Stephen to Gogol and begs the doctor to save her husband's hands. Gogol removes the hands from Rollo's corpse and transplants them onto Orlac. He performs this operation in secret, and leads Yvonne and Stephen to believe that the pianist has retained his own hands, misshapen by the accident.

Stephen's post-surgical treatment proves long, painful and expensive. Soon the couple face bankruptcy, and still Stephen can't play as he once did. So again Yvonne approaches Gogol for help. Gogol, apparently, hoped Yvonne's gratitude for his surgical skill would evolve into affection. When he realizes this has not worked, Gogol grows bitter and frustrated. "Is there no room in your heart, even pity, for a man who had never known love but who has worshiped you since the day he first walked into that absurd theater?" Gogol pleads. Lorre's voice becomes sharper, more nasal, than in his earlier scenes.

Yvonne admits she was aware of Gogol's feelings for her, and had even "traded on them" to enlist his help. But she says she can offer him nothing besides friendship in return for his assistance. "There is something about you…" she begins. "That repulses you?" Gogol finishes her sentence. "Frightens me," Yvonne corrects.

Throughout the next few scenes, Lorre ratchets up his delivery. His line readings grow faster, his tone grows increasingly harsh and nasal and he adds more demonstrative flourishes with his eyes and hands.

Gogol meets with Stephen, who complains that his hands "have a feel for knives" and "want to kill." Still trying to conceal the true origin of the pianist's hands, Gogol tells Yvonne that the trauma of her husband's accident has affected Stephen's mind and that she should leave him. This sends Yvonne into a rage. Orlac responds with a feverish outburst: "I, a poor peasant, have conquered science. Why can't I conquer love? Don't you understand? You *must* be mine." Lorre's voice grows strained and shrill, his eyes bulge (even more than usual), and his posture becomes noticeably stiffer. He looks like a rubber band stretched to the limit.

In the next scene, he snaps. While preparing for an operation, Gogol engages in an internal dialogue with his obsessed inner self. The "bad Gogol" appears in a mirror, dressed in a suit and snappy fur-lined overcoat; he taunts the "good Gogol," dressed in medical scrubs: "Nothing matters to you but one thing—Yvonne! Yvonne!" Lorre's "bad Gogol" fumes like a *cum laude* graduate from the Snidely Whiplash School of Villainy. After this scene, Gogol descends into total madness—and Lorre cuts loose with some of the most feverish and florid work of his career.

During the film's final two reels, Gogol frames Stephen for murder and unwittingly confesses this to Yvonne. (Unbeknownst to him, she has taken the place of her own wax likeness in Gogol's sitting room.) He boasts to his "waxwork" Yvonne: "She'll come here now, flesh and blood, not wax like you, and he, he shall be shut up in the house where they keep the mad." During the film's closing moments, Lorre smiles and staggers and swoons like a comic drunk from the days of Mack Sennett. He cackles nonstop. His face is wet with perspiration. His eyes hold a vacant faraway look. Gogol has lost all contact with reality. When Yvonne tries to escape, Gogol believes his statue has come to life. "I *am* Pygmalion! ... My love has made you live!"

Even though 1935 reviewers remained cool toward *Mad Love*, most singled out Lorre for praise. *The New York Times* reported that Lorre, "with his gift for supplementing a remarkable appearance with his acute perception of the mechanics of insanity, cuts deeply into the darkness of the morbid brain.... He is one of the few actors in the world who can scream: 'I have conquered science; why can't I conquer love?'—and not seem a trifle silly." Charles Chaplin, after screening *Mad Love*, called Lorre "the greatest living actor."

Modern critics remain effusive in their praise of Lorre's work in *Mad Love*, although most—even the esteemed William Everson—seem to focus overmuch on his late-reel pyrotechnics. In *Classics of the Horror Film*, Everson praises "the lecherous, heavy-breathing, giggling mania of a totally bald Lorre." It's true enough that Lorre's marvelously entertaining, almost madcap work in the film's later sequences proves unforgettable. But that work is only the completion of a perfect arc, the final brushstrokes of an acting masterpiece.

Other Notable Performances

Lorre owes his standing as a "horror star" largely to his monumental performance in *Mad Love*.

While he proved equally adept in comic roles and (infrequently) as a heroic lead, Lorre made only a handful of films that can be placed confidently within the horror genre. Plus, several of those—*You'll Find Out* (1940), *The Boogie Man Will Get You* (1942), *The Raven* (1963) and *The Comedy of Terrors* (1963)—were horror comedies. The omnibus *Tales of Terror* (1962) was two-thirds straight horror, but Lorre appeared in the lone comedic segment. Films like *M, Stranger on the Third Floor* (1940) and *The Face Behind the Mask* (1941) remain borderline horrors at best. *20,000 Leagues Under the Sea* (1954) and *Voyage to the Bottom of the Sea* (1961) are science fiction, not horror. Only *The Beast with Five Fingers* (1946) and *Invisible Agent* (1942) are lead-pipe-cinch horror films. And *Invisible Agent* plays more like an espionage thriller than a monster movie.

No matter how many of his pictures you count as horror, however, Lorre retains his status as one of the screen's preeminent purveyors of murder and mayhem.

The star gave one of his best, least appreciated portrayals in *Stranger on the Third Floor*. Lorre, despite extremely limited screen time, dominates this film. He packs every line, every gesture with meaning. Never again would the actor accomplish so much with so few lines. His performance in

Lorre contributed another chilling performance in *Stranger on the Third Floor* (1940). Despite limited screen time, he dominates the film. (Photograph courtesy Ted Okuda.)

Stranger could serve as a sort of Cliff's Notes for Lorre's entire catalogue of movie madmen.

A strong case could be made that Lorre's work in *The Face Behind the Mask* ranks as the very best of his career. He is stunning. This dark melodrama provides another part that seems tailor-made for Lorre's gifts. He plays a man who is rejected by society and turns to crime after his face is horribly scarred in a fire.

Lorre gave one of his most delightful and best-remembered performances as the effete Joel Cairo in *The Maltese Falcon*. His finest hour as a heroic lead came in an overlooked gem called *The Mask of Dimitrios* (1944), one of his post–*Falcon* collaborations with Greenstreet.

His acerbic wit and impeccable timing (not to mention his ever-ready ad libs) enabled Lorre to shine in many of his comedic roles, particularly the three pictures he made for American International Pictures, *Tales of Terror, The Raven* and *The Comedy of Terrors*. During an era when too often the actor seemed bloated, miscast and disinterested, these films gave moviegoers reason to remember why they loved Lorre in the first place.

JOHN CARRADINE

During a career that spanned six decades, John Carradine appeared in some of the very best movies ever made—and in many of the very worst. Along the way, he sired a screen dynasty and carved out a name for himself as one of Hollywood's most colorful characters. After a while, it became difficult to separate John Carradine the actor from John Carradine the legend.

William Reed Carradine (his given name) was born in New York City in February 1906 to an upper-middle-class family. He was a precocious child, gifted artistically, who fell in love with theater in general and Shakespeare in particular after attending a performance of *The Merchant of Venice* as a teenager. Before he turned 20, Carradine took to the road as an itinerant painter and actor. He drifted across America to

John Carradine had many great films, and many more poor ones, on his résumé by the time he posed for this publicity still.

Hollywood, where he began landing occasional bit parts in movies. Around this time, legend has it, he also marched up and down the streets of Hollywood in a Victorian cloak, reciting Shakespearean speeches at the top of his lungs.

During this era, Carradine made brief appearances in a few Universal horror classics, including *The Black Cat* (1934) and *Bride of Frankenstein* (1935). Later, Carradine (dubiously) claimed that he turned down the role of the Monster in the original *Frankenstein* (1931). Carradine, cast as a sadistic jailer, scored a breakthrough in the Civil War era prison melodrama *The Prisoner of Shark Island* (1936), directed by John Ford. He earned rave reviews and won a contract from 20th Century–Fox. He also contributed memorable supporting performances to Ford's greatest triumphs, *Stagecoach* (1939) and *The Grapes of Wrath* (1940). Although he had sympathetic parts in those two films, he was typically cast as the heavy. His performance in *Jesse James* (1939) cemented his status as one of Hollywood's premier villains.

In retrospect, Carradine's Hollywood ascension seems almost inevitable. Few stars have ever filled a movie screen like John Carradine. To employ a hackneyed phrase, the camera loved him. It's virtually impossible to take your eyes off his tall, lanky figure or his elongated face whenever he's in frame. Of course, this is a gift any actor would covet, but it sometimes worked against him. That's because, like many of the great horror stars, at heart Carradine remained a self-confessed "ham," ready to lapse into arch theatricality at any opportunity. (Only a chronic extrovert would shout Shakespeare at puzzled cab drivers on Hollywood Boulevard.) From Carradine, who possessed such astounding personal charisma to begin with, even a mildly risible performance could seem over the top.

"It isn't that he hasn't the sensitivity necessary to play any role," director Edgar G. Ulmer told *Modern Monsters* Magazine (as quoted in Tom Weaver's book *John Carradine: The Films*), "it's that, thanks to his Shakespearean training, he's almost *too strong* for the screen."

When his contract at Fox ran out, Carradine freelanced. At first this proved very lucrative. Carradine started his own Shakespearean theater troupe, funded with income from his film roles. To keep the troupe in business, Carradine began taking almost any and all roles offered. So the character star began appearing in chintzy productions like Monogram's *Voodoo Man* (1944), which damaged his reputation. When Carradine began making the rounds on Poverty Row, he simply was looking for quick paychecks. To his surprise, he also found one of the greatest roles of his career.

Bluebeard **(1944)**—John Carradine left a legacy of outstanding performances of all sorts—in leading roles and supporting parts, as the hero and the heavy, in Westerns, horror films, dramas and comedies. However, a special place of honor must be reserved for Carradine's turn as the demented painter in director Edgar G. Ulmer's Poverty Row miracle, *Bluebeard*.

Bluebeard appears to be the only horror project that Carradine approached with the same sobriety of intent he brought to his mainstream roles. His work as a supporting player in A-budget pictures almost always proved controlled, thoughtful and convincing. In contrast, his performances within the horror genre, although usually colorful and entertaining, were routinely broad, sometimes overwrought and almost never naturalistic.

Granted, it's difficult to deliver a well-considered, unaffected performance while performing in trash like *Frankenstein Island* (1981). With *Bluebeard*, he enjoyed a part worthy of his best efforts. Gaston Morrell unquestionably ranks as the best-written character Carradine ever portrayed in a horror film. Carradine also benefited from the guidance of Ulmer, the most talented director with whom he would work in horror films (unless you count his bit part in James Whale's *Bride of Frankenstein*).

"John Carradine was a person I could hang on to," Ulmer told interviewer Peter Bogdanovich (as quoted in Bogdanovich's book *Who the Devil Made It*). "He knew what we were trying to do." What Ulmer was trying to do was craft an understated psychological thriller, not dissimilar to the films producer Val Lewton was producing across town at RKO. One can only assume that Carradine preferred this more literate, character-driven approach to the sort of thing he was doing in other horror shows of similar vintage. For instance, in his first starring role in a horror film, Universal's *Captive Wild Woman* (1943), he played a wacky scientist who transforms an ape into a woman (played by talentless ingénue Acquanetta).

Whether inspired by the material or led by Ulmer, however, Carradine is at his quietest and most powerful in *Bluebeard*. With his subtle, even reticent performance, he sketches an evocative portrait of a sensitive but damaged character driven by dark impulses beyond his control.

As the film opens, all Paris is clutched in the grip of terror. Several young women have fallen victim to a mysterious strangler nicknamed Bluebeard. Police are combing the city for clues to his identity. Gaston Morrell (Carradine), mild-mannered proprietor of a marionette show and sometimes painter, seems an unlikely suspect. After a chance meeting on the street, Morrell invites Lucille (Jean Parker) to attend his puppet show. After the show the two flirt, and Gaston commissions Lucille, a seamstress, to fashion some new costumes for his marionettes.

Gaston places his hand on Lucille's chin and studies her profile. When Lucille asks, "Are you trying to decide how you'll paint me?," Gaston grimaces. He turns his head, a gesture symbolic of Gaston's desire to turn away from his compulsion to kill. "I'm not going to paint you," he croaks in a tight-throated voice, his face hidden in shadow. Throughout this scene, Gaston remains passive. To underscore this, Carradine restricts his supple baritone to its most soothing tones.

Gaston returns to his apartment, where he finds his jealous lover, Renee (Sonia Sorel, Carradine's real-life second wife), awaiting him. When she confronts him, again Gaston attempts to move away, turning his back on Renee to walk upstairs. She forces the issue, and Gaston slowly turns to face her. In close-up, Carradine pivots from three-quarter profile to stare directly into the camera. His lips are pursed, his eyes burn. "I warn you, you'll regret it," Carradine reads with steely determination. His withering stare provides another bit of visual shorthand, signifying that Gaston has given in to his compulsion. If Gaston gives you The Look, you're a goner.

Gaston removes his cravat and uses the tie to strangle her. As Gaston chokes Renee, the camera remains focused on Carradine's face. His brow furls, his mouth opens slightly, and then his face grows slack again. In just a few seconds, he conveys

Left to right: Constance (Carrie Devan), Babette (Patti McCarty) and Lucille (Jean Parker) don't realize that kindly puppeteer Gaston Morrell (Carradine) is secretly the notorious killer known as Bluebeard.

rage, sadness and, finally, distaste. When Gaston carries away Renee's body, Carradine's scrunched nose and curled lips suggest disgust. It's the look of a man lugging a soiled diaper to the garbage pail. Gaston, we surmise, is repulsed by his own behavior.

As the passive Gaston, which is to say, in the scenes where he isn't throttling anyone, Carradine's technique is so subtle that it's barely visible. He ambles in and out of scenes like an animated rag doll. He is particularly effective when Lucille visits Gaston to discuss the costumes she is to sew (and to continue their flirtation). As they chat, Lucille mends Gaston's cravat. She doesn't realize the necktie was torn during Renee's murder. Seated next to Lucille on a sofa, Gaston again gazes at the young woman's profile. "You're quite charming, quite unlike anyone I've ever painted before...." Carradine's voice trails off. He sits motionless, but his very stillness informs us that gears are turning in Gaston's head. Just then, Lucille interrupts, handing the puppeteer his freshly mended cravat. "All fixed," she says. "Now you can use it again." Silently, Carradine fixes his eyes on the tie and then back up to Lucille, as the scene fades out. It's a tiny look, but one that informs audiences that Gaston, like viewers, appreciates the bitter irony of Lucille's words.

The police, assisted by Lucille's sister (who, improbably, happens to be dating the detective assigned to the Bluebeard case), lay a trap for Gaston. He escapes, but not before bumping off both Lucille's sister (Teala Loring) and his Mephisthophelean manager (Ludwig Stossel). In his haste fleeing the scene, Gaston leaves the murder weapon behind — the cravat Lucille mended. When the detective shows the tie to Lucille, she recognizes it and leaves to confront Gaston. The film halts its rush to the finale long enough for Gaston to explain himself to Lucille.

Gaston reveals that, as a struggling art student, he took in a sick young woman. While she recovered from a fever, he painted the her, using her as the model for a canvas of the Maid of Orleans. His unwitting model recovered and disappeared. Gaston's painting won a competition. (As Gaston speaks, these events play out in flashback. Essentially, Carradine serves as narrator for an extended montage, his voice swelling and relaxing as the action dictates.) Exuberant, Gaston decided to seek out his unwitting model, to share his joy with her — only to learn that Jeanette, the woman he painted as the mother of Christ, was, in fact, a prostitute.

"This was the real Jeanette, a low, coarse, loathsome creature," Carradine seethes. "Suddenly the sight of that Jeanette did something to me, something indescribably infuriating…. Every time I painted again, I painted Jeanette. So I tried making puppets because I could make them out of wood." The flashback ends. Carradine paces like a caged tiger, squinting, his voice growing shrill. "When they became Jeanette, I could take out my fury on them." To demonstrate, he grabs a marionette and twists its head off. "Every girl I painted turned out to be Jeanette. I couldn't prevent it. I couldn't help myself. Every time I painted her, I had to kill her again. Finally, life came to mean nothing to me, not even my own."

Throughout this lengthy monologue, Carradine is positively astounding. Gaston seems wounded, even tortured, but nevertheless he radiates menace. Like a dangerous animal trapped in a corner, Gaston at his most vulnerable is also at his most ferocious.

Bluebeard received mixed notices in 1944. Most of the accolades went to Carradine. *Photoplay* opined, "John Carradine gives one swell performance." *Motion Picture Daily* went further: "Carradine as the psychiatric painter surpasses any performance he's given lately, or ever." Carradine's portrayal still earns rave reviews. Film historian Gregory Mank, in a biography of Carradine penned for Weaver's book, refers to *Bluebeard* as "the actor's greatest leading movie performance."

It is that, and more. Among other laurels, Carradine's work in *Bluebeard* may be crowned the finest performance ever given in a Poverty Row production. In a perfect world, this scintillating portrayal would have bolstered Carradine's fading reputation and helped him garner larger and more important roles in higher class, bigger-budget productions. Unfortunately for Carradine, as well as movie fans, it didn't work out that way.

Other Notable Performances

Carradine could always be relied upon when entrusted with quality material. In fact, he seemed to give his best performances in supporting roles in high-caliber productions. He brought the perfect note of threadbare dignity to his role of the morally ambiguous gambler in John Ford's *Stagecoach* (1939), and just the right blend of spiritual yearning and battered idealism to his part as the disillusioned minister in Ford's *The Grapes of Wrath* (1940). The latter film features the most moving and resonant work of Carradine's entire career. Carradine's most frightening performance may have been his portrayal of butchering Nazi general Reinhard Heydrich in *Hitler's Madman* (1943). Carradine acts circles around everyone else in the cast of that picture. He also contributed outstanding performances to *Prisoner of Shark Island* (1936) and *Captains Courageous* (1937).

Horror fans' ongoing affection for Carradine stems, in large part, from his two appearances as Dracula in a pair of Universal "monster rallies," *House of Frankenstein* (1944) and *House of Dracula* (1945). The tall, gaunt Carradine cuts a spidery, alien-looking figure in Dracula's cape. This is one instance (or, two instances, to get technical about it) where Carradine's overpowering, almost mesmerizing screen presence definitely worked in his favor. He is particularly impressive in *House of Dracula*, which gives the Count more screen time and a more proactive role in the plot.

During this same era, Carradine delivered an effective and surprisingly low-key portrayal as the Egyptian mystic commanding the mummy, Kharis, in *The Mummy's Ghost* (1944). And he offered delightfully over-the-top performances, bordering on the comic, in *Captive Wild Woman* (1943) and *The Invisible Man's Revenge* (1944), cast as a mad scientist on both occasions.

While playing Hamlet with his troupe, Carradine fell in love with his Ophelia, actress Sonia Sorel. Unfortunately Carradine was already married and had two sons (an adopted stepson, Bruce, and a son named John who would later act under the name David). Divorce, alimony and child support placed additional financial burdens on Carradine, as did his subsequent marriage to Sorel and the task of supporting the three sons he gave his second wife (Christopher, Keith and Robert). Carradine also racked up legal fees by attempting to gain custody of his two sons from his first marriage.

Under this sort of financial pressure, Carradine's career buckled. Eventually, his assignments consisted almost exclusively of the sort of bottom-of-the-barrel dreck he formerly took on simply to earn extra cash. It's almost inconceivable, but this distinguished actor was relegated to vehicles such as *Billy the Kid Versus Dracula* (1966), *Silent Night, Bloody Night* (1973) and *Demented Death Farm Massacre* (1986). The less said about Carradine's later films, the better. Suffice it to say that even a talent as great as Carradine needs halfway decent material.

As the 1940s gave way to the 1950s, and for most of the rest of his life, Carradine was forced to try and make a silk purse out of a sow's ear. Always able to trade on his magnificent screen presence, he remained fun to watch. But only occasionally could what he was reduced to doing be categorized as good acting.

GEORGE ZUCCO

He left behind a lifetime of roles too small for his talent.

Film critic Paul Zimmerman used those words to eulogize actor Robert Ryan, but the sentiment applies just as well to George Zucco. Often Zucco was much better than the films in which he appeared. Especially while working in the horror genre, he brought exceptional craftsmanship and impeccable taste to productions that didn't deserve either commodity. As film historian Gregory Mank wrote in a feature article on Zucco in *Filmfax* magazine (February-March, 1992), "This British stage actor exuded sophistication, intelligence and professionalism, which often saved an otherwise mundane melodrama."

Like his contemporaries Peter Lorre and John Carradine, Zucco alternated between supporting parts, usually as the heavy, in "respectable" A-budget dramas and leading roles in B-grade (or even lower grade) monster movies. In both worlds, he excelled.

Zucco's icy, understated style set him apart from the overheated overacting of most other screen villains. If a less maniacal, more reasonable-sounding way to read a line existed, Zucco would find it. He seldom stooped to on-screen apoplexy. Zucco could convey unspeakable fury by simply narrowing his eyes, or maybe cocking his head.

George Zucco (his real name — who would change his name to George Zucco?) was born in January 1886 in Manchester, England. As a teenager he and his family immigrated to Canada, where he worked on a farm and developed a lifelong affinity for animals. By 1908 he had joined a barnstorming theatrical troupe. When World War I broke out, Zucco returned to his homeland and enlisted to defend Queen and country. During a battle in France, he nearly lost his right arm. The arm was saved, but it never functioned properly again. He permanently lost the use of two fingers on his right hand. The greatest acting of Zucco's career, in fact, may be the masterful way he hid this disability from audiences. Most fans are completely oblivious to his impediment.

After the War, Zucco returned to London and resumed his stage career. He played all sorts of roles, but it was a supporting part in the acclaimed play *Journey's End* that, in 1929, brought him theatrical notoriety. The play also catapulted to stardom its director, James Whale, and Zucco's co-star, Colin Clive. Several years later, Hollywood beckoned to Zucco. He answered the call, contracting with Hollywood's most prestigious studio, MGM. When his MGM contract expired, Zucco became one of cinema's busiest freelancers.

His standout performance as the nefarious Prof. Moriarty in *The Adventures of Sherlock Holmes* (1939) solidified Zucco's credentials as Hollywood's classiest criminal. The actor quickly graduated from mainstream villainy to full-throttle horror, starring in shockers like *The Mummy's Hand* (1940) at Universal, and a succession of horror shows for Poverty Row's PRC. One of those projects was a Universal B-movie that debuted on the bottom half of a double-bill with *Son of Dracula*—just the sort of unglamorous place where, in retrospect, fans might have expected one of Zucco's finest performances....

The Mad Ghoul (1943)—

The eyes, according to that deathless cliché, are the windows to the soul. Except, perhaps, for the eyes of George Zucco. His eyes are more like funhouse mirrors, twisting and distorting the actor's mild-mannered personality. They reveal the mania of his evil characters rather than Zucco's own gentle soul.

Author Gregory Mank, one of the few film historians to write at length about the actor, often refers to Zucco's "pinball eyes." It's a good comparison, not only because Zucco's eyes are almost perfectly round, like pinballs, but because they seem constantly in motion, bouncing off the walls and lighting up. We're drawn to Zucco's eyes in part because he remains otherwise passive. Restricted by his war injury, Zucco could not engage in broad physical displays. The actor was graced with a melodious voice, but typically he delivered his lines in only the most dulcet of tones. He avoided shouting, cackling and other high-volume histrionics.

George Zucco as most fans remember him, fez and all, from *The Mummy's Hand* (1940).

This placid façade only made Zucco's villains seem more confident, more powerful and more dangerous. Meanwhile, his roving, blazing eyes convinced audiences that something unspeakably wicked lurked behind that polished, calm exterior. That's certainly the case with Dr. Alfred Morris, Zucco's character in *The Mad Ghoul*. Morris remains aloof, imperious, and cold as a stone—a conniving, egomaniacal sociopath. But Morris is also something else—an incurable romantic.

Unlike the run-of-the-mill madmen Zucco played for PRC, Morris isn't after power or fame or revenge. He commits his crimes in the name of love, or at least of desire. As Dr. Morris, Zucco radiates all the power and authority characteristic of the Typical Zucco Villain but, in addition, brings a measure of pathos that sets this character apart from all his other horror roles.

Morris discovers an ancient potion that enables him to place subjects in a state of "living death." He can return his subjects to normal with a special concoction of herbs and other elements. Unfortunately, one of those elements must be extracted from the heart of a living or recently deceased victim. At first he experiments only with monkeys, but even this upsets his squeamish assistant, Ted (David Bruce), who complains that there must be "something evil in all this."

"Moral concepts," Morris responds dismissively. "I'm a scientist. To me there is no good or evil, only true or false." Zucco delivers the line matter-of-factly, as Morris injects a monkey with the "antidote" made from the heart of another monkey. Zucco looks away from the camera and appears engrossed in the procedure. This provides effective visual shorthand for Morris' ethics (or lack thereof). The issue of right and wrong is so unimportant to Morris that he doesn't look away from his work even momentarily. He dismisses Ted's concerns out of hand, without even a glance.

Morris devotes considerably greater attention to Ted's fiancée, Isabel (Evelyn Ankers). She joins Morris and Ted for a drink, but seems distracted. Morris guesses (correctly) that she is no longer in love with Ted, and assumes (incorrectly) that she has fallen in love with Morris himself.

"It had to happen," Morris says. He is seated next to Isabel, a professional singer, on a piano bench. He didn't bother to look at Ted earlier, but now he stares at Isabel. Zucco remains in profile throughout the following monologue, delivering his lines almost straight into Ankers' ear. His tone is hushed, underscoring the secretiveness of his message: "It had to happen. In some ways, Ted is only a child. In his field, he's brilliant, but his field is narrow. For you, music has opened up a great new world. You've traveled, you've outgrown him. It's perfectly natural you should turn to a more sophisticated man, a man who can share your great joy in music, a man who knows the book of life and can teach you how to read it."

Morris decides to kill two birds with one stone by making the unsuspecting Ted the subject of a human experiment with the "living death" gas. He turns his assistant into a zombie, robs a grave and collects the heart from a desecrated corpse. Using the stolen heart, he brews up the zombie antidote and restores Ted to his former self—but not before leaving his assistant a post-hypnotic message: "You will forget Isabel. Isabel doesn't want you. She doesn't love you. She loves me." He also removes from Ted all memory of the grave robbery.

Shortly afterward, the monkey that Morris and Ted had previously revived returns to its zombie state. Suddenly Morris realizes the same thing will happen to Ted—and that he will be forced to continue robbing graves or even killing to keep his assistant from remaining a zombie forever. Lovesick Ted wants to leave Morris' service to join Isabel on a concert tour. Morris urges him to stay. "Ted, we've got to find a permanent cure," he says. Zucco seems visibly shaken with anxiety. He clenches his fists and almost bounces on the balls of his feet.

Zucco's finest moment comes when Morris lunches with Isabel. She reveals that the man she's fallen for isn't Morris at all, but her accompanist, Eric (Turhan Bey): "You've seen how we feel about each other. I can't understand Ted not seeing." For a moment, Zucco's eyes seem almost blank, as Morris sits in stunned silence. "We see what we want to see most of the time," Morris says, finally. Zucco's eyes dart up to look at Isabel, then back down at his own hands, as if ashamed. "Even I, a scientist, have such moments of weakness." Zucco reads the line with quiet heartache.

Dr. Morris (George Zucco) meets a gruesome fate during the finale of *The Mad Ghoul* (1943). The film isn't top-flight, but Zucco's performance is.

Morris, however, isn't about to give up on Isabel. He tries ordering the zombified Ted to murder Eric and then commit suicide. But the plan is foiled when Isabel intervenes. Morris continues trying to keep Ted from remembering anything about these incidents, convincing him that he is suffering from some mysterious ailment. Ted eventually figures out what's really happening. Morris vacillates between rationalization and outright lies as he pleads with his enraged assistant: "When we killed, it was self-defense. Besides, they can't touch us, nobody knows anything!" Then he claims Ted's exposure to the gas "was an accident, you understand? An accident!"

Despite his pleas, Morris meets a ghastly demise. Ted exacts revenge by exposing Morris to the zombie gas. Morris crawls off to a graveyard as he sinks into his zombie state, clawing at the dirt over a fresh grave. This eerie denouement called for Zucco to appear in Jack Pierce fright makeup.

With its outlandish storyline and gory plot elements — not only zombie-ism and murder, but robbing graves and cutting out victims' hearts — *The Mad Ghoul* ranks among the most, well, ghoulish of Universal's horror shows from the 1940s. Perhaps as a result of these lurid elements, 1943 reviewers afforded the film no more respect than the schlock productions that Zucco was making at PRC. Some newspapers failed to review the film at all, and those that did dismissed it out of hand — and Zucco's performance along with it.

Even in recent years, relatively little has been written about *The Mad Ghoul*. Authors Tom Weaver and John and Michael Brunas write in *Universal Horrors* that "Zucco tempers his stock villain mad scientist with an affecting vulnerability." Mank, in the same *Filmfax* article quoted above, opines, "Zucco plays the mayhem with such polish, such sophistication, that the melodrama transcends the hokum and becomes genuinely exciting—and even a bit moving."

The Mad Ghoul, unheralded though it may be, remains Zucco's most creative horror portrayal. Moreover, of all the performers and performances covered in this book, George Zucco and *The Mad Ghoul* may be the most undervalued.

Other Notable Performances

Zucco made a sublime Moriarty in *The Adventures of Sherlock Holmes* (1939), the second film to feature Basil Rathbone as Sherlock Holmes and Nigel Bruce as Dr. Watson. The same year he contributed a brief but outstanding supporting performance as the Procurator in director William Dieterle's sumptuous remake of *The Hunchback of Notre Dame* (1939). Zucco contributed other short but scintillating performances to the classic films *The Black Swan* (1942) and *Madame Bovary* (1949). He menaced Johnny Weissmuller's King of the Apes in *Tarzan and the Mermaids* (1948), a performance not dissimilar to his many mad scientist roles. And he displayed good comic timing in the Bob Hope pictures *The Cat and the Canary* (1939) and *My Favorite Blonde* (1942).

Zucco's first and best-remembered role in a straight horror film came as the high priest Andoheb in *The Mummy's Hand* (1940). Cast as the devout protector of a long-dead Egyptian princess, Zucco attacks his role with feverish zeal. One testament to the enduring popularity of this performance is that, more than 40 years after the actor's death, when the first figure model kit to feature a likeness of Zucco was offered for sale, that kit depicted Zucco as Andoheb.

Dead Men Walk (1943) gave audiences two Zuccos in one—both of them excellent. Zucco plays twin brothers, one a saintly scientist, the other a bloodthirsty vampire. The star's presence—he's on screen almost constantly in *Dead Men Walk*, playing one brother or the other (and sometimes both)—lifts this production to something near respectability. Zucco also enjoyed a memorable bit as Lampini, owner of the Chamber of Horrors in *House of Frankenstein* (1944).

The Mad Ghoul represents only one of Zucco's many turns as a mad medico. Again and again, in films such as *The Mad Monster* (1942, where he transformed Glenn Strange into an overall-wearing werewolf), and *The Flying Serpent* (1946, where he commanded an ancient Central American monster), Zucco's sober, slick performances redeemed woefully shoddy material. These aren't great movies, or even good movies, but they're fun to watch—thanks to Zucco.

Playing on Poverty Row permanently damaged the careers of John Carradine and Bela Lugosi. It's a tribute to his talent and professionalism that starring in these lowly productions didn't harm Zucco's stock with the major studios. Through the late 1940s and into the '50s, Zucco continued to work for big leaguers MGM, 20th

Century–Fox and RKO, appearing alongside major stars like Gene Kelly, Judy Garland, Ingrid Bergman, Gregory Peck, Charles Laughton, Tyrone Power and James Mason.

Sadly, Zucco suffered a devastating stroke during the filming of *The Desert Fox* (1951) and never worked again. He spent the final nine years of his life in a nursing home. He was survived by a wife, Stella, and a daughter, Frances, herself an actress. Frances died of throat cancer just two years after her father. The two were interred side by side.

LON CHANEY, JR.

Few stars have taken more knocks than Lon Chaney, Jr. Although immortalized as a horror legend, Chaney's work often generates more snickers than shivers. His hyper-histrionic performances in pictures like *The Alligator People* (1959) and Universal's odious Inner Sanctum mysteries (1943–45) have achieved the same sort of fame (or perhaps infamy) as Bela Lugosi's Monogram work. "Campy" is too bland a term to describe such spectacular misfires.

Yet — despite all the evidence to the contrary — Chaney was not a bad actor, merely an extremely limited one. Within a narrow spectrum of roles, Chaney could perform very impressively. He was most effective when cast as a sweet-natured, dim-witted, ne'er-do-well struggling against forces beyond his control. He was least effective when cast as virtually anything else.

His inability to convincingly affect a suave or menacing demeanor left Chaney poorly equipped for most horror roles. Conversely, when cast in non-horror roles, Chaney usually performed quite well. His downfall was that most producers couldn't set aside the erroneous equation, based on the actor's name: "Chaney = Horror." As a result, this most limited of all horror stars became the most frequently miscast.

For Lon, Jr., born Creighton Tull Chaney in Oklahoma in 1906, life was a struggle from the outset. Born prematurely, weighing just two and a half pounds, he nearly died in infancy. His soon-to-be-famous father watched over the child dutifully, displaying a degree of concern and affection for Creighton that, according to most accounts, seems to have quickly dissipated. Chaney, Jr., himself once suggested that his father physically abused him.

While we will never know the truth of this allegation, clearly the relationship between father and son was strained. Senior's staunch disapproval of his son's desire to pursue a dramatic career contributed to this rift. Chaney, Sr., transferred Creighton out of Hollywood High (where his classmates included Fay Wray and Joel McCrea) when the father learned other show biz kids were encouraging his son's interest in acting. After high school, Creighton worked as a butcher and a fruit picker. When his father died in 1930, the General Water Heater Corporation employed Creighton as a boilermaker. Two years after his father's death, Creighton quit that job to begin, at last, his long-delayed acting career.

Creighton took his lumps, appearing in dozens of Western programmers (usually has the black-hatted heavy) working under contract at 20th Century–Fox (and eventually taking the name Lon Chaney, Jr.). When his contract expired, Chaney chose to freelance, hoping to land a wider range of parts as a free agent. Instead, he quickly fell back into playing Western heavies simply to put food on the table. Then he lost his modest inheritance in a divorce settlement.

Shortly afterward he earned his long-awaited Big Break, winning the role of Lennie in a Los Angeles stage production of John Steinbeck's *Of Mice and Men*, a bona fide Broadway hit. Chaney earned rave reviews and retained the role in director Lewis Milestone's 1939 screen adaptation of the play. Chaney's touching performance in the movie jump-started his floundering film career.

Amiable Lon Chaney, Jr., poses for this Universal publicity still.

He followed *Of Mice and Men* with his first horror-fantasy role, *One Million B.C.* (1940), and took small character parts in pictures like *North West Mounted Police* (1940). But Chaney remained an actor without a studio contract, and thus without any promise of steady work—not an enviable position during the height of Hollywood's studio system, unless you were already a popular star.

Finally, Universal stepped forward and offered Chaney, Jr., a contract, counting on the Chaney name to add momentum to the studio's re-entry into the horror film market. After a two-year gap in its production of screen chillers, the studio had released a major hit in late 1939 with *Son of Frankenstein*, and was gearing up to crank out a whole new wave of horror shows. At first Chaney and Universal seemed like a good fit. Chaney's first two Universal horrors—the underrated *Man Made Monster* and the wonderful *The Wolf Man* (both 1941)—gave Chaney parts worthy of (and appropriate for) his abilities. The blockbuster success of *The Wolf Man* kicked Universal's second horror cycle into high gear, established Chaney as a box office draw and fixed the actor, in the minds of Universal brass, as a "horror star."

At that point, however, Chaney lost any chance of securing a serious dramatic role, at least from Universal. He became a parody of himself as he trotted through four Wolf Man sequels and fared even worse as the Frankenstein Monster (in *The Ghost of Frankenstein*, 1942) and Count Dracula (in *Son of Dracula*, 1943). Perhaps most damaging were a trio of assignments he hated — as the mute, mindless mummy Kharis in *The Mummy's Tomb* (1942), The *Mummy's Ghost* and *The Mummy's Curse* (both 1944) and six appearances in the critically reviled Inner Sanctum mysteries.

To make matters worse, the studio dropped the "Jr." from his screen credits and began billing him as "the master character creator," begging comparisons with his father that the son could never win. Chaney, Jr., lacked his father's expressive facial features and his natural gift for pantomime — not to mention his skill with make ups and years of vaudeville training. When cast as the Frankenstein Monster, Dracula and the Mummy, Chaney also suffered in comparison with Boris Karloff and Bela Lugosi. Plus, with the exception of *Son of Dracula*, Chaney's scripts were vastly inferior to those of the 1930s originals. Chaney's woes were only exacerbated by alcohol, to which he increasingly turned to for solace.

By the time the 1940s — and the second horror cycle — came to an end, it was already clear that Chaney's 1939–42 heyday had been a mere blip of commercial success and critical acclaim in an otherwise unremarkable career. He hit bottom following the production of *Abbott and Costello Meet Frankenstein* (1948). After filming his fifth and final appearance as death-craving Larry Talbot, Chaney himself attempted suicide, taking an overdose of barbiturates. Chaney survived and rebounded, but by the early '50s, he was relegated to thankless, often mute, henchman roles in subpar shockers such as *The Black Castle* (1952). He even returned to making low-budget Westerns. A few bright moments remained, but most of his best work was behind him.

Nevertheless, he had at least one shining moment on which to reflect:

The Wolf Man (1941)

— If Bela Lugosi defined the classic screen vampire, then Chaney, Jr., personified the werewolf. His impassioned portrayal of Larry Talbot, the Wolf Man, richly deserves its place among the pantheon of landmark horror characters.

Time and time again Chaney entered his horror film roles with all the grace of a Sumo wrestler squeezing into a VW Beetle. He was too gruff or too folksy or too flabby or too *some*thing for most of his horror assignments. But *The Wolf Man* fit him as comfortably as an old pair of sneakers. The story presents an eerie parallel with his personal life. Chaney plays Larry Talbot, wayward son of Sir John Talbot (Claude Rains), a wealthy European aristocrat. The father-son relationship is distant and icy. Certainly Chaney could empathize with Talbot's drive to win approval from his wealthy, aloof father.

"Tradition ... insists that the Talbots be the stiff-necked, undemonstrative type. Frequently, this has been taken to very unhappy extremes," Sir John admits in an early scene. "Don't I know that!" Larry replies. (Chaney's voice rings with good humor, but betrays Talbot's yearning for paternal approval.) Larry has returned to the Talbot estate after an 18-year absence. When Sir John suggests they set tradition aside and treat one another warmly, Larry instantly concurs — but the best the two men can manage is a firm handshake. Larry continues to refer to his father as "Sir."

The film's early sequences establish Larry as a carefree, happy-go-lucky fellow, not terribly bright but extremely likable. While testing his father's new telescope,

"Even a man who is pure of heart and says his prayers by night...." Larry Talbott (Lon Chaney, Jr.) in his lycanthrope state, from *The Wolf Man* (1941).

Larry spots Gwen (Evelyn Ankers) and watches her as she dresses. He rushes to visit the girl at her father's shop, where he behaves like a different sort of wolf, hounding Gwen to join him for a moonlit stroll. Gwen hesitates. She is already engaged to someone else. Larry is doggedly persistent. At one point he picks up a walking stick adorned with a silver wolf's head and a five-pointed star. Gwen explains the star is a pentagram, the sign of the werewolf.

LARRY: *Werewolf? What's that?* (Chaney never takes his eyes off Ankers. His playful tone makes clear that Larry remains more interested in the girl than the legend.)
GWEN: *That's a human being who at certain times of the year changes into a wolf.* (She offers this explanation as matter-of-factly as a native of Hershey, Pennsylvania, might explain, "That's the chocolate bar factory.")
LARRY: *You mean runs around on all fours and barks and snaps and howls at the moon?* (Chaney poses the question with incredulous amusement.)
GWEN: *Worse than that, sometimes.*
LARRY: *What big eyes you have, Grandma!*

With repeat viewings, and especially after seeing Chaney's four other Wolf Man outings, this scene develops a haunting, deeply ironic air. Larry is so wrapped up in wooing Gwen he completely ignores her warnings about lycanthropy. Over the course of the next hour of screen time, Larry disintegrates from a breezy bachelor full of zest for life into a cursed soul who craves death. It's the widest range of emotions Chaney would ever be called upon to portray in a single role, and he remains convincing throughout this transformation. This is pure conjecture, but perhaps the challenging breadth of the role may have caused Chaney to doubt his ability to pull off a suitable portrayal. Could some of the heart-wrenching fear Larry displays in the film's later scenes reflect Chaney's own performance anxiety? If so, then, ironically, Chaney's misgivings worked in his favor.

Larry begins his descent into desperation with an act of bravery. When a werewolf (Bela Lugosi) attacks Gwen's friend, Jenny (Fay Helm), Larry attempts to rescue her, bashing in the animal's skull with his silver-tipped cane. But during the struggle, the beast bites him. The local constable becomes suspicious when his men discover Larry's walking stick near the body of a gypsy fortune-teller (the werewolf, reverted to human form). Larry insists he killed a wolf, not a man. His father, the constable and a physician patronize him with half-hearted yes-yesses. "They're treating me like I was crazy," Larry mutters to himself. (Chaney's voice grows higher, whinier, as the film progresses.) Even Gwen, who seemed to accept the idea of werewolfery earlier, is skeptical. "Perhaps the story I told you about the werewolf confused you," she offers. "Why does everyone insist *I'm* confused?" Larry counters, exasperated.

Soon Larry makes his first (off-screen) transformation into his wolf state. Jack Pierce's famous makeup seems more cuddly than terrifying nowadays, but Chaney's game antics beneath all that yak hair and spirit gum remain admirable. He yaps, growls and snarls with gusto, and pads through the dry ice fog on his toes in a reasonably effective, animalistic fashion (more feline than wolf-like, but close enough).

Larry tries to explain his plight to his father, but the elder Talbot dismisses Larry's explanation out of hand. Sir John agrees to tie Larry to a chair and lock him in his room, but only to help his son free himself from his "mental quagmire." In the film's daringly downbeat denouement, Larry frees himself, attacks Gwen and is killed by his father, who clubs his son to death with the same walking stick Larry used to kill the first werewolf. Before his father's eyes, Larry transforms from wolf back into man as if to say, "I told you I was a werewolf!" After falling apart for most of the preceding 70-odd minutes, Larry finally looks restful, at peace.

Critics in 1941 were less than dazzled by Chaney's performance. *The New York*

Times noted only that Chaney "appears vaguely [out of the fog], bays hungrily and skips back into the mufti." But audiences embraced Chaney's portrayal immediately and, over the years, writers (including mainstream voices such as Leonard Maltin and Gene Shalit) have done the same. William Everson, in *Classics of the Horror Film*, calls Chaney's Wolf Man "top drawer." Writer John Stell, in his essay on the film in the Midnight Marquee Actors Series volume *Lon Chaney Jr.*, notes correctly, "Larry Talbot is the best performance Chaney ever gave in a horror film." In *Universal Horrors*, authors Tom Weaver and John and Michael Brunas write that the Wolf Man "is among his handful of first-rate performances," and note Chaney's "brash, easygoing charm in the first reel and his dramatic intensity in the later scenes."

Chaney's Wolf Man quickly entered the canon of universally recognized Universal monsters. Karloff's Frankenstein Monster and Lugosi's Dracula remain the only rivals to the character's enduring popularity. In 1998, when the U.S. Post Office unveiled its horror film commemorative stamps, Chaney was immortalized alongside Karloff, Lugosi and, yes, his father (in this contest, he and his father finished in a tie — one stamp apiece).

Chaney reprised his role as Larry Talbot four times — in *Frankenstein Meets the Wolf Man* (1943), *House of Frankenstein* (1944), *House of Dracula* (1945) and *Abbott and Costello Meet Frankenstein* (1948) — and performed capably in each film. Some fans and critics argue he was even better in *Frankenstein Meets the Wolf Man* than in the original. But none of the sequels offered Chaney the opportunity to portray such a wide range of emotions as the original *Wolf Man*. As the series progressed, Larry Talbot became a one-note character. Larry's obsession with ending his lycanthropic misery by finding a way to die degenerated into an unintentional, macabre joke — an unfortunate fate for such a splendid character.

Other Notable Performances

Revealingly, Chaney's finest performance was not in a horror film at all, but rather as Lennie in *Of Mice and Men*. His moving portrayal in that picture, along with his fine supporting performance as the weak-willed ex-sheriff in the classic Western *High Noon* (1952), hints at what Chaney might have accomplished had he escaped horror typecasting and pursued a career as a character player.

Monster movie fans can at least admire Chaney for his unflagging devotion to the genre. He appeared in scores of horror pictures and holds the dubious honor of being the only man to portray all of Universal's Golden Age monsters (the Wolf Man, the Frankenstein Monster, Dracula and the Mummy).

Aside from his many appearances as Larry Talbot, Chaney's finest contributions to horror cinema came in *Man Made Monster* and *Spider Baby* (1964). *Man Made Monster* marked Chaney's first project with director George Waggner, who would later direct *The Wolf Man*. As in *Wolf Man*, Chaney plays a dim witted but likable fellow who is transformed into a monster against his will (in this case, by mad scientist Lionel Atwill). In director Jack Hill's dark comedy *Spider Baby*, Chaney brings an unexpected, tongue-in-cheek sense of humor and a surprising note of pathos to his role as the caretaker of a family of cannibals.

Chaney's most underrated performance is probably *Strange Confession* (1945), among the least-frequently screened of the notorious Inner Sanctum mysteries. The film, a remake of the 1934 Claude Rains vehicle *The Man Who Reclaimed His Head*, has its share of weaknesses, but for once Chaney isn't one of them. He offers a solid, at times touching portrayal as a scientist slowly driven insane by the Machiavellian machinations of his conniving employer (J. Carrol Naish).

In these and a handful of other pictures, Chaney was able to step out of his father's oppressive shadow and establish a memorable screen identity all his own. Under the circumstances, few actors could have fared as well.

VINCENT PRICE

Evil never looked so good. Refined, poised, ever-graceful Vincent Price wore screen villainy like an Armani suit. He understood that it's more effective to generate a subtle, understated sense of menace — madness masked by a polite, polished veneer — than to cackle and jabber like a slobbering maniac. Time and again, Price not only accomplished this difficult assignment, but made it look easy. He was equally convincing when cast as a sniveling coward, and he possessed the finest comic timing of any horror star, yet Price is best remembered as a purveyor of well-mannered malevolence.

Off-screen, Price's greatest passions were visual arts, fine food and a good joke. Although known for his exquisite taste and rapier wit, Price was an intellectual who remained accessible to the common folk. He was involved in ambitious effort by Sears to sell fine art to the general public. His frequent appearances on television talk shows and quiz shows earned high ratings. And he never hesitated to sign an autograph (often accompanying the signature with a quickly sketched self-portrait).

Although I never had the good fortune to meet Price, I had the pleasure of speaking with his charming daughter, Victoria, about her father. She cites her father's insatiable curiosity as one of his defining personality traits. Price was always interesting to be around, she says, because he himself always found something to be interested in. This attribute comes across on the screen. There are wonderful Vincent Price performances and there are awful Vincent Price performances, but there are no boring Vincent Price performances. Usually, he seems to be having a great time.

In his 1973 film *Theater of Blood*, Price portrayed Edward Lionheart, a Shakespearean ham who exacts revenge on a circle of film critics who denied him a coveted acting award. At one point a theater patron refers to Lionheart as "that *vigorous* actor." Like Lionheart, Price often could be categorized as (overly) vigorous. But even his most theatrical portrayals are spiced with playful zest and abundant good humor. His propensity to overact usually evidenced itself as good-natured hamming, and even at his hammiest Price remained likable and amusing, if not always frightening. Consistently, however, Price's most impressive performances are his most restrained.

Unlike many of his companions in the horror cinema firmament, Price in his lifetime never knew hardship or scandal. He was born to wealth and privilege, part of a blue-blooded lineage that dates at least as far back as Colonial Massachusetts. Price's father owned a profitable candy company and could afford to put his young son through the best private schools in St. Louis, Missouri. Vincent majored in fine arts at Yale and traveled widely throughout Western Europe during his summer vacations. Appearing in college plays whetted his appetite for a dramatic career. When New York producers scoffed at his résumé of student productions, Price traveled to England, lied about his experience back in the States and quickly landed his first professional role.

A few months later at London's Gate Theatre, he appeared as Prince Albert in the play *Victoria Regina* and became an overnight sensation. Price continued in that role for two years, making his Broadway debut

Vincent Price strikes a characteristic pose, cocked eyebrow and all, for this publicity shot.

when the London smash came to America. When *Victoria Regina* ended its run, Price joined Orson Welles' prestigious Mercury Theatre for two productions and signed on for his first film role, opposite Constance Bennett in *Service De Luxe* (1938).

Price's success in *Victoria Regina* led producers to cast him mostly in regal or gothic roles. Prophetically, his most impressive performances from this period came in films with horrific undercurrents, such as *Tower of London* (1939), *The House of the Seven Gables* and *The Invisible Man Returns* (both 1940). In each case, however, his work was upstaged — in *Tower of London* by co-stars Basil Rathbone and Boris Karloff, in *House of the Seven Gables* by co-star George Sanders, and in *The Invisible Man Returns* by the picture's Oscar-winning special effects (which kept Price's face off-screen for all but the film's final two minutes).

Between pictures, Price honed his craft by appearing in several plays, both on and off Broadway. He scored a major triumph in *Angel Street* as the despicable Dr. Manneringham. Price continued to deliver convincing supporting portrayals in movies such as Otto Preminger's classic noir thriller *Laura* (1944), MGM's swashbuckling spectacular *The Three Musketeers* (1948) and the lamentably overlooked Ronald Colman comedy *Champagne for Caesar* (1950). Although clearly an actor of formidable talent, stardom did not appear to be in the cards for Price.

This hardly fazed Price, who was more concerned with launching a second career as a museum curator. Along with a group of fellow art aficionados, including Edward G. Robinson, Price financed the Modern Institute of Art in Los Angeles in 1948. This venture folded after two years, but Price's devotion to fine art remained undaunted. Later, he was appointed to the board of directors of the Los Angeles County Museum, to the Fine Arts Committee of the White House and to the Latin Arts and Crafts Board of the U.S. Department of the Interior.

Just when it seemed Price would be a character actor for the rest of his career, Price starred in a little picture called *House of Wax*.

A 3-D remake of director Michael Curtiz's Golden Age classic *Mystery of the Wax Museum* (1933), with Price in the role originated by Lionel Atwill, *House of Wax* became a surprise blockbuster, earning more than $5 million. Suddenly, Price was a star. With the resurgence of screen horror in the late 1950s, demand for the actor's services skyrocketed. He appeared in hits like *The Fly* (1958) and two pictures by gimmickmeister William Castle, *House on Haunted Hill* and *The Tingler* (both 1959). Throughout the 1960s, Price appeared in ten pictures based on the stories of Edgar Allan Poe, many directed by low-budget legend Roger Corman, and some penned by the brilliant Richard Matheson. His unnerving performances in these popular films led to Price's coronation as the new King of Horror.

Throughout the 1970s and '80s, Price's film appearances dwindled in number but not in quality. With a memorable cameo in director Tim Burton's oddball parable *Edward Scissorhands* (1990), Price bid farewell to the genre that had made him a household name. Throughout the latter half of his career, Price seemed more at ease with his status as a horror star than any other actor so pigeon holed. While other stars pined for opportunities outside the genre, Price appeared to genuinely enjoy appearing in scary movies. "I don't mind being typecast as a villain," he once informed an interviewer (as quoted in Victoria Price's book, *Vincent Price: A Daughter's Biography*). "All of us get typecast in people's minds.... If they don't know you for something [specific], they don't know you at all."

***Tales of Terror* (1962)**—Not only does this movie offer viewers three Vincents for the Price of one, it provides an ideal showcase for its star's vaunted versatility. Virtually every strength Price brought to his various horror assignments can be found in one or more of the three vignettes in this picture, adapted (very loosely) by Richard Matheson from Edgar Allan Poe short stories.

In the first segment, "Morella" (arguably the strongest of the trio), Price offers in an understated, naturalistic performance. He would virtually reprise this role, striking the same notes of bitterness and yearning, in his final Poe feature with Roger Corman, *The Tomb of Ligeia* (1965).

In "Morella," Price portrays Locke, a brooding recluse who is visited by his long-lost daughter, Lenora (Maggie Pierce). Staggering drunk, with his hair and clothes disheveled, Locke looks as dilapidated as his cobweb-filled house. "Are you all alone here?" Lenora asks. "I was ... until you came," Locke replies, caustically. With remarkable economy of dialogue, Price quickly and vividly establishes Locke's sour, nihilistic demeanor. Locke tries to ignore his uninvited guest, scowling and swilling whiskey. Then he turns to a portrait of his late wife, Morella, and announces with mock

Locke (Price) is none too happy to receive his long-lost daughter Lenora (Maggie Pierce) in *Tales of Terror* (1962), a movie that gives fans three Vincents for the Price of one. (Photograph courtesy Bryan Senn.)

congeniality: "Your murderer has returned." (Morella died shortly after giving birth to Lenora.)

"I wanted to kill you," Locke confesses to Lenora. "I went into the nursery and I took you out of your cradle and I almost hurled you out of the window!" Then Lenora reveals that she has contracted a terminal illness. Stunned by this news, Locke begs his daughter's forgiveness. Years of self-torment begin to melt away. Price looks like he is awakening from a dream.

Shortly afterward, Lenora discovers that her father has kept her mother's decaying corpse in the house, rather than burying her. This macabre development provides the opportunity for a moving monologue by Price. Locke is beginning to comprehend the madness of the drunken, morose state in which he has spent the years since his wife's death. Price's face goes slack. In the sheepish tones of a man confessing a sin to his priest, or perhaps an infidelity to his wife, he explains:

"The thought of imprisoning her beauty in a box and putting her underneath the ground...." His voice trails off as his face wrenches in distaste. Then his face relaxes again and he continues. "I was deranged, Lenora, insane with grief. I only wanted to kill myself. I almost did kill myself, a dozen times. I don't know what kept me from it. I could not bury her."

In contrast to the emotionally hard-hitting "Morella," the film's second segment, "The Black Cat," is played strictly for laughs. (The plot owes as much to another Poe story, "The Cask of Amontillado," as to its namesake.) Price contributes another fine performance — this time a side-splittingly funny supporting role as Fortunato, "the foremost wine taster in the world today." And again, Price's performance foreshadows later film appearances. The success of this segment led to two more AIP comedy-horror roles (in *The Raven* and *The Comedy of Terrors*, both 1963).

In "The Black Cat," prissy Fortunato is challenged to pit his skill at identifying wine (label and vintage) against that of a crude drunkard named Herringbone (Peter Lorre). Although exasperated by Herringbone's crass behavior (the drunkard gulps from a goblet, while Fortunato daintily sips from a shallow tasting cup), the wine taster cannot hide his admiration for his opponent's skill at identifying label and vintage. "I must say, you seem to know your wine, sir!" Fortunato acknowledges.

Later, after walking his soused opponent home, Fortunato cannot hide his admiration for Herringbone's wife, Annabelle (Joyce Jameson). Fortunato and Annabelle soon launch a torrid romance. (Fortunato fawns over his mistress and calls her "heart of my heart," a line Price reads with sickening earnestness.) When Herringbone learns of the affair, he invites Fortunato over for a friendly glass of wine — poisoned wine. "I am genuinely dedicated to your destruction," Herringbone calmly explains after Fortunato has drunk the deadly dose. Fortunato's reaction, eyes popping with astonishment and panic, is pure Price — unsettling yet hilarious.

The last of the three *Tales*, "The Case of M. Valdemar," again finds Price in a meaty supporting role, this time opposite Basil Rathbone. In the film's first two segments, we met Price the consummate actor and Price the underrated comedian. This final vignette brings us face to face with Price the lovable ham.

He plays the title character, a wealthy man dying of brain cancer. "To escape a pitiful and painful decline into death," Valdemar engages the services of Carmichael (Rathbone), a hypnotist. Carmichael agrees to aid Valdemar, provided Valdemar participate in a macabre experiment. Carmichael, using his hypnotic control over Valdemar, wants to extend the moment of death as long as possible (why this would be desirable is never explained).

Carmichael secretly lusts for Valdemar's widow-to-be, Helene (Debra Paget). Valdemar wants his wife to remarry after his demise, but with kindly Dr. James (David Frankham) — not with Carmichael. What Valdemar hasn't counted on is that Carmichael, improbably, is able to extend "the moment of death" interminably. Although his heart and lungs have stopped, Valdemar is trapped between this world and the next. His disembodied voice (filtered through a spooky, tremulous echo effect) cries out for release: "Give me peace!" Valdemar moans in vain even as his body begins to deteriorate, turning chalky as it lays in state.

Carmichael vows to sever his control over Valdemar, but only if Helene agrees to marry him instead of Dr. James. Incensed at Carmichael's treachery, Valdemar wills his corpse to animation. Carmichael recoils in horror as the zombie-like form begins to disintegrate. For a spectacularly ghastly climax, Valdemar's body seizes Carmichael and melts into a puddle of protoplasmic goo, killing the hypnotist in the process.

Price's delivery is far more, um, *stylized* in this segment than in "Morella" or even "The Black Cat." Perhaps Price felt his performance needed some extra octane to keep from being outdistanced by Rathbone's arch theatricality. In any event, the approach suits Matheson's script, which calls on Price to appear weary but benevolent (on his deathbed), then frightened and agonized (in his astral form) and finally enraged and ruthless (as the reanimated corpse), all in the space of a scant 20 minutes. It would have been impossible to convincingly evoke all of those emotions in a naturalistic manner in the time allotted.

Tales of Terror may be Price's most under-appreciated work. Contemporary observers brushed the picture aside and Price along with it. The *New York Times* critic dismissed Price's efforts by noting that Rathbone (as opposed to Price) "at least bothers to act." Recent criticism has provided a little more support. Philip Hardy's *Encyclopedia of Horror Films* refers to Price's performance in the third segment as "fine," and *The Video Hound's Golden Movie Retriever* calls his performance in the first segment "excellent." Nevertheless, probably because the film itself ranks among the lesser entries in the AIP Corman-Poe series, *Tales of Terror* almost never enters into discussions about the actor's best work. It should.

The Masque of the Red Death (1964)

—AIP's Poe adaptations seemed to bring out the best in Price, especially those helmed by Corman. Price's success in these vehicles is even more remarkable since, according to virtually every actor who has ever appeared in a Corman film, the director provides notoriously little guidance for his players. Watching actors in a Corman film is like reading an author's "raw copy" before an editor has polished the text. All the mistakes are visible. Yet Price made very few errors in Corman's Poe pictures, which also include *House of Usher, Pit and the Pendulum, Tales of Terror, The Tomb of Ligeia, The Raven* and *The Haunted Palace*.

Time and again in these films Price hits just the right note, finding the correct tenor for each role. His perfect pitch fails him only rarely (during parts of *Pit and the Pendulum* and *The Haunted Palace*). Without a strong hand to keep him in line, Price's work tends toward the robust, but each of these performances is carefully crafted, rich in subtle nuances absent from Price's work in other pictures from the same period (such as *Diary of a Madman* and *Master of the World*).

Perhaps Price flourished in these pictures because he respected the material; he held a genuine affinity for Poe. Whatever the reason, Price gave Corman some of the actor's best-loved and most enduring characterizations. The finest of this lot was his portrayal of Prospero, the debauched Italian prince who revels within the safety of his castle while outside his subjects are ravaged by plague, in *The Masque of the Red Death*.

As the film opens, preening Prospero (decked out in a frilled hat, flowing cape and sequined blouse) tours his dominion. When two of his subjects balk at Prospero's invitation to attend a banquet, the prince orders the men killed. A beautiful peasant girl, Francesca (Jane Asher), pleads for mercy. Prospero's traveling companion, Alfredo, remarks after spying the lovely waif: "Have such eyes ever known sin?" "They will, Alfredo, they will," Prospero answers. Price's voice is melodious.

When a woman of the village is discovered with the dread plague of the Red

Prince Prospero (Price, center) taunts Gino (David Weston) as guards hold the young man at sword's point in this scene from *The Masque of the Red Death* (1964). Francesca (Jane Asher), Gino's fiancée and the object of Prospero's desire, looks on helplessly.

Death, Prospero orders Francesca to accompany him back to his castle. Then, with a cavalier wave of the hand, he commands: "Burn the village to the ground." Price oozes oily charm and radiates icy indifference to human suffering.

Prospero is equally cool to his own wife, Julianna (Hazel Court). When Julianna discovers Francesca bathing in her boudoir, he asks: "Must she always bathe in my bedroom?" "We shall find you another room," Prospero replies. Price's delivery of this line, blending superb comic timing with his trademark sneer, is priceless.

Later, Price enjoys a bravura monologue. While his guests stand in awe, Prospero lectures on the subject of terror. Price orates with Shakespearean zest, presenting much of the dialogue in a silky stage whisper: "Terror? What is terror? ... Is it to awaken and hear the passing of time? Or is it the failing beat of your own heart? Or is it the footsteps of someone who, just a moment before, was in your room?"

Prospero gets snide kicks from degrading his guests, commanding them to imitate various animals: a pig, a worm and a jackass. On the heels of such sadistic heartlessness, Price brings a measure of pathos to Prospero as the prince explains why he has forsaken God to worship Satan: "Can you look around this world and believe in the goodness of a God who rules it? Famine, pestilence, war, disease and death, they rule this world.... If a god of love and life ever did exist, He is long since dead. Someone, something rules in His place."

Given a bombastic reading, these lines might have sounded like cookie-cutter Gothic Villain dialogue. Price's sensitive, quiet reading suggests unexpected vulnerability beneath Prospero's bitter cynicism. Maybe this is an act that Prospero is putting on to seduce Francesca. Or perhaps Prospero is not simply malevolent, but rather misguided.

This undercurrent of pathos brings an intriguing uncertainty to the film's later movements, as when Prospero tells Francesca, "I want to save your soul so you can join me in the glories of Hell." Price reads the line with utter conviction. Might the prince, applying his own twisted logic, truly believe he is acting in the peasant girl's best interests?

Prospero also deserves some respect as a devout practitioner of his faith (even if that faith happens to be Satanism). Instead of exploiting this element for cheap shock value, Price approaches the rites of Lucifer with the same reverence that Catholics afford Holy Communion. The film's climax succeeds only because Price has convinced us of Prospero's zealotry.

The personification of the Red Death (a masked, red-cloaked specter) infiltrates the palace to claim Prospero and his guests. At first Prospero believes the Red Death is Satan himself. Price grovels giddily. When the red apparition removes his mask, however, he wears Prospero's face—indicating that death has come for the prince. "Each man creates his own heaven, his own hell," the Red Death explains. Price's look of stunned agony as he is overtaken by plague remains the film's most unforgettable image.

Along with *Conqueror Worm*, *The Masque of the Red Death* ranks among Price's most critically laurelled work. Contemporary reviewers seemed to enjoy the film—and Price's performance in it—more than they felt they should. *The New York Times'* Eugene Archer wrote that Price played "with gusto ... scowling and smirking all over the place."

Recent criticism has offered more intellectual insight. Hardy, in his *Encyclopedia*, writes, "Price, initiating tortures with a characteristic air of sadistic glee, also conveys a genuine philosophical curiosity as to the unknown territories into which his quest for evil may lead him. One readily believes in this world of his, where good and evil are not merely words but ideas to be tested and perhaps found wanting."

The Masque of the Red Death features Price at his most colorful, energetic and entertaining.

Conqueror Worm (a.k.a. Witchfinder General) (1968)

—Embraced by many critics as the finest performance of his career, *Conqueror Worm* finds Price at the pinnacle of his ability. He was never more believable or more chilling than as Matthew Hopkins, "witchfinder general." Although his screen time is limited, the long shadow of Price's lecherous inquisitor dominates the film.

Such impact was not achieved without significant struggle for all concerned. As usual, Price wanted to chew the scenery. By his own admission, the actor battled daily with uncompromising director Michael Reeves. "What he wanted from me was a low-key, menacing portrayal," Price told *Filmfax* magazine interviewer Gregory J.M. Castos. "He got it, though I fought him almost every step of the way. But I think it's one of the best film performances I've ever given."

Price's presence is confined primarily to two long sequences. The first begins as Hopkins and his assistant, Stearne (Robert Russell), interrogate a priest accused of witchcraft. Price's matter-of-fact delivery ("A simple confession, that's all we ask") makes Hopkins' villainy only too convincing. He looks blasé as Stearne repeatedly stabs the priest in the back, searching for "the Devil's mark." Hopkins, it's obvious from Price's detached demeanor, has done this countless times before and has no compunction about torturing and killing yet again, even if the victim is a man of God. The witchfinder perks up only when he spots the priest's lovely niece, Sara (Hilary Dwyer), fleeing from the rectory.

Hopkins overtakes the girl and, when Sara protests his treatment of the priest, suggests, "Perhaps in private talk you might be able to shed some light on his innocence." The words are sanctimonious, but Price's delivery is flavored with the honey of seduction. As he speaks, Hopkins' eyes remain fixed on Sara's bosom. "Perhaps in the quiet of your room tonight, you might be able to prove him guiltless," he coos.

That evening, Hopkins sneaks away from Stearne to visit Sara at the rectory. Hopkins agrees to let the priest live (albeit in prison) if Sara services him. "Men sometimes have strange motives for what they do. My motive in coming here was ... to find the truth. Justice must be done," Hopkins explains as he unbuttons her bodice. With a single raised eyebrow and a small lilt in his voice, Price makes Hopkins appear as lascivious as a drooling, raincoat-clad pervert.

The next night, Stearne follows his master to the rectory and discovers Hopkins' dalliance. At the first opportunity, Stearne returns and viciously rapes Sara. When Hopkins learns of this, he immediately loses interest in the girl and resumes torturing the priest. When the cleric won't confess, the witchfinder simply lies and claims the priest confessed! The priest is promptly hanged and the girl abandoned. After collecting nine guineas from the local prefect, Hopkins and Stearne ride off.

Sara's betrothed, Richard (Ian Ogilvy), a young soldier who had been away at war, begins trailing them to seek revenge. Hopkins' response, once he learns of this threat, betrays his willingness to abuse his authority as well as his supreme confidence. "You forget our powers," smug, self-righteous Hopkins scoffs. "[Richard] could be a witch." No one does smug better than Price. Succinctly, he makes it clear that Hopkins fears the young soldier on his trail as much as he would a groundhog in his garden.

Although not cowed, Hopkins resents this distraction and vents his frustration on his "witches." Price's voice crackles with venom as the witchfinder unveils "a new method of execution. A fitting end for the foul ungodliness of womankind." Hopkins watches (Price's eyes fixed, his jaw set) as a convicted witch is strapped to a tall ladder and lowered into a bonfire. Clearly, Hopkins enjoys the sight.

After this sick spectacle, Hopkins spots Sara, who is hiding in the same village. He quickly apprehends the girl, as well as Richard, who had come to visit his wife. Two of Richard's comrades-in-arms arrive to free their friend and, in the resulting

"Witchfinder General" Matthew Hopkins (Price) and the magistrate of Lavenham (Peter Haigh), right, oversee a local witch-burning in *Conqueror Worm* (1968). Price battled director Michael Reeves throughout the production, but later acknowledged that his performance was one of his best.

confusion, Richard grabs an axe and begins hacking away at Hopkins. He knocks the witchfinder to the floor and repeatedly chops into his back and shoulders as the villain writhes and moans in agony. Finally, one of Richard's rescuers finishes the deed by blasting Hopkins with a musket.

It's a tribute to Price's performance that to some audiences this brutal method of dispatch did not seem excessive. *New York Times* critic Howard Thompson reported that viewers "cheered when Price was hacked to death."

Perhaps the most impressive aspect of Price's performance in *Conqueror Worm*, however, is the power it has when the star isn't even on the screen. Hopkins, like a super-powered bogeyman, lurks behind every scene, creating a free-floating sense of anxiety. When Sara hides out in the tiny village, audiences can't help worrying that Hopkins will arrive and discover her (which, of course, he does). When Richard leaves in search of Hopkins, viewers yearn for the soldier to find his quarry, and fret when at first the witchfinder evades him. Of course, much of this tension is generated by Reeves' sophisticated direction and the film's intelligent script (co-written by Reeves with Tom Baker). But none of these virtues would have helped if Price wasn't so vibrantly villainous, so vividly vile. Even when Price is off-screen, Hopkins lingers, the same way the sight of a bursting flashbulb remains even after you shut your eyes.

Price received warm notices during the initial release of *Conqueror Worm*. Elsewhere in his *New York Times* review, Thompson wrote, "Price has a good time as a materialistic witch-hunter and woman disfigurer and dismemberer, and the audience ... seemed to have a good time as well." Over the years, reviewers have continued to shower Price's performance with accolades. Gene Wright, in his book *Horrorshows*, calls the portrayal "awesomely intimidating." Author David J. Hogan, in a *Filmfax* cover story on Price, called it "marvelously convincing" and gushed that "the performance may be the finest of Price's career; it's certainly the most sobering."

This avalanche of critical praise is well-deserved. Price's carefully seasoned, slightly undercooked portrayal of Matthew Hopkins rates among the finest ever served by the actor.

The Abominable Dr. Phibes (1971)

— Boris Karloff had the Frankenstein Monster and Imhotep, the living mummy. Bela Lugosi had Count Dracula. Lon Chaney had Erik, the Phantom. Lon Chaney, Jr., had Larry Talbot, the Wolf Man. Those characters became cultural touchstones, and together they established the mythology of horror cinema.

History denied Vincent Price such a mythic role. It is the only important credential missing from his résumé as a horror icon. The closest Price came to creating a timeless monster was his blood-curdling, serio-comic portrait of Dr. Anton Phibes, a character too offbeat to be fully embraced by most audiences.

A renowned musician, trained theologian and amateur inventor, Phibes plots some of the most ingenious, wittiest and utterly ghastly murders ever filmed. His motive is revenge. Phibes' beloved wife, Victoria, died on the operating table while undergoing emergency surgery. Rushing to his wife's side, Phibes was badly burned in a car crash and is believed dead. He is actually quite alive (although horribly disfigured) and has hatched an elaborate plot against the nine members of the medical team that was unable to save Victoria. For each of them he plans a murder based on the Biblical Curses of Egypt.

Bringing this colorful villain to life posed several challenges. Since Phibes masks his charred-skull visage with a false nose and other makeup, Price's range of expression is limited to slow, carefully measured movements. Because Phibes speaks through a mechanical device implanted in his neck, Price's voice is electronically altered, his delivery flat and robotic. Phibes' dialogue is compulsively repetitive. Throughout the film he chants lines like, "Nine killed her, nine shall die," with musical, mathematical precision. The happy byproduct of these claustrophobic restrictions is that they hold Price's worst tendencies in check.

Price is especially effective during the ritualistic celebrations that follow Phibes' murders. Phibes, who has sculpted wax busts of each of his intended victims, places an amulet bearing a Hebrew symbol representing the victim's means of destruction around the neck of the wax effigy. Then he takes a blowtorch and melts the face of the statuette until each resembles his own mangled features. He winds up his mechanical orchestra, the Clockwork Wizards, who play a ragtime number while Phibes dances with his beautiful, mute and possibly robotic assistant Vulnavia (Virginia North). Finally, Phibes, an accomplished organist before his "death," sits at his keyboard playing a requiem and reciting paeans to his late spouse: "My love, my sweet queen, my noble wife. I alone remain to bring delivery of your pain."

The monomaniacal intensity (revealed in his blazing eyes as he melts the wax replicas and in his feverish line readings) that Price lends these sequences generates an eerie ambiance as disconcerting as the killings themselves.

Phibes' origin and motivation are revealed slowly, as the film's storyline unspools and Phibes prowls from victim to victim. In an unforgettable early scene, he joins his prey at a masquerade ball and provides

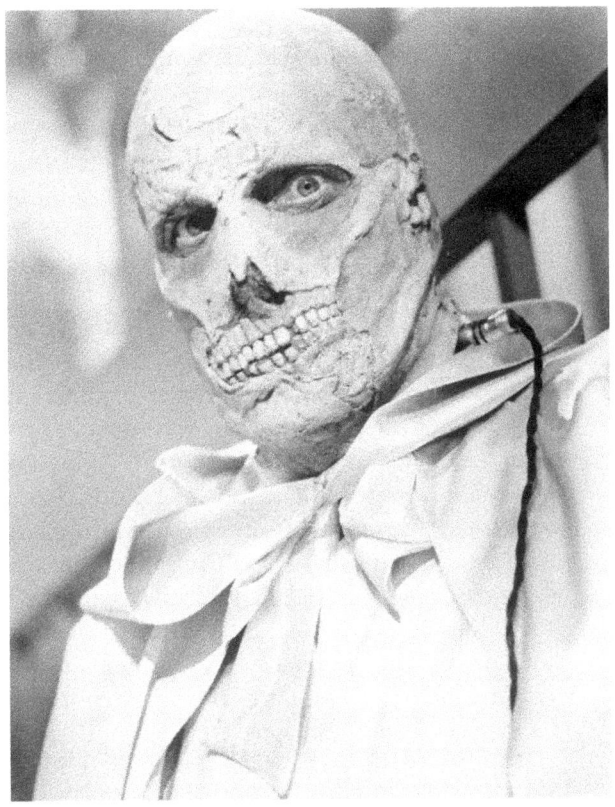

Price as the hideously disfigured Phibes in *The Abominable Dr. Phibes* (1971), one of his subtlest and most effective portrayals.

the unsuspecting medico with an elaborate frog headpiece. As he latches the mask in place, Phibes activates a vise-like mechanism that slowly begins to crush the victim's skull. Phibes, festooned in a chicken mask, patiently watches from the background as the doctor tries vainly to remove the headpiece. His victim writhes in agony and finally collapses, as blood pours from beneath the mask. Phibes takes no pleasure in this enterprise; his reaction is chillingly matter-of-fact. He stays to make sure his work is finished, then quickly disappears.

Flush with success, however, Phibes grows bolder. He bumps off another physician (who happens to be an amateur pilot) by filling the gentleman's biplane with flesh-eating rats. Phibes placidly lounges in a field of daisies (literally stopping to smell the flowers) and observes his handiwork through a telescope. As the plane spirals downward, a half-grin slowly creases Phibes' face. He relishes his victory with a brief round of applause.

In the film's climax, Phibes confronts the chief surgeon of the medical team, Dr. Vesalius (Joseph Cotten), with a particularly devious scheme representing the Plague of the First Born. He has kidnapped Vesalius' son and locked the boy to a table. The key to the lock has been implanted near the youngster's heart. Vesalius has six minutes (that's how long Victoria lived on the operating table) to surgically remove the key and free his son before acid, descending from a device in the ceiling, will drip onto the child's face.

Phibes does his best to distract the doctor, peeling off his makeup to reveal his skull-like face and taunting Vesalius mercilessly. "I have killed but nine times in my life," Price rasps. "How many times have you killed?" But at least he gives Vesalius a sporting chance (which, ultimately, enables the doctor to free his son). Phibes retreats to a secret chamber, lies down in a luxurious coffin next to his dead wife and begins embalming himself. He has saved the final curse — of darkness — for himself.

Rather than dashing off Phibes as just another mad genius bent on revenge, Price envisions Phibes as a man struggling to reconcile his desire for order, for justice, in a world that often proves unpredictable and capricious. Audiences identify with Phibes, despite his heinous crimes, because at some point nearly all of us have wondered, "Why is this happening to me?" Phibes takes such sentiments a step further by demanding retribution, imposing his own twisted idea of order and justice.

None of this makes Phibes any less intimidating. Nor is Phibes weakened by the macabre comic touches Price brings to certain scenes (like his daisy-sniffing in the airplane sequence). The character may not have become an icon like the Frankenstein Monster or Dracula, but in Phibes Price crafted something nearly as rare and valuable — a true original. Never in cinema history would there be another character quite like Price's jocular, dancing psychopath (although Robert Englund's Freddie Krueger would bear some striking similarities).

The Abominable Dr. Phibes unfailingly elicits strong reactions from its audience. Its queasy blend of gruesome violence, "sick" humor and eerie music delights some and disgusts others. Perhaps as a result of their visceral response (positive or negative) to the picture as a whole, few critics (in 1971 or since) have singled out Price's performance for comment. Philip G. Hardy's *Encyclopedia*, for instance, notes only that Price "is deprived of his most characteristic instrument, his voice," which is not only inadequate, but inaccurate. *MonsterScene* editor William N. Harrison, however, in a cover story on the Phibes films, praised Price for instilling in Phibes "a sense of gloom and tragic, perverse dignity."

Rich in pathos and in humor but still quite frightening, no single film displayed the range of Price's gifts more impressively than *The Abominable Dr. Phibes*, not even the disappointing sequel, *Dr. Phibes Rises Again*. The latter film was played primarily for laughs, and Price (to his detriment) was given much more latitude to mug and ham. Although enjoyable in a different way, Price's second turn as Phibes is well below the standard set by the original.

Other Memorable Performances

Price established himself as a horror icon with a single performance — as mad sculptor Henri Jarrod in *House of Wax* (1953). Price's work is evocative and exciting, the equal of Lionel Atwill's fine work in the original *Mystery of the Wax Museum*. *House of Wax* marked one of very few times Price appeared in heavy makeup in a traditional monster role. If nothing else, this movie proves that Price could have excelled in such assignments, had they remained in style. The film was a commercial triumph but a critical dud. Reviewers like *The New York Times*' acerbic Bosley Crowther considered the film the avatar of bad taste. "Its performance by Vincent Price as the monstrous hero ... is in a consistently stiff and graceless style," Crowther complained. Critics have debated *House of Wax*'s comparative flaws and virtues ever since. Price's performance has received relatively little attention. Philip Hardy, like many writers, flatly states that "the film made a horror star of Price," without bothering to explain why the role vaulted Price to such heights. Here's why: Because Price is wonderful in it.

Prior to this star-making turn, Price gave a pair of convincing performances playing sniveling cowards in both *Tower of London* (1939) and *Laura* (1944). The former film, a bastardization of Shakespeare's *Richard III*, features Price as the prissy Duke of Clarence, who drowns in a vat of wine. In the latter picture Price enjoys a juicy supporting part (essentially a red herring role) in director Otto Preminger's sublime *film noir*. Most critics agree that *Laura* remains the best movie in which Price appeared. Price made the most of a showy supporting part in *The House of the Seven Gables* (1940) playing the Good Brother, Clifford, to George Sanders' scheming Bad Brother, Jeffrey. Jeffrey frames Clifford for murder in order to gain control of the family mansion, where a treasure is supposedly hidden. In his best pre–*House of Wax* performance, Price believably transforms himself from a pampered aesthete to a grizzled ex-con over the course of the picture.

Price as the mangled Henri Jarrod from *House of Wax* (1953), the film that cemented his reputation as a horror star. (Photograph courtesy Bryan Senn.)

Price's comedic flair, glimpsed in the "Black Cat" segment of *Tales of Terror* and parts of *The Abominable Dr. Phibes*, was given fullest expression in *Champagne for Caesar* (1950), where he played an eccentric soap tycoon, and in and Corman's Poe parody *The Raven* (1963), playing an irascible sorcerer engaged in a battle of wills with another wizard (Boris Karloff).

The Raven marks another memorable portrayal by Price in a Corman-Poe film. So does his quiet, understated performance in *The Tomb of Ligeia* (1965). Many fans would argue this role ranks among his very finest work, although Price is equally good in the "Morella" segment from *Tales of Terror*. Price also contributed enjoyable, under-appreciated performances in gimmick king William Castle's *House on Haunted Hill* (1959) and the *House of Wax* knock-off *The Mad Magician* (1954). Both films serve as prime examples of Price's smiling psychopath shtick.

When Price's performances failed as touching works of naturalistic brilliance, they usually succeeded as thrilling romps of stylish theatricality. As a result, almost any Price performance is worth watching — for one reason or another.

PETER CUSHING

Peter Cushing was a dynamo, a perpetual motion machine.

A lesser actor, if magically granted Cushing's distinctive, clipped and understated delivery, might get by on his vocal skills alone. But Cushing never did; he refused to simply stand around and read his lines. Try watching a Cushing movie with the sound turned off. You may be amazed how much information about his character the actor telegraphs through his body language and his clever use of props. The way Dr. Frankenstein holds a scalpel or Prof. Van Helsing wields a mallet and stake not only convinces the audience that these gentlemen know their trades, but informs viewers about the characters' state of mind — focused or distracted, triumphant or anxious.

Tireless dedication to these details of his craft enabled Cushing to deliver high-quality work with uncanny consistency. Cushing's most ardent fans often boast that the actor "never gave a bad performance." This outlandish-sounding statement may be nearly true. Throughout his career, the star delivered one spellbinding portrayal after another. Seeing his name in a film's opening credits was something like a guarantee — the movie might or might not be good, but Cushing's presence assured that, at least while he was on screen, there would be something exciting to watch.

Cushing ranks alongside Lon Chaney, Boris Karloff and Peter Lorre as one of the most polished craftsmen in the history of horror cinema. Accolades have rained on Cushing's work for decades. But he worked hard for every scrap of recognition. The camera did not love him the way it did photogenic stars such as Bela Lugosi, John Carradine or his frequent co-star Christopher Lee. Whatever he lacked in natural charisma, however, Cushing more than compensated for with intensity and determination.

Peter Wilton Cushing was born in May 1913 in Surrey, England, the son of a surveyor. He idolized cowboy star Tom Mix as a youngster, acting out scenes from Mix's Western yarns in the backyard. After appearing in school plays, Cushing that decided he wanted to become a professional actor, but his father had other ideas and arranged for his son to take a job in the local surveyor's office. During off-hours, Cushing auditioned for stage roles, only to be turned away time after time. His application for admission to the Guildhall School of Music and Drama was rejected on account of young Cushing's poor diction. Undaunted, the would-be thespian took speech lessons and practiced relentlessly, applying the same stringent work ethic he would later bring to his screen roles. Finally, in 1936, after three years of workaday drudgery, he was offered his first professional theater job — as a part-time actor and full-time stagehand. Without hesitation, he quit his day job, even though his new salary would be half of his pay as a surveyor.

Three years later he traveled to Hollywood. Cushing earned bit parts in movies, including director James Whale's *The Man in the Iron Mask* (1939) and the Laurel & Hardy comedy *A Chump at Oxford* (1940), then graduated to supporting roles in features such as director George Stevens' *Vigil in the Night* (1940) and leading roles in one-reelers. Just when success seemed within his reach, however, the actor grew homesick and returned to England.

Peter Cushing, always so energetic on screen, looks a bit tired in this publicity still.

The most significant result of Cushing's return to England was that he met his future wife, Helen Beck. The couple married in 1943 and remained united for decades. In his autobiography, Cushing writes that Helen gave him the confidence he needed to realize his untapped potential as an actor. After his marriage, Cushing began assembling an impressive résumé of supporting roles in British movies, including Laurence Olivier's Academy Award–winning production of *Hamlet* (1948). In the 1950s Cushing emerged as a star in the fledgling medium of live television. He scored lofty ratings and won critical praise for his performances in a series of televised dramas, including a superb BBC adaptation of George Orwell's *1984* (1954). By 1956, when Hammer Films producer Michael Carreras contacted him, Cushing was already a household name in Great Britain. Television brought Cushing stardom, but Hammer would bring him immortality.

Over the next three decades, he would emerge as one of the most respected and beloved actors ever to specialize in horror films. His unwavering professionalism and unyielding commitment to excellence gave movie buffs every reason to adore Cushing. How could audiences resist a performer who always gave his best, especially when his best was so good? As author Bill Warren observes in his book *Keep Watching the Skies!: American Science Fiction Movies of the Fifties*, Cushing "even in shoddy films, borders on perfection."

Ironically, Cushing's amazing consistency makes it difficult for individual roles to stand out. Since almost all his portrayals are so strong, it's challenging to separate his very finest from his nearly-as-good. Nevertheless, a handful of his performances surpassed Cushing's usual excellence and entered the canon of classic horror portrayals.

Horror of Dracula (a.k.a. Dracula) (1957)

— His role as Prof. Van Helsing in *Horror of Dracula* serves as a sort of Rosetta Stone for all of Cushing's performances. Through it, careful observers can decipher the entire lexicon of the actor's technique. Almost all of his favorite devices are showcased here.

He reinvents Van Helsing, transforming the character from the feeble academician described by Bram Stoker into a swashbuckling, vampire-slaying superhero, a figure as vibrant and energetic as Cushing himself. Unlike Stoker's Van Helsing, Cushing's version of the character makes a worthy foil for Count Dracula, able to match his crafty nemesis gambit for gambit and, if necessary, fist for fist. His remains by far the most compelling vampire hunter ever presented on screen.

Co-star Christopher Lee dominates *Horror of Dracula*'s opening reels. Cushing makes his first appearance 23 minutes into the 82-minute film. Once Cushing appears, however, this becomes *his* movie. Van Helsing serves as the audiences' point-of-view character for the remainder of the story; they share his determination to end Dracula's bloody reign of terror, and his anxiety when at first the vampire appears to be unstoppable. Cushing's tense performance provides the emotional core of the picture.

He is seen first in a full-length, fur-collared overcoat, a narrow-brimmed hat, gloves and a scarf. Outwardly and inwardly, Cushing's Van Helsing remains tightly wrapped. The professor has arrived at an inn to inquire about his friend, Jonathan Harker (John Van Eyssen, who fell prey to Dracula in the film's opening reel). As he questions the innkeeper, Cushing's erudite delivery—slightly nasal and rich with rolled Rs—makes it seem unimaginable that the performer was once shunned for his diction.

Acting on a tip from a barmaid, Van Helsing sets out on foot toward Castle Dracula. Nearing the castle, he is almost run over by a fast-moving horse-drawn hearse. As the carriage speeds away, Cushing braces himself, steely-eyed. Then he springs into action. Cushing dashes out of frame and into the next shot. He sprints toward the castle and bursts through the door, without knocking and without hesitation. He scans the deserted castle, picks up possible clues and sets them back down again with quick, efficient motions. Throughout the film, Cushing's movements retain this urgency. He remains energetic and confident, courageous in the face of evil.

Soon Van Helsing discovers Harker, now a vampire himself, sleeping in a coffin in the cellar. Cushing picks up a mallet and stake and then pauses to cast a forlorn look at his former friend, whom he now prepares to destroy. His look of pity strikes another note that will resonate throughout his characterization. Cushing seizes every opportunity to underscore Van Helsing's sensitivity and compassion.

A signature Cushing sequence shortly follows. Returned home, Van Helsing

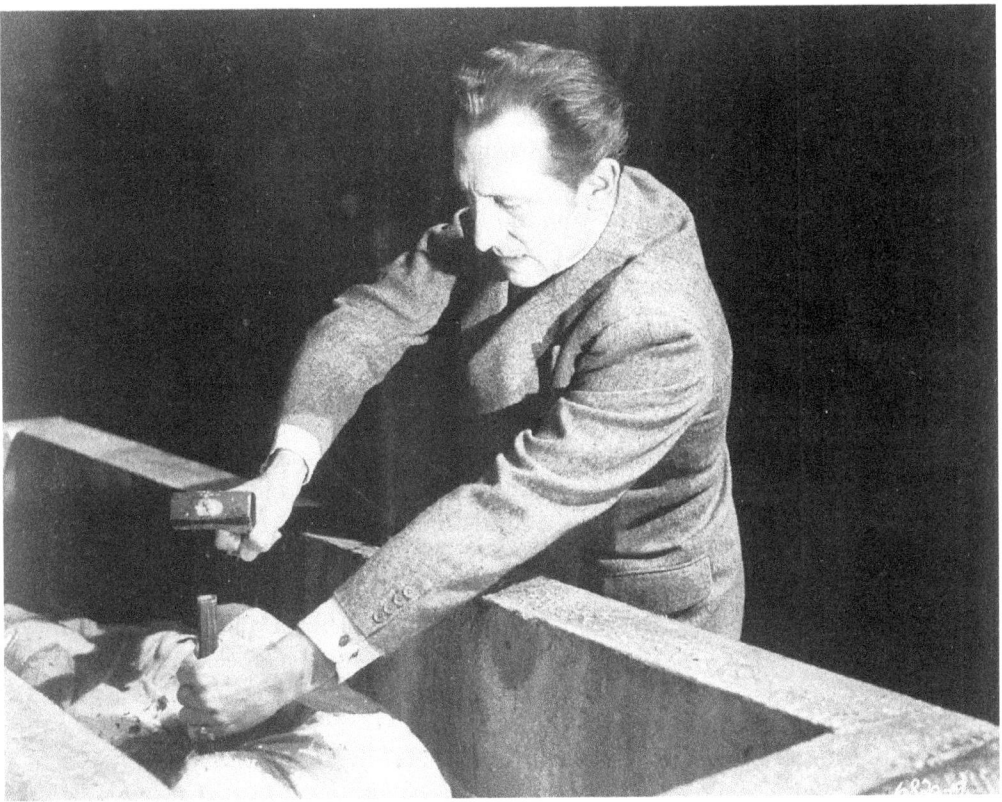

"There is no other way." Prof. Van Helsing (Cushing) stakes Lucy (Carol Marsh) in *Horror of Dracula* (1957).

reviews his notes on vampirism, listening to a dictograph recording of his own voice as he thumbs through a notebook. This scene runs about 90 seconds and exists purely to spell out (through the recorded exposition) the Hammer house rules about vampires. It's the sort of thing that usually brings movies to a screeching halt. Yet Cushing, working with the simplest of props — a notebook and a pencil — works out several fascinating bits of business that make the sequence seem action-packed. Cushing tilts his head toward the dictograph and rubs his forehead, to make it clear he is paying close attention. As he listens, he flips pages in the notebook, jots notes and scans its pages, hungry for information. Sitting more or less still in his own study, Van Helsing appears to be working just as hard as when he was rushing from room to room through Castle Dracula.

Van Helsing and his friend, Arthur (Michael Gough), confront Arthur's daughter, Lucy, now one of Dracula's vampire "brides." First they chase the vampire away from her targeted victim, a young girl. It's near sunrise, so Lucy flees to her coffin inside the nearby family crypt. Before going in after Lucy, Van Helsing pauses to attend to the frightened child. Cushing removes his fur-collared coat and drapes it around the girl. "You look like a Teddy Bear now," he tells the girl, in a surprisingly affectionate tone. It's entirely different from the strident tenor Cushing has used so far. With the girl, his movements are slower, too. Carefully, he removes a crucifix necklace and places it around the girl's neck, then pats her on the head and smiles. As he turns away from the girl, however, Van Helsing's familiar look of grim determination reappears on Cushing's visage. This sequence informs audiences that despite his driven, hard-edged exterior, Van Helsing remains at heart kind and gentle. Cushing understood that this was necessary to round out and humanize his character, and he wrings every drop of pathos from this brief scene.

Arthur and Van Helsing proceed into the crypt where the iron-willed professor explains to his friend that Lucy (Carol Marsh) must be destroyed with the hammer and stake. Lucy is now "only a shell, possessed and corrupted by the evil of Dracula. To liberate her soul and give her eternal peace, one must destroy that shell for all time," Cushing lectures sternly. Then he pauses and adds in a softer, almost apologetic voice, "There is no other way."

As Arthur turns away, Van Helsing looks down at Lucy. Cushing purses his lips and sets his jaw. He fidgets just enough with the hammer and stake to let viewers know Van Helsing does not enjoy what he is about to do. Then, wincing, he whacks the stake three times, driving it deep into her chest. When it's done, Cushing looks at Lucy, gulps as if sickened, and turns away mournfully. He leads Arthur back to Lucy's side. Now that all signs of vampirism have vanished from the body, Cushing allows Van Helsing a tiny smile. We gather that Lucy's soul has been saved, and that this warms Van Helsing. Audiences must surmise that it is moments like this — and the satisfaction of helping troubled souls find peace — that motivates Van Helsing to continue his gruesome and terrifying battle against the unholy.

The *danse macabre* that is *Horror of Dracula* culminates in a poetic *pas de deux* between Cushing and Lee — the film's carefully choreographed climactic confrontation between Van Helsing and Dracula. The two battle each other literally fang and nail in one of the greatest action sequences ever lensed for a horror film. Van Helsing chases the Count back to his castle and, in the dusty library, Dracula pounces on his pursuer.

Dracula grabs Van Helsing around the neck. Cushing's frantic attempts to free himself, throwing his body left and right, make Lee's grasp seem unimaginably powerful. Van Helsing winces and feigns passing out as Dracula chokes him. Then, when the vampire bares his teeth and leans in for the kill, Cushing's eyes pop open and he pushes Lee away. Like dueling samurai warriors, Lee and Cushing stare into one another's eyes and move in unison — Cushing taking a step back whenever Lee takes a step forward. Suddenly Van Helsing notices a ray of light shining through a hole in the heavy drapes. Cushing bounds onto a long table near the window. Then a stuntman rushes to the end of the table and leaps onto the curtains, ripping them down and bathing the room in sunlight. It's a tribute to Cushing's athleticism that audiences not only accept the idea that Van Helsing could run and jump this way, but may be surprised to learn that Cushing didn't perform the stunt himself!

Cushing's eyes burn as brightly as the sunlight streaming in through the window. As Lee writhes on the floor in apparent agony, Cushing grabs a pair of candlesticks and clangs them together to form a crude cross. Breathless, gasping for air but still wearing the same look of steely resolve, he holds the Count at bay as sunlight burns Dracula to cinders. The imaginative gambit of turning two candlesticks into a makeshift crucifix only seems plausible because Cushing has already sold viewers on Van Helsing's fervent belief in the power of Christ.

Even as *Horror of Dracula*'s last few feet of film unspool, Cushing continues adding subtle but impressive flourishes. With his foe vanquished, he pulls on a glove and gingerly rolls his shoulder, suggesting he may have pulled something amid all his running and jumping. It's a minor touch, but it's fresh and insightful, true to the character and to the moment. It's prototypical Peter Cushing.

When the film was released, British critics, who knew and respected Cushing from his television work, were more upbeat in their notices than American writers. American reviewers lambasted *Horror of Dracula* because they resented Hammer's willingness to present horror in bright, blood-red color. Yet some found at least faint praise for Cushing's work. *The New York Times* called his performance "proper and precise," and *Variety* labeled it "impressive."

In recent years, film historians have devoted more attention to Lee's performance in the title role than to Cushing's marvelous Van Helsing. Tom Johnson and Deborah Del Vecchio are one exception. In their book *Hammer Films: An Exhaustive Filmography*, they write, "What Cushing did [in *Horror of Dracula*] is as impressive as Lee's accomplishment. He took a rather bland character (especially next to Dracula!) and created the most dynamic hero in horror films."

Actually, in terms of creating a fully rounded, believable character, Cushing's accomplishment surpassed Lee's.

The Revenge of Frankenstein (1958)

—Despite his superb work in *Horror of Dracula*, and even though he returned to star in several subsequent Hammer Dracula films, Cushing never became identified with Van Helsing. That's probably because he was already linked in minds of fans with a different character—Baron Victor Frankenstein.

In retrospect, this association seems inevitable. The obsessed Baron presents a fun house mirror reflection of Cushing's own personality—a warped vision of the actor's determination to leave his mark on his chosen profession. When in peak form, Cushing almost visibly radiated intensity, throwing off passion the way the sun throws off ultraviolet rays. This was never more apparent than in his appearances as Frankenstein; when he's seen in close up in these films, the screen seems to almost pulse with life. Cushing played the sociopathic scientist in *The Curse of Frankenstein* (1956), his first Hammer film, and reprised his role in five of the studio's six Frankenstein sequels—reaching an artistic zenith with *The Revenge of Frankenstein*, the second entry in the series. In many respects, *Revenge* proved an eccentric picture. Quirky and ripe with ironic dark comedy, the film recalls the subversive horrors of James Whale rather than its straightforward predecessor—or most other Hammer films.

This unusual approach gave Cushing, for the first time, a starring role that showcased the actor's adroit comedic timing. He resumes his crackling, high-watt characterization where *Curse* left off, but amps up his performance with his sardonic wit. All of Cushing's Frankenstein portrayals remain remarkably good. But the wellspring of black humor Cushing brings to *Revenge* enriches his performance immeasurably, lending it an extra dimension lacking in his other Frankensteins.

Revenge picks up just minutes after the conclusion of *Curse*. In its opening sequence, Frankenstein escapes the guillotine by bribing a guard. Afterward, working under the name Dr. Stein, he establishes a practice in the remote village of Carlsbruck. By day the industrious physician splits his time between his office, where he tends to the oversexed hypochondriac daughters of the community's elite, and his free clinic, where he treats the unwashed felonious riffraff of the town's underbelly. By night he continues his illicit experiments in a secret lab. Cushing's body language makes clear that Frankenstein's confidence remains undeterred. In these early scenes he wears a devilish Eddie Haskell grin and occasionally hums a little tune. As he pulls on his jacket, he places a flower in his lapel and pauses to sniff the bloom.

Cushing attacks his part with so much joy and chutzpah that audiences have little choice but to sympathize with Frankenstein. Pitted against the stuffed shirts of the Carlsbruck Medical Council, his Baron emerges as an acid-tongued anti-hero. The council comes to call on Frankenstein in his clinic, interrupting the doctor as he tends to a patient. Cushing seems entirely focused on preparing a hypodermic. (One of the reasons the actor was so good in the Frankenstein films was because these movies give him so many fascinating props to toy with.) "I am the president of the Medical Council," announces one of the interlopers (Charles Lloyd Pack). "Congratulations," Cushing replies flatly, and proceeds with the injection. He doesn't waste a sidelong glance on his "esteemed" visitors.

If Frankenstein is cool toward his guests, he's no warmer toward his patients. Cushing gives the doctor a frosty bedside manner. After examining a patient's arm, he curtly states, "You must have it off." He reads the line with all the compassion of a traffic cop instructing a motorist, "You can't park there." Frankenstein's patient protests. "If you'd rather die it's up to you," Cushing responds in a disinterested tone. As the patient begs to keep his arm, Cushing coolly checks his pocket watch. When, finally, the patient explains that he's a pickpocket, Cushing cocks an eyebrow and quips, "You'll have to find another trade — or use the other hand."

The patient is persuaded, the amputation is performed, and afterward Cushing enjoys one of his finest scenes in the film. As in the Dictaphone scene from *Horror of Dracula*, the action of the sequence is deceptively simple: Frankenstein washes his hands and enjoys a modest dinner. Once again, Cushing transforms the mundane into the sublime. He cleans his hands briskly but thoroughly, as if preparing for an operation. Then he proceeds to carve a baked chicken with surgical precision. His movements are graceful yet decisive.

Ambitious young Dr. Hans Kleve (Francis Matthews) barges in on Frankenstein's supper. Hans realizes that "Dr. Stein" is really Dr. Frankenstein — and he tells Frankenstein this. Cushing — once again with body language alone — makes clear that Frankenstein remains unperturbed. He continues to dissect the chicken, to carve a block of cheese and consume his repast nonchalantly.

Frankenstein agrees to take on Hans as his assistant, and afterward relates his version of the story told in the first film. Frankenstein's original creation "should have been perfect," Cushing reports bitterly. His voice drips with disdain for those who

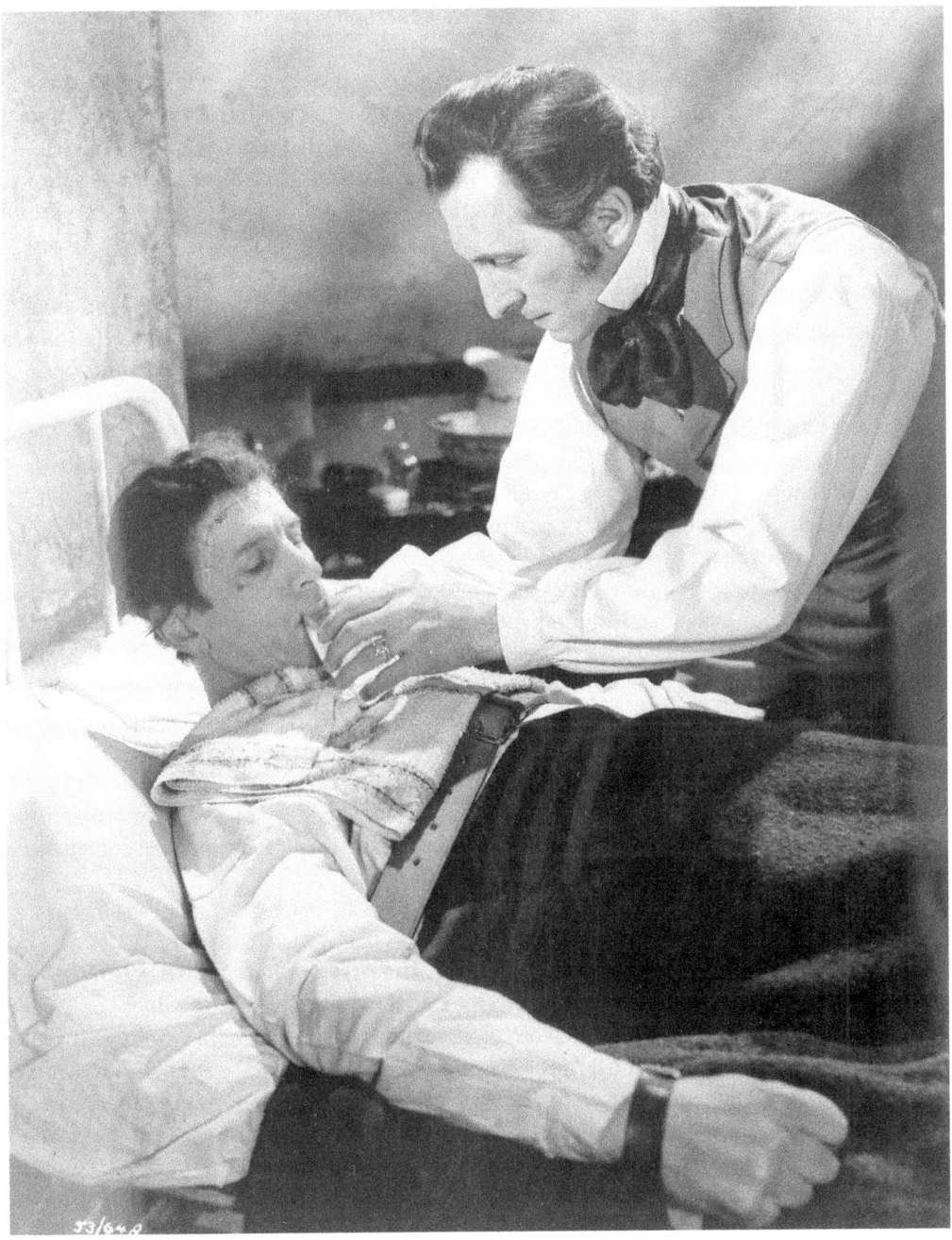

Dr. Victor Frankenstein (Cushing) displays his bedside manner with brain-transplant patient Kurt (Michael Gwynn) in this scene from *The Revenge of Frankenstein* (1958).

interfered with his plans. "I made it to be perfect. If the brain hadn't been damaged, my work would have been hailed as the greatest scientific achievement of all time." Then his voice drops slightly. His nostrils flare. "I swore I would have my revenge," he continues, rolling the word "revenge" around his tongue like a fine cognac.

Frankenstein informs Hans that this time "the operation will be a *complete* success." He states this without a shred of doubt in his voice, as if it were a cosmic truth whispered into his ear from the mouth of God. This intractable conviction and Herculean power of will remains by far the most striking and memorable element Cushing brought to his characterization. In film after film, no matter how many times Cushing's Frankenstein fails, the scientist remains certain that next time he will succeed; that he cannot possibly fail again. For him, defeat is literally inconceivable.

Cushing enjoys another memorable exchange with Matthews in a later scene. Hans spots Frankenstein feeding raw meat to a caged chimpanzee. Cushing, in a detached tone, explains that after being the subject of an earlier experiment, the chimp "et his wife." Cushing's face creases with a small grin as he delivers the line. "He ate another monkey?" Matthews asks. "What else would he be married to?" Cushing replies with the perfect dash of comedic bile. Frankenstein remains unconcerned that the chimp has gone cannibal. "I didn't try to correct it," he explains matter-of-factly. "He's been through enough and he's perfectly happy and in good health." Cushing is not only very funny in this scene, but his nonchalant, almost bored delivery underscores what a pure sociopath Frankenstein really is. Even society's deepest ingrained taboo—against cannibalism—holds no revulsion for him.

Unfortunately, such subtleties were lost on American movie critics in 1958. Most of them were too busy bashing Hammer horror in general to pay any attention to Cushing's performance in particular. The British press was somewhat more favorable. A critic from the *Monthly Film Bulletin* called Cushing's performance "stylish and diffident." Contemporary critics have been more effusive. In *Keep Watching the Skies!*, Warren notes that in *Revenge of Frankenstein* Cushing "plays Victor Frankenstein with delicacy, insight, humor and Frankenstein's own precision." He concludes that Cushing "is the ultimate Dr. Frankenstein of the movies."

By the same token, Dr. Frankenstein is the ultimate Peter Cushing of the movies.

Mania (a.k.a. The Flesh and the Fiends, a.k.a. The Fiendish Ghouls, a.k.a. Psycho Killers) (1959)

—Of all Cushing's finely crafted characterizations, none are more convincing, more balanced, more wholly realized than that of Dr. Knox, the unscrupulous surgeon of *Mania*. Due to the delicate blend of conflicting elements that comprise Knox's personality, Cushing had to present himself as aloof but not cruel, as sarcastic but not bitter and, for the film's conclusion, as sympathetic but not maudlin. The extraordinary demands of the role inspired Cushing to a rarified level of excellence.

Filmed by upstart Triad Pictures, *Mania* represented a calculated effort to cash in on the demand for British gothic horror generated by the breakthrough success of the early Hammer chillers. Producers Robert Baker and Monty Berman hired Cushing hoping for a characterization similar to his popular Frankenstein persona. They received what they hoped for—and more. Cushing's approach to Knox did prove similar to his Frankenstein, at least on a surface level. He lights up Knox with the same current of electric intensity and gallows humor he brought to *The Revenge of Frankenstein* the previous year. But Dr. Knox is much more than an ersatz Frankenstein. Compared to Knox, Victor Frankenstein seems a relatively simple part. Unlike

Frankenstein, Knox is no monomaniacal sociopath. Cushing centers the character around a core of kindness, of good intentions gone astray.

The star enjoys a noteworthy introduction as Knox addresses his pupils. He looks like a strange combination of the disarming (he wears a huge, cartoonish bowtie) and the disconcerting (he also bears one grotesque, heavy-lidded eye). Playing a fiery orator, Cushing lectures his students on the value of anatomical research — using human corpses. "Death is not only your enemy, it is your friend," he rumbles in a powerful and unusually gravelly voice. "Death is an incident producing clay. Use it, mold it, learn from it." He punctuates the statement by clenching his hands into fists.

With evangelical fervor, he preaches that good science demands cold, reasoned detachment. "Emotion is a drive which dulls the intellect," Cushing sternly lectures a failing medical student. His harsh tone makes clear that, at least in his professional pursuits, Knox practices what he preaches; he expresses no sympathy or compassion. The chief problem facing medical science, Knox seems to believe, is the shortage of bodies available for anatomical research. "Yes, in Parliament, with 500 walking corpses there, you'd think they could spare one. The member from Edinburgh would do nicely," Cushing quips. The first third of the film is laced with this sort of caustic humor, which Cushing handles deftly (and dryly). Later he taunts a clergyman by denying the existence of the soul. "I can show you the heart, can you show me the soul?" he asks. Then, in a voice dripping with sarcasm, he lists several possible residences for the elusive soul — "Beneath the arm pit? Between the eyes? Deep in the abdomen?"

As acerbic as he may be with his contemporaries in the medical community (whom he clearly disdains), Knox remains kind toward his daughter Martha (June Laverick). This dichotomy enables Cushing to demonstrate that Knox may be cold but he is not cruel.

Knox's quest for dissection fodder leads him to begin receiving subjects of suspect origin from an overeager pair of grave robbers, Burke (George Rose) and Hare (Donald Pleasence). When his partner, Dr. Mitchell (Dermot Walsh), raises concerns over the origins of the corpses, Knox balks. "I know nothing and care less" about Burke and Hare, he sneers. Then he leans forward, pushing his face close to Mitchell's. "I will teach anatomy using the best specimens available, to turn out doctors who will replace quacks." He stresses that his goal is to produce surgeons "who will fight for humanity." Cushing punctuates the word "fight" by clenching his fists again. "The individual is not important."

Despite his brave words, Cushing paces and wrings his hands when Burke and Hare are arrested. He quickly regains his composure. To demonstrate this, Cushing's performance grows subtly more still. He stops his nervous movements and his facial expression softens. Then he walks into his classroom as if nothing has happened. Even though an angry mob shouts for his blood outside the classroom window, Knox coolly proceeds with his lecture. "Today's lesson is neurology," he calmly states. Cushing seems poised, centered, like a basketball player sizing up a free throw amid the din of an opposing crowd.

Knox must testify at a hearing conducted by the medical council. On his way

Dr. Knox (Cushing) looks with kindness on his beloved daughter, Martha (June Laverick), in *Mania* (1959). Knox means well, but....

home he encounters a young girl who asks him for money to buy candy. The doctor smiles warmly and kneels before the girl. It's been a while since a stranger approached Knox with kindness, and Cushing seems relieved. He explains that he doesn't have any money with him, but that he will be happy to give her some if she will follow him to his home. "No thank you," the girl answers. "You might try to sell me to Dr. Knox."

Cushing stares blankly for a moment, as the girl walks away. Then his features melt into a heartbroken look of realization: He's become the bogeyman. His shoulders drop. He looks like he just took a kick in the stomach. He rises, unsteady, his lips trembling, then shuffles away, fidgeting with his cane. This heart-rending epiphany may be the finest single scene of Cushing's entire career. Only the coldest-hearted viewer could remain unmoved by this sequence.

Afterward, he explains to Martha that he is turning over a new leaf. Knox realizes that his ambition overpowered his desire to help humanity. He will try to do better. Cushing's delicate, reverent handling of these lines convinces viewers that Knox is sincerely repentant. "As a child, I believed in God and the Devil," he explains in soothing, sonorous tones. "It took a child to show me what I am now." He stares at his reflection in the window glass, his chin resting in his hand, and says to himself in a sad, confessional voice, "You are an ogre, Dr. Knox." His tone is not bitter, or even disheartened. If anything, Cushing sounds strangely satisfied—as if he has finally found the solution to a particularly puzzling riddle.

As always, Knox soldiers on to the lecture hall. He begins moving toward the classroom in a slow, defeated shuffle. As he approaches the classroom, however, he begins to walk faster, more assuredly. Cushing's gait reveals that medicine and teaching continue to energize Knox. He enters a class divided between his supporters and his detractors. He cleans his smudged glasses, shores up his bruised dignity and leads his students in reciting the Hippocratic Oath. Knox may yet be redeemed.

None of this seems to have moved 1959 critics. American reviewers, if they bothered to write about the film at all, dismissed *Mania* out of hand as another low-budget, lowbrow shocker. Cushing's work went unappreciated, maybe even unnoticed. Even in recent years, *Mania* hasn't received the same amount of attention as Cushing's Hammer classics. However, historians who have taken the time to study the film have come away impressed—both with the film and with Cushing's work. Critic Jonathan Rigby, in his book, *English Gothic: A Century of Horror Cinema*, writes, "Cushing is on top form here, whether dealing with grubby suppliers in smooth, resistless, mellifluous tone, or rounding with a melodramatic, bird-like flourish on his enemies on the Medical Council."

This is arguably Cushing's single best portrayal.

Twins of Evil (a.k.a. Twins of Dracula, a.k.a. The Gemini Twins, Hammer) (1971)

—The 12 years that passed between *Mania* and *Twins of Evil* took their toll on Cushing. Where he once appeared lithe and athletic, Cushing now looked gaunt and brittle. His hair, once streaked with gray, was now gray and streaked with color. His days of racing across castle sets and bounding onto tables were over. Yet, while his body may have withered, Cushing's spirit remained untouched. He continued his dogged pursuit of perfection. And, with his portrait of witch-burning zealot Gustaf Weil in *Twins of Evil*, he caught it.

Weil may be the only Cushing character to rival Dr. Knox in terms of depth and complexity. This demanding role required all the skill he brought to *Mania* a dozen years earlier. Cushing's stunning performance proved he was still able to scale the heights of his previous triumphs. He is not only convincing but also strangely moving, even though Weil ranks among the least sympathetic of Cushing's characterizations.

During the film's opening sequences, it appears that Weil will be the story's heavy. Cushing is first seen posed on horseback, wearing a black pilgrim frock and a mournful look. As the leader of a band of witch-hunting vigilantes known as the Brotherhood, Weil oversees the burning of a young girl. "Oh God, have mercy on this poor unfortunate creature," he pleads, as he puts a torch to the kindling. As the woman screams in agony, he closes his eyes, clasps his hands together and says, "Brothers, let us pray."

Later the prim Weil receives his recently orphaned twin nieces and chides them for their immodest dress. (Although they are in mourning, they wear green, low-cut dresses and matching feathered hats.) "What kind of plumage is this? For birds of

Gustaf Weil (Cushing) carries the decapitated head of his vampire-niece during the conclusion of *Twins of Evil* (1971). Weil is one of the most complex characters Cushing ever portrayed. (Photograph courtesy Bryan Senn.)

paradise?" Cushing sneers. "Your parents are not yet cold in their graves," he says, spitting the words out venomously, and flashing a look of disgust.

The local royalty, Count Karnstein (Damien Thomas), derides Weil. "Some men like a musical evening," Thomas taunts. "Weil and his friends find their pleasure by burning innocent girls." The town's kindly schoolteacher, Anton (David Warbeck), also criticizes Weil's "reign of terror."

Despite all the evidence to the contrary, however, Weil isn't the story's villain. In truth, he's one of its heroes—a sort of misguided Van Helsing who perpetrates loathsome violence in order to save souls. At a meeting of the Brotherhood, Cushing vows to "seek out the devil worshippers and purify their spirits so that they may find mercy at the seat of the Lord by burning them!" He howls the last three words, bringing a loud roar from the congregation.

Later, with only his wife as audience, Weil elaborates: "The aristocracy of this country is decadent." Cushing sounds tired, exhausted from his long campaign. "Their whole lives are devoted to sinful pleasures, the pursuit of lust." He paces round his dining room table. He speaks in urgent yet hushed tones. "Is it any wonder that the Devil comes among us?" By now his voice has begun to ring again with the fervor of his faith. "God's will *shall* prevail." As Cushing delivers the final line, he holds up his hand as if swearing an oath. The actor's feverish intensity in this scene convinces us that Weil, unlike Vincent Price's Witchfinder General, is not a self-serving hypocrite but a devout (although misinformed) believer. It's his sincerity that frightens.

Weil proves to be correct in his belief that sorcery and devil worship lurk behind the murders: Count Karnstein, who turns out to be a vampire, seduces one of Weil's nieces, Freda (Madelaine Collinson), into vampirism. When Weil learns that Freda is a vampire, he exclaims, "The Devil has sent me twins of evil!" Cushing redeems this corny-sounding line with his incredulous, anguished-sounding reading.

He captures Freda and carts her away to the town jail. On the way, Cushing hangs his head and wears a glassy-eyed look of disappointment. In the film's early scenes, the stern Weil stood straight and held himself with almost military precision. Following his comeuppance, he slouches and leans. After imprisoning Freda, Weil returns home to interrogate the other twin, Maria (Mary Collinson).

Weil's wife (Kathleen Byron) prevents him from "beating the devil out of" the uncorrupted twin. She criticizes him for his harsh treatment of the girls. "Have you ever thought that you might have helped to beat the Devil *into* her?" Cushing closes his eyes and briefly turns away, stung. "The young must be chastised," Weil replies, probably repeating words he heard as a boy. Cushing's voice trembles. He seems on the verge of tears. He staggers away, grabs a beam for support. In a softer tone, he adds, "I have tried always to be a good man." He delivers the line with his eyes closed, looking exhausted. This powerful sequence forces a paradigm shift for viewers—who must now begin to feel some degree of sympathy for Weil. This is one of very few times when viewers feel pathos for a Cushing character yet remain frightened of him. Once the corner is turned, however, Cushing steers audiences toward further pathos.

Freda escapes and places the innocent twin, Maria, in her cell. Weil mistakes Maria for Freda and nearly burns her alive. Cushing squints and fidgets with his torch as he gathers his nerve to burn "Freda." Suddenly Anton interrupts and informs him he has the wrong twin. The innocent girl is freed. Afterward, leaning against a tree for support (again), he humbly begs, "Lord, please forgive me." In the film's finale, Anton takes over the more vigorous, physically demanding sequences that Cushing would have performed 15 years earlier. But the most poignant moment remains reserved for Cushing. Weil serves as an almost Biblical sacrifice in the battle to defeat Karnstein, offering up his own life to save that of his niece.

Once again Cushing's brilliant work went almost unnoticed. In 1971, most of the media attention went to the buxom Collinson twins, the first twin centerfolds in the history of *Playboy* magazine. Cushing's work remains under-appreciated even today, and *Twins of Evil* receives little critical attention. However, Gene Wright, in his book *Horrorshows*, writes, "Peter Cushing, looking more emaciated than ever, is at the top of his form as a fanatic witch hunter out of Hawthorne."

Cushing's superb, multi-faceted portrayal deserves more thoughtful comment. Gustav Weil ranks among the actor's most gripping creations.

Other Notable Performances

A comprehensive look at all the "other notable performances" given by Cushing could fill the rest of this book. Nearly every performance he ever gave remains enjoyable for one reason or another — even when, later in his career, he became resigned to do-nothing parts in execrable pictures. Consider, for instance, the laughably awful crime drama *Shatter* (1973). The movie comes alive only during Cushing's too-few, too-brief appearances. His smoldering portrayal of a tough-talking British agent brings not only excitement but also dignity to a movie in short supply of class. Cushing stands out like a Rolls-Royce in a parking lot full of pickup trucks.

In his second Hammer role, and one of his most underrated performances, Cushing appeared as an intrepid scientist on the trail of the elusive Yeti in *The Abominable Snowman* (1957). In many respects, his energetic turn as the scientist-hero in this film presaged his characterization of Prof, Van Helsing.

In Hammer's bloody re-telling of *The Hound of the Baskervilles* (1959), Cushing made one of cinema's most compelling Sherlock Holmeses. Again, his approach remained very Van Helsing–like, although Cushing's Holmes lacks the morose, haunted quality of the actor's work from *Horror of Dracula*. If Hammer had elected to continue its Holmes series, Cushing may have rivaled Basil Rathbone as the supreme Holmes of the silver screen.

If that had happened, however, Cushing might not have been available for other horror classics, such as *The Mummy* (1959). Again cast as a heroic scientist, Cushing delivers another brilliant performance. The physicality of his work in this film ranks among the finest of his career, especially during the film's early sequences, when a broken foot hobbles his character.

Many Cushing fans argue that the star's finest Frankenstein performance came in *Frankenstein Must Be Destroyed* (1968). His work in this film is truly chilling and marks a radical departure from his previous Frankensteins. This time around, the mad Baron remains devoid of humor and completely unsympathetic. He even rapes his assistant's pretty young fiancée (Veronica Carlson). The script does not allow for any of the fine shadings or complexities of Cushing's very finest portrayals. As a result, Cushing remains limited to a one-note performance, although he strikes his single note beautifully.

The "Poetic Justice" sequence from the 1972 anthology film *Tales from the Crypt* features another of Cushing's most remarkable performances. It's certainly his most touching. He's cast against type as Arthur Grimsdyke, a meek, kindly old man who putters around in a woolen cap and a sweater, making toys for neighborhood children and taking in stray dogs. Grimsdyke remains very much in love with his deceased wife, with whom he contacts via an oujia board. This seems all the more poignant since Cushing lost his beloved real-life wife, Helen, just months prior to shooting this film. His bereavement is heartbreakingly authentic.

Unfortunately, trusting, gentle Grimsdyke has an enemy, Elliot (Robin Phillips), a neighbor who covets his property. When Grimsdyke's wife sends a message through the Oujia Board ("DANGER"), it never occurs to the selfless old man that the warning could be meant for him: "Danger? Who to?" he asks aloud. "Is it one of the children?" Elliot pulls strings that force Grimsdyke to lose his dogs, gets the old man fired from his job collecting trash, and then drives all the children away. Finally, he sends Grimsdyke a mailbag full of vicious valentines that drive the old man to hang himself. Cushing's teary-eyed, trembling reading of the cruel cards proves heartrending. He makes it difficult to endure this sequence with a dry eye. Only the brevity of this piece — it runs about 15 minutes— prevents "Poetic Justice" from taking a place among Cushing's greatest works.

In a role that, like *Twins of Evil,* harkened back to *Mania,* Cushing contributed a striking portrait of a well-meaning but overzealous scientist in *The Creeping Flesh* (also 1972). He injects his daughter with an experimental serum derived from an ancient corpse, with disastrous and ironic results. Again, Cushing's performance proves heartbreaking.

While horror fans likely remember Cushing best as Frankenstein, or maybe Van Helsing, moviegoers at large recognize Cushing more readily for his final great performance, as Grand Moff Tarkin in *Star Wars* (1977). With his radiant, nearly demonic performance as the icy Imperial magistrate who cavalierly orders the murder of an entire planet, Cushing made Tarkin as menacing a villain as Darth Vader himself. The *Star Wars* sequels were weakened by Cushing's absence.

But, since his death in 1994, movies in general have been weakened by Cushing's absence.

CHRISTOPHER LEE

Standing six feet, four inches tall, Christopher Lee towers over other performers— in more ways than one. Few actors occupy the screen as commandingly as Lee, with his razor-sharp features and bass fiddle voice. Beyond simple physicality, Lee rivets audiences with mysterious aura and lordly demeanor. He is best known for playing stiff-necked European aristocrats, which follows naturally since Lee himself is descended from a long line of stiff-necked European aristocrats.

Christopher Frank Carandini Lee was born in London on May 27, 1922. He was the son of the Contessa Estelle Maria Carandini, and part of one of the eldest noble lineages in Italy. Lee's parents divorced when their son was four years old, and when his mother remarried a few years later, the young man gained a new step-cousin — Ian Fleming, destined to create super-agent James Bond. Patrick Macnee, who gained fame as super-agent John Steed on television's *The Avengers*, was a boyhood chum of Lee's. Perhaps inevitably, given such associations, Lee became a real-life spy. After three unhappy years at Wellington College, Lee quit school in 1939. About two years and an assortment of dead-end jobs later, he joined the Royal Air Force, where eventually he was assigned as an intelligence officer.

After World War II, still searching for a career, Lee hit on the idea of becoming a movie actor. He had appeared in school plays and had a fine, classical baritone. Initially, however, few producers would consider him. At 6'4", he loomed over his co-stars, especially his prospective leading ladies. Eventually, Hammer Films offered the struggling young actor a series of roles that would transform his height from a curse into a blessing.

Superficially, Lee recalls John Carradine, another tall, lean actor with ample charisma and a lengthy filmography, including many horror movies. However, a more revealing comparison might be between Lee and Lon Chaney, Jr. While there is no physical resemblance, or any meaningful similarity in their technique, Lee and Chaney, Jr., share a different sort of bond. Both can be remarkably effective, but only within a limited spectrum of assignments.

Chaney, Jr., made numerous attempts to branch out but never convincingly played any role other than the likable roughneck. Lee has appeared in comedies and dramas alike, playing both heroes and (more commonly) villains in leading roles and supporting parts. The multilingual performer has acted in English, Italian, German and French. Despite all this, Lee remains most effective playing the aloof, austere aristocrat. Despite the actor's many natural gifts, a survey of Lee's performances in the horror genre reveals an overabundance of one-dimensional characters and a relative dearth of pathos or humor. The Internet Movie Database's entry on Lee ventures that the actor typically "portrays characters who are intelligent, unsympathetic, aggressive, humorless, ruthless and totally evil." There are, of course, exceptions to these broad generalizations.

Christopher Lee looks steely-eyed for this publicity photograph.

Lee and Chaney are opposite sides of the coin: Chaney's misfortune was that his limited range left him unsuited for many horror roles. Lee's prevailing tendencies, on the other hand, make him ideal for mysterious, menacing characters.

Perhaps that's why, despite limited range, Lee has been able to accomplish so much within the genre. Along with Peter Cushing, he co-founded the Hammer horror dynasty. With all due credit to clever producers Anthony Hinds and Michael Carreras and gifted director Terence Fisher, Hammer's horror line could not have survived without the drawing power of Cushing and Lee. Largely because of this, Lee remains a beloved icon for a generation of horror fans.

Here's a closer look at two of the performances that have earned him such devotion.

Horror of Dracula (1958)

—Lee remains best recognized for playing the title character in the long-running series of Hammer Dracula films, inaugurated with this superb gothic. By a sizable margin, Lee ranks as the most popular performer to follow Bela Lugosi's iconic performance as the nefarious count.

The most effective Dracula to reach movie screens between Lugosi and Lee was John Carradine, who essayed the role in Universal's *House of Frankenstein* (1944) and *House of Dracula* (1945). However, Carradine's stiff, pseudo–Shakespearean take on the character falls fairly close to the Lugosi version. Lee would take the character in daring new directions and, in the process, create a new icon all his own.

Lee's long, lithe physique served him well as Dracula. His agile, athletic and amorous Dracula redefined the character for a new generation of horror fans. Stoker's Count never appeared so dangerous, cunning or seductive in the character's previous screen incarnations. For moviegoers who came of age in the 1960s, Lee eclipsed Lugosi to become *their* Count Dracula.

Jimmy Sangster's *Horror of Dracula* script focuses more on Prof. Van Helsing (Peter Cushing) than on the Count himself. Lee's screen time in the picture is restricted primarily to the film's opening sequence and its finale. He virtually vanishes from the picture during the interim, his presence limited to a sprinkling of brief interludes. Yet, Lee's presence is so powerful, especially during the film's spine-tingling opening sequence, he casts a shadow over the entire film. Although seldom seen, Dracula seems to be constantly hovering in the background, as if he might leap from behind the curtain at any moment.

Lee's entrance is a stunner. Just over seven minutes into the picture, as Jonathan Harker (John Van Eyssen) nervously surveys the foyer of Castle Dracula, Lee suddenly appears at the head of the stairs (accompanied by a spike in James Bernard's score)—a striking figure cloaked in black, looking back at Harker with icy, expressionless eyes. His cape flows elegantly as he descends the stairs. Lee moves with cool confidence, not even bothering to look down at the steps. He moves quickly and speaks with a refined British accent. From the outset, Lee's Dracula is the antithesis of Lugosi's immobile, slow-talking, eerily foreign Count. The only real similarity is in the costuming: Both Draculas choose evening clothes and slick back their hair.

Lee's opening line is perfunctory, almost banal: "Mr. Harker, I am glad that you arrived safely." His tone is disarming, even pleasant. "I am Dracula, and I welcome you to my house." He helpfully carries Harker's grip upstairs and apologizes for his lack of servants. (The maid, he claims, is away due a death in the family.) But something behind Lee's watery eyes informs us that all this is for show. Dracula has some malevolent design and Harker is merely a pawn.

Our suspicions are soon confirmed, when Dracula interrupts Harker's seduction by the Count's vampire "bride" (Valerie Gaunt). Lee looks utterly bestial, his face curled into a snarl, with blood on his lips and dripping from the corners of his mouth. Even his eyes are bloodshot. He growls, leaps over a table and savagely hurls Gaunt to the floor. Lee's unbridled ferocity seems even more shocking in contrast to his genteel behavior earlier. Dracula and his "bride" struggle. Harker interrupts and is thoughtlessly tossed aside. Throughout this sequence, Lee conveys a degree of physical power lacking from the classic Lugosi-style Dracula, who was more likely to mesmerize his enemies than knock them senseless. He has no dialogue in this scene, yet it ranks among Lee's most effective. He is startling and terrifying.

Dracula (Lee) and his "bride" (Valarie Gaunt) struggle in *Horror of Dracula* (1957). Lee's performance rewrote the book on one of the screen's great villains. (Photograph courtesy Mark A. Miller.)

Later sequences elaborate on the sexual allure of Lee's vampire. His encounter with Mina (Melissa Stribling), for instance, plays less like an attack and more like a romantic rendezvous. As Lee draws near to her, her lips quiver, suggesting arousal. Lee caresses her cheeks and neck with his hands and pulls her face close to his. He runs his lips and nose along her forehead, cheeks and lips, soaking in the smell of her skin and the taste of her lips before going for her throat. As he plunges his teeth into her neck, he pushes her back onto the bed. While there was an implied erotic element to previous screen vampires, the movies had never seen a Dracula as overtly sexual as this.

The movie builds to a climactic confrontation between Dracula and his nemesis, Van Helsing (Peter Cushing). Van Helsing and Mina's husband, Arthur (Michael Gough), rush to Castle Dracula, where they discover Dracula burying the still-alive Mina as a dog might bury a bone. She screams, but Lee cheerfully chucks a shovel full of dirt in her face. When he spots Van Helsing and Arthur, Dracula bolts into the castle, providing another display for Lee's vigor and grace.

Van Helsing rips down the curtains in Dracula's library, trapping the vampire in a shaft of light from the rising sun. Lee's look of agony and shock when the sunlight strikes him is priceless. Van Helsing holds the Count at bay with a makeshift cross (made from a pair of candlesticks). Lee recoils, revolted. Finally, as Dracula's hand crumbles to dust, Lee howls with fear and impotent rage. To the very end, Lee's eyes dart around the room, as if looking for means of escape, some way of turning the tables on his opponent. He never surrenders, never repents. It is a fitting end for the screen's most vicious Dracula.

Future entries in Hammer's Dracula series would also limit Lee's screen time, sometimes to agonizing extremes. In *Dracula, Prince of Darkness* (1966), for example, Lee receives top billing but is actually on screen fewer than 11 of the film's 90 minutes (not counting pre-credit stock footage from *Horror of Dracula*). Some of Hammer's Dracula sequels are effective nonetheless. But, as a consequence, Lee was denied the chance to significantly advance the character beyond what he established in *Horror of Dracula*. Instead, his Dracula became a one-dimensional bogeyman, an insatiable, soul-sucking force of nature, used more as a plot device than as a fully developed as a character.

Lee himself became notoriously disgruntled with Hammer's treatment of the character. "I felt increasingly frustrated and increasingly despondent," Lee vents during the DVD audio commentary for Hammer's *Scars of Dracula* (1970), just one of the forums Lee has used to voice his displeasure over the years. "I kept saying to them, 'Look, you have a great, great character who is heroic, romantic, erotic, created by Bram Stoker in an immortal classic and what are you doing with him? You are writing the stories first and then you are trying to fit the character in.'" Eventually Lee's unhappiness became visible on screen, through his increasingly disengaged performances in the later sequels.

Dracula was an investment of diminishing returns for Lee. No wonder then that, in the initial wake of *Horror of Dracula*, Lee steered clear of the character. He declined to appear in Hammer's initial follow-up, *The Brides of Dracula* (1960), which ironically proved the best of Hammer's Dracula sequels. However, once Lee stepped back into Dracula's cape, he seemed incapable of removing it. He starred in a total of seven Hammer Dracula films, as well as director Jess Franco's *Count Dracula* (1970) and two spoofs, *Uncle Was a Vampire* (1959) and *Dracula and Son* (1977).

Nevertheless, his work in *Horror of Dracula* stands as a monumental piece of work, a landmark in horror film history. Although at the time critics hated the film and Lee along with it, audiences responded. As Jonathan Rigby writes in his book *English Gothic*, Lee's Dracula "forced petrified baby-boomers around the world to choke on their popcorn."

"Lee's performance of Dracula is a revitalization of the character," Gary Svehla states with succinct accuracy, in an essay from the book *Dracula: The First 100 Years*. Although Lugosi's more stately Dracula remained the stereotype for the character, Lee's feral, overtly sexual vampire seemed more in tune with its times, or at least in tune with the coming decade of the 1960s. His portrayal would inform many future Draculas, particularly in European films.

However, none of the imitators—or even Lee himself—could recreate the unique power of Lee's performance in *Horror of Dracula*. Like Dracula himself, it is deathless.

The Devil's Bride (a.k.a. *The Devil Rides Out*) (1967)

—With his performance in this film, Lee proved how effective he could be in a complex role, when working at the peak of his talent. Here, Lee validates his ability to play something other than the stone-faced heavy and, in the process, proves once and for all that subtle, multi-layered characterizations, although elusive, are not beyond his grasp.

Lee, who seldom created villains who were at all likable, here presents us with an even rarer gem—a hero who's a little bit scary. *The Devil Rides Out* wasn't Lee's first or only appearance as a heroic character in a horror film. He offered a compelling turn as a do-gooding physician who foils Anton Diffring's scheme to gain eternal life in *The Man Who Could Cheat Death* (1959); and played a monster-busting professor in *The Gorgon* (1964). Both of those performances, however, remained as thin as most of his villainous roles. His characters seemed impossibly righteous and courageous. As *The Devil Rides Out*'s Duc de Richleau, Lee offers a far better shaded portrayal.

Like many of Lee's villains, the Duke is a cold, imperious authority figure who will stop at nothing to achieve his goals. His companions follow his orders implicitly, in part because they remain as intimidated by their friend as by their enemies. Nevertheless, compassion motivates de Richleau. Despite his blustering, de Richleau remains vulnerable—he knows fear and, at times, doubts his ability to guide his friends from disaster.

Lee never looked better than in his period (1920s) costume—dark three-piece suit and bowler hat—and Van Dyke beard. As usual, Lee radiates an air of nobility. He moves with stiff, straight-backed, military precision. As the film opens, de Richleau and his friend Rex (Leon Greene) pay an unannounced social call on de Richleau's young charge Simon (Patrick Mower), whose deceased father served with him during World War I. Simon awkwardly explains that he is entertaining guests, members of an "astronomical society" he has joined. The Duke quickly surmises, from snippets of conversation, that Simon has joined a coven of Satanists. He sprints upstairs to examine Simon's telescope, stored in a chamber where the coven performs its secret rites. There, de Richleau first commands, then pleads with Simon to turn his back on the cult.

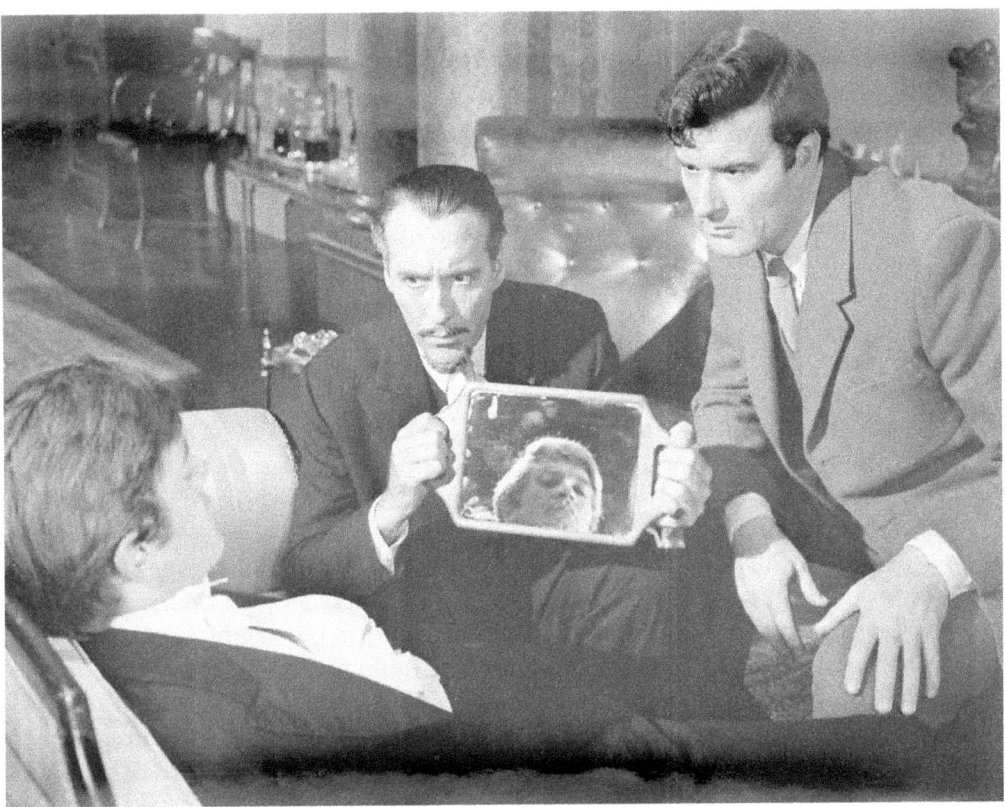

The Duc de Richleau (Lee) hypnotizes young Simon (Patrick Mower) while his friend Rex (Leon Greene) watches, in this scene from *The Devil's Bride* (1967).

He grabs Simon by the lapels and growls, "You fool! I'd rather see you dead than meddling with black magic!" Lee's eyes burn with rage, and his voice fills with gravel. But, clearly, Simon remains even more frightened of Mocata (Charles Gray), the leader of the coven.

Realizing that intimidation won't work, de Richleau relaxes and reveals his true emotions—fear and concern. "I'm sorry, Simon, but I feel like a father watching his son try to pick hot coals out of a fire." Now Lee's eyes are fixed and tense with dread. When this gambit also fails, the Duke begins to lecture. "I'm considerably older than you are, Simon. And although I've never spoken of it, I've made a very deep study of these esoteric doctrines." He walks closer, and places his hand on Simon's shoulder. This time, however, it's not a violent, grabbing motion, but a tender gesture. His voice grows soft, although his eyes remain just as sternly fixed. "I beg of you, as I've never begged anything in my life before, give up this desperately dangerous adventure and leave this house immediately." Lee's earnest reading convinces us that de Richleau will do anything — even grovel in front of his friends — to keep Simon from harm. This proves a key sequence because it establishes that, however rigid and short-tempered he may appear later in the film, the Duke is motivated by genuine concern for Simon's well-being.

When this tactic also fails, the Duke resorts to brute force. He knocks Simon unconscious with a swift right cross to the chin, then hauls the young man away like a sack of potatoes. This ruthless pursuit of his goals—however well-intended those goals may be—makes de Richleau both a powerful ally and a man to be wary of. Lee reinforces the Duke's steely exterior as he painstakingly persuades Rex that the danger Simon faces is real and not fancy.

The power of darkness, de Richleau informs Rex, "is a living force which can be tapped at any given moment of the night." Lee delivers this line with such icy resolve, this provides one of the most chilling scenes in the film. The unflappable conviction Lee brings to this sort of dialogue convinces viewers that the Satanist threat is real, despite lackluster special effects (such as the appearance of a goat-faced Lucifer), which threaten the film's credibility.

The Duke disappears from the screen for long stretches and the film carries on from the perspective of Rex, who falls in love with—and attempts to save—Tanith (Nike Arrighi), a young woman who, like Simon, is about to become initiated into the cult. As in *Horror of Dracula*, Lee's presence lingers even while he is off-screen.

The plot of the movie would be almost indecipherable without exposition provided by de Richleau. He spells out for his friends, and by extension the audience, exactly what they are facing, how certain spells work and the significance of particular objects and rites. This sort of exposition would present a challenge for most actors, but it works perfectly in Lee's hands. Delivering these sorts of speeches seems entirely in character for the professorial Duke, and his clipped, impatient delivery of this dialogue only underscores de Richleau's sense of urgency and frustration with delay.

Eventually, magic mumbo jumbo from de Richleau and timely ghostly intervention save the Duke and his friends from disaster and damnation. Afterward, during the story's coda, viewers glimpse a side of Lee rarely captured on film—relaxed, warm, smiling. De Richleau wears an easy grin and seems more than just relieved, but actually happy. When Simon says, "Thank God" (that the ordeal is over), de Richleau replies with the film's final line: "Yes, Simon, He is the one we must thank." Once again, Lee strikes the perfect note, sounding devout and thankful without seeming overly pious and clubbing audiences over the head with the theme of the film.

The Devil Rides Out was not a box office success and didn't receive great reviews upon its initial release. The film didn't reach the U.S. until 1968 where, under the title *The Devil's Bride*, it found itself in the considerable wake of Roman Polanski's *Rosemary's Baby*. Most critics were dismissive, misjudging it as a *Rosemary's Baby* rip-off. However, some reviewers—like *The New York Times'* Howard Thompson—at least gave good marks to Lee. Thompson described de Richleau as "a steely aristocrat, played by suave dignity by Christopher Lee."

Film historians have elevated the film's status. Many critics now consider *The Devil Rides Out* one of director Terence Fisher's finest works. And many hail Lee's performance as one of his best. Even notorious Lee-basher William K. Everson, in *More Classics of the Horror Film*, concedes, "Christopher Lee (normally a rather pompous and dull actor) in the completely straight role of the Duke de Richelieu also gives a well-controlled but intense performance that is also, quite easily the best of his career." Authors Tom Johnson and Deborah Del Vecchio, in their book, *Hammer Films: An Exhaustive Filmography,* correctly surmise that Lee's "stern demeanor usually does not lend itself to heroic roles, but in this case it worked."

In *The Devil Rides Out* it works beautifully.

Other Notable Performances

Lee first earned notoriety for his carefully studied, physically inventive appearance as "The Creature" in Hammer's seminal shocker *The Curse of Frankenstein* (1957). It's a performance of enduring interest, the most compelling portrayal given in the role since Boris Karloff's landmark collaborations with James Whale. Lee's confused, shuffling creature behaves like a robot with several wires crossed or some key circuit disconnected. It tries to perform simple, normal actions, but its body can't execute the command correctly. The creature moves in flailing, herky-jerky motions and then, in frustration, explodes in bursts of mindless rage. This makes sense, because in the film the Creature receives a damaged brain. Unlike the Universal Frankenstein films, however, Hammer's Frankenstein pictures focused on Baron Frankenstein (Peter Cushing) rather than on his creation. As a result, Lee's creature isn't fully realized as a character in its own right. Also, Lee's screen time is severely limited, although he makes the most of what he gets.

Many of Lee's finest performances came in supporting roles. These include his convincing portrayal of the weak-kneed Sir Henry Baskerville in *The Hound of the Baskervilles* (1962); his blood-curdling appearance as the ironically named killer Resurrection Joe in *Corridors of Blood* (1958); and his one-of-a-kind performance as the sadistic playmate of kinky Daliah Lavi in director Mario Bava's *The Whip and the Body* (1963). This film, as well as any other, capitalized on Lee's strange combination of menace and sex appeal. Lee's charming yet chilling portrayal of a witty warlock in *The Wicker Man* (1975) almost indisputably ranks as the very finest of Lee's supporting parts. The star has often cited this performance as his personal favorite.

Lee's forays outside the genre have earned only limited success, but he made a memorable foil for Agent 007 as *The Man with the Golden Gun* (1974). And he gave one of his most menacing leading performances as the title character in Hammer's offbeat *Rasputin, the Mad Monk* (1966), which cannot be categorized as a horror film with any measure of certainty.

Most recently, Lee earned accolades in Peter Jackson's *The Lord of the Rings* films, 2001's *The Fellowship of the Ring* and 2002's *The Two Towers,* in which he played the evil wizard Saruman. Director George Lucas gave Lee more screen time in *Star Wars Episode II: Attack of the Clones,* trusting him with the juicy role of Count Dooku, the evil emperor's secret emissary. Lee commanded attention in this role the same way Cushing did as Grand Moff Tarkin in the original *Star Wars.*

Lee is a reliable and amazingly prolific performer. His résumé includes a staggering total of nearly 200 motion pictures—so far. At the time this book was being written, Lee was preparing to reprise his role as Count Dooku in Lucas' final *Star Wars* film. Given his recent successes, still more roles should be forthcoming. For Christopher Lee, the best may be yet to come.

OTHER HORROR STARS

Boris Karloff and Bela Lugosi gained instant worldwide fame for their breakthrough performances in *Frankenstein* and *Dracula* (both 1931). But for every Karloff and Lugosi, the movies gave us a J. Carrol Naish and a Michael Gough — stars who toiled for years in horror pictures without landing that elusive signature role that might have made them household names. These horror luminaries may be lesser known, but it's not because they were lesser talents (or at least, not *always* for that reason). Their performances often proved exciting and memorable, if not as scintillating as the best work of their better-known counterparts.

Here's a quick nod to horror cinema's second-tier stars:

If anyone other than Lon Chaney could be considered cinema's first "horror star," that person would be German actor **Conrad Veidt**. Veidt played the Somnambulist in Robert Wiene's *The Cabinet of Dr. Caligari* (1920), one of the finest and most influential films of the silent era, horror or otherwise. He gave his most affecting performance in the title role of Paul Leni's classic almost-horror film *The Man Who Laughs* (1928), playing a nobleman-turned–sideshow-performer whose face is frozen in a permanent smile. Veidt's other horror and borderline-horror credits include the anthology film *Eerie Tales* (1919), the title role in F.W. Murnau's lost *Dr. Jekyll and Mr. Hyde* (1920), *The Count of Cagliostro* (1921), Leni's *Waxworks* (1922), Wiene's *The Hands of Orlac* (1924), *The Man Who Cheated Life* (a.k.a. *The Student of Prague*, 1926), a retelling of the Faust story, and *Rasputin* (1930). Eventually Veidt immigrated to America, where he was usually cast as a Nazi. Most viewers remember him for one of his last roles, as Major Strasser, the Nazi shot by Humphrey Bogart at the end of *Casablanca* (1942).

Erich von Stroheim ranked among the most innovative filmmakers of the silent era, but the multi-talented actor-director-screenwriter alienated studio executives with his dictatorial behavior and continual cost overruns. Films such as *Foolish Wives* (1922) garnered rave reviews and sold lots of tickets, but turned little profit because von Stroheim shots reels and reels of unused footage. By the mid–1930s he was finished as a director, although he continued to work in front of the camera. With his bald pate and piercing round eyes, von Stroheim seemed a natural for screen villainy. His unnerving performance as a demented ventriloquist in the 1929 talkie *The Great Gabbo* stands as his greatest contribution to the horror genre. He also excelled as a mad medico in the 1935 chiller *The Crime of Dr. Crespi*. Posters for that film billed von Stroheim as "The Man You Love to Hate." Von Stroheim's best-known film appearances came in director Jean Renoir's classic *Grand Illusion* (1937) and Billy Wilder's timeless *Sunset Blvd.* (1950). In the latter film he earned an Oscar nomination for his portrayal of Gloria Swanson's husband-turned-butler.

Basil Rathbone rose to fame playing suave, swashbuckling villains in movies such as *Captain Blood* (1935) and *The Adventures of Robin Hood* (1938), then attained immortality in the title role in the lengthy and eternally popular Sherlock Holmes film series of the 1930s–40s. Rathbone was blessed with a resonant baritone and striking, angular features. Those attributes served him well in a trio of *Bluebeard*-like thrillers—*Love from a Stranger* (1937), *The Mad Doctor* (1941) and *Fingers at the Window* (1942)—in which he played romantically inclined psychopaths. His work in *The Mad Doctor* is particularly disquieting. Rathbone owes his horror star status in large part to these films, and to his histrionic performance in the title role of *Son of Frankenstein* (1939). He demonstrated exceptional range with a comic turn as a cataleptic Shakespearean ham in *The Comedy of Terrors* (1963).

The tortured soul of **Colin Clive** donned his mortal coil in January 1900 in St. Malo, France. He lived just 37 years, the last of those plagued by alcoholism, and made fewer than 20 films. Yet his place in horror movie history remains assured, thanks to his riveting, neurotic performances as Henry Frankenstein in director James Whale's *Frankenstein* (1931) and *Bride of Frankenstein* (1935). Clive's jittery, paranoid portrayal of pianist Stephen Orlac in *Mad Love* (1935) surpassed even his Frankensteins. Unfortunately, co-stars consistently upstaged Clive—in the Frankenstein films, Boris Karloff's Monster trumped his performance; and in *Mad Love*, Peter Lorre's Dr. Gogol eclipsed him. Clive and Whale both rose to prominence with the British stage production *Journey's End*. Unfortunately, Clive, cast as an alcoholic World War I army officer, developed a real-life addiction during the run of the play. He and Whale reunited for an acclaimed screen version of the play in 1930. Clive also contributed outstanding performances in *Jane Eyre* (1934) and *History Is Made at Night* (1937).

Tod Slaughter helped pioneer the British horror film. He enjoyed a lengthy career on the stage, operating a touring theatrical troupe that specialized in hoary Victorian melodramas. Slaughter served as the troupe's star villain and packed in patrons throughout provincial Britain. Beginning in the late 1930s, Slaughter teamed with producer George King to turn his productions into cinematic chillers. The results were decidedly mixed, but the best of these efforts—*Sweeny Todd: The Demon Barber of Fleet Street* (1936) and *The Face at the Window* (1939)—retain some measure of interest, if only for Slaughter's cyclone-like screen presence. His arch shenanigans would have made Bela Lugosi blush.

J. Carrol Naish may be the most gifted "horror star" never to gain true stardom. Although his ancestry was Irish, the dark-eyed, wavy black-haired Naish frequently was cast as Italian, Mexican, gypsy, American Indian and even Asian characters. Affected nationalities notwithstanding, Naish's work was usually convincing and often touching. He snared Oscar nominations for his portrayal of an Italian prisoner of war in the Humphrey Bogart tank saga *Sahara* (1943), and for playing an impoverished Mexican father in *A Medal for Benny* (1945). He also contributed a superb performance as farmer Zachary Scott's neighbor and nemesis, in director Jean Renoir's rural drama *The Southerner* (1945). Horror fans remember Naish primarily for his touching portrait of Daniel, the lovesick hunchback who moons over Elena Verdugo in *House of Frankenstein* (1944). More commonly, Naish was cast as the oily villain. That was the case with *Strange Confession* (1945), probably his finest horror portrayal. Naish, a duplicitous chemical magnate, steals his employee's wife and causes the death of an innocent child—driving mild-mannered Lon Chaney, Jr., to mayhem. Naish enjoyed a rare starring role in the gruesome Poverty Row horror show *The Monster Maker* (1944), playing a scientist who infects his victims with a disfiguring disease. His other genre credits include *Dr. Renault's Secret* (1942), *Calling Dr. Death* (1942), *Jungle Woman* (1944), *The Beast with Five Fingers* (1946) and *Dracula vs. Frankenstein* (1971), his ignominious final film.

Character actor **Martin Kosleck** fled Gestapo persecution in his homeland only to become typecast as a Nazi when he reached Hollywood. When Hitler rose to power, the actor was tried in absentia for treason on account of his anti-fascist politics, was found guilty and sentenced to death. In American films he played Adolf Hitler's propaganda minister, Joseph Goebbels five times, and portrayed a platoon of other storm troopers, SS officers and spies. When he wasn't cast as a Nazi, Kosleck could often be found in B-grade monster movies. Fright film fans remember him for his portrayal of a warped artist who uses homicidal maniac Rondo Hatton as an instrument of revenge in the 1946 chiller *House of Horrors*. As in most of his horror vehicles, Kosleck gave performances far better than his undistinguished material deserved. His other genre appearances include *The Mad Doctor* (1941), *The Mummy's Curse* (1944), *The Frozen Ghost* (1945), *She-Wolf of London* (1946) and *The Flesh Eaters* (1964).

It's something of a stretch to call **Rondo Hatton** an actor. Hatton, in his youth a handsome athlete, was exposed to poison gas while serving in World War I. The gas damaged his pituitary gland and caused him to contract a disease known as acromegaly. This condition slowly deforms the bones in the head, hands and feet, as well as the external soft tissues. After the War, as his condition worsened, he worked as a newspaper reporter, then began taking bit parts in movies. Universal Studios hired Hatton to portray a killer known as the Creeper in the 1944 Sherlock Holmes mystery *The Pearl of Death*. Subsequently, the studio used him as a sort of living, breathing special effect in *The Jungle Captive* (1945), *House of Horrors, The Spider Woman Strikes Back* and *The Brute Man* (all 1946). The studio press department built up Hatton as a star, even though he could barely speak intelligibly, let alone act. Hatton was dead before *The Brute Man* premiered, a victim of the condition that had brought him fame.

Hatton's career blazed a trail for ex–pro wrestler **Tor Johnson**, whose intimidating appearance helped him earn supporting and even occasional leading roles in low-budget horror and sci-fi films, despite his total lack of acting ability. Johnson made occasional cameos in mainstream movies during his wrestling career, but is best remembered for his awful performances in the terrible productions of hapless would-be auteur Edward D. Wood, Jr., including *Bride of the Monster* (1956), *Plan 9 from Outer Space* (1958) and *Night of the Ghouls* (1959). The chillers Johnson made without Wood weren't much better: *The Black Sleep* (1956), *The Unearthly* (1957) and *The Beast of Yucca Flats* (1961), Johnson's last and possibly worst picture. He played the title role. Don Post Studios created a fright mask using Johnson's likeness, which sold very well.

If this book were devoted to science fiction movies, then stars such as **John Agar, Robert Clarke, Arthur Franz, Marshall Thompson** and **Kenneth Tobey** would merit considerably more attention. But these fondly remembered, granite-jawed hero-types usually plied their trade in sci-fi flicks.

Rondo Hatton poses for a publicity still from *The Spider Woman Strikes Back* (1946).

An A-list star and Oscar champion (having won Best Actor honors for *The Lost Weekend* in 1945), **Ray Milland** starred in one of the most spine-tingling of all ghost movies, *The Uninvited* (1944), and played the Devil himself in *Alias Nick Beal* (1949). When his popularity began to wane in the early 1960s, Milland returned to horror films to extend his career — sometimes, it seemed, at any cost. In 1962 he directed and starred in the early post–apocalyptic thriller *Panic in Year Zero!* and took the lead in one of director Roger Corman's Edgar Allan Poe adaptations, *The Premature*

Burial. The following year he landed the title role in Corman's *X — The Man with the X-Ray Eyes*. Although hardly the stuff of Academy Awards, these were leading roles in respectable genre films, and Milland delivered solid performances in them all. Over the next 20 years, however, Milland slid into cheaper, lower-class fare such as *Frogs* (1972), *The House in Nightmare Park*, *Terror in the Wax Museum* (both 1973), *The Uncanny* (1977) and *The Attic* (1981). His career reached a low watermark with *The Thing with Two Heads* (1972), in which he played a racist whose head is transplanted onto the body of an African-American convict (former football star Rosey Grier). This remains one of the most ignominious roles ever accepted by an Oscar recipient.

The Mexican film industry built a thriving horror film cycle of its own, beginning in the late 1950s. Three stars emerged from Mexico and gained cult followings with fans around the world. **Abel Salazar** was the prime mover in the Mexican horror cycle. His 1956 film *The Vampire* marks the beginning of the surge in popularity of these pictures. The multi-talented Salazar was born in Mexico City in 1917 and in 1941 began his screen career as an actor. In addition to acting, Salazar produced and co-wrote several films, starring in many of his own productions. He usually cast himself as the hero, roles well-suited for a star with his handsome features and smooth demeanor. Following the breakthrough success of *The Vampire*, Salazar made a succession of horror pictures, including *The Vampire's Coffin* (1957), *The Man and the Monster* (1958), *The World of the Vampires*, *The Witch's Mirror* (both 1960), *The Living Head*, *The Brainiac* (both 1961), perhaps the finest of all Mexican-made horrors, *The Curse of the Crying Woman* (1961).

Salazar often co-starred with Spanish émigré **German Robles**. The template for their partnerships was struck with *The Vampire*, in which Robles played Count Karol de Lavud (the film's substitute Dracula) to Salazar's Dr. Enrique (its ersatz Van Helsing). It was a relationship similar to the one worked out by Christopher Lee and Peter Cushing at Hammer, only Salazar was more involved behind the scenes than either of those stars. Robles' striking features, which were more angular and fierce-looking than Salazar's, along with his willingness to attack bloodthirsty roles with gusto, made him a perfect foil for Salazar. Following *The Vampire*, the duo re-teamed for *The Vampire's Coffin*, *The Living Head* and *The Brainiac*. Robles' credits without Salazar include appearances in a Mexican rip-off of *Abbott & Costello Meet Frankenstein* titled *The Castle of the Monsters* (1957) and a 1959 television serial devoted to the vampire grandson of Nostradamus. This serial was later re-edited and released as four feature films.

The Mexican cinema also gave us the one and only **Santo**. Born Rudolfo Guzman Herta, Santo gained fame as the silver-masked wrestler known only as El Santo ("The Saint"). The mysterious Santo emerged as a cultural phenomenon in Mexico, appearing in comic strips and eventually movies. He made more than 50 movies in his 24-year screen career, initially starring in stories in which he worked alongside detectives, solving mysteries and body-slamming the bad guys. Then his adventures took a turn for the weird, as Santo began a popular and long-running series of battles with various supernatural villains: *Santo vs. the Vampire Women* (1962), *Santo in the Wax Museum* (1963), *Santo vs. the Martians* (1966), *Santo in the Treasure of*

Dracula (1968), *Santo vs. Frankenstein's Daughter* (1971) and *Santo and the Blue Demon vs. Dracula and the Wolf Man* (1973), among many others. American producers sometimes Anglicized the name "Santo" and billed the star as "Samson." His acting talents were limited, but Santo represented an improvement over Rondo Hatton and Tor Johnson. When Santo died in 1984, he was buried with his mask on. More than 100,000 people turned out to pay their respects at his memorial, which was held in Mexico City.

Michael Ripper seemed to pop up in every movie ever made by Hammer Films. Actually, he appeared in a mere 35 of the studio's productions between 1948 and 1972. Nevertheless, he came to personify the company in a way unmatched by even stars Peter Cushing and Christopher Lee, who were often seen in non–Hammer films. In fact, one day on set Lee asked Cushing, "Why do I get the impression the two of us are appearing in a Michael Ripper production?" At least that's the way Lee related the anecdote at the Monster Rally film convention in Arlington, Virginia, in 1999, which both Lee and Ripper attended. Ripper might have inherited Dwight Frye's crown as the genre's only "supporting star," but he never received a role as juicy as Frye's Renfield from *Dracula* or Fritz from *Frankenstein*. His most prominent horror roles were sizable supporting parts in *The Reptile* (1966) and *The Mummy's Shroud* (1967). He excels in both.

If, like Frankenstein in his lab, it were possible to cobble together the prototypical "horror actor," the result would likely be **Donald Pleasence.** His cue-ball head, boiled-egg eyes and velvet-lined voice were tailor-made for the genre. He could appear icy and menacing, or sensitive and meek with equal ease. Despite these striking physical attributes and ample talent, Pleasence never found the breakthrough role that might have made him a horror superstar like his contemporary and countryman, Peter Cushing. This wasn't due to lack of effort: His filmography includes well over 100 movies. Pleasence began his acting career on stage in London in 1939. He served in the RAF during World War II, was shot down and waited out the rest of the conflict in a POW camp. Like Cushing, he gained notoriety in a series of BBC productions. In fact, he appeared alongside Cushing in a 1954 teleplay of George Orwell's *1984,* and their careers remained strangely intertwined. Pleasence gave one of his finest performances as grave robber–turned-murderer William Hare in the Cushing vehicle *The Flesh and the Fiends* (a.k.a. *Mania,* 1959). Pleasence landed his best-recognized horror role, as psychiatrist Dr. Sam Loomis, in John Carpenter's *Halloween* (1978), after Cushing turned down the part. A sampling of Pleasence's other horror and sci-fi credits includes *Fantastic Voyage* (1966), *THX 1138* (1970), *From Beyond the Grave* (1973), *Dracula* (1979), *Escape from New York* (1981), *House of Usher* (1988) and *Buried Alive* (1990), as well as numerous *Halloween* sequels. Pleasence is also remembered for his portrayal of James Bond's arch-nemesis, Ernst Blofeld, in *You Only Live Twice* (1967).

Distinguished British character actor **Michael Gough** searched throughout his lengthy career for a signature role, and finally found it in an unlikely place — the Bat Cave! Today he's recognized for his appearances as Bruce Wayne's butler, Alfred, in the film series launched by director Tim Burton's *Batman* in 1989. Although his credits include classic films such as *The Man in the White Suit* (1951), *Richard III* (1955),

The Boys from Brazil (1978) and *Out of Africa* (1985), prior to *Batman* Gough was best remembered for his horror films of the late 1950s and early '60s. Gough made a memorable appearance as Arthur Holmwood, the disbelieving, disapproving husband of Mina Holmwood, in Hammer's *Horror of Dracula* (1957). Afterward Gough emerged as a poor man's Peter Cushing. His splendid portrayal as a duplicitous impresario provided one of the few bright spots in Hammer's dreary *The Phantom of the Opera* (1962). And he made a straight-faced appearance in *Dr. Terror's House of Horrors* (1965). More often than not, however, Gough descended into self-parody in abysmal horror shows, including *Konga* (1961), *Black Zoo* (1963) and *Horror Hospital* (1973). His condescending performances in these pictures make it clear that Gough didn't share Cushing's enthusiasm for horror. By the mid–1970s he had put the genre behind him.

In the studio's ongoing attempts to develop a third horror star to supplement Peter Cushing and Christopher Lee, Hammer tried to outfit Shakespearean-trained **Oliver Reed** for the part. He shrugged off this guise and attained fame on his own terms, but not before leaving behind some memorable horror performances. Genre fans remember Reed for his titular role in *The Curse of the Werewolf* (1961), the finest of his Hammer outings. He also appeared in *The Two Faces of Dr. Jeykyll* (1960), *The Damned* (1963), *Paranoiac* (1963) and several pirate films for the company. When his association with Hammer ended, he returned to the genre periodically—for *The Shuttered Room* (1967), *The Devils* (1971), *Burnt Offerings* (1976), *Maniac* (1977), *The Brood* (1979), *Dr. Heckle and Mr. Hype* (1980), *Spasms* (1980), *Venom* (1981), *House of Usher* (1988), *Gor* (1988) and *The Pit and the Pendulum* (1990). But he was best known for non-genre work, including the appropriately titled musical *Oliver!* (1968, directed by his uncle, Carol Reed), *I'll Never Forget What's-His-Name* (1967), *The Three Musketeers* (1974) and *The Four Musketeers* (1975). He made a memorable final appearance in the Oscar-winning *Gladiator* (2000).

Barbara Steele deserves recognition as the first (and, so far, only) woman to break into the boys' club of horror stardom. She burst onto the scene with a stunning appearance in director Mario Bava's landmark 1960 chiller *Black Sunday* (a.k.a. *The Mask of Satan*), in which she essayed dual roles, playing a debauched, 200-year-old vampire and the vampire's virginal young descendent. Steele's hypnotizing screen presence and otherworldly beauty—she seemed simultaneously scary and sexy—made her an instant favorite of moviegoers. Especially male moviegoers. Steele soon became a doe-eyed, blood-spattered fetish object for adolescent boys who liked horror movies. In America, she appeared alongside Vincent Price in director Roger Corman's *Pit and the Pendulum* (1961). Throughout the 1960s and early '70s she starred in a series of European shockers, including *The Horrible Dr. Hichcock*, (1962), *Castle of Blood*, *The Ghost* (both 1963), *The Long Hair of Death* (1964), *Nightmare Castle* (1965) and *Curse of the Crimson Altar* (1968). Each of these films is known by several alternate titles. Unfortunately, assessing Steele's actual acting ability (such as it may or may not be) proves rather difficult, since invariably other actresses dubbed Steele's voice for the American release of her films. Her presence, however, adds interest to any picture.

Paul Naschy, born Jacinto Molina Alvarez, is an incredibly prolific Spanish star,

Barbara Steele, the only woman to break into the boys' club of horror movie superstardom, in a scene from her breakthrough horror vehicle *Black Sunday* (1960).

screenwriter and sometimes-director best known for his long-running series of low-budget shockers about a werewolf named Waldemar Daninsky. Naschy's range as an actor is extremely limited, and his performances are often inexpressive (and usually poorly dubbed by other actors). However, his films can be remarkably imaginative. Although most include nudity and graphic violence, Naschy's pictures also exude a delightful kind of innocence. They are childish, in the best sense of the word. For a sampling of Naschy at his best, try *Werewolf Shadow* (a.k.a. *Werewolf vs. the Vampire Women,* 1971), *The Hunchback of the Morgue* (1972), *Horror Rises from the Tomb* (1973) or *House of Psychotic Women,* a.k.a. *Blue Eyes of the Broken Doll* (also 1973).

Cameron Mitchell and **Howard Vernon** also enjoyed long careers and made many appearances in low-budget European chillers. Mitchell is best remembered for playing the lead role in director Mario Bava's watershed "giallo" thriller *Blood and Black Lace* (1963). Mitchell's lengthy filmography also includes memorable appearances in *Island of the Doomed* (1967), *Nightmare in Wax* (1969) and *The Toolbox Murders* (1978), all of which are known by multiple titles. Vernon remains etched in the minds of horror fans for his title performances in director Jess Franco's *The Awful Dr. Orloff* (1962) and *The Diabolical Dr. Z* (1965). Vernon remained a frequent Franco collaborator. The pair teamed for *Night of the Blood Monster* (1970), *A Virgin Among the Living Dead* (1971), *Dracula vs. Frankenstein, The Demons* (both 1972) and three Dr. Orloff sequels, among many other pictures. Again, all of these carry many alternate titles.

During the early 1970s, **Robert Quarry** and **Ralph Bates** both threatened to emerge as new horror stars. Although interesting and capable performers, neither found that special role to make stars on the level of their contemporaries Peter Cushing, Christopher Lee and Vincent Price. Quarry came closest, portraying the nefarious vampire Count Yorga in *Count Yorga, Vampire* (1971) and *The Return of Count Yorga* (1972). He also appeared in *Dr. Phibes Rises Again, Deathmaster* (both 1972), *Sugar Hill* and *Madhouse* (both 1974). Bates was the only actor to play Victor Frankenstein in a Hammer film other than Peter Cushing (he essayed the role in 1970's *The Horror of Frankenstein*). He also contributed an underrated leading performance to *Dr. Jekyll and Sister Hyde* (1971). His other genre credits include *Taste the Blood of Dracula* (1970), *Lust for a Vampire* (1971), *Fear in the Night* (1972) and *Murder Motel* (1975). Bates also starred in the short-lived television series *Moonbase 3* (1973).

Robert Englund provided the face of one of the 1980s' most recognizable screen bogeymen, Freddie Krueger. He brought a refreshing balance of menace and sardonic humor to the role, reaching an artistic zenith with his caustic

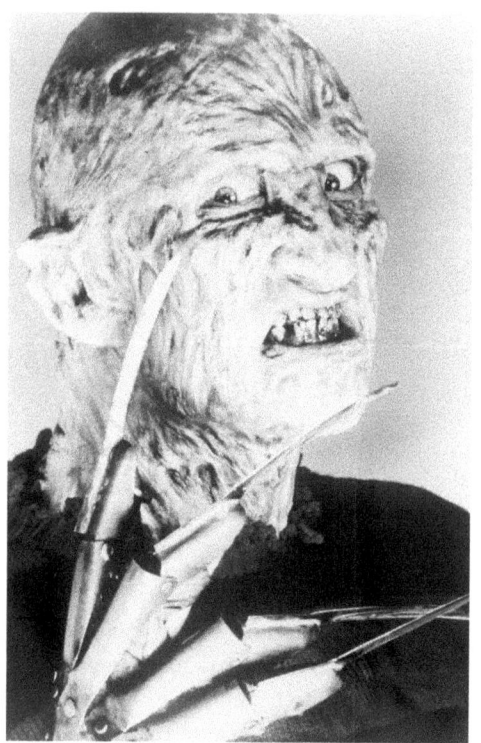

Robert Englund, pictured here as Freddie Krueger from *A Nightmare on Elm Street* (1984), remains the closest thing to a horror star that movies have produced in recent memory. (Photograph courtesy Bryan Senn.)

performance in *A Nightmare on Elm Street III: Dream Warriors* (1987). Englund studied acting at UCLA's film school and landed minor roles in two horror films—*Dead and Buried* and *Galaxy of Terror* (both 1981)—before director Wes Craven tapped him to portray Krueger in the first *Nightmare* film (1984). Unfortunately, he's enjoyed little success in any screen role other than that of Krueger. His title performance in director Dwight Little's 1989 *Phantom of the Opera* proved as forgettable as the movie itself. Craven developed a syndicated television series for Englund, *Nightmare Café* (1992), but it quickly fell before the ratings chopping block. Englund tried his hand at directing in 1988 with *976-EVIL*, but the movie flopped. Englund returned as Krueger in *Freddie vs. Jason* (2003). He remains the closest thing to a horror star to develop in recent memory.

Englund notwithstanding, Christopher Lee reigns as horror's final super star—not only the last survivor of a generation of screen legends but, in all likelihood, the last horror super star the cinema will ever produce.

Since the demise of Hollywood's studio system, actors who achieve success in horror films need not continue to perform exclusively in that genre. For instance, after his acclaimed performance in *The Silence of the Lambs* (1992), Anthony Hopkins wasn't forced to portray a succession of Hannibal Lecter wannabes. Hopkins played light comedy (*The Road to Wellville* [1994]), drawing room drama (*Howard's End* [1992]), romances (*The Remains of the Day* and *Shadowlands* [both 1993]), biopics (*Chaplin* [1992] and *Nixon* [1995]) and even a swashbuckler (*The Mask of Zorro* [1998]). Aside from an ill-advised appearance in *Bram Stoker's Dracula* (1992) and two long-delayed *Lambs* sequels, he has steered clear of horror. If Lugosi or Karloff had been given as much say in their assignments, the history of horror cinema might have unfolded quite differently.

More importantly, contemporary horror films are driven by directorial flash, gore and special effects, not by engrossing characterizations. Directors such as George Romero, Wes Craven and John Carpenter have developed into the genre's true stars. If, like their screen creations, Karloff or Lugosi returned from the grave, they would discover very few horror roles worthy of their talents. By the same token, there aren't enough well-written horror parts to cultivate any new horror screen idols. This should only make us cherish the work of Karloff and company that much more.

PART TWO
Mainstream Actors

The names March, Perkins and Hopkins may not conjure up images of cobweb-swept castles and fog-shrouded marshes as do the names Karloff, Lugosi and Cushing. Nevertheless, Fredric March, Anthony Perkins and Anthony Hopkins all contributed watershed performances to horror cinema. They are three "guest stars"—performers not readily associated with horror—who have left an indelible impression during their "visits" to the genre. They are far from the only three.

In fact, nearly all the horror performances to earn Academy Award consideration were given by actors with long-established credentials in mainstream movies. March's kinky Jekyll and Hyde and Hopkins' erudite Hannibal Lecter remain the only two horror characterizations to earn Oscar statuettes for Best Actor in a Leading Role. Karloff and Lugosi, along with nearly all the other horror luminaries, were never even nominated for an Academy Award. This betrays the snobbery of Oscar voters. Nevertheless the Academy's apparent anti-horror bias makes the achievements of March, Hopkins and others all the more remarkable. No matter who gives it, how outstanding must a horror performance be in order to break through and earn an Academy Award nomination?

Casting a popular, respected performer in a horror film hardly guarantees a good performance. Respected mainstream performers have imploded more often than they have succeeded in horror roles. Witness Kenneth Branagh's barking, cackling meltdown in *Mary Shelley's Frankenstein* (1994). His performance seems even worse since it comes from a former Oscar nominee. Branagh's work has plenty of company in its misery. Future Oscar winner (for his supporting role in *A Streetcar Named Desire* [1951]) Karl Malden seemed stiff and ill-at-ease in his horror entry, *Phantom of the Rue Morgue* (1954). Screen legend Humphrey Bogart (who won an Academy Award for *The African Queen* [1951]) appeared completely at sea in *The Return of Doctor X* (1939). Oscar winner (for *A Free Soul* [1931]) Lionel Barrymore phoned in his performance in *Mark of the Vampire* (1935).

When so many have failed, why have other guest stars thrived in horror roles? Part of the answer lies in the rare, almost symbiotic relationship between character and actor present in all great portrayals, regardless of genre. Other factors, however, remain specific to the horror *oeuvre*: The great horror performances are works of tremendous daring. To succeed in horror roles, mainstream stars must be unafraid to risk their most valuable asset—their carefully crafted and marketed screen personas. These actors must display further courage by offering performances with emotional depth. They must invest their characters with insights unearthed from their own dark sides, or obtained by plumbing their own darkest fears.

Perhaps most importantly, these performers must approach their horror roles with the same professionalism and sobriety of purpose they bring to their other projects. Too many actors apparently think that appearing in a monster movie gives them license to froth and jibber like some second-rate Lugosi wannabe. The following performances prove there's no substitute for taking your work seriously:

Fredric March in *Dr. Jekyll and Mr. Hyde* (1931)

—Robert Louis Stevenson's classic yarn has been filmed more than 25 times—and that tally doesn't include knock-offs or parodies. Over the decades, hundreds of actors have essayed the role(s) of Jekyll and Hyde on stage and on film. Yet, Fredric March's Oscar-winning 1931 portrayal remains the standard by which all others are judged. It established the same sort of benchmark that Lugosi's Dracula set for screen vampires. Universally hailed as a triumph by 1931 critics, March's performance would stand for 60 years as the most heralded portrayal in the history of horror cinema.

Unlike Karloff and Lugosi, who were introduced to film audiences through horror films, March was an established star when he made his *Jekyll and Hyde*, an Academy Award nominee the year prior for his work in *The Royal Family of Broadway*. As a result, March was able to sidestep the quagmire of typecasting. March reaped all the benefits an Oscar victory can bring an actor, and continued to land leading roles in prestigious pictures. He won a second Academy Award in 1946 for *The Best Years of Our Lives* and was Oscar-nominated for *A Star Is Born* (1937) and *Death of a Salesman* (1951). March never needed to appear in another horror film and — unless you count the romantic fantasy *Death Takes a Holiday* (1934) or the whimsical *I Married a Witch* (1942)— he didn't.

March's Jekyll and Hyde was the first characterization in the genre to overtly meld eroticism and menace, opening the door for a horde of sexually repressed madmen. Echoes of March's portrayal can be heard both within and beyond the horror genre, in performances as varied as Leslie Banks' Count Zaroff in *The Most Dangerous Game* (1932), Anthony Perkins' Norman Bates in *Psycho* (1960) and Robert DeNiro's Travis Bickle in *Taxi Driver* (1975), among countless others.

The key to March's brilliance lies not in his ferocious Mr. Hyde, but rather in his compelling Dr. Jekyll. March's Jekyll is a simmering kettle of sexual frustration. Victorian morality forces Jekyll to suppress his healthy desire for his bride-to-be. Eventually, these urges become twisted and emerge as his deviant Hyde persona. If this approach sounds routine, that's only because March's take on the character established such an influential precedent.

Before March, screen incarnations of the good doctor (notably John Barrymore's overrated silent version) painted Jekyll as something just shy of a saint — prim, noble and resolutely proper. Such stateliness helped draw a bold demarcation between the decorous Jekyll and the lascivious Mr. Hyde. March understood that Wally Westmore's ghastly, simian Hyde makeup would mark this line clearly enough. This freed the actor to enrich his portrayal of Jekyll with glimmers of the doctor's darker impulses, making the physician's transformation into the sadistic, perverted Hyde more believable. At times the Good Dr. Jekyll seems nearly as roguish as Hyde himself.

Jekyll chafes at the bonds of propriety, bristling visibly when his friend Dr. Lanyan (Holmes Herbert) chastises him with the expression, "It isn't done." "It's the things that one *can't* do that tempt me," March counters curtly. At a dinner party, Jekyll and his fiancée, Miriam (Rose Hobart), retreat from the dance floor to the garden. There, seated on a bench, March's eyes swell with lust. "I do love you seriously," he says in a strained voice. "So seriously it, it frightens me." In closeup, his hungry eyes roll over her body. Then he gives her a deep, lingering kiss— the kind that would soon be outlawed by the Production Code.

Miriam's father, Gen. Carew (Halliwell Hobbes), balks when Henry suggests cutting short the couple's planned ten-month engagement so the lovers can be wed immediately. "It isn't done," the old man scoffs. "It's positively indecent." Betraying a latent bent for violence, Jekyll later carps to Lanyan, "Pity I didn't strangle the old walrus!" March spits out the words bitterly, unleashing a tiny fragment of Jekyll's pent-up anger.

March enjoys two showcase scenes, one as Jekyll and the other as Hyde, both with lovely young "dance hall girl" Ivy Pierson (Miriam Hopkins). The first of these occurs as Jekyll and Lanyan return home from the dinner party. The pair trip across a bully brutalizing Ivy. Jekyll gallantly rescues the girl and carries her up a flight of stairs to the safety of her boudoir. This sets the stage for the most erotically charged sequence of horror's Golden Age.

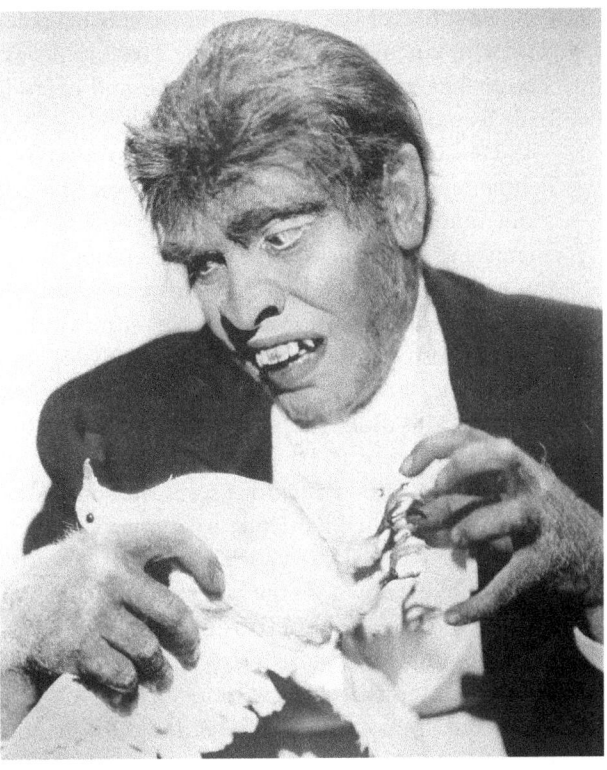

A bird in the hand: Fredric March, in full Hyde makeup, poses for this evocative publicity still.

Ivy feigns injury to keep the handsome young doctor in her room. She claims her leg is injured and seizes the opportunity to show Jekyll her thigh. March, sounding more amused than concerned, warns her not to wear her garter so tight because it restricts circulation. Ivy grabs his hand and presses it to her thigh, flashing Jekyll a look that makes it clear blood is flowing freely to all her body parts. She coos that Jekyll is "the kind a woman would do something for."

March's work here is his most subtle and convincing in the film. He conducts himself with outward decorum, but the arch of his eyebrows and his wry grin reveal that the doctor takes special enjoyment in this examination. He retains his prim reserve when Ivy coyly asks Jekyll to turn around while she undresses. She then peels off her garters and stockings and tosses them to his feet. Finally, when Ivy—now naked beneath a thin sheet—pulls Jekyll nearly on top of her for a goodbye kiss, desire conquers decorum and March meets her embrace with wanton enthusiasm. This kiss, even more randy than the one he gave Miriam in the garden, brings March's first bravura sequence to a breathless crescendo.

Later, however, Jekyll is chagrined by his moral lapse. "I want to be clean not only in my conduct but in my thoughts and desires," he tells Lanyan. When Gen. Carew takes Miriam on a lengthy journey out of the country, Jekyll's desires finally boil over, and he unleashes Hyde to quench his carnal thirsts.

Not only is March's Jekyll the most believable, fully sketched version of the good doctor in cinema history, March's Hyde ranks as the screen's fiercest and cruelest. The apelike makeup is unnerving in and of itself, but March makes the character truly fearsome.

He invests Hyde with a host of subtle physical traits independent of Jekyll's mannerisms. He speaks in a different voice (Jekyll lilts, Hyde rasps) and walks with a different gait (Jekyll strolls, Hyde prowls). He enlivens the character with lusty energy and a surprising dash of dark humor. "I'll grant you I'm no beauty, but under this exterior you'll find the very flower of a man," Hyde tells Ivy, with tongue firmly in cheek. March—who prior to this film was best known as a light comic actor—revels in such moments. He (and thus Hyde) appears to be having tremendous fun as he brandishes his cane at onlookers, trips a waiter and intimidates Ivy until she submits to his desires. It's virtually impossible to pull your eyes from March's Hyde when he's on-screen. He is magnetic.

The star's other standout scene demonstrates Hyde's brutality. The setting is an opulently furnished flat Hyde has rented for Ivy. In a telling bit of throwaway business, Hyde viciously kicks the head of a bearskin rug as he stalks across the room. Then he plops down on the bed to read the newspaper. When a notice informs him that Jekyll's fiancée has returned from a journey abroad, Hyde decides to bid Ivy farewell—but not before a final night of torment. "The last evening is always the sweetest," March declares with mock sorrow. Whatever physical abuses Hyde inflicts on Ivy remain tastefully off-screen, but his mental cruelty proves terrifying enough. He forces the young woman to proclaim that she loves him, and goads her into singing for him, even though she looks utterly terrified throughout.

During this sequence, Hyde warns Ivy, "You belong to me." If she steps out of line while he's away, March snarls venomously, "I'll show you what horror means!" This simple declarative sentence ranks among the most unnerving single lines in the history of the genre, alongside Lugosi's "Children of the Night" speech, Anthony Perkins' observation that "we all go a little crazy sometimes," and Anthony Hopkins' languid recollection of liver, fava beans and a nice Chianti.

The scene closes with another dose of black humor, as Hyde raises Ivy's skirt and claws at her garter. "Look how tight your garter is," March hisses through his makeup teeth. "It will bruise your pretty, tender flesh." His mocking delivery parodies his own work in the earlier scene.

As Jekyll struggles vainly to break free from Hyde, the doctor disintegrates into a pathetic jumble. As Jekyll deteriorates, Hyde becomes even more energized. Throughout the film's final reels, March clubs victims, bounds up and down stairs and flees from police with remarkable athleticism. This late burst of adrenaline helps March's performance race to its conclusion with even greater power. His enthralling portrayal only improves as the film proceeds.

None of this was lost on 1931 audiences, who made the film a smash hit. The critical reception proved just as warm. In addition to winning an Oscar statuette, March earned rave reviews from newspaper critics nationwide. Even squeamish observers like *The New York Times'* resident horror hater, Mordaunt Hall, came away impressed. "Mr. March's portrayal is something to arouse admiration," Hall opined.

Over the years, most critics have continued to laud March's work. "March's acting ... is occasionally highly theatrical, but it remains one of his best performances," William K. Everson wrote in *Classics of the Horror Film*. "For perhaps the only time when a player has essayed this type of role, one really believes in the separation of personalities."

Moreover, one really believes each of the individual personalities. Both Jekyll and Hyde are fully realized characters, and the skill March demonstrates in crafting them makes his performance one (or perhaps two) of the greatest achievements by an actor in horror cinema history.

Charles Laughton in *Island of Lost Souls* (1933)

— By the time *Island of Lost Souls* reached theaters the mad scientist had become horror cinema's first full-blown cliché. *Frankenstein* paved the way in 1931. In less than two years, *Dr. Jekyll and Mr. Hyde*, *Doctor X*, and *The Mask of Fu Manchu* followed its well-traveled path, with *The Vampire Bat* and *The Invisible Man* on their way. Still, nothing audiences had seen before could have prepared them for Charles Laughton's unctuous, unsettling Dr. Moreau.

Thanks in large measure to Laughton's commanding portrayal, *Island of Lost Souls* proved the definitive screen treatment of H.G. Wells' frequently filmed novel *The Island of Dr. Moreau*. Working alongside (and overshadowing) horror legend Bela Lugosi, Laughton authored one of the richest and most disquieting portrayals in horror cinema history. In his book *Golden Horrors*, author Bryan Senn calls Laughton's Moreau "the greatest mad doctor of them all." This may be a mild overstatement, since the competition for that honor includes Peter Cushing's exquisite Victor Frankenstein. But if Moreau isn't the hands-down greatest, he's certainly the scariest.

None of this, however, was what Charles Laughton had in mind for his first starring film role. Reportedly, he hated the part. Soon he would land a project more to his liking — the title role in *The Private Life of Henry VIII* (1933), for which he won an Oscar. Despite a propensity toward the baroque and a reputation for being "difficult" on the set, Laughton earned the adoration of fans and respect of colleagues. He was nominated for Best Actor twice more, for *Mutiny on the Bounty* (1935) and *Witness for the Prosecution* (1957). The actor brings all his formidable skills to bear on *Island of Lost Souls*.

In retrospect, Laughton's distaste for *Island of Lost Souls* seems puzzling. Throughout his career, the actor displayed a special flair for macabre subjects; he proved to be one of the genre's most frequent and most welcome guests. Already he had contributed an outstanding supporting performance to another Golden Age horror masterpiece, *The Old Dark House* (1932). Later, he offered a heart-wrenching turn as Quasimodo in *The Hunchback of Notre Dame* (1939), charmed audiences in the supernatural comedy *The Canterville Ghost* (1944) and shamelessly chewed the scenery opposite Boris Karloff in *The Strange Door* (1951). Laughton's lone directorial effort was the spine-tingling *The Night of the Hunter* (1955), in which he elicited an astounding lead performance from Robert Mitchum as a psychotic minister.

The role of Moreau gave the disgruntled Laughton an opportunity to indulge

Dr. Moreau (Laughton), center, meets one of the most gruesome fates in cinema history during the climax of *Island of Lost Souls* (1933). (Photograph courtesy Bryan Senn.)

his worst tendencies. Given his lack of enthusiasm, the star might easily have slid into snide, over-the-top histrionics. Fortunately, his performance never betrays his dissatisfaction. Instead, Laughton responded with a surprisingly subtle, reserved portrayal. Through most of the film, his Moreau remains soft-spoken, mild-tempered. On the surface he seems to be the sort of harmless, bookish eccentric you might find hanging out at the local coffee house.

No wonder, then, that castaway Edward Parker (Richard Arlen) misreads the doctor. When he — and the audience — first meets Moreau, the doctor could not appear more docile. The smiling, nattily attired gent generously offers to shelter castaway Parker for the evening, and to shuttle his guest to the mainland the next day. As the plot unfolds, Laughton allows the true Moreau to emerge. Moreau is charming but devious, equal parts genius and sadist. He lords over a race of half-man, half-animal monsters he has created in a lab known as "The House of Pain." His perverse plan is to mate Parker with his Panther Woman, Lota (Kathleen Burke).

This scheme suggests a bent toward bestiality, but for the most part Moreau's proclivities remain elusive. In a stroke of brilliance, Laughton leaves Moreau strangely asexual. He talks about reproduction only in the most detached, scientific manner. "Is [Lota] capable of being attracted? Has she a woman's emotional impulses?" he wonders aloud, in a purely academic tone. He shows no sexual interest in Lota — or in Parker, for that matter. Yet he looks on with voyeuristic delight after arranging a rendezvous between the Panther Woman and her intended lover. When Lota nuzzles up to Parker, Moreau giddily confers with his assistant (Arthur Hohl). "Did you see that, Montgomery? She was tender, like a woman." Laughton breaks into a beady-eyed grin. "How that little scene spurs the scientific imagination onward!"

If the scientific benefits of these experiments seem dubious, perhaps that's because their true purpose is to feed Moreau's bloated ego. The scientist seems much more interested in power than in sex. He gets his kicks lording over the island's "natives." When the man-beasts become unruly, Moreau bangs a gong to call the populace to order. Then, as the Sayer of the Law (Lugosi) recites, "His is the hand that makes, ... that heals, his is the House of Pain," Moreau smugly basks in the worship of his misshapen creations. Laughton breaks into a tiny, condescending smile that, under the circumstances, looks scary as hell. He seems to gather in his subjects' fear and dread the way a flower soaks up sunlight.

Later, Parker breaks into the House of Pain and interrupts Moreau while the doctor is vivisecting one of his man-beasts. This forces Moreau to explain to Parker how he transformed various species of animals into the island's current half-human denizens. Laughton mentions "plastic surgery, blood transfusions, ray baths." Parker is aghast at this revelation.

"Spare me your youthful horrors, please," Laughton winces. He waves his hand dismissively and turns his back on Parker. As the two men continue talking, Laughton casually lounges across the vivisection table — straps, buckles and all — with his legs crossed, as if this instrument of torture were some macabre deck chair. In a drowsy voice, he describes the trials of teaching his creations to speak.

"Oh, it takes a long time and infinite patience to make them talk," he reports wearily. Laughton almost yawns. Then his eyes narrow and his lips curl into a coy grin. He chuckles deviously and adds, "Someday I'll create a woman and it will be easier." (Parker does not yet realize that Lota is also one of Moreau's creations.) Finally, in a dreamy voice, Moreau asks Parker: "Do you know what it means to feel like God?" Laughton makes this potentially bombastic line seem introspective. His quiet, controlled approach only makes the line more chilling.

Laughton enjoys another terrific scene with Arlen after Parker finally discovers that Lota is, indeed, one of Moreau's creations. He bursts into Moreau's quarters as the doctor is pouring himself a cup of tea. "Moreau, you don't deserve to live!" he bellows. Laughton seems unperturbed, and continues to prepare his tea. Briefly, he looks up. "Beg your pardon?" he asks politely. Since Moreau never seems to lose his temper, he never seems to be out of control of the situation. Parker rails indignantly, but Moreau never so much as blinks. "You're an amazingly unscientific young man," Laughton notes with a bemused grin, as he drops a sugar cube into his teacup. Parker responds by slugging Moreau, knocking him flat on his back — and spilling his tea.

While Moreau's eerie asexuality and icy confidence are frightening, his most repellent and terrifying trait remains his utter lack of compassion for his creations. Laughton vividly demonstrates this when he realizes that Lota has begun to regress back into her panther state. At first the scientist appears dejected. Then Moreau realizes that Lota has been crying. Suddenly, Moreau is overjoyed. The tiny moment that elapses as Moreau makes this realization, and as his spirits rise, represents a tremendous bit of acting on Laughton's part.

"You see this?" he asks Montgomery. "The first of them all to shed tears—she *is* human!" Laughton smiles, flushed with excitement. He even begins to giggle, a boyish, jubilant giggle. Lota cringes. For her, this means another round of agonizing treatments in the House of Pain. No matter to Moreau. "Get everything ready ... this time I'll burn all the animal out of her!" he shouts with glee.

Laughton remains smug, heartless and irretrievably evil, even as Moreau faces an uprising from his creations. He cracks his bullwhip and expects his "natives" to meekly retreat. They refuse. Laughton must have understood that only a purely evil villain could deserve Moreau's gruesome fate—perhaps the most ghastly death in screen history. Moreau's man-beasts lay him across a gurney in the House of Pain, break into his cabinet of surgical tools and perform a primitive vivisection on their former "god."

Island of Lost Souls remains a powerful, chilling spectacle, especially by the standards of its era. Although most 1933 reviewers lacked the stomach for the picture as a whole, many praised Laughton's work. Even lily-livered Mordaunt Hall of *The New York Times* wrote, "The general effect of the film is enhanced greatly by Mr. Laughton's urbane impersonation." Subsequent critiques have been even more favorable. Historian Steve Kronenberg, in *Monsters from the Vault* magazine, ventured, "With Moreau, Laughton created a timeless depiction of absolute evil, while lending his own peculiar, perverse spin on madness."

Nearly 70 years have passed since *Island of Lost Souls* debuted. In the decades since, hundreds of additional mad scientists have matriculated to movie screens. Yet Laughton's erudite and unrepentant Dr. Moreau remains at the head of the class.

Claude Rains in *The Invisible Man* (1933)

— There's never been a performance quite like Claude Rains' stunning screen debut. The film billed its star quite appropriately as "The Invisible One." Audiences saw the actor's face for only a few seconds at the end of the picture. Yet Rains' portrayal left an indelible impression on horror cinema.

With *The Invisible Man*, Rains achieved two remarkable triumphs. First, he supplied the yardstick by which all future invisible protagonists would be measured. Since 1933, everyone from Vincent Price to Chevy Chase has played an invisible character. None of them have equaled Rains. More importantly, Rains' Invisible Man stands as one of the most memorable debuts in cinema history—alongside Lauren Bacall in *To Have and Have Not*, Burt Lancaster in *The Killers* and Julie Andrews in *Mary Poppins*, among others. Although strictly speaking not his first screen role (he had a supporting role in a forgotten 1920 silent film), *The Invisible Man* was Rains' first screen work in America, his first in talking pictures and the one that launched in earnest a storied career.

Director James Whale selected Rains, then a little-known British stage performer, based solely on the actor's voice. Film historian Paul Jensen explains Whale's stratagem in the DVD documentary *Now You See Him: The Invisible Man Revealed*:

"There must be a way back." Jack Griffin (Rains) laments his fate in *The Invisible Man* (1933). (Photograph courtesy Bryan Senn.)

"Claude Rains has the greatest voice in the world, and if he can't be seen at least the voice will have the presence."

Whale certainly did not choose Rains for the role based on a brilliant screen test. Rains' first sound test was apparently disastrous. "It was mannered and theatrical and overblown," Rains' daughter, Jessica, reports in the same documentary. Yet the florid gesticulations that failed him so miserably in his screen test served him surprisingly well in his turn as Dr. Jack Griffin, the title character in *The Invisible*

Man. Although Griffin is invisible, Rains (or parts of Rains) almost always remain visible on screen. And whatever part of Rains remains visible — the flailing arms of an apparently empty shirt, the skipping legs of a pair of trousers swiped from a bobby — those parts are constantly in motion, constantly transmitting information or reinforcing the dialogue.

While it's true that only a strong vocal talent could have succeeded in the role, Rains doesn't simply stand around and enunciate. His performance is a seamless mesh of vocal prowess and inventive physicality. Rains punctuates the dialogue with imaginative bits of business that bring his character to life. Author William K. Everson, in *More Classics of the Horror Film*, suggests that Rains' "pantomimic style, the gestures of the head and hands, are obviously patterned on those on Lon Chaney in *Phantom of the Opera*, though enlarged on to a considerable degree." If so, Rains' performance has a noble bloodline indeed.

Throughout the film — helped by Whale's low-angle shot selection — Rains seems to occupy more space than physically possible for a man of his height and build. In the movie's opening scene, he trudges through the snow in his overcoat, hat, scarf and glasses, lugging a suitcase. When he makes his head-turning entrance into the Lion's Head Inn, it seems only natural for all eyes to fix on Rains. We can't take our eyes off him either. Then, from under a swath of bandages and a heavy scarf, comes his first line of dialogue. It's a terse demand: "I want a room and a fire." His clipped, forceful delivery informs us that Griffin may be weary and half-frozen, but remains steadfastly focused. He's not to be taken lightly.

The first of Rains' many bravura scenes comes a few minutes later, when the innkeeper's wife (Una O'Connor) disrupts Griffin's experiments. He's searching for the formula that will return him to visibility. "A whole day's work ruined by a foolish, ignorant woman!" Rains rolls the "r" on "ruin," and his inflection suggests an aural sneer. He smashes a beaker into a framed picture of the woman, then strides over to a nearby table, opens his notebook and drops into a chair. "There must be a way back. God knows there's a way back," he says to himself, hunched over the notebook, his temples resting against his clenched fists. "If only they'd leave me alone." Audiences can almost see his brow furrowing beneath his bandages.

Griffin's outburst brings the innkeeper to the room, demanding that his guest vacate at once. At first, Griffin pleads. "I implore you to let me stay. I beg you," Rains says in a voice rife with anguish. As the innkeeper ignores him and begins breaking down Griffin's chemistry equipment, the tenor of Rains' delivery changes. Suddenly he's louder, sterner, enraged. "Leave that alone and *get out of here!*" Griffin demands. Then he bashes the innkeeper over the head with a heavy book and pushes him down the stairs.

This leads to the film's most famous sequence, when Griffin strips before a crowd of gawking locals in order to escape the local constable (E.E. Clive). "You're *crazy* to know who I am, aren't you?" Rains roars, and again inserts that rolled-R sneer. Griffin proceeds to pull off his false nose, toss aside his dark glasses and peel away his bandages. As the onlookers stare in shock, Griffin begins to laugh. The mad ("Nyeah-ha-ha-ha-ha-ha!") cackle Rains invents for Griffin ranks alongside Dwight Frye's Renfield Laugh among the most famous expressions of delight in all of horror cinema.

Rains lifts his arms and his entire body rocks with laughter. His body language grows more and more exaggerated throughout this movement of the film, beginning when the innkeeper bursts into his makeshift laboratory and concluding with Griffin's rampage through town. The Invisible Man steals a bicycle, smashes a window, knocks over a baby carriage and tosses an old man's hat into the creek.

From that sequence forward, Rains' voice and posture reflect the shifting tides of Griffin's psyche as he sinks into chemically induced madness. Griffin pays an unexpected and unwelcome call on his former colleague, Dr. Kemp (William Harrigan). Seated in a rocking chair, he recounts to the terrified Kemp how he ingested a solution of chemicals to render himself invisible. "The drugs I took seemed to light up my brain," Rains reports, in a distant, intoxicated voice. He speaks with his head titled back, as if he were looking at the stars. Quickly, however, his spacey aloofness morphs into bloodthirsty delirium. "I realized the power I hold—the power to rule, the power to make the world *grovel at my feet!*" His voice flashes with fire, then abruptly cools. He resumes calmly, rocking in the chair. "We'll begin with a reign of terror—a few murders here and there," he suggests in a deceptively sweet, singsong tone.

By the time Griffin's fiancée, Flora (Gloria Stuart), arrives at Kemp's house for a visit, the Invisible One has gone completely round the bend. When Flora ventures that her father—Griffin's superior—might be able to help him find an antidote to the invisibility serum, Griffin scoffs and declares that her father "has the brain of a tapeworm, a maggot next to mine!" Rains spits out the words like they were mouthfuls of soured milk, then chews his way through another delirious rant. "Even the Moon's frightened of me, frightened to death," Griffin proclaims. Rains stands in front of an open window, bathed in moonlight, his arms crossed over his chest. "The whole world's frightened to death." Especially in this sequence, Rains' theatrical delivery aids him. Only a colorful, rococo performance could have worked for this material.

The Invisible Man provided ideal on-the-job training for Rains. Since his part didn't require the subtlety of most screen acting, it enabled him to adapt his skills to the new medium. After this film, Rains appeared in several more horror and borderline horror projects, including *The Man Who Reclaimed His Head* (1934), *The Clairvoyant* (1934), *The Mystery of Edwin Drood* (1935), *The Wolf Man* (1941) and in the title role of Universal's color remake *Phantom of the Opera* (1943). As his career progressed, Rains' grasp of film technique improved dramatically and the young star matured into one of the finest craftsmen in screen history. He received four Academy Award nominations and contributed splendid performances to scores of classic movies, perhaps most memorably as the evil Prince John in *The Adventures of Robin Hood* (1938), as Police Prefect Louis Renault in *Casablanca* (1942) and as Alexander Sebastian, the Nazi who marries Ingrid Bergman, in Alfred Hitchcock's *Notorious* (1946). In the hearts and minds of horror buffs, however, he remains Jack Griffin, the Invisible One.

The mastery of Rains' work in *The Invisible Man* was overshadowed during the film's initial release by the superb visual effects of John P. Fulton. Most reviewers ignored Rains entirely—or, perhaps, looked right through him. Later critics have brought his artistry into view. In *Golden Horrors*, author Bryan Senn writes that, "Through his intelligent, powerful voice and expressive body language, Claude Rains creates a character who, although faceless, become more real (indeed, more *visible*) than many other star portrayals."

Rains' portrayal stands as one of the most satisfying and durable from the Golden Age of movie horror.

Laird Cregar in *The Lodger* (1944)

— Laird Cregar's star burned briefly but brightly. Cregar illuminated his frequently dark roles with the fire of his own tortured soul, and he was never more incandescent than in *The Lodger*.

The hulking actor, who claimed to be a direct descendent of John Wilkes Booth, stood six-foot-three and weighed 300 pounds when he signed his contract with 20th Century–Fox. He earned that contract with an impressive performance in a self-produced one-man show in which he played Oscar Wilde. Like Wilde, Cregar was a giant of a man, a brilliant artist and a homosexual. To his dismay, all those things worked against him in Hollywood.

He quickly became typed as "the heavy" due not only to his massive bulk, but also because of his convincing screen villainy in pictures such as *I Wake Up Screaming* (1941), *The Black Swan* and *This Gun for Hire* (both 1942). In his 1943 comedy, *Heaven Can Wait*, director Ernst Lubitsch cast Cregar as the Devil himself. Perhaps a lesser actor would have resigned himself to these sorts of parts, but Cregar yearned for more. All the while, his private life kept his career in jeopardy in the closeted world of 1940s Tinsel Town. If the public learned the truth about him, his career would be ruined. Cregar had to live with that knowledge, and with the realization that studio executives might use this against him if he refused to accept an assigned role.

By the time he made *The Lodger*, Cregar was already growing desperate to change both his screen image and his self-image. When *Lodger* co-star Merle Oberon flattered Cregar by suggesting he could win leading man roles if he lost weight, Cregar seized on the idea that transforming his physique would provide a panacea for all his problems. He began dieting with anorexic obsession. In less than a year, Cregar would starve more than 100 pounds from his body — and die of a heart attack.

His performance in *The Lodger* stands as the finest Jack the Ripper in screen history — quite a feat, considering the nefarious serial killer has appeared in scores of films over the decades, beginning as early as 1924 and continuing as recently as *From Hell* in 2001. Cregar appears to grasp some inner truth missing from all other screen Rippers. He seems so close to the role — or, perhaps, the role seems so close to him — that at times Cregar's portrayal becomes difficult to watch. Playing this heartbroken misfit character, so full of self-loathing and conflicting impulses, Cregar appears to be channeling his own anguish and confusion.

Slade, Cregar's character in *The Lodger*, yearns for acceptance but is driven by destructive psychological forces beyond his control. He is as complex and tormented a villain as the movies can offer. As author John McCarty writes in his *Movie Psychos and Madmen*, "One sees in [Cregar's] eyes and hears in his placid voice a conscious desire to be delivered from his madness even as he clings to that madness and

Laird Cregar delivered the performance of his life in *The Lodger* (1944).

subconsciously urges it on." In this conflicted role, Cregar treads a treacherous course between menace and pathos. One false step, in one direction or the other, and his performance would descend into either schmaltz or camp. In his surefooted handling of the material, Cregar makes it impossible not to feel compassion for Slade, but never allows audiences to feel so much sympathy for the character that they stop being afraid of him.

Director John Brahm delays Cregar's entrance for the first few minutes of the film, as the police discover the Ripper's latest victim. Then, dramatically, Cregar steps out of the fog, a shadow-draped figure in a black cape and bowler hat carrying a medical bag. Something brooding and dangerous lingers behind his sleepy-looking eyes. He raps on the door of a household with a room to let and introduces himself as "Mr. Slade" (an assumed name). He is a large, soft man with an even softer voice. He speaks with the mannered care of someone trying desperately not to offend — or, perhaps, not to reveal. Never has precise elocution sounded so creepy. Through much of the film, his voice remains distant, as if he is in only tenuous contact with reality.

The landlady, Ellen (Sara Allgood), rents Slade a room with two modest adornments — several portraits of "old-time actresses" and a large Bible. In this telling, the Ripper's victims are all actresses or former actresses. (In reality, the Ripper preyed on hookers, but the Production Code would not allow on-screen depictions of prostitutes.) When Ellen returns the next day, she discovers that he has turned all the paintings to the wall. "There was something peculiar about those pictures," he explains. Cregar's body language expresses Slade's discomfort. He stands straight-backed, stiff, and speaks hesitantly, with a slight tremble in his voice — obviously ill at ease. "I don't suppose you ever noticed it, but wherever you went in this room the eyes of those women seemed to follow you about. That can ... get on one's nerves."

There's something peculiar all right, but not with the pictures. He's seen constantly thumbing through and occasionally quoting from that oversized Bible. And, as he reveals to the landlady's niece, Kitty (Oberon), the River Thames fascinates him. "Have you ever held your face close to the water and let it wash against your hands as you look down into it?" he asks. Cregar, very quiet and very still, stares at Oberon with unspoken longing. "Deep water is dark and restful and full of peace."

His odd behavior makes Kitty and Ellen suspicious. Kitty begins to seriously wonder if the family's lodger may, indeed, be the Ripper when she discovers him burning his black medical bag in the oven. Earlier the same day, the police revealed that the Ripper was seen carrying such a bag. "I'm sorry if there's an odor, but there was something I had to do," Slade apologizes weakly, explaining nothing. As his character grows more agitated, so does Cregar's performance. He steps more quickly when he moves and his eye movements become more frequent and furtive. The tempo of his speech quickens and he grows shorter of breath. Visibly, he grows less and less at ease.

Kitty visits Slade in his room. He speaks to her with the Bible sitting in his lap, staring blankly at the wall. As Slade quotes Solomon, Cregar's voice again sounds dreamy and distant. But soon his tone turns bitter, as he begins to talk about actresses. "Women of the theater are painted and powdered to look beautiful" but are ugly inside, he announces disdainfully. When Kitty, herself a young actress, takes issue with this remark, Slade explains that his brother, a gifted artist, fell in love with an actress and that the relationship drove his brother to suicide. Slade stares at a miniature self-portrait painted by his brother. Cregar looks at the painting with a bizarre intensity that seems to infer some unnatural bond between Slade and his brother. Through this look, and in the way he delivers those lines about the brother, Cregar introduces the possibility that Slade was incestuously, homosexually fixated on his sibling.

If this is true, the Ripper's crimes against actresses are not merely displaced revenge murders brought on by his brother's death, but something more deeply bound to the killer himself. By killing objects of desire, he hopes to terminate his own suppressed desires. The dazed state in which we find Slade during the film's earliest moments seems to suggest that these killings, like the river, leave him "full of peace." Since, however, he cannot escape himself, this peacefulness always soon abandons him, forcing him to kill again. None of this exists, in as many words, in the film, but Cregar's performance makes it possible to read these depths into the characterization.

"You wouldn't think anyone could hate a thing and love it, too," Cregar explains, leaning very close, tantalizingly close to Kitty as he almost whispers this line. "A man can destroy what he hates and love what he destroys. I also know that there is evil in beauty and that if the evil is cut out...."

Inevitably, Slade chooses to make Kitty his next victim. He decides to attend her performance at a Whitechapel music hall. As the film rushes toward its climax, Cregar's simmering portrayal reaches full boil. As Kitty performs the sexy "Parisian Trot"— a sort of poor woman's can-can — Slade looks on with his mouth agape and eyes wide. He seems at once revolted and attracted. Slade hides in the dancer's dressing room and startles her when she returns there following the number.

"I'm going away and I'm going to take you with me," he announces, after stepping out from behind a screen. Cregar's vocal delivery modulates between the calm, distant tone he used in the early scenes and his harsher, louder tenor from later in the film. His movements around the room speed up and slow down, but his body remains coiled and tense. His herky-jerky body language suggests that emotional forces beyond Slade's control are rippling through the killer's mind. "You're so exquisite, more wonderful than anything I've ever seen. It's such lovely women as you that drag men down," he laments. Cregar moves over to Oberon and places his hand on her shoulder. "You corrupt and destroy men ... but when the evil is cut out of a beautiful thing, only the beauty remains."

Cregar's voice grows more strident and breathless with each line. He clutches Oberon's throat and draws the knife from within his cloak. "I love you and I hate the evil in you. I have never known such beauty as yours or such evil in such beauty. Men will not look at you as they did tonight!" Cregar virtually shouts that final sentence. He is sweating and his breath is coming in gasps, frothing over in bug-eyed frenzy at this point. But he's built toward this moment so skillfully throughout the film that this seems the logical endpoint for Slade.

Detectives burst in and shoot Slade in the neck, but the killer escapes and leads the police on a harrowing chase through the theater. During this final sequence, holding his hand to his bleeding throat, crawling along a catwalk in a desperate attempt at escape, Cregar turns Slade over entirely to his darker impulses. Finally, the killer is reduced to something sub-human, a bloodied, wild-eyed, cornered beast. As Cregar has drawn the character, we believe this is the way it had to end for Slade who, ultimately, proves unable to escape his own inner demons.

Most 1944 critics were duly impressed by Cregar's performance. In the decades since, however, *The Lodger* has slipped into relative obscurity. In his book *Hollywood Cauldron*, historian Gregory Mank praises Cregar's "outlandishly perverse performance" as "the most haunted and haunting of screen Rippers."

Ironically, the smashing critical and commercial success of *The Lodger* only tightened the grip of typecasting on Cregar. He strived to transform himself by losing weight and beginning a romantic relationship with a woman. But Fox producers insisted on reuniting him with Brahm for another gaslight-era chiller, *Hangover Square*. Cregar protested bitterly but eventually agreed to do the film. Watching *The Lodger* and *Hangover Square* back-to-back, Cregar looks shockingly thin and sickly in the latter film. Cregar himself would never see *Hangover Square*. After the picture wrapped, he checked himself into the hospital for elective abdominal surgery, related to his weight loss plan, but suffered two heart attacks following the operation. The second attack proved fatal. He was just 28 years old. *Hangover Square* was released posthumously.

Anthony Perkins in *Psycho* (1960) — This one changed everything.

If, as author David Skal once said to me, "serial killers have become our new vampires," then Norman Bates is our new Count Dracula. The characterization is as pivotal in the development of the modern horror film as Bela Lugosi's Dracula was to the launching of horror cinema's Golden Age. Sadly, *Psycho* overwhelmed Anthony Perkins' career the same way *Dracula* consumed Lugosi's.

Psycho remains one of the most celebrated and most scrutinized films of all time. Its place in cinema history is assured, and its impact on the development of the horror genre cannot be overstated. One statement commonly made about *Psycho* is that this picture transplanted horror from Carpathian castles to audiences' own backyards. This may be too broad a generalization, since *Psycho* was hardly the first film to feature a psychopath on the loose in a contemporary setting, or even the first memorable film of this type. Nevertheless, *Psycho* resonated in the public consciousness in a way unequalled by any of its predecessors. One of the primary reasons for that resonance is Perkins' Norman Bates.

Sources agree that director Alfred Hitchcock gave Perkins wide latitude to embellish Norman, adding nuances not in Joseph Stefano's script or in Robert Bloch's source novel. For instance, it was Perkins' idea to have Norman munch candy corn throughout the film. According to author Charles Winecoff's biography of Perkins, *Split Image*, Perkins also chose Norman's wardrobe and even restructured a scene he shared with Martin Balsam to incorporate overlapping dialogue. "People like Tony [Perkins] and Balsam are intelligent men and you leave them to it," Hitchcock told interviewer Peter Bogdanovich (quoted in Bogdanovich's book, *Who the Devil Made It*).

In the DVD documentary *The Making of Psycho*, Stefano indicates that Hitchcock had Perkins in mind for the part from the beginning. While writing the screenplay, Stefano said, "I perceived a young man, vulnerable, good-looking, kind of sad, makes you feel sorry for him. Hitchcock said, 'What about Tony Perkins?' And of course that was practically what I had described." Yet even Stefano was surprised by how fully Perkins brought the character to life. "He had an incredible grasp on Norman Bates and the situation he was in. I think Tony Perkins must have known what it was like to be trapped."

Indeed, Perkins appears to have been as deeply connected to Norman as Laird Cregar was to Slade. Like Cregar, Perkins was a gay man forced by the attitudes of his day and the politics of Hollywood to closet his sexuality. Perkins channeled the anguish and frustration caused by this into his role as the sexually conflicted Norman. But, for Perkins, that was only the beginning; there are other striking parallels between Perkins and Norman. Like Norman, Perkins was an only child who lost his father at a young age (when Perkins was five) and who, as a result, was raised by an overbearing single mother in a household of suddenly and drastically reduced means. Perkins and Norman made a perfect — eerily perfect — match.

Norman Bates (Anthony Perkins) covers his mouth to squelch a scream when he discovers Mother's handiwork in *Psycho* (1960). (Photograph courtesy Bryan Senn.)

Perkins' performance, however, is much more than a collection of fortunate coincidences. It's a work of supreme insight and great daring, a multi-layered portrayal as rich and enduring as any ever given in horror cinema, and one that only improves as the viewer returns to it again and again. The closer you watch Perkins' work in this film, the more treasures you discover.

Perkins' performance functions on two levels—the first, when the viewer initially sees the film (before you realize that Norman and Mother are one in the same), and the second when you see it again (after the secret is out). The first time through, viewers perceive Norman as shy and awkward, troubled but likable. Later they discover he is far more disturbed than it seems on the surface. Initially, Perkins' work seems straightforward. However, subsequent viewings reveal that Perkins has laced his performance with sly humor. Dialogue, such as Perkins' fidgety assertion that "Mother, my mother — what's the phrase? 'She isn't quite herself today,'" takes on new meaning once viewers know the punchline.

Norman is running from the house on the hill to the motel office in the pouring-down rain when we first glimpse Perkins. He pulls the lapels of his jacket together but does not open the umbrella he's carrying. When the audience gets its first clear look at him, he's soaked and rumpled. Perkins delivers his dialogue in timid stops and starts as he shows Marion (Janet Leigh) around her cabin. "And the, um, over there," he stammers and nods, since Norman is too embarrassed even to speak the word "bathroom."

Soon Perkins enjoys one of his finest scenes, when Norman chats with Marion over sandwiches and milk in the motel's parlor. At first he maintains that gawky, stammering delivery, as he and Marion begin an odd conversation about taxidermy and the eating habits of birds. When the chat becomes more personal, Perkins withdraws, leaning back in his chair and absently stroking one of Norman's stuffed birds. Then Marion asks a more pointed question ("Do you go out with friends?"). He suddenly snaps to attention, putting both feet on the floor and wringing his hands. "Well, um, a boy's best friend is his mother," Perkins replies nervously. At least, it sounds and looks like nervousness the first time the viewer hears and sees it. Watch closely the second time around, and you may detect the slightest mischievous twinkle in his eyes. Perkins understood that lines like this would play very funny to audience members in on the joke. His deft reading preserves those comic possibilities without tipping his hand to first-time viewers.

Throughout this lengthy scene, Perkins shifts from anxiety to titillation to despair to anger and back again with great eloquence and subtlety. The shifting tides of Norman's emotions are visible on Perkins' face, and resonate in the tenor of his voice, but he never seems to be Acting. He even delivers one pivotal bit of dialogue off-camera. "You know what I think?" Perkins asks, as Janet Leigh nibbles at her sandwich. "I think we're all in our private traps, clamped in them, and none of us can ever get out." His words practically reverberate with longing. "We scratch and claw, but only at the air, and only at each other. And for all of it, we never budge an inch."

Marion suggests that Norman consider committing his mother to an asylum. In a bitter, choked voice very near to tears, Perkins croaks, "People always mean well. They cluck their thick tongues and shake their heads and suggest oh so very delicately." According to Winecoff, this line may have been re-written by Perkins. The film's most chilling line, however, belongs to Stefano. It comes soon after, when, as Norman's agitation begins to cool, Perkins delivers his shaky apology for Mother's behavior: "It's not as if she was a maniac, a raving thing. She just goes a little mad sometimes. We all go a little mad sometimes."

Perkins proves equally mesmerizing in a later sequence that contains no dialogue at all — as he cleans up the bathroom in which "Mother" has murdered Marion. He rushes into Marion's room, catches sight of her butchered corpse and reels back, covering his mouth with his hand, shivering and sickened. Then, nervous but resolute, the dutiful, even fastidious son begins to literally mop up the scene of the crime. He turns off the still-running shower, wraps Marion's body in the shower curtain and dumps it in the trunk of her car with the rest of her belongings. He then mops the floor and washes out the bathtub. As he proceeds, the nervousness drains from him — Perkins' facial expression slackens and his movements become almost mechanical.

Finally, he rolls Marion's car into the swamp to dispose of the evidence. As it sinks into the murk, he placidly plucks and chews kernels from that ever-present bag of candy corn. When the car momentarily stops sinking, Perkins clasps his hands in front of his mouth as if in prayer. After a short pause, the car sinks the rest of the way, disappearing into the bog, and Perkins flashes an eerie grin that indicates something beyond relief, something approaching triumph. Quietly, this simple grin provides one of the few clues in his performance that all may not be as it appears between Norman and Mother.

The film closes with a close-up of an even more memorable Perkins grin. He is seated in a chair in a cell at the police station, wrapped in a blanket, when a fly lands on his hand. The camera dollies in on Perkins, his eyes burning with delight, his face fixed in a death's-head smile. (The image of a skull is briefly superimposed.) "I'm not even going to swat that fly," audiences hear via voiceover narration (not provided by Perkins). "I hope they are watching. They'll see. They'll see and they'll know. And they'll say, 'Why, she wouldn't even hurt a fly.'" That's good dialogue, but Perkins' eerily confident grin transforms it into great dialogue — at once amusing and spine-tingling. With successive viewings, we realize that this is the final note of the symphony that is Perkins' performance, the melding point between the humor and the menace that have served as theme and counter-theme throughout his portrayal. And, as viewers step away from the film — for the first time or the fiftieth — that final note rings in their ears.

Critical response to *Psycho* was divided. Many critics panned the film. Others praised it. *The New York Times* panned it and later praised it (giving it a negative review upon its release but later placing it on its list of the Ten Best Films of 1960). In any case, most of the credit — or blame — for *Psycho* went to its celebrity director, Hitchcock, and not to Perkins. The *New York Daily News* was one of the few to single out Perkins, writing: "Anthony Perkins' intelligent performance, the best of his career, makes the picture what it is, which is better than it would be without him." In 1961, Perkins won the British equivalent of the Academy Award and France's Victoire de Cinema. Back home, insiders such as columnist Hedda Hopper lobbied the Academy for an Oscar nomination on behalf of Perkins. When the Oscar nominees were announced, however, it was not Perkins but co-star Leigh who was nominated (for Best Actress in a Supporting Role). She lost.

Since then, *Psycho* has been canonized. It's indelibly affixed to every list of the greatest thrillers ever made and finished Number 18 on the American Film Institute's "100 Movies, 100 Years" list of the 100 greatest American films. As acclaim for *Psycho* has grown, so has appreciation for Perkins' performance. Critic Roger Ebert puts it succinctly in his book *The Great Movies*: "Perkins does a great job of establishing the complex character of Norman, in a performance that has become a landmark."

None of this, however, was gained without a tragic cost to Perkins himself. Before *Psycho*, Perkins had been typed, primarily, as the likable but troubled young man. Such roles earned him fame on Broadway in *Tea and Sympathy* and *Look Homeward, Angel*, and in early films such as *Friendly Persuasion* (1956) and *Fear Strikes Out* (1957). After *Psycho*, there was no returning to those sorts of parts. Leigh, in the *Psycho* DVD documentary, explains: "He was not Norman Bates, but he was so brilliant that the people said, 'Yes you are. You are too Norman Bates.'"

Perkins tried playing a wide variety of characters, and turned in some other good performances (perhaps most memorably as Joseph K. in Orson Welles' 1963 adaptation of Franz Kafka's *The Trial*), but audiences never really embraced Perkins in any role other than Norman Bates. As the years passed, his roles grew smaller and less frequent. After decades of resistance, Perkins finally caved in and agreed to reprise his most famous role for a pair of subpar sequels, *Psycho II* (1983) and *Psycho III* (1986). Perkins performed capably in both films and also directed the latter, but *Psycho II* wasn't the blockbuster that Perkins (and Universal Pictures) had dreamed of, and *Psycho III* flopped entirely. From there, what was left for Perkins? Cheap Spanish productions, made-for-TV movies (including *Psycho IV: The Beginning* in 1990), straight-to-video misfires and a premature death at age 60 from AIDS.

Norman Bates killed Perkins' once-promising career as surely as he killed Marion Crane. But, in exchange, he gave Perkins a kind of immortality. After more than 40 years, Norman, forever intertwined with Perkins, remains one of the most recognizable characters in the history of motion pictures.

Duane Jones in *Night of the Living Dead* (1968)

— It was one of the most turbulent years in American history. In 1968, Martin Luther King, Jr., was assassinated in Memphis, and African-Americans rioted in cities across the nation. Congress passed the Civil Rights Act. Meanwhile, Alabama Governor George Wallace founded the American Independent Party and ran for the presidency on a pro-segregationist platform. This was also the year that presidential nominee Robert Kennedy was assassinated, the year of the Tet Offensive in Vietnam and of the antiwar riots at the Democratic National Convention in Chicago. It seemed that the survival of the world, or at least of the United States, was teetering in the balance.

Enter director George Romero, screenwriter John Russo and actor Duane Jones, who together would craft *Night of the Living Dead*. This endlessly fascinating film pushed horror cinema toward its gore-splattered future while remaining connected with the genre's Old Dark House past. Its themes seem timeless, yet they echo loudly the troubles of its era. As a result, *Night of the Living Dead* has emerged as one of the most discussed and written-about horror films of all time. Despite all this analysis, however, relatively little attention has been devoted to Jones' stunning lead performance, and the vital ingredient it provides in the overall success of the film.

The scenario recalls Alfred Hitchcock's *The Birds* (1963): A lonely knot of people trapped in a boarded-up house fends off attacks by mindless creatures in a world that has suddenly begun to rip itself apart. The crucial difference is that in Hitchcock's film, the trapped heroes represent a family unit; in Romero's film, they are a random assembly of different ages, backgrounds and races. Ben (Jones), a black man, emerges as the group's leader.

In the audio commentary for the 30th Anniversary Edition DVD of *Night of the Living Dead*, screenwriter John Russo says that no one considered the "social ramifications" of casting an African-American in the film's lead role. Jones was "just the best actor who auditioned for the part." Even if you accept that Russo and Romero didn't envision the socio-political possibilities of this casting choice, you must think that Jones himself did.

After *Night of the Living Dead*, in which he made his screen debut, Jones devoted much of his career to promoting and participating in African-American theater companies as an actor and a director. A former English professor, he also served as director of the Maguire Theater at the Old Westbury campus of New York State University and served as artistic director at the Richard Allen Center in New York City. His few subsequent film appearances were mostly in small, Afrocentric productions such as *Ganja & Hess* (a.k.a. *Vampires in Harlem*, 1972). Obviously, Jones was well-educated and politically astute. How could such a man not understand that his performance could make a subtle yet powerful statement? Jones brings to his role nuances that no white actor could have, enriching both his character and the film as a whole.

The film's earliest scenes chronicle Barbara's (Judith O'Dea) terrified flight from a cemetery, where a zombie has murdered her brother, to the secluded farmhouse, where the rest of the action will take place. Jones makes his entrance 13 minutes into the film, rushing out of his pickup truck, which has run out of gas, and into the house. Barbara has slipped into a state of shock, dazed and incommunicative.

Ben enters the house, carrying a tire iron, and makes a quick scan of the place. He tries the phone, to no avail, and is sickened by the sight of a half-devoured corpse at the top of a staircase. Jones moves with urgency and acute awareness of his surroundings. His actions are efficient, determined and carefully thought-out. Although clearly frustrated with Barbara, he remains compassionate. "I know you're afraid," he says. "I'm afraid, too. But we have to try to board the house up together." Jones leans close to her, makes eye contact and takes hold of her arms, as one might do when explaining something to a frightened child.

Later, as he disassembles the dining room table (he needs the wood to board up the windows), he relates to Barbara his first encounter with the zombies at a place called Beekman's Diner. Zombies surrounded the diner and attacked its inhabitants *en masse*. Although he's telling Barbara, Jones' distant, introspective delivery makes clear that Ben is really talking to himself, hoping the memory will lose its power as he puts it into words. His voice grows quieter and his movements with the table become slower. Finally, he pauses and says, "I can still hear the man screaming...." He stares at the floor for a second, then resumes talking, more agitated. He has abandoned the table entirely. His hands now free, he illustrates his story with broad, sweeping motions. His throat tightens and his voice grows distressed as he describes running through a line of zombies with the pickup truck. "They scattered through the air, like bugs..." he says, choking back tears.

Earlier Ben said he was scared, but not until this scene do we glimpse how profoundly all this has affected him. It's a humanizing moment, one that galvanizes our sympathies. Jones must have recognized it was vital to the success of the film that audiences identify with his character, and his delicate handling of this scene — overtly emotional but never maudlin — is simply riveting.

For the sake of contrast, consider the 30th Anniversary Edition of *Night of the Living Dead*. Released to DVD, this version inserts newly shot footage into Romero's original film. Some of that new footage is devoted to dramatizing the events as they unfold at Beekman's Diner. Unfortunately this gambit backfires, since it distracts viewers from Ben's telling of the story, undercutting both the power and the purpose

Ben (Duane Jones) defends the farmhouse from attacking zombies in *Night of the Living Dead* (1968).

of the original sequence. It's crucial that audiences identify with Ben at this point in the film because soon Jones' character — a nice and capable guy at heart — will be pushed to his breaking point. If audiences don't connect with Ben now, the later scenes lose their emotional impact.

Ben must forcibly restrain Barbara when, overwrought, she decides to leave the house in search of her dead brother. He grabs her. She slaps him. So Jones sets his jaw and, with a look that, without words, says, "Okay, you asked for this," decks Barbara with a right cross. Jones' tender demeanor, as he checks on her before venturing upstairs, informs us that punching Barbara was necessary but not pleasant for Ben.

Harry Cooper (Karl Hardman) makes an appearance. Along with his family and a young couple, Harry has been hiding in the cellar of the farmhouse until this point — which aggravates Ben. The two men treat each other with suspicion and disdain. Ben questions Harry's explanation of why he and the others didn't come up sooner to help him board up the house. "Now wait a minute," Jones begins, with his brow furrowed and his voice raised. As he continues, his tone turns from one of irritation to indignation. He sounds like a man who's been lied to and misled too often in the past. "You just got finished saying you couldn't hear from down there, now you say it sounded like the place was being ripped apart. It would be nice if you got your story straight, man!"

At this point, the thematic undercurrents of the picture begin to bubble to the surface. Middle-aged, white Harry and young, black Ben argue at length about what course of action to take. Harry wants to hide in the cellar. Ben wants to remain upstairs. This sequence — as Hardman insists "the cellar's the safest place!" and Jones roars, "The cellar is a deathtrap!" — is loaded with symbolic value. It's a shadowy reflection of the inter-racial and inter-generational conflicts raging throughout the country at the time, as people of different ages and points of view argued vehemently about how to resolve the many crises they faced, in a world gone crazy.

Jones excels during these heated exchanges with Hardman, not because he is a black actor, but because he is a gifted actor, one who is unafraid to call upon his own experience for emotional fuel. Nevertheless, his ethnicity gives him a different and, in this context, more explosive vein of emotions to mine. How often had white men referred to educated, erudite Jones as "boy" or "nigger"? How often had he, like so many other African-Americans, been forced to use the "colored" restroom or been refused service in a restaurant? How many Harry Coopers had Jones known in his lifetime?

Frustrated, Ben tries to banish Cooper to his beloved basement. "Now get the hell down in the cellar," he says. Jones' voice is calm but his tone is acidic. "You can be the boss down there. I'm boss up here." Indeed, Ben has emerged as the leader of this rag tag band of refugees, but has done so based on his disposition and ability (and the fact that he discovered a rifle and ammunition in the house). Jones' weary face informs us that, unlike Harry, Ben does not desire authority; he only desires survival. Ironically, however, all Ben's best-laid plans go awry. An attempt to refuel the pickup truck turns into a debacle, and the young couple is killed.

Ben rushes back to the house and finds that Harry has locked him out. Jones kicks in the door and aims a withering stare at Harry, who cowers near the entrance to the cellar. Belatedly, Harry helps Ben board up the doorway. Once the doorway is secure, Ben turns to Harry. Jones' face is wet with perspiration and his eyes are burning with righteous fury. He bashes Harry in the face three times, chases him across the room and lifts him up from the floor to deliver a fourth roundhouse right. Then he throws Harry into a chair, holds him down by the shoulders and, with veins popping, shouts in his face: "I ought to drag you out there and feed you to those things!" But, of course, he doesn't — even though Harry would have gladly let Ben be eaten alive by the zombies.

Later, exhausted, seated in a hard wooden chair and reloading the rifle, Ben even offers to carry Harry's wounded child a mile or more to the family's overturned car. Before that can happen, the zombies, who have gathered by the dozens, begin attacking the house. While Jones tries to prevent them from entering the house, Harry steals Ben's rifle and makes for the cellar. At last, Ben snaps. He grabs the weapon from Harry. Jones grits his teeth, as if sucking up his willpower. Ben aims the rifle and pulls the trigger, shooting Harry in the stomach. As Harry crumples to the floor, Jones' face creases with a tiny, enigmatic grin — of relief or of victory? In any case, the look is short-lived. The sound of the zombies pounding at the door suddenly jolts him back to reality. He turns toward the door but pauses to glance back at Harry. The look on Jones' face is one of wide-eyed horror, expressing the sudden recognition of what he's done. This look reassures us of what we already know — that before all this started, Ben never imagined he was capable of killing anyone.

Here, in this single look, in this single fragment of Jones' performance, we find encapsulated the true power of Romero's vision. In the end, the most frightening thing in *Night of the Living Dead* isn't the zombies, or even their gruesome dining habits. What's truly horrifying is the way people treat one another. Romero's haunting supposition is that we, as a species, are unable to overcome our fears, prejudices and petty jealousies, and that ultimately this will lead to our destruction. That in the end Ben is forced to retreat to Harry's cellar reflects the director's fatalism, as does this film's bitterly ironic finale.

Thanks in no small measure to Jones, *Night of the Living Dead* emerged from the drive-in movie circuit, where it made its debut, and eventually gained recognition as one of the truly great horror movies and one of the finest films of the 1960s. In 1988, critic John Kobal asked dozens of esteemed film critics from around the world to list their Top Ten favorite films and used the results to compile his book, *The Top 100 Movies*. *Night of the Living Dead* made the list, appearing alongside the likes of *Citizen Kane*, *Singin' in the Rain*, *8½*, *Rashomon* and *Battleship Potemkin*. At Number 97, *Night of the Living Dead* finished one spot higher than *Psycho*.

Nevertheless, the last thing critics then or now talk about in relation to *Night of the Living Dead* is the acting. Despite all the verbiage devoted to the movie, it's virtually impossible to find a critique that mentions Jones by name and examines his performance in detail. In his outline of the film, Kobal notes only that "the main character is a black man, a fact which is never once mentioned in the film, and he still dies in the end, shot by white rescuers who mistake him for one of the culprits." Which is fine, except that Ben isn't merely "a black man" but a fully sketched human being with which audiences strongly identify. His death at the end of the film is powerful only because Jones has created such a believable and likable character.

Biographical data on Jones is also scarce but Hardman, who also co-produced *Night of the Living Dead*, told me that Jones was very intelligent and somewhat introverted. A co-worker of mine during my years as a newspaper reporter knew Jones from his years as a New York academic and described him the same way. She also said that Jones always became visibly uncomfortable whenever anyone mentioned *Night of the Living Dead*. Sadly, this gifted, smart, sensitive man was also deeply troubled. Jones died in July 1988 at age 50. According to Hardman, Jones "took his own life."

Michael Rooker in *Henry, Portrait of a Serial Killer* (1986) —

Posters for this film proclaimed, "He's not Freddie. He's not Jason. He's real."

Well, sort of.

The title character in director John McNaughton's controversial chiller is based on real-life serial killer Henry Lee Lucas. In fact, all the key characters in the story have real-world namesakes, and many of the episodes depicted in the film mirror actual events. Moreover, McNaughton relates the tale in a gritty, documentary-like style.

Yet, despite all these claims to realism, it is with this film — and with Michael

Rooker's startling performance — that the serial killer fully emerges as an archetypal monster, the latter-day equivalent of the vampire or the werewolf. Through his well-crafted portrayal, and with able support from McNaughton and the film's script, Rooker creates an indefatigable bogeyman, forever roaming the highways and side streets in search of fresh targets. His Henry represents not just Lucas but every serial killer — including the one who may be watching your house at this very moment. His characterization taps into the audience's collective nightmares unlike any previous screen psycho.

The 1970s and early '80s gave us no short supply of slashers. The most recognizable of these — Freddie Krueger, Jason Vorhees and Michael Myers — behaved less like monsters than like comic book super-villains. They bore masks and uniforms (Freddie's trademark sweater, for instance) and displayed eccentric but predictable patterns of behavior, which recurred throughout their serialized exploits. These characters sold plenty of movie tickets, but did so without plugging into the zeitgeist with any true resonance. By the mid–1980s, audiences weren't likely to be honestly, deeply frightened by any character so cartoonish as Freddie or Jason.

Rooker and McNaughton must have recognized this. They labor to make Henry everything Freddie and Jason are not. Rooker's Henry is the kind of guy you wouldn't notice if you were standing next to him in the grocery store checkout line. More than anything else, Henry is that most ubiquitous and potentially dangerous of American fixtures — the faceless stranger. Rooker's shrewdly reasoned performance reflects a key understanding of what's scary — that the less we understand, the more we fear. Although his acting remains naturalistic, Rooker betrays as few insights as possible to Henry's inner self. We get a few contradictory glimpses; he allows us nothing more. In the end, all we know with certainty about Henry is that he loves to kill people, that he's very good at it, and that he's unlikely to be stopped. Rooker's enigmatic characterization functions like a blank canvas, onto which viewers paint their own phobias.

In 1986, when *Henry* was filmed, the real-life Lucas had gained a grisly form of celebrity by confessing to hundreds of murders. Many of those confessions proved to be false, but there's no doubt that he killed his mother, as well as 82-year-old Kate Rich and Lucas' teenaged girlfriend, Becky Powell. No one is really sure how many other murders Lucas committed, but some of those were committed with the assistance of accomplice Otis Toole. *Henry* is the story of a serial killer, his roommate and sometime accomplice Otis (Tom Towles) and a girl named Becky (Tracy Arnold). However, *Henry*'s plot strays from reality, and Rooker's character differs from the real Lucas in significant and revealing respects. It's through these artistic liberties that Henry is elevated from tabloid headlines to the stuff of myth.

The film's opening sequence shows us two faces of Rooker's character — the unassuming, even likable Henry met by casual acquaintances and the raging, animalistic killer known only to his victims. We see Rooker pay a warm compliment to a waitress at a diner, in a surprisingly reedy, timid voice ("Nice smile you got there"). Seconds later, in a flashback, we hear him snarl with rage as he kills a young woman with a bottle ("Die, bitch!"). Rooker refuses to let us reconcile these two faces.

Henry climbs into his beat-up Chevy Impala and drives to the mall parking lot.

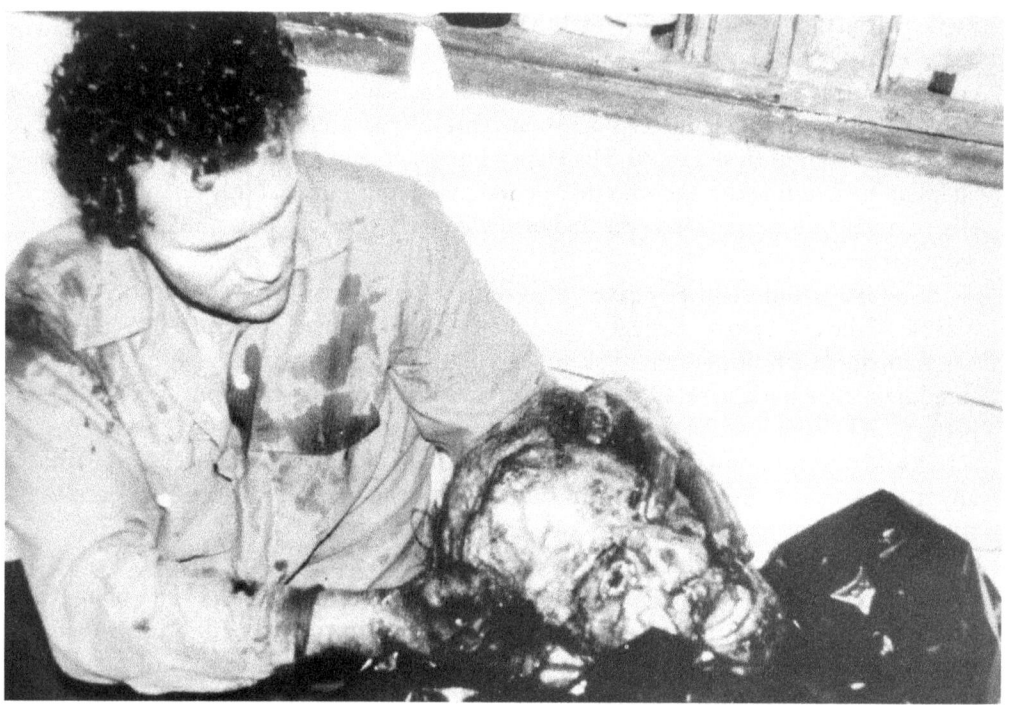

Henry (Michael Rooker) toys with the body of one of his victims in this particularly unsettling photograph from *Henry, Portrait of a Serial Killer* (1986).

Poker-faced, he patiently sizes up the women leaving the mall, looking for potential prey. He settles on a young woman and follows her as she drives to her happy-looking suburban home. Even when the young woman's husband comes out to greet her, foiling Henry's initial designs, Rooker's face remains blank. His eyes are emotionless, dead, like a shark's eyes, as he drives away.

Later, Henry meets Becky. In the film, Becky is Otis' sister. In reality, Becky Powell was Toole's niece. In the film, Otis is Henry's roommate. In reality, Toole claimed he and Lucas were lovers as well as partners in crime. Although Otis is portrayed as bisexual in the film, Henry is presented as asexual. Even when, later, he and Otis pick up a pair of hookers, Henry can only gain release through murder.

Rooker's most dialogue-heavy scene, and the one most potentially revealing about Henry, is an after-dinner conversation between Henry and Becky in the greasy kitchen of their grungy apartment. Becky and Henry discuss their childhoods. Rooker rests his head against the wall and stares off into space as he speaks. He seldom looks directly at Becky, and does not seem to be connecting with her in any real sense, despite the intimacy of the discussion. Becky tells Henry that her father repeatedly sexually abused her when she was a child. Rooker, staring out from under heavy, drunk-looking eyelids, asks, "You didn't get along with your daddy, huh?" It's a straight-faced question, not sarcasm. Rooker's clueless delivery tells us that Henry has no comprehension of sexuality, or of love, and even less understanding of women.

To Henry, women are truly and completely objectified. They are plastic dolls. He likes to play with them, and then rip their heads off.

Becky, after some hesitation, asks if (as Otis told her earlier) Henry really killed his mother. "I guess I did," Rooker replies with a sneer. It's a mild, almost indifferent sneer, indicating only that he resents being asked the question, not that he harbors any lingering pain or remorse about the murder. Rooker's face remains impassive as Henry explains that his mother was a prostitute, and that often she would force him to watch her as she turned tricks. (This corresponds with the real-life Lucas.) "She beat me a lot, too," Rooker rasps. "She'd beat me when I wouldn't watch it and sometimes she'd beat me and make me wear a dress and watch 'em doin' it. Then they'd laugh at me." That's powerful stuff, but Rooker's deadpan, glassy-eyed delivery doesn't inspire empathy — except in Becky. She grabs his hand and tells him, "I feel like I've known you forever and ever."

Faced with this show of affection, Henry seems confused. Rooker's eyes remain glazed over. His head wobbles. He looks at the floor, swallows and licks his lips. "Yeah, I killed my mama," he continues in an even huskier voice. He ends his tale with, "I shot her, I shot her dead." Becky is confused. Otis told Becky that Henry killed his mother with a baseball bat. Earlier, Henry told Becky he stabbed his mother to death. When she asks him about this, Rooker again looks stunned. He pauses, open-mouthed, and blinks slowly. "Oh yeah." Rooker repeats the same cycle of mannerisms as before — looking at the floor, swallowing, licking his lips, then rasps: "That's right, I stabbed her."

The three versions Henry gives of his mother's murder, combined with the knowledge that he's killed women with a knife, a gun, a broken bottle, by drowning and strangulation, may suggest that, in his mind, Henry is killing his mother over and over again, in a different manner each time. But this analysis is challenged by later revelations in the film, when Henry explains why he varies his *modus operandi*. It would also be appropriate to wonder if Henry's story proves inconsistent simply because he's lying. The real Lucas turned out to be a compulsive liar. In any case, the final result is that even this potentially revealing sequence remains cryptic, open to multiple interpretations. The inner Henry — whoever he may be — remains elusive.

Rooker and McNaughton (who co-wrote the film's script with Richard Fire) alter other key aspects of Henry's personality. In the film, Henry restrains Otis when Otis tries to kiss Becky. "Don't do that, Otis, she's your sister," Rooker warns, turning his head sideways at Otis, like a confused dog. Later, Henry prevents Otis from molesting the body of one of the duo's female victims. The real Lucas bragged about engaging in incest and necrophilia, as well as Satanism and other nefarious acts not depicted in the film.

Rooker and McNaughton must have realized that depicting Henry as a necrophiliac would have pushed audiences too far. Besides, the contradictions make Henry that much more unknowable. Who but a complete sociopath could commit such grotesque crimes? On the other hand, if Henry understands and abides by societal mores against incest and necrophilia, can he truly be a sociopath? Also, the film Henry, while no great intellect, is considerably brighter and better mannered than the real Lucas. Ironically, the film posits that Henry, the more intelligent and socialized of the two, is more dangerous than Otis. In most respects, Henry seems like a regular guy. Yet his appetite for murder consumes him. His entire life is structured to allow him to continue to kill. Nothing else matters.

Henry's plot involves parallel seductions, as Henry attempts to induct Otis into serial killing and Becky tries to entice Henry into a romantic relationship. Both of these endeavors fail, since Otis lacks the self-discipline and intellectual capacity to kill and get away with it, and Henry lacks the self-awareness and emotional capacity to love and be loved. As a result, Otis eventually poses a threat to Henry, and Henry in the end proves dangerous to Becky.

Otis discovers Henry is a killer in dramatic fashion: Henry and Otis pick up a pair of prostitutes in Henry's car and are engaging in sexual acts with their respective "dates," Henry in the back seat and Otis in the front seat. Suddenly, Henry becomes enraged and strangles his "date." When the hooker in the front seat cries out, Henry grabs her and quickly snaps her neck. After this sequence, McNaughton cuts immediately to a scene some time later. Otis looks sickened, but Henry is unfazed, calmly eating a hamburger and take-out coffee. "You want some fries?" he asks nonchalantly.

Significantly, Rooker's only real display of passion in the film comes when Henry talks about killing. Describing the act to Otis, he rubs his hands together expectantly. "It's always the same, and always different," Rooker says in a voice ripe with yearning. In this sequence, Rooker illustrates Henry's love of murder. In a later one, Rooker demonstrates the level of cool detachment he is able to maintain from his crimes. "If you shoot somebody in the head with a .45 every time you kill somebody, it becomes like your fingerprint, see?" Rooker explains. "But if you strangle one and stab another and one you cut up and one you don't, then the police don't know what to do. They think you're four different people." He delivers his lines in the flat, mildly frustrated tone of a high school English teacher struggling to help his pupils grasp the concept of a split infinitive.

In a sequence toward the end of the film, Rooker dramatizes Henry's unquenchable thirst, his almost sexual longing, for the kill. Henry and Becky return from dinner out. Otis is passed out on the couch. Becky takes Henry into her bedroom, removes her shirt and begins kissing Henry and unbuttoning his shirt. Rooker looks at her with confusion rather than desire. When Otis barges in, interrupting the couple, Henry looks relieved rather than frustrated. Henry decides to go out for cigarettes and "air." Inflamed by Becky's advances, he prowls the streets in search of a victim, in search of release.

From the outset, *Henry* was a lightning rod for controversy. Although produced in 1986, it didn't receive wide distribution until 1990, and when it did, due to its graphic subject matter, it was given an X rating. In essence, this restricted the movie to the "art house" circuit, since most mainstream theaters at the time refused to book X-rated films. It was further hindered because many newspapers refused to accept ads for films rated X. Despite these obstacles, *Henry* became a cult hit. Even critics who piled derision on the picture praised Rooker's performance. Although too controversial for Academy Award recognition, *Henry* was nominated for Best Picture at the Independent Spirit Awards, and Rooker took home the Silver Space Needle trophy for Best Actor. As history has placed the film in perspective, historians have showered Rooker with praise. In his book *Movie Psychos and Madmen*, author John McCarty praises Rooker's "frightening, low-keyed, dead-eyed intensity."

Because *Henry* was so poorly distributed upon its initial release, it remains a picture many people have never seen. As a result, Rooker's performance will never attain the kind of iconic status as Anthony Perkins' Norman Bates or Anthony Hopkins' Hannibal Lecter. But no one who sees *Henry* will ever forget Rooker's portrayal. Of all the performances covered in this book, Rooker's remains by far the most disturbing.

Anthony Hopkins in *The Silence of the Lambs* (1991)

There can be no doubt about the enduring popularity and historical significance of Lon Chaney's Phantom of the Opera, Boris Karloff's Frankenstein Monster or Anthony Perkins' Norman Bates. Each of these films was released 40 or more years ago, and each characterization has withstood the test of time. It's a riskier proposition to venture which recent performances will pass the judgment of history. I'm willing to wager, however, that Anthony Hopkins' cannibalistic killer, Hannibal Lecter, will one day be empanelled among Hollywood's supreme rogues gallery.

Already, in just over a decade since the film's release, Lecter has entered the public consciousness like few other movie madmen. The sensational commercial and critical success of *The Silence of the Lambs* has a great deal to do with this, of course, but Lecter lingers in the cultural vernacular as more than just a character from a popular film. He is remembered and discussed by film as if he had a life independent from the movie. Like the Phantom, the Frankenstein Monster and Norman Bates, Lecter has made the jump from finely wrought character to pop culture icon. In the American Film Institute's 2003 "100 Heroes and Villains" poll, Lecter was named the top screen villain of all time.

This represents the highest possible compliment to Hopkins, whose performance exemplifies the power of playing realistically a character that is not at all realistic. Hopkins' portrayal both frightened and amused audiences. More than that, however, it held filmgoers in awe. The advertising campaign for *Superman: The Movie* promised audiences, "You will believe a man can fly." *Silence of the Lambs* might well have promised, "You will believe a man armed only with a fountain pen can outwit the FBI, escape an entire police force and get away with multiple murder."

In this, Lecter has less in common with Norman Bates than with another pop culture idol, secret agent James Bond. Like Bond, Lecter is a man of superior intelligence, keen powers of observation, dry wit and refined taste. Like Bond, he is apparently indestructible and capable of extricating himself from seemingly hopeless situations. And, like Bond, he is at heart an assassin, an impossibly perfect killer. Various actors have played Bond with verve and panache, but none of them have done so with any great degree of realism. Hopkins' steadfast commitment to naturalism makes the impossible seem plausible, and brings Lecter to life to a degree that has always escaped Bond.

On the Bravo Network program *Inside the Actors Studio*, Hopkins told interviewer James Lipton that when he read the script for *Lambs* he immediately recognized Lecter was "a life-changing role." According to Hopkins, director Jonathan

Demme gave him flexibility to develop the character as he saw fit. The star understood intuitively that he could inspire more chills by playing a charming villain and decided to approach the role "very calmly and penetratingly." His entire performance is built around this keystone idea. Almost invariably, Hopkins makes the quieter choice. His occasional broader strokes are carefully chosen for maximum impact.

It was Hopkins' idea to give the character slicked-back hair and a tight-fitting uniform so that Lecter would appear "graceful and dangerous, like a shark." Lecter is mesmerizing from his first appearance. FBI trainee Clarice Starling (Jodie Foster) arrives at Lecter's cell to interview him. She finds him standing perfectly vertical, with his arms at his side, like a human exclamation point. His eyebrows are raised slightly, curious, expectant. "Good morning," he says softly.

Lecter maneuvers Starling closer to the glass so he can get a better look at her identification. But the twinkle in Hopkins' eyes and the slight tilt of his head make it clear that Lecter is soaking in every detail of Starling, not just her ID. Hopkins literally bristles with awareness ("That expires in a week"). Hopkins gives a tiny wink, as he shifts his eyes from Starling's badge to her face. "You're not real FBI, are you?" Hopkins' tone of voice remains soft, playful. He seems amused. His curiosity is piqued even more than before. Starling sits but he remains standing, and breaks into a beaming grin.

"Memory, Agent Starling, is what I have instead of a view," Lecter says later in the interview. Coming from a lesser actor, that line might have sounded maudlin. Hopkins reads it with only a hint of sadness and completely without regret or despair. When Lecter criticizes Starling for her "ham-handed segue" into the survey she has brought for him to complete, Hopkins sounds like a disappointed college professor. Indeed, theirs seems to be a teacher-pupil relationship. He quizzes her repeatedly. "Why do you think he removes their skins, Agent Starling? Thrill me with your acumen," Hopkins asks in the same cool, professorial tone, but with a grin this time.

Eventually, Lecter accepts the survey and begins to flip through it. But quickly his emotions shift. Hopkins' voice grows colder, reproachful. "Oh, Agent Starling, you think you can dissect me with this blunt little tool?" Then Hopkins begins to mock Starling's West Virginia accent. This wasn't scripted, nor was it worked out in rehearsals. Hopkins says it came to him while shooting the scene. It just seemed like something Lecter would do. During their scenes together, Hopkins and co-star Foster developed an improvisational rapport, each ad-libbing bits of dialogue and adding unscripted touches that fleshed out their already brilliantly written roles.

This sequence builds to the film's most famous passage of dialogue. Hopkins matter-of-factly recounts, "A census taker once tried to test me. I ate his liver with some fava beans and a nice Chianti." Then he makes a bizarre slurping sound. This slurping noise was another on-the-spot ad lib, and one of the few, carefully chosen moments in the film where Hopkins elects to go over the top. Because his delivery to this point has been so controlled and so polite, this grotesque vulgarity—which shocked Foster herself during shooting—seems to come out of nowhere. As a result, it seems even more bizarre and unnerving. It makes us wonder, what other unpleasant surprises might Dr. Lecter have in store?

Hopkins' approach to Lecter's next scene, another interview with Starling in his cell, informs us at once that Lecter has gained control of his situation — and of Starling. Instead of standing, Lecter is seated casually on the floor with his back to the wall and his legs stretched out before him. Hopkins' body language alone tells us that Lecter is confident and relaxed. He realizes he has command of the situation, since he has knowledge Starling needs. At this point, Hopkins' performance becomes slyly comic.

When Starling informs Lecter she has discovered the remains of one of the psychotic psychiatrist's former patients, he quips: "Best thing for him, really. His therapy was going nowhere." As always in this film, Hopkins' comic timing is impeccable. This callous humor, Hopkins seems to understand, will impact viewers on two levels. Audiences will laugh at the joke, but the joke will make them realize how unfeeling and utterly indifferent to human life Lecter truly is.

By the time we reach Starling's third interview with Lecter, the serial killer has begun to openly toy with his "pupil." She must obtain from him information to help her apprehend a new serial killer, known as Buffalo Bill. But Lecter won't give away what he knows. He demands a quid pro quo exchange, trading information about the killer for information about Starling's childhood. He teases her, withholding key data. Hopkins' playful, delighted demeanor in this sequence demonstrates how much pleasure Lecter takes in the control he holds over Starling. (How often does a caged man gain control of anything?) Simultaneously, Hopkins is able to signal Lecter's growing fascination with Starling. He sits in rapt attention as Starling recounts her father's death and her move to live with an uncle on a sheep farm. We already understand that Lecter is an elitist. He is easily bored and despises mediocrity, but is fascinated by Starling because in her he senses something extraordinary. All this we know because of the way Hopkins listens to Foster. It does not exist in screenwriter Ted Tally's dialogue. Hopkins inserts it between the lines.

Lecter's and Starling's final quid pro quo exchange takes place in a Memphis police station, where Lecter has been transferred as part of a deal to reveal the identity of Buffalo Bill. Locked in a cell that resembles a giant birdcage, he placidly reads a paperback collection of poetry. Lecter does not see Starling enter the room, yet he recognizes her even before she speaks. Hopkins spins in his chair, puts the book down and stares admiringly at his visitor. "People will say we're in love," he coos. Indeed, the intimate rapport established between Lecter and Starling does suggest some degree of romantic attraction. However, the way Hopkins' icy blue eyes fix on Starling betrays that Lecter harbors no genuine compassion for Starling (or for anyone else). Lecter is, at best, sexually infatuated, which seems a logical extension of his ever-predatory personality.

To the end, their relationship remains primarily teacher-pupil. Lecter realizes he may not see Starling again, so he gives her what amounts to a final exam. Hopkins quotes Marcus Auerlius, then asks, "What does he do, this man you seek?"

"He kills women?" Starling answers uncertainly.

"No!" Hopkins raises his voice and rolls his eyes. "That is incidental," he corrects her testily. "He covets," Hopkins explains, holding the "s" on "covets" to produce a serpentine sound. He leans forward in his chair and glares at Clarice intently. We realize Lecter is frustrated with his star student's inability to deduce the solution.

This final interview is cut short, and the film's most grisly sequence follows. Lecter uses the innards of a pilfered ink pen to pick the locks on his handcuffs and overpower his two jailers. Hopkins hisses like a snake and bares his teeth as he slaps the cuffs on one guard. He gnaws on the other's guard's face like an animal, then returns to the handcuffed guard and beats the man to death with his own billy club. Hopkins wields the club with trance-like detachment. Afterward, he pauses to listen to a symphony playing on a tiny cassette player in his cell. With his bloody hands, he pretends to conduct the orchestra. This is the only scene of Lecter actually engaging in violence during the film. All Lecter's other crimes are only described in dialogue.

Yet, due to the ferocity Hopkins brings to his flashes of anger at Clarice, and the heartless humor he aims at his victims, we have no doubt about Lecter's ability or inclination to commit unspeakably heinous acts. In most respects, the quiet sequences in Lecter's cell are at least as frightening as this bloody assault. After the movie, viewers are more apt to recall Lecter's dialogue — lines like "Love your suit!"— than the image of Lecter, covered in blood, bashing in a man's skull.

The Silence of the Lambs is a film of dazzling artistry and technical precision, as perfect a chiller as has yet been produced. It garnered seven Oscar nominations and won five statuettes. And Hopkins' isn't the only great performance in the film. Yet even amid this splendor, Hopkins' artistry stands out. Perhaps the most telling evidence of the power of Hopkins' performance is that almost no one quibbled when he was nominated as Best Actor in a Leading Role, even though he's on screen for just 23 of *Lambs*' 118 minutes. Hopkins could justifiably have been nominated for Best Supporting Actor. Even with such limited screen time, however, he dominates the film. Audiences were more likely to leave theaters chattering about Lecter than about the film's titular "primary" villain, Buffalo Bill (Ted Levine).

Hopkins' Academy Award triumph ended a 60-year drought of Best Actor Oscar wins by actors appearing in a horror film. On his way to that victory, he earned nearly every critic's prize to be reaped among the 1992 harvest of acting awards. He also garnered a steamer trunk full of ecstatic reviews.

Hopkins reprised his role, but was let down by absurd material, in the misguided sequel *Hannibal* (2001). This ridiculous picture plays like an unintentional parody — more Austin Powers than James Bond, with ravenous swine standing in for Dr. Evil's mutant sea bass. Hopkins served a third turn as Lecter in the *Lambs* prequel, *Red Dragon* (2002), a marked improvement over *Hannibal* but still not a patch on the original. Hopkins' performance had become almost reflexive. He trots out his trademark collection of poses, gestures and other Hannibalisms, but takes few risks. As a result, for once Lecter fails to dominate the film.

None of this, however, lessens the brilliance or impact of his original performance. Hopkins'— and Lecter's— place in history remains assured.

And you'll never look at fava beans the same way again.

Haley Joel Osment in *The Sixth Sense* (1999)

— *The Sixth Sense* isn't told from the point of view of Cole Sears (the little boy who "sees dead people"), but Cole's plight provides the story's emotional center. To a degree not immediately apparent on our first viewing of the film, we see the world as Cole sees it. His relationship with psychiatrist Malcolm Crowe (Bruce Willis) forms the focal point of the story, the glue that holds this film together and makes its surprise ending seem like a genuine psychological epiphany, instead of a cheap movie gimmick.

That's a lot to heap on the shoulders of a pre-teen kid.

Writer-director M. Night Shyamalan realized this when he wrote the script, and feared that he would never find a young actor skilled enough make the character work. "Cole's role is so difficult and so complex, it seemed impossible," Shyamalan says in an interview included on *Sixth Sense* DVD. Haley Joel Osment, 11 years old when the film premiered, won this pivotal role with an impressive audition. Despite his young age, Osment was already a veteran performer. He began acting at age five, when he played Forrest, Jr., in *Forrest Gump*. Afterward, he earned recurring roles in three television series; made guest appearances on several more television shows; and played small roles in other films. His performance in *The Sixth Sense* is not the work of a gifted amateur, but of a trained professional.

"He's the most talented child actor I've ever seen," co-star Bruce Willis says in another DVD interview. "I'd rank him with some of the best adult actors I've ever worked with."

However, it's impossible to fully appreciate Osment's performance unless you put out of your mind Osment's age. Sure, his is by far the best portrayal by a young actor in a horror film. Accept that as a given and try to factor it out of the equation. Taken on its own merits, making no allowances for the age of the actor, Osment's work remains powerful, moving and surprisingly unaffected. Although he spends much of the film in tears, he never seems to be posing or overreaching.

Perhaps this is because in Cole, Osment saw a shadowy reflection of himself. Both Cole and Osment are boys with extraordinary gifts which separate them from other children their age. Osment understands Cole and does not feel sorry for him. "Cole's a fighter," Osment says in another DVD interview. "He isn't just a depressed, sad little boy."

This insight, more than anything else, provides the key to Osment's success. Audiences sympathize with Cole automatically, because he's a child in danger. If Osment milked the role for still more pathos, his portrayal would quickly grow maudlin or morose, possibly both. Instead of emphasizing Cole's fear, Osment consistently underscores Cole's courage. As a result, viewers may begin by pitying Cole, but eventually they come to admire him.

Before audiences meet Cole, they see Dr. Malcolm's notes about the boy. Cole, the product of divorced parents, suffers from "acute anxiety," is "socially isolated" and has a "possible mood disorder." Then, suddenly, Osment is on screen, as Cole exits his little apartment. Malcolm's notes seem to spring to life. Osment pulls a pair of eyeglasses from his satchel and puts them on. The glasses are much too big for him, and have no lenses. Osment looks around furtively before moving far from the door. Then he begins to walk, a fast, nervous walk that becomes a run. He dashes into a nearby church. When Malcolm enters, Cole is playing with tin soldiers amidst the pews. Everything about Osment's performance in this brief sequence — his facial expressions as he exits the apartment, his posture, his gait — illustrates Cole's isolation and nervousness.

In another early scene, Cole is eating breakfast when his mother, Lynn (Toni Collette), steps out of the kitchen to treat a spot on the boy's tie. She returns to the kitchen a few seconds later and discovers that every drawer and cabinet door in the room has suddenly opened. Cole lies, and says he was searching for Pop-Tarts. Then he asks, "What are you thinking, Mom? Anything bad about me?" Osment's timid reading of this line informs us that Cole isn't sure he wants to know the answer to this question. Throughout the film, Osment convinces us that even though Cole is pursued by the spirits of the dead, his deepest fear is that he will become isolated from his mother. This is a perfectly normal fear for any child, and could only be amplified when Mom represents the single warm, supportive relationship in his life.

At least, she is the single warm, supportive relationship in Cole's life until Malcolm appears. During their first two meetings, Cole keeps Malcolm at a distance. "You're nice, but you can't help me," Osment says, forlornly. Soon, though, Malcolm's candor wins over the boy. When Cole bitterly refers to himself as a "freak," Malcolm tells him, "That's bullshit!" Osment's eyes pop open in wide amazement. "You said the S-word!" he says, incredulous. No adult has previously spoken to Cole as if he were a fellow grownup.

Later he is hospitalized for minor injuries suffered at the hands of his classmates. When Malcolm comes to visit the boy, Cole finally opens up. The scene begins with a long speech by Malcolm. Throughout this sequence, Osment listens and reacts with subtle but meaningful facial expressions. Osment's look of surprise when Malcolm calls Cole "a really cool little boy" is priceless. "I'm going to tell you my secret now," Osment says after gathering his breath. This brings us to the now-famous line, "I see dead people," which was featured prominently in the film's trailer and was parodied by comedians incessantly during the film's initial release. It became a catchphrase, even a cliché, but it represents a pivotal moment in the film. It comes 50:31 into this 107-minute picture. After this, we will fully enter Cole's world, and will see what he sees. Osment whispers the line with intensity and conviction, teary-eyed and a little bit ashamed. Again Cole is afraid, not of the ghosts, but that revealing his ability will cost him Malcolm's friendship and support (which it nearly does).

Osment's is far from a one-note performance. He shows us Cole's frustration with a teacher who addresses his pupil with a mixture of contempt and condescension. "I don't like people looking at me like that," Osment says, in a rare flash of anger. He goes on to taunt the teacher with the instructor's childhood nickname, "Stuttering Stanley." Later Osment plays a moment of joy, in a brief shot of him riding in a shopping cart being pushed by his mother. He rides in the front of the cart, with his eyes closed and his arms outstretched exuberantly.

Yet for most of the film, Osment is called upon to soldier through one unnerving episode after another. For Cole, even a midnight trip to the bathroom can be terrifying. Osment opens the bedroom door a crack and peeks out carefully. Then he walks that nervous-fast walk to the bathroom. As he walks he holds his arms at his sides, as if trying to occupy as little space as possible, hoping that way he will pass unnoticed. And he frowns, another keynote in Osment's performance. His frown communicates Cole's nervousness, but it also tells us something else. It's one of the

Dr. Malcolm (Bruce Willis, left) takes Cole (Haley Joel Osment) to the home of a recently deceased girl in this chilling scene from *The Sixth Sense* (1999).

outward signs of the boy gathering up his courage. Osment frowns frequently in this film, almost as often as he whispers and sobs, but he never cowers.

Malcolm understands Cole's bravery, and encourages the boy to face his fears and talk with the ghosts who haunt him. Maybe they need help. The ghost of a sick little girl appears in Cole's bedroom. At first, Osment runs and hides behind a chair, sobbing in terror. But after a moment, still bleary-eyed, he purses his lips with determination and approaches the girl. "Do you want to tell me something?" he asks in a shaky voice.

For Cole, telling his mother about his ability is an even more frightening proposition.

Toward the end of the film, while they are trapped in a line of cars backed up from a traffic accident, Cole finally decides to reveal his secret to his mother. It is the single bravest act he will perform in the entire film. Osment looks at her, unsure, still summoning up his courage. "I'm ready to communicate with you now," he says matter-of-factly. More tears ensue, but this time they are tears of relief when, helped by some information obtained from his grandmother's ghost, Cole is able to reveal his secret and convince his mother that he's not crazy. This sequence could have descended into schmaltz, but it doesn't. Osment has so effectively convinced us of Cole's fear of estrangement from his mother that the scene unfolds with as much tension as any in the film. The scene's tearful finale plays as release rather than jubilation. The movie's famous surprise ending, which involves Malcolm, quickly ensues, but the sequence with Cole and his Mom in the car has already provided *The Sixth Sense* with its emotional climax.

As a result of his stunning work in this film, Osment became one of the youngest actors ever honored with an Academy Award nomination. His category was Best Actor in a Supporting Role, and although he lost (to Michael Caine, who was nominated for *The Cider House Rules*) he deserved to win. Osment went on to star in director Steven Spielberg's offbeat science fiction yarn *AI: Artificial Intelligence* (2001). Once again he delivered a memorable performance in a remarkably demanding role, as a robot child who yearns to become a flesh-and-blood boy. His work in this film is inventive and sometimes deeply moving, but it is not the equal of his work in *The Sixth Sense*. Then again, few performances are.

We are unlikely ever to see another portrayal quite like Osment's Cole Sear, from Osment or from anyone else.

Other Mainstream Actors

A comprehensive examination of remarkable "guest" performances could fill a volume about the size of the New York City Yellow Pages. I cannot do justice to them all here. Nevertheless, a dozen or so additional characterizations cry out for attention.

Max Schreck's Count Orlok in director F.W. Murnau's *Nosferatu* (1922) stands as one of the most nightmarish visions in the history of cinema, a visage so bone-chilling it was reprised in precise detail in two later films, director Werner Herzog's 1979 *Nosferatu* remake and in the 2000 chiller *Shadow of the Vampire*. The iconic power of Schreck's characterization, achieved not only through makeup and costuming but also with posture and facial expressions, cannot be denied. But Orlok isn't much of a character. He functions more as a cipher for the audience's fears of plague and other unholy terrors. **Emil Jannings** contributed an equally powerful portrayal as Mephisto in Murnau's *Faust* (1926). Of the two performances, Jannings' is the better realized. Mephisto is as frightening as Count Orlok, but also possesses a personality. Jannings' portrayal, along with Schreck's Count Orlok and Lon Chaney's Phantom of the Opera, represent the zenith of horror acting during the silent era.

Leslie Banks' unnerving screen debut as the cunning Count Zaroff in *The Most Dangerous Game* (1932) should not be overlooked. Zaroff is the jaded hunter who, tired of hunting animals, has turned to hunting people (a pastime he refers to as "outdoor chess"). Banks' performance was one of the earliest to link the urge to kill with sexual dysfunction. Apparently, Zaroff can only function sexually after being aroused by murder. "What is woman ... until the blood has been quickened by the kill?" he says. Banks' sly, multi-layered characterization makes clear that Zaroff, despite his aloof demeanor, yearns for the approval of his fellow hunter, Rainsford

Zaroff (Leslie Banks, left) and Bob Rainsford (Joel McCrea) tangle during the finale of *The Most Dangerous Game* (1932). (Photograph courtesy Ted Okuda.)

(Joel McCrea). Banks is especially effective in the film's second half, as he stalks McCrea and Fay Wray. Costumed in a Satanic-looking, jet-black hunting outfit, he radiates menace, stalking his prey with palpable intensity. He tiptoes through the jungle, carrying a bow loaded and cocked, eyes focused like lasers on the trail ahead.

Eccentric **Ernest Thesiger** illuminated two of director James Whale's Golden Age masterpieces, *The Old Dark House* (1932) and *Bride of Frankenstein* (1935). In both of these roles, as Horace Femm and Dr. Pretorius, Thesiger was decadence personified. Femm is a hedonist gone to seed, the perfect counterpoint for his insanely puritanical sister, played by Eva Moore. Pretorius is the agent of scientific (and possibly homosexual) seduction who coaxes Henry Frankenstein (Colin Clive) into creating a second monster, this time a female. Both of these delightful performances sing with Thesiger's wicked, sardonic wit. Thesiger also appeared in *The Ghoul* (1933) and *They Drive By Night* (1938).

Robert Montgomery's clever work in the borderline-horror film *Night Must Fall* (1937) is often ignored, despite the fact that it earned him a Best Actor Oscar nomination. Academy voters were impressed with the range displayed by Montgomery, an actor better known for light romance and comedy. He's eerily effective here, playing an eager-to-please young handyman who ingratiates himself to a wealthy spinster (Dame Mae Whitty). The spinster's niece (Rosalind Russell) begins to suspect that the handyman may be a murderer. Montgomery, who presents his character as a man who's lost touch with own identity, skillfully alternates between being charming and disconcerting.

Stanley Ridges' unjustly maligned work in *Black Friday* (1940) deserves more praise than in all likelihood it will ever receive. Ridges serves as a focal point for fans' ire, simply because he's not Boris Karloff or Bela Lugosi. Originally, producers planned to co-star Karloff in the Ridges role and Lugosi in the Karloff role. When Karloff opted for the role originally envisioned for Lugosi, Ridges was brought in and Lugosi was relegated to a brief and thankless supporting part. None of this, however, diminishes the effectiveness of Ridges' performance. He's surprisingly convincing as a man whose mind is being taken over by the personality of a dead gangster. His sober, evocative performance helps make *Black Friday* one of the more interesting variations on the Jekyll and Hyde theme.

Ernest Thesiger in his most celebrated role, as Dr. Pretorius from *Bride of Frankenstein* (1935). (Photograph courtesy Bryan Senn.)

The performances of **Gunnar Bjornstrand** as Death in *The Seventh Seal* (1957) and of **Robert Mitchum** as the Rev. Harry Powell in *The Night of the Hunter* (1955) would certainly rank among the very finest horror performances, if either film could be categorized as horror with any degree of certainty. Unfortunately, neither one can. Yet both are chilling, iconic characters which have been copied repeatedly over the decades. How many screen characters—or even real people—have tattooed their knuckles with "L-O-V-E" and "H-A-T-E" like Mitchum in *Night of the Hunter*? Powell is perhaps the most enduring characterization to emerge from Mitchum's long and distinguished career. Mitchum gave us a second superb, spine-tingling performance in another not-quite-horror film, *Cape Fear* (1962).

Bjornstrand's character seems to have leaped to life from a medieval tapestry. Like Lugosi's Count Dracula, his Death was ripped off or parodied in countless subsequent films, and quickly became something of a cliché. But within the context of

The Seventh Seal, he is perfection: Cold and aloof as Death must be, yet unexpectedly sympathetic toward those he claims and, ultimately, just as lost as they are.

Robert DeNiro's bloodthirsty Travis Bickle, from *Taxi Driver* (1976), is another characterization I would have eagerly granted greater analysis if the film could be labeled horror. As it stands, Bickle remains the most terrifying psycho to appear *outside* the genre.

Niall MacGinnis, Carl Boehm, John Amplas and **Terry O'Quinn** all contributed career-best performances in well-remembered shockers.

In *Curse of the Demon* (a.k.a. *Night of the Demon*, 1957), MacGinnis sketched a chilling portrait of a Satanist grappling to rein in forces beyond his control — including his own mother. His is a bracing, complex portrayal, capable of sending chills down audiences' spines one moment, generating pathos the next and supplying a few gallows chuckles along the way.

In *Peeping Tom* (1960), Boehm created one of the screen's most blood-curdling psychopaths, Mark Lewis, who films his victims as he murders them, then watches the movies for his own amusement. Mark wasn't born a killer, but as Hannibal Lecter might explain, was made one "through years of systematic abuse." The most haunting aspect of Boehm's portrayal is that the innocent little boy remains visible, trapped inside the grownup psycho.

In *Martin* (1977), Amplas also balances child-like innocence with adult mania. His edgy yet heartsick portrayal creates both pathos as menace and provides the emotional core for this perennially underrated chiller about a troubled man who may or may not be a vampire. Thanks in large part to Amplas, this remains George Romero's finest film not involving flesh-eating zombies. Yet, Amplas' career went nowhere and (perhaps as a result) his work here is seldom mentioned among the premier horror performances of the 1970s. It should be.

Finally, in *The Stepfather* (1987), Terry O'Quinn scared audiences out of their wits with his portrayal of a homicidal maniac who's over-committed to the idea of "family values." O'Quinn lays it on with unrestrained gusto and walks away with one of the most stylish and unforgettable genre performances of the decade.

This quartet of unforgettable characters proves that small-name actors sometimes deliver big time performances.

Willem Dafoe's performance in *Shadow of the Vampire* (2000) deserves attention, if only because (as of this writing) it's the most recent horror performance to be nominated for an Academy Award. Dafoe plays Max Schreck, the actor who played Count Orlok in F.W. Murnau's classic *Nosferatu*. The film's conceit is that Schreck was a real vampire. Dafoe does an amazing Schreck imitation, but mimicry is not the same thing as acting.

This is as good a place as any to note that originally I planned to include a fourth and final section in this book devoted to ensemble cast performances. (I'm still disappointed that I won't be able to use my proposed chapter title, "A Good Cast Is Worth Repeating.") This section would have dealt with films in which the entire cast is impressive, but no single performer stands out.

For the record, I do not buy into the old saw that when one actor is brilliant, one should credit the actor; when all the actors are brilliant, one should credit the director. Unfortunately, it proved ungainly to attempt in-depth analysis when addressing an entire cast. I would like, however, to mention a few films especially worthy of attention:

The Picture of Dorian Gray (1945) features superb performances by all involved, especially George Sanders, Angela Lansbury and Hurd Hatfield. *Dorian Gray* ranks as perhaps the overall best-acted chiller of the 1940s, rivaled only by the cream of the Lewton crop. *The Haunting* (1963) is another film almost overburdened with great portrayals. Even Russ Tamblyn, in a role that might have been little more than throwaway comedy relief, brings something credible to the piece.

Mel Brooks' spoof *Young Frankenstein* (1974) features one of the finest ensemble casts ever assembled for a comedy. Absolutely everyone in this picture is riotously funny. Even the supporting players carve out hilarious characters, such as Cloris Leachman's Frau Blucher and of course Marty Feldman's "Eye-gor." Star Gene Wilder deserved, but did not receive, an Oscar nomination for his sidesplitting performance in the title role.

In more recent memory, writer-director John Landis' gloriously cockeyed *An American Werewolf in London* (1981) revolves around a trio of carefully calibrated characterizations, which enables the film to maintain its tricky balance between terror and humor: David Naughton as the werewolf, Jenny Agutter as Naughton's girlfriend and Griffin Dunne as his back-from-the-dead-and-progressively-decomposing victim.

Although neither of them can be placed definitively within the borders of horror, *The Hunchback of Notre Dame* (1939) and *Jaws* (1975) also merit mention. In addition to Charles Laughton's heartrending Quasimodo, *Hunchback* boasts outstanding performances by Maureen O'Hara, Sir Cedric Hardwicke, Thomas Mitchell and Edmond O'Brien. Even George Zucco, in a glorified cameo, proves memorable. *Jaws* features astonishing portrayals by Roy Scheider, Richard Dreyfuss and Robert Shaw.

PART THREE
Leading Ladies

In *Scream* (1992), Sidney Prescott (Neve Campbell) describes horror movies as "some stupid killer chasing some big-breasted girl who can't act who's always running up the stairs when she should be going out the front door. It's insulting."

Unfortunately, this bleak assessment of women's place in horror cinema contains an element of truth. However, the problem isn't so much that women appearing in horror films couldn't act; it is rather that for decades they received little opportunity to do so. Yes, women, including Fay Wray, Evelyn Ankers and Barbara Shelley (to name just a few) made valuable contributions to the development of horror cinema. They brought badly needed shades of warmth, wit and sex appeal to projects which otherwise might have turned out monotonously dark. Their efforts helped win the hearts of audiences during the genre's adolescence, and earned them the ardent devotion of generations of fans.

The sad truth, however, is that they accomplished all this in spite of rather than because of the parts they were given. Generally speaking, actresses appearing in horror films were called upon to do little more than stare doe-eyed when their leading man glanced at them and shriek convincingly when the monster scooped them into its arms. With rare exceptions, during screen horror's Golden Age and even into the 1950s, actresses were denied the opportunity to create the kind of deathless, larger-than-life characters that made icons of their co-stars, whomever their male counterparts might be — Lon Chaney, Jr., Christopher Lee or, in Wray's case, an animated gorilla.

During this era, gifted actresses routinely found parts worthy of their talents in other genres, but seldom in monster movies. Actresses popular enough to have some say in their roles almost invariably avoided horror films. Studios sometimes purposefully insulated actresses from the genre. For instance, while Universal's *Frankenstein* (1931) was in pre-production, a young ingénue named Bette Davis was considered for the role eventually played by Mae Clarke. The studio pulled Davis out of the production because executives, who thought Davis had the potential to become a major star, feared that appearing in the film might stigmatize the actress. (Ironically, 30 years later a horror picture would reinvigorate Davis' flagging career.) Universal's attitude toward the genre reflected the sentiments of many in the industry. The message could not have been clearer if studios had stamped horror scripts with a warning label: "Appearing in this film may be hazardous to your career."

This goes a long way toward explaining why most of the watershed performances by women in the horror genre have appeared since the demise of the studio system and the rise of a new breed of horror picture. This new model horror movie was hammered out against the backdrop of the American feminist movement of the 1960s. Audiences began to reject old-fashioned "shrinking violets" and to embrace female characters who behaved more like the empowered women of post-feminist America. Although plenty of big-breasted-girl-running-up-the-stairs-when-she-should-be-going-out-the-front-door roles lingered, screenwriters gradually began to create more female characters with backbone and intelligence, and more scripts revolved around female-centric topics such as marriage, childbirth, parenting, aging and sex roles.

As a result, actresses began to discover in horror films believable, three-dimensional characters whose attitudes and concerns reflected their own experiences. These were roles in which talented women could — and did — express the full measure of their abilities, creating characters as significant and iconic in their own way as those crafted by Karloff, Lugosi, Price or Cushing: Rosemary Woodhouse, Carrie White, Lori Strode, Clarice Starling and others.

The following survey includes these and several more unforgettable characters, beginning with a pair of pioneering roles from the Golden Age....

Gloria Holden in *Dracula's Daughter* (1936) — Gloria Holden was

one of the many actresses who looked on horror films with disdain. From all accounts, she was aghast at being assigned *Dracula's Daughter* as her first starring role. Throughout the remainder of her career, she refused even to discuss the film, as though if she ignored it long enough the movie would vanish from her filmography. Exactly the opposite happened. With the possible exception of her next picture, the Oscar-winning *The Life of Emile Zola* (1937), *Dracula's Daughter* has outlived every other movie Holden ever made. And her performance as Countess Zaleska remains by far the best remembered of her career.

The British-born actress made her film debut with an uncredited role opposite Dracula himself, Bela Lugosi, in the serial *The Return of Chandu* (1934). Perhaps it was Lugosi's fate that gave Holden reason to dread this assignment. In the five years that had passed since *Dracula* had ushered in the era of talking horror pictures, Lugosi had proven unable to separate himself from his role as the undead Count. He had been unrelentingly typecast and his fortunes were already sinking (so much so that, even though he was under contract to appear in *Dracula's Daughter*, he was written out of it). Now Holden was asked to step into his cape.

If Holden knew anything about the film's pre-production history, she may well have had additional concerns. Universal had been trying to come up with a Dracula sequel for years, but was unable to find an acceptable script. John L. Balderston, who wrote the original *Dracula*, turned in an initial treatment in 1934. It was Balderston's idea to make the vampire in the sequel female, and to exclude Dracula himself from the action. Dracula was written in and out of the production as various writers turned in additional treatments. Finally screenwriter Garrett Fort delivered a screenplay which integrated elements both from Balderston's treatment and from Bram Stoker's short story "Dracula's Guest" and added an original angle that would prove revelatory: The idea of making the titular character a sympathetic, reluctant vampire.

Various actors were assigned to *Dracula's Daughter* and then removed as the script went through rewrite after rewrite and the film was delayed and delayed again. Universal initially announced that the movie would star Lugosi, Boris Karloff and Colin Clive. When the casting carousel finally stopped, however, Holden was left to play Countess Marya Zaleska, the "daughter" of Dracula.

Despite, or maybe even because of, Holden's distaste for the role, her performance remains masterful and moving. Her disdain for the part translates into a kind of self-loathing that perfectly suits her troubled character. In the original *Dracula*, Lugosi has a single line suggesting that the Count may be lonely or unhappy with his lot in (un)life: "To die, to be *really* dead — that must be glorious!" But relatively little is made from this, and the bravado Lugosi displays in his other sequences undercuts the idea that he is anything other than an enthusiastic King of the Undead. Holden, on the other hand, never seems entirely at ease. Her Countess seems believably repulsed by her own actions because they repulsed Holden herself.

"I don't believe any woman has ever been asked to play such a poisonous role before," she told reporters while the film was in production. "[The screenwriter] has made me an insatiable fiend."

This insatiable fiend makes her initial appearance nearly 11 minutes into the 71-minute film. When we first glimpse Holden, she is swathed in a black-hooded cloak. Only her beautiful, glistening, piercing eyes are visible. (This image proved so striking that Universal recreated it for the film's original one-sheet movie poster — a stark solid-black background except for Holden's mesmerizing eyes, highlighted in spooky green and yellow hues, with the film's title set in dripping green letters and a red-lettered warning: "Look out! She'll Get YOU!" This simple, bold design represented a pronounced departure from the studio's typically elaborate advertising art.)

Holden reveals her face when Zaleska performs an arcane funeral rite over Dracula's body, which she swiped from the local constabulary. In a fog-shrouded park she purifies the body with fire, salt and finally prayer. Holden dreamily intones her ritualistic recitation with a kind of detached indifference that suggests Zaleska performs this ceremony out of some sense of duty, not out of affection for her vampiric "father." Zaleska withdraws a cross from beneath her cloak and, with her head turned so she cannot see it, holds it over Dracula's burning body: "In the name of the all–Holiest and through this cross, be the evil spirit cast out until the end of time." Holden looks pained, as if handling the cross causes her acute discomfort. But when it's over, her expression immediately brightens.

Her servant, Sandor (Irving Pichel), approaches. Her first words to Sandor, viewed on the script's printed page, look jubilant: "Free—free forever! Free to live as a woman, to take my place in the bright world of the living!" But Holden's insightful performance transforms these words into an expression of relief rather than joy; and, even then, relief tempered by nervous anticipation. Clearly she yearns to escape the curse of vampirism, but she has lived so long as one of the undead that she is ill prepared to return to life among the living (if such a return is even possible).

Zaleska's portrayal of the monster-in-torment foreshadows Lon Chaney, Jr.'s, Larry Talbot/Wolf Man, but without the morbid self-pity that afflicted that character in its later appearances. In the *Wolf Man* sequels, Talbot yearned not just to be cured, but for death. Zaleska wants life, freedom.

The screenplay refers to vampirism as if it were a sort of addiction, which Zaleska is unable to defeat. In recent years, however, another interpretation has emerged: That Zaleska's condition parallels lesbianism. The most commonly cited reason for this association is a strikingly homoerotic episode between Zaleska and a female victim. But there are other indicators: During the 1930s, homosexuality was widely considered a mental illness and gay people sometimes turned to psychologists to "cure" them, as Zaleska does later in the film. She longs to be a "real woman" and speaks of her "attacks" with shame and recrimination ("I can't tell you [about it], it's too ghastly"), the way in which a cowed lesbian might approach her "unnatural" desires. *Dracula's Daughter* presents vampirism as an inescapable part of the vampire's

Countess Zaleska (Gloria Holden) performs a strange ritual over the burning body of her vampire "father" in *Dracula's Daughter* (1936).

being — like a person's height or eye color, an essential, permanently encoded characteristic — that cannot be divested from that person's individual identity. Today, many argue that homosexuality is a similarly ingrained trait.

Whether such comparisons entered Holden's mind as she prepared for her role or (more than likely) not, her performance only seems more impressive when viewed in this light. Whatever its origin, Holden strikes a note of desperate longing and sustains it throughout most of the film. In one memorable scene, Zaleska, seated at a piano, tells Sandor, "Dracula's destroyed, his body is in ashes. His spell is broken. I can live a normal life again, even play normal music again." Holden's delicate handling of these lines again darkens dialogue that might otherwise have sounded brighter; her tone is slightly stilted and phony-sounding, suggesting that her optimism is forced. It's as if deep down inside she realizes she is fooling herself — although she is not yet willing to admit this. Zaleska begins to play a bright, cheerful melody, but her song quickly transforms into a somber, minor-key piece.

Deflated, she gives in to her urges. Sandor wraps her cloak around the Countess' shoulders and Zaleska leaves to claim the film's first victim. When they return, Holden carries herself in a noticeably different manner. Previously, she stood straight and tall, with the high-necked carriage one would expect from a woman of noble birth. Returning from the kill, Holden slouches slightly. She appears tired, disheveled and ashamed. She removes her cloak and hands it to Sandor. "There's blood on it again," she reports with disgust.

At a dinner party, Zaleska meets Dr. Jeffrey Garth (Otto Kruger), a psychiatrist who assures her he can "release" her from "any obsession." "Release?" Holden asks, looking wide-eyed at Kruger. He advises her to "meet and fight" her impulses, assuring her she can defeat them if she has enough willpower. He mentions that they sometimes lock alcoholics in a room with a bottle of booze to test the subject's ability to resist temptation. Holden devours his every word as if she were starving and his pronouncements were bread. She hungers for hope, acceptance, normalcy.

Acting on Garth's advice, Zaleska instructs Sandor to picks up a young girl and brings her back to her studio to serve as a model while the Countess paints. When Sandor returns with a beautiful young blonde named Lili (Nan Grey), the stage is set for the film's most powerful sequence.

"Don't be afraid, my dear," Zaleska tells Lili. Holden's voice sounds hollow and her demeanor is aloof. She is struggling not to reveal her true motivations — either to Lili or to herself. "I'm doing a study of a young girl's head and shoulders. You won't object to removing your blouse, will you?" she asks. But as her eyes settle on Lili's naked shoulders, her tone becomes slightly breathier and less distant. Something else — something like lust — begins to creep into her voice. Holden's nostrils flare and her eyes open wider. She stares at Lili intently. Lili becomes concerned. "Won't I do?" she asks. Suddenly Zaleska's shaky will crumbles, overcome by her compulsion. "Yes, you'll do very well indeed," she replies. Holden's voice is ripe with unbridled desire now. She closes in on her victim, her eyes fixed in a glassy stare, wearing an enigmatic half-smile. Afterwards, she returns to Garth, repentant. "You're the one person who stands between me and utter destruction," she pleads with breathless anxiety, gulping her words. "I know the truth now." Holden's voice cracks, fighting tears. "There's nothing ahead for me now but horror."

Garth, however, has grown suspicious of his patient. His friend, Dr. Von Helsing (Edward Van Sloan), has warned him that a new vampire, possibly one of Dracula's offspring, may be at large in London. Eventually Garth discerns that Zaleska is this vampire, and tries to help Scotland Yard apprehend her. She is stung by his betrayal. "You're no longer the sympathetic Samaritan are you, Mr. Garth? You're a policeman," Holden charges bitterly. Zaleska feels rejected, betrayed. But she emerges from this strangely energized. No longer concerned with curing her vampirism, she — for the first time — begins to embrace it. As this occurs, the physicality of Holden's performance, as well as the delivery of her dialogue, changes in subtle ways. Her previous hangdog expressions vanish; she holds herself with greater grace and moves with almost balletic precision. Instead of frowns and furtive glances, she smiles easily and with cool confidence. Thanks to all this, as well as subtle changes in lighting and costume, Zaleska suddenly looks even more radiant, in an elegant, austere and utterly foreign way. She looks as if she could, after all, truly be the child of Lugosi's dashing but deadly count.

Emboldened, she hatches a nefarious scheme worthy of her "father." She kidnaps Garth's secretary (and love interest) and spirits the young woman (Marguerite Churchill) to Transylvania. She offers to free his secretary if Garth will join her as one of the undead. The psychiatrist calls her "insane." "Insane? To offer you eternal life?" Zaleska responds, incredulous. Her reply only vocalizes what Holden has already effectively portrayed in her newfound demeanor: The Countess has finally come not only to accept but to revel in her vampiric nature. Garth capitulates. But Sandor, who has been goading Zaleska throughout the film to embrace her vampirism, slays her with an arrow shot for a crossbow — jealous that Garth and not himself is to receive the "gift" of eternal life.

Holden crumples to the floor wordlessly. As the film fades out, we catch a final glimpse of the Countess. Our opening view of Zaleska focused on her eyes, and so does this one. But now they are glassy, expressionless, dead.

Despite the overall high quality of *Dracula's Daughter* and Holden's superb work in it, the film was neither a critical nor financial success upon its initial release. A backlash against horror films had begun, and *Dracula's Daughter* suffered along with the rest of the genre. Most publications lambasted it. *Variety* was a notable exception, praising both the film and Holden's performance: "The heavy portions are more than adequately handled by Gloria Holden."

As with many of the classic horror pictures, however, film historians sought to correct these oversights. "In the plum title role, Gloria Holden is equally adept at enlisting the audience's sympathy as she is at conveying the full menace of her celebrated parent," write authors Tom Weaver and John and Michael Brunas in their book *Universal Horrors*. "With eerie grace and sensitivity, Gloria Holden dominated *Dracula's Daughter*. Indeed, she makes several episodes unforgettable," author Gregory Mank opines in his book *Women in Horror Films, 1930s*. In fact, many critics (including me) consider *Dracula's Daughter* a superior film to the 1931 *Dracula*, and Holden's performance a masterwork on par with Lugosi's.

Not that any of this brightened Holden's opinion of the film. Mank, in *Women in Horror Films*, reports that as late as 1991 (shortly before her death) Holden still referred to *Dracula's Daughter* as "that awful thing." Holden's film career continued for 22 years after *Dracula's Daughter*, but never again would she land a role as memorable as this one. She had the honor of playing Alexandrine Zola in *The Life of Emile Zola*, which won the 1937 Academy Award for Best Picture. But she is remembered as Countess Zaleska, not Madame Zola. Although she never appeared in another full-blooded horror movie, Holden played a psychic in director Tod Browning's final film, *Miracles for Sale* (1939).

The financial disappointment of *Dracula's Daughter* conspired with a number of other factors to make this the final horror classic released by Universal during the first wave of horror cinema's Golden Age, a cycle that began five years earlier with the release of the Lugosi *Dracula*. Fortunately, horror films would regain their marketability, and a second wave of Golden Age horrors would begin at Universal with *Son of Frankenstein* in 1939. (Otherwise, *Dracula's Daughter* might have been remembered as the horror movie that killed horror movies!)

As it stands, Holden's performance forms a poetic bookend to Lugosi's work in the original film. These two masterful performances serve as the alpha and omega of the initial wave of horror's Golden Age.

Simone Simon in *Cat People* (1942)

—All the great horror performances—indeed, all great performances, period—contain a keystone characteristic, a single choice upon which the actor constructs his entire characterization: The eerie stillness of Boris Karloff's Imhotep, the heartfelt fervor of Peter Cushing's Van Helsing or the aching loneliness of Anthony Perkins' Norman Bates.

In the case of Simone Simon's "Cat Woman," Irena Dubrovna, the keynote is more difficult to summarize. It is not restricted to her vocal delivery, to the physicality of her performance, or even to the prevailing mood that seems to underlie her portrayal, although it influences all of those aspects. Perhaps the most succinct way to describe this mercurial quality is as a wellspring of gentleness. Simon treats her role as if it was made of crystal and she was afraid she might break it. Although impressive in itself, the sensitivity and subtlety of her work in *Cat People* also perfectly fits her character, a woman who walks an emotional tightrope throughout the film, a single footfall away from disaster and damnation.

Visionary producer Val Lewton conjured up *Cat People* with Simon in mind from the beginning, a strategy that appears sound in retrospect but which puzzled observers at the time. Many in Hollywood considered Simon damaged goods.

A native of Marseilles, France, and a former model, Simon began her film career in 1931. She appeared in more than a dozen French movies over the next four years, mostly playing supporting roles, often in comedies. In 1934 she appeared in *Le Voleur*, directed by Maurice Tourneur, father of *Cat People* director Jacques Tourneur. She signed a contract with 20th Century–Fox and arrived in Hollywood in 1935, accompanied by much ballyhoo and promoted as the studio's new Continental sex siren.

Unfortunately, her relationship with the studio quickly deteriorated. She was unable to finish—or, in some cases, even begin—three projects due to illness. Producer Darryl F. Zanuck removed her from *Danger—Love at Work* because director Otto Preminger was unhappy with her performance. The films she completed failed to distinguish themselves at the box office. Then, in 1938, Simon became embroiled in a Hollywood scandal. She accused her personal secretary of stealing funds from her accounts. In response, the secretary characterized Simon as a predatory hedonist with a bent toward promiscuity and wild parties. For Fox, the sensational headlines provided the final straw. The studio dropped Simon's contract.

To the surprise of almost everyone, Simon rebounded from her Hollywood debacle. She returned to France and delivered an outstanding performance opposite French megastar Jean Gabin in director Jean Renoir's gripping thriller *La Bete Humaine* (1938). She also appeared in a handful of plays before returning to America for an acclaimed supporting role as the Devil's temptress in director William Dieterle's *All That Money Can Buy* (a.k.a. *The Devil and Daniel Webster*, 1941).

Despite her recent reversal of fortune, however, few would have dared cast Simon in a major role in an important film, much less built the entire project around her. Make no mistake, *Cat People* was a very important film for both Lewton and RKO–Radio Pictures. It would be the first product from RKO's newly assembled horror unit, which Lewton supervised. The struggling studio was counting on *Cat People* not only to make money, but to establish RKO as a serious competitor with Universal in the production of fright flicks. With all this on the line, Lewton and writer DeWitt Bodeen customized the film to Simon's unique presence and abilities. Her foreign-ness is integral to the role, as is her alluring sexual charisma. Plus, since Fox's efforts at making a star of Simon had failed, the actress was not yet pigeonholed as a heroine or a villainess, an element essential to the movie's is-she-or-isn't-she-a-monster structure.

Irena (Simone Simon) extends her claws in this cheeky publicity photograph for *Cat People* (1942). Writer-producer Val Lewton designed the project around Simon's talents.

Given her central place in the picture's conception, it's hardly surprising that the first character we meet in *Cat People* is Irena. She is standing outside the panther cage at the zoo, her brow crinkled, furiously scribbling in a sketchbook. She rips out page after page, ripping her sketches, crumpling them up and tossing them toward a nearby trashcan. When her rubbish falls to the ground, Ollie Reed (Kent Smith) approaches to playfully chastise her. Simon plays it coy and — no pun intended — kittenish. Without seeming overly flirtatious, she makes clear that Irena enjoys Ollie's attention. In fact, the whole sequence seems like a typical Hollywood "Meet Cute" scene until Irena and Ollie walk away and the camera reveals what Irena has been sketching — the panther, punctured by a sword.

Irena brings Ollie back to her nearby apartment for tea. At first, she appears to be a fairly normal, happy young woman — chatting, making tea and humming a folk song from her native Serbia. Then, as the sun begins to set, the roaring of lions can be heard in the background. "Many people in this building complain the roaring keeps them awake," Simon chuckles. "To me, it's like the sound of the sea is to others — natural and soothing. I like it." These lines recall Lugosi's "Children of the Night" speech from *Dracula*, but Simon handles her dialogue far differently. Where Lugosi was self-consciously weird and off-putting, Simon remains relaxed and warm. "I like the dark, it's friendly," Irena adds, as she brings the tea. Again, Simon chooses not to milk this line for all its worth. What makes this work is that Irena doesn't see anything creepy about her affection for the roar of lions and the embrace of darkness. In trying not to sound intentionally scary, Simon takes the scariest approach of all.

Later, Simon delivers a lengthy monologue in which she retells a horrific legend from her village — a macabre tale of devil worship, practiced by witches with the ability to turn themselves into cats: "Little by little, the people changed. People bowed down to Satan and said their masses to him. They had become witches and were evil." Even during this eerie oration, however, Simon remains restrained. She tilts her head to the left, slows her speech slightly, allows the smile to slowly drain from her face. Irena seems ashamed, full of remorse and regret. But Simon skillfully avoids the trap of sounding like she is telling a scary story, even though she is. This, of course, only makes her tale even scarier.

Cat People is a film of bravura set pieces: the pet shop scene, the bus scene and the swimming pool scene. However, Simon's best work occurs between those famous sequences. Her fascinating portrait of Irena becomes the connective tissue between these sequences and keeps us enthralled until the next big scare arrives.

Inevitably Ollie and Irena profess their love for one another. Then Ollie notes that the two of them have never kissed. To his disappointment, Irena suddenly pulls away from him. Simon repositions herself, so that she is at a right angle to his eyes. She looks withdrawn and frightened. She fidgets nervously, tugging on her fingertips. She gulps, pauses, bites her lip and remains silent until forced to respond. "I've lived in dread of this moment." Simon frowns and looks ruefully at Ollie. "I never wanted to love you.... I fled from the past. Some things you could never know — or understand. Evil things — evil." She looks away from him again, despondent.

Irena believes that she is descended from the mythic shape-shifting witches of her village, and that if she gives in to her sexual desires or other "sinful" feelings (such as anger or jealousy) she will transform into a murderous beast. Despite this, the infatuated Ollie asks Irena to marry him and lovesick Irena accepts. Ollie doesn't take his wife's fears seriously. Irena becomes disturbed when another Serbian "cat woman" approaches the couple during their wedding reception, but Ollie shrugs it off: "Oh, Irena, you crazy kid!"

He becomes more concerned when later that evening Irena refuses to consummate their marriage. "I want to be Mrs. Reed, really. I want to be everything that name means to me and I can't. Oliver, be kind, be patient," she pleads. "Give me time, time to get over that feeling there is something evil in me." Again, Simon seems deeply ashamed, torn between her physical desires and her self-loathing.

To emphasize their separation, she speaks to him from the other side of a closed door. Simon slides down the door, dropping to her knees in anguish. Ollie approaches the door from the opposite side. As if she can sense his presence, her trembling hand begins to reach for the doorknob. Simon's body language changes slightly. She's suddenly more alert, limber, lusty. Before she reaches the doorknob, the lions begin to roar in the distance. Her hand falls away, and Ollie walks off.

Irena's plight may be read as a dark reflection of conflicted, Puritanical attitudes about sexuality — namely, that marriage is good but sexual desire is evil. Simon, product of a more permissive French culture, certainly understood how hypocritical American sexual mores could wreak havoc on a young woman's life. Scandal drove her from Hollywood a few years prior, even though the revelation that a young, handsome, unmarried *male* star had made many sexual conquests would not have merited a single headline.

Playing Irena, Simon may or may not have mined her own emotions created by the scandal, but clearly she tapped into something. Although she addresses her role with restraint and delicacy, in close-up something dark lingers behind her eyes, like storm clouds on the horizon. Once again, this perfectly suits her character. Bottled-up Irena is so set on keeping her emotions in check that she warns her husband, "Oliver, we should never quarrel. Never let me feel jealousy or anger. Whatever is in me, is held in, is kept harmless, when I'm happy."

As a result, the couple's relationship disintegrates into a passionless parody of marriage, devoid not only of sex but even of anger. Their walk together becomes a death march, full of frustration, fear and dread. Ollie confides his frustration to his co-worker, Alice (Jane Randolph), but this only incites Irena's jealousy (setting the stage for the "cat-woman's" pursuit of Alice and the spine-tingling bus and swimming pool sequences).

Ollie tries sending her to psychiatrist Dr. Judd (Tom Conway). "Do you sincerely believe if your husband were to kiss you, you would change into a cat and rend him to bits?" Dr. Judd asks, incredulous. Yet Irena is equally as dismissive of him. "When you speak of the soul, you mean the mind and it is not my mind that's troubled," she tells him with obvious disdain. Eventually, however, Irena caves in and acts on Dr. Judd's advice. She throws away all her gloomy cat icons and other reminders of her homeland and tries to live normally. She prepares a romantic dinner for Ollie and seems, finally, to be ready to try to make love to him. Ollie, however, has had enough. He informs Irena that he has fallen in love with Alice, and wants a divorce. "It's better this way," he says.

Simon's work here is heartbreaking. She looks dazed. "Better? Better for who?" Simon smiles bravely but her entire body wilts, as if all the strength were draining out of her. She turns away from him and collapses onto a couch, burying her face in the cushioned back of the sofa. Then she raises her head slightly, so that only her eyes are visible above the rear of the couch. "I love silence. I love loneliness," she declares without tears but deeply hurt. She tells him to go and as he leaves, her fingernails rip claw marks into the upholstery of the couch. Like a wounded animal, the cat-woman will soon lash out.

Simon reprised her role as Irena in Lewton's offbeat sequel *The Curse of the Cat People* (1944), a light fantasy with a completely different tone than the original film. *Curse* focuses on a friendless, moody child named Amy (the daughter of Ollie and Alice, from the first film). Earning her father's disapproval, Amy (Ann Carter) believes in magic, and spends much of her time dreaming and wishing. When Amy wishes for a playmate, Irena's ghost appears to console and befriend the child. In a touching counterpoint to her work in *Cat People*, Simon's unearthly Irena appears as a gentle, unburdened soul who has found peace at last in the beyond.

Simon also claimed the lead in one of Lewton's non-horror pictures, *Mademoiselle Fifi* (1944). Unfortunately, her success at RKO did little to improve her place in the Hollywood pecking order. After her association with Lewton ended, she found herself plying her trade at Poverty Row studios Monogram and Republic, biding her time until World War II ended and it was safe to return to France. She worked regularly in the French cinema through the mid-1950s and appeared in another international classic, director Max Ophuls' *La Ronde*, in 1951. Although she officially retired in 1956, she returned for a cameo appearance in the 1972 picture *La Femme en Bleu*.

As the opening salvo in Lewton's conquest of the horror genre, *Cat People* ranks among the most-studied of all chillers. Yet Simon's work has garnered relatively little critical attention. Analysis usually focuses on cinematographer Nicholas Musuraca's evocative lighting, Jacques Tourneur's meticulously calibrated direction and DeWitt Bodeen's unusually literate script (co-written by Lewton, uncredited). All of those are pivotal factors in the success of the film, but Simon deserves considerable credit. Author Greg Mank argues this in his book *Women in Horror Films, 1940s*: "Subtle, sexy and curiously tragic, Simone Simon's Irena was the true spark of Lewton's *Cat People*, which made show business history."

Indeed, *Cat People* may well be the most vital film to emerge from the second wave of horror's Golden Age. Launched by Universal's *Son of Frankenstein* in 1939, this second cycle of horror shows would include far more chillers than the genre's first wave, none more influential or better crafted than *Cat People*. The critical and commercial success of this film validated Lewton's mature, subtle approach to the genre and paved the way for seven more innovative films that changed the face of scary movies forever. Simone Simon's lovingly crafted portrayal of the doomed, heartsick Irena is the single most important element in the success of the single most important horror movie of the 1940s.

Bette Davis in *What Ever Happened to Baby Jane?* (1962)

—Bette Davis was, arguably, the most gifted woman ever to step in front of a movie camera. You could make a case for a handful of other actresses as the finest in screen history, but Davis must be mentioned in any such conversation. When the American Film Institute named its Top 50 actresses of all time, as part of its "100 Years, 100 Stars" poll, Davis finished No. 2, trailing only four-time Academy Award winner Katharine Hepburn. Davis won two Oscars herself and was the first woman ever to win the AFI's Lifetime Achievement Award.

The Academy nominated Davis for Best Actress five years in a row, from 1938 to 1942. At her best, she delivered performances so enduring they border on the mythic: Julie Marsden from *Jezebel*, Charlotte Vale from *Now, Voyager*, Margo Channing from *All About Eve*. "Baby" Jane Hudson from *What Ever Happened to Baby Jane?* is another of those performances.

Davis was a titanic talent and a powerful personality, but by the early 1960s she was something else, too—washed-up. At least, that was the prevailing opinion. She had been in this position before, in the late 1940s. At that time, Davis' last several films had underperformed at the box office. *Beyond the Forest* (1949) was an outright flop. After that failure, Warner Bros. elected not to renew her contract. Executives there, and elsewhere, believed the actress was past her prime. But in Hollywood, all a performer needs to get back on top is the right project, and Davis found it in *All About Eve* (1950), a smash hit that earned her an Oscar nomination and placed her back among Tinsel Town's elite.

Twelve years later (and Davis 12 years older), and history was repeating itself. Davis' name on the marquee wasn't packing in fans the way it used to. Her last several films had lost money. Naysayers were convinced that this time, at age 54, Davis was finished for good. Always strong-willed and iconoclastic, Davis drew attention to her situation in 1961 by placing a sarcastic "Job Wanted" ad in the Hollywood trade papers. She needed another *All About Eve* to turn things around. What she got was something quite a bit different, but no less reinvigorating.

Director Robert Aldrich and co-star Joan Crawford approached Davis with a project based on Henry Farrell's novel about a psychotic former child star who torments her crippled ex–movie idol sister. The material was, to say the least, outré, but Davis recognized the film's potential and not only accepted the project but threw herself into it with what can only be described as reckless abandon.

If *Baby Jane* had backfired, it could easily have been the film that wrecked Davis' career permanently. Never classically beautiful (Universal president Carl Laemmle famously ventured that the young Davis had "as much sex appeal as Slim Summerville"), Davis for decades carefully nurtured and protected her screen image. Now she enthusiastically dismantled it, designing for herself a startlingly grotesque makeup and wig.

Audiences first see Davis' Jane Hudson following an 18-minute flashback preamble to the main action of *What Ever Happened to Baby Jane?*. Davis is swilling Scotch and scowling at a stack of her sister's fan letters (which she soon throws in the trash). Her face is saggy and ancient-looking, far older than her actual age, painted much too heavily with lipstick, eyeliner and rouge. She looks like a prototype for Cesar Romero's Joker from the *Batman* television series. Her hair is frizzy and unkempt. Her gait is a graceless, bow-legged shuffle. From our first glimpse, Davis leaves no room for doubt: Jane Hudson is coarse, sodden and hideous.

Jane lives in near-seclusion with her sister, Blanche (Crawford). Blanche lost the use of her legs in a car accident many years earlier, cutting short a brilliant movie career. Police suspected, but were unable to prove, that Jane — a former child star on vaudeville but at the time of the accident a struggling actress riding her sister's coattails — intentionally ran over her sister. Blanche, apparently, has been in Jane's care ever since, despite bouts of mental illness on Jane's part. Lately, a local television station has been playing Blanche's movies, reviving interest in her career — and also reviving Jane's psychotic jealousy.

Blanche is watching one of her old pictures on television when Jane walks into her room. "Enjoying yourself?" Davis asks sourly, as she snaps off the television.

"I was watching!" Blanche protests.

"Then you're an idiot," Davis sneers, her words oozing contempt.

"I won't have you speak to me like that!" Blanche declares. But Davis merely holds her sneer and slams the door in her sister's face, not even dignifying Blanche's complaint with a reply.

It was no great stretch for Davis to act as if she despised Crawford. At Warner Bros., where the two were under contract in the 1930s and '40s, the actresses became bitter rivals, competing for plum roles, studio publicity and sometimes men. The acid-tongued Davis once said of Crawford, "I wouldn't piss on her if she was on fire." Crawford's feelings toward Davis were no less acrimonious. Even after Crawford's death years later, Davis could find no charity for her former co-star. "You should never say bad things about the dead, you should only say good," Davis told reporters. "Joan Crawford is dead, good!"

Baby Jane marked the first collaboration between these two notorious arch-enemies, a pairing that could produce either magic or disaster. It turned out to be the former, of course. The two stars' hatred for each other radiates from almost every frame, as the on-screen tension ratchets up to pressure-cooker levels.

But Davis brings much more to her role than her animosity toward Crawford. In the plight of the aging, forgotten Jane Hudson, she may have heard echoes of her own fears and anxieties. She was herself an aging woman in an industry that celebrates only young women. In Hollywood, actresses' careers usually begin to falter once they reach age 40 (if not sooner), whereas their male co-stars can work into their sixties and beyond. Hollywood movies simply aren't written for older women, a problem that has, if anything, only worsened in the 40-plus years since *Baby Jane*. Davis seems to tap into her own resentment over the detrimental impact aging had on her career, along with (in all likelihood) other frustrations. It all boils over in her explosive, uninhibited portrayal of Jane Hudson, perhaps the most venomous and heartless psychopath in movie history.

"You miserable bitch!" Davis snarls in the kitchen as Blanche rings the call bell from her upstairs room. She plods up to her sister's room as if every step were painful, as if she resents having to move at all. Jane begins to terrorize and starve her sister, serving her a dead parakeet and later a dead rat.

Later, Jane, again (or still) drunk, tinkers at a piano while the melody to her schmaltzy childhood hit "I've Written a Letter to Daddy" plays in her head. In a chair near the piano rests a near-life-sized doll of 12-year-old "Baby" Jane Hudson, a relic from her young celebrity. Watery-eyed Davis begins to sing "I've Written a Letter to Daddy" in purposefully jagged tones, and caresses the face of the doll, tracing the outlines of her character's youthful face.

When the song ends, Jane continues with her old act, staring at herself in a full-length mirror as she performs, feigning the childish speech and movements of her glory days. As Davis recites the line, "I wish that you could tell me, because I'm far too young to know...," she steps under a harsh, white overhead light that makes her look impossibly older, shadows underscoring her every wrinkle and crag. She sees herself in the mirror. Davis gasps, her face freezing into a look of complete horror. She yelps and covers her face with her hands, sobbing.

Jane longs desperately, madly, to recapture the beauty, popularity and, perhaps most of all, power she possessed during her youth. Blanche wants to sell the house and put Jane into a rest home (or perhaps an asylum), but Jane won't hear of it. "You aren't ever going to sell this house and you aren't ever going to leave it, neither!" Davis stabs a finger in Blanche's face. She sashays around her sister's wheelchair, lording over her sibling, flaunting her strength and mobility. "You wouldn't be able to do all these awful things to me if I weren't still in this chair," Blanche sobs. Davis rolls her eyes and smiles condescendingly, as if restraining laughter. "But ya are, Blanche! Ya *are* in that chair!" she roars. With her delivery of this famous line, Davis demonstrates not only that Jane lacks pity for her sister but that she takes sadistic delight in Blanche's suffering.

By removing her sister's call bell and telephone, and sending away the maid, Jane orchestrates a situation that gives her complete control over Blanche. "When I was on the stage, you had to depend on me for everything, even the food you ate came from me. Now you have to depend on me again so, you see, we're right back where we started." Around this point in the film, Davis' performance begins to change noticeably, as her character slips deeper into madness. Davis visibly regresses, adopting childlike speech patterns and immature gestures (such as covering her ears to avoid hearing something unpleasant). She takes on the demeanor of a petulant little girl, instead of a bitter old woman. Jane Hudson is becoming "Baby" Jane again.

She even plans a theatrical comeback, hiring an unctuous accompanist, Edwin Flagg (marvelously played by Victor Buono), and ordering recreations of her old costumes. She returns from the costume shop and discovers that Blanche has crawled out of her wheelchair and down a flight of stairs to reach a telephone and call for help. On the phone, Blanche describes Jane as "emotionally disturbed." Hearing this, Davis' features curl into the face of an enraged gargoyle. Blanche suddenly notices Jane standing in the doorway and hangs up the phone. Davis stomps over and begins to kick her helpless sister viciously around the floor. (Davis took advantage of this sequence to deliver one real-life kick to Crawford's ribs, resulting in minor injuries to her co-star.) When Blanche lapses into unconsciousness, Davis unceremoniously drags her across the floor by a wrist.

The housekeeper, Elvira (Maidie Norman), returns and confronts Jane, who she discovers has locked Blanche in her room (although Elvira does not realize how badly Blanche is hurt). Elvira is the employee and Jane the employer, their roles in this instance are very different: Elvira is the parent, and Jane is the errant child. Elvira demands that Jane open the door. Jane refuses ("You can't make me!") and makes lame, infantile excuses. When the maid threatens to call the police, Jane gives her the key but warns, "You'll be sorry." Davis' babyish reading of this line is simply

"I've Written a Letter to Daddy": "Baby" Jane Hudson (Bette Davis) and accompanist Edwin Flagg (Victor Buono) rehearse for Jane's delusional comeback.

terrifying. Moments later, Jane sneaks up behind Elvira and bashes in the housekeeper's head with a hammer. Davis approaches her victim with the mischievous half-grin of a kid making a crank phone call. Jane remains completely oblivious to the agony of her now-dying sister, lost in the golden fog of her childhood memories. When Blanche begs for help, Davis shrieks and covers her ears: "Every time I try to think of something nice, you remind me of the bad things. I only want to think about the good things." Then she begins to reminisce about rehearsing her act with her father on the beach, as crowds would gather to catch a glimpse of the famous Baby Jane Hudson. Davis really sells this, a dreamy look in her eye, even tugging on her skirt to imitate a girlish curtsy.

For the film's finale, she drags her sister to the beach. While Blanche lies rolled up in a blanket, dying, Jane walks barefoot along the water's edge, plays with a bucket in the sand, bounces a ball with a few young girls and buys ice cream cones. When Blanche begs for Jane to call a doctor, again Jane covers her ears. "Please stop!" she cries, as if *she* were the injured one. And in a way, of course, she is: a once-proud woman demolished, reduced to a pathetic and grotesque parody of girlhood.

With *Baby Jane*, Davis proved the naysayers wrong and revitalized her career yet again. The film was a blockbuster with audiences and earned Davis her final Oscar nomination. She continued making movies for another 27 years, working practically up to her death from breast cancer in 1990. For her, *Baby Jane* opened up a whole new realm of possible roles, and she subsequently appeared in a number of horror and borderline-horror films, including *Dead Ringer* (1964), *The Nanny* (1965), *Burnt Offerings* (1976), *Return from Witch Mountain* (1978) and *The Watcher in the Woods* (1980). For television, she made *Madame Sin* (1972), *Scream, Pretty Peggy* (1973) and *The Dark Secret of Harvest Home* (1978). Her final film was the horror-comedy misfire *Wicked Stepmother* (1989).

The success of *What Ever Happened to Baby Jane?* spawned numerous copycats, many with similar titles, each featuring an aging actress as a demented killer. Crawford starred in *Strait-Jacket* (1964), Geraldine Page appeared in *Whatever Happened to Aunt Alice?* (1969), Debbie Reynolds and Shelley Winters co-starred in *What's the Matter with Helen?* (1971) and Agnes Moorehead headlined *Dear Dead Delilah* (1972). Davis herself returned to this *oeuvre* for Aldrich's follow-up, *Hush ... Hush Sweet Charlotte* (1965), co-starring with Olivia de Havilland (after Crawford bowed out).

However, none of those subsequent films recaptured the lightning that electrified *Baby Jane*. And none of those actresses, not even Davis herself, could equal the audacity or brilliance of Davis' triumph in the original movie. Jane Hudson stands among the most daring and gloriously over-the-top portrayals in horror movie history. It is a fitting monument to a larger-than-life performer.

Mia Farrow in *Rosemary's Baby* (1968)

—Few horror films focus so intently on women's issues as *Rosemary's Baby*, which concerns itself with marriage, pregnancy, childbirth and the maternal instinct. As author Gene Wright writes in his book *Horrorshows*, "In essence *Rosemary's Baby* is a woman's picture, [but] not from a sexist point of view." The genius of the film lies in the way it carries women's everyday anxieties to their ultimate extreme. For instance, Rosemary's husband isn't merely preoccupied with work, he has betrayed her to a satanic cult to advance his career. Rosemary's pregnancy turns hellish in the literal sense of the word, and her child is truly a "little devil."

Further, few horror films focus so intently on a single actress as *Rosemary's Baby*. Director-screenwriter Roman Polanski turns the film into a first-person narrative, relating the story entirely from Rosemary's perspective, even entering the character's dreams. She is on screen virtually every minute of the film. Given all this, selecting the right actress to play Rosemary was critical.

Polanski placed the weight of the entire project on the girlish shoulders of Mia Farrow.

Prior to *Rosemary's Baby*, Farrow was recognized for her role on the *Peyton Place* television series, but still best known as the daughter of actor John Farrow and actress Maureen O'Sullivan (Jane to Johnny Weissmuller's Tarzan), and as the wife of Frank Sinatra. Farrow surely understood the potential of this role, which had "breakthrough" written all over it. In addition to the project's singular focus on her character, author Ira Levin's source novel had been a runaway bestseller in 1967, providing the movie with a built-in audience. This was Farrow's chance to gain recognition for her abilities rather than her associations.

In retrospect, her part must have resonated with the actress on a deeper level as well. Although she was childless at the time, Farrow would devote much of her life to childbirth and parenting. By 1994, Farrow had borne five children and adopted nine more. In a strange coincidence, she and her large family lived in a building adjacent to the Dakota, where *Rosemary's Baby* was filmed.

Farrow brings these motivations, as well as her remarkable natural talent, to bear on her role and carries the film with her richly shaded yet refreshingly unaffected performance. Her portrayal divides, roughly, into three equally impressive phases: early on, as the happy and hopeful newlywed Rosemary; later as the terrified, pain-stricken, pregnant Rosemary; and finally as the defensive, almost feral, mother Rosemary. During the course of this remarkable progression, Farrow is called upon to hit nearly every note on the emotional scale. And she strikes each one flawlessly.

Farrow's cleverly calibrated delivery brings rich nuances to Polanski's script, in some cases providing a new layer of meaning that conflicts with the face value of the dialogue. In one key scene, for instance, Rosemary guilt-trips her husband, Guy (John Cassavetes), into joining the elderly couple next door for dinner. Guy is reluctant. "I told them they could count on us," Farrow says. Since the scene plays out as Rosemary is preparing to tile the floor, Farrow's face isn't even visible. She sits on her knees, fiddling with a tape measure, her back to the camera. Yet, by inflection alone, Farrow interjects an unspoken but unmistakable "I'll resent it if you say no" undercurrent into Rosemary's statement. When Guy caves in and agrees, Rosemary says, "Okay [we'll go], but only if you want to." But Farrow's tone is one of triumph, not acquiescence.

Dinner with the neighbors, Roman Castavet (Sidney Blackmer) and his wife Minnie (Ruth Gordon), becomes uncomfortable when Guy dismisses religion as "show biz." The Castavets enthusiastically agree. Farrow only looks at her plate, fidgets and remains silent. When pressed, Rosemary reveals, "I used to be Catholic, but now I don't know." Yet again, Farrow's reading suggests a separate truth — that she's still a Catholic, or at least Christian, in her heart but is no longer practicing so as not to displease her atheist husband. At the very least, Rosemary clearly harbors some vestige of her girlhood faith.

Events take a turn for the weird after dinner with the Castavets. Actually, events are already pretty weird, but now Rosemary becomes aware of their weirdness. Guy lands a coveted part in a new play, but only after the actor originally assigned the role is mysteriously struck blind. Soon he becomes absorbed in preparing for the play. Rosemary, who wants to start a family, feels neglected. Then an apologetic Guy announces to Rosemary that the time is finally right to "make a baby." He supplies all the prerequisites for a romantic evening: fresh roses, candlelit dinner, soft music — and drugged chocolate mousse. After dinner, Rosemary staggers to the bedroom and collapses onto the bed, half-conscious. Still she insists, "We have to make a baby."

Rosemary makes a baby, all right, but with Satan rather than Guy. The Castavets belong to a coven of witches who have called Lucifer out of Hell for the occasion. They stand around chanting and paint runic symbols on Rosemary's naked body.

Farrow and Polanski both handle this pivotal sequence masterfully. Because she did not eat her entire serving of the drugged mousse (she didn't like the taste), Rosemary drifts in and out of consciousness. We see the event as Rosemary sees it, as a boat ride with friends that morphs into something altogether different. Farrow's eyes pop open and she shrieks, in a moment of horrified clarity, "This is no dream, this is really happening!"

Yet, in the morning, and for much of the rest of the film, Rosemary struggles to sort out what is real from what is illusory. She senses something is wrong, but can't quite put the pieces together.

Rosemary is momentarily distracted from her fears when she learns that she is pregnant. The doctor's office telephones her with the news. Farrow clutches the receiver to her chest, throws her head back and beams joyously. Later she looks at herself in the mirror, her face cradled in her hands, and half-whispers to her reflection, "You're pregnant!" Her eyes sparkle with wonder and joy. She celebrates by getting a stylish new, short hairdo.

Her happiness is short-lived. Rosemary's (and Farrow's) appearance begins to change, and not in the way that pregnant women are supposed to change. She loses weight. She looks pale, reedy, washed-out. Dark circles appear around her eyes, which, with her close-cropped blonde hair, give her face the look of an animated skull. Some of the change in Farrow's appearance can be credited to the makeup artist, but Farrow seems to have actually lost some weight for these sequences as well. In one scene, Farrow's ribs are visible through her clingy red party dress. She looks emaciated, like she's spent the last few months at Auschwitz instead of her luxurious Manhattan apartment. She also moves differently — more slowly and with discernable difficulty. Her easy smile vanishes.

The pain disappears as inexplicably as it arrived, and Rosemary's spirits brighten. When she feels the baby move within her, she is jubilant. "It's alive. Guy, it's moving. I can feel it kicking!" she says with wonder. The rapture in Farrow's words perfectly captures the joy and awe I heard in my wife's voice the first time she felt our daughter kicking in her womb.

None of this, however, allays Rosemary's suspicions about the Castavets and their friends. Those only deepen. She's convinced that the neighbors are part of a coven of witches and want to use her baby as a human sacrifice. When she realizes that Guy is in on the scheme, she turns not only paranoid but panic-stricken — and the physicality of Farrow's performance changes yet again. She becomes jittery, never at rest.

Rosemary decides to contact her kindly former gynecologist, Dr. Hill (Charles Grodin), for help. Crammed into a phone booth on a sweltering summer day, Rosemary waits for a return call from Dr. Hill. Farrow holds the receiver against her face, her eyes staring like lasers, whispering shakily, half-crazed with terror and recognition. "All of them, all in it together. All of them witches."

Dr. Hill invites her to his house, where Rosemary launches into a hysterical recap of the film's events. Farrow races through her freaked-out monologue urgently, her voice crackling with fear: "They're very clever people. They planned everything right from the beginning. The made some sort of deal with Guy. They gave him success and he promised them our baby to use in their rituals." She pauses and adds, "I know this sounds crazy." Indeed it does.

No wonder, then, that Dr. Hill, fearing for her sanity, calls for Guy and Rosemary's regular physician, Dr. Sapirstein (Ralph Bellamy), to come and collect Rosemary. They take Rosemary, who's now in labor, back to the apartment. There the cult engulfs her, pawing at her and dragging her down onto the bed. Farrow flails her arms and legs and convulses her entire body, attempting to free herself. Sapirstein prepares a hypodermic and administers a sedative, despite Rosemary's blood-curdling screams: "Help me, somebody help me!" Farrow writhes on the bed, rolls her head back and forth and weeps in agony. Her reaction makes this scene petrifying.

When Rosemary awakes, she is tied to the bed. She has given birth. "The baby, where is it?" she demands immediately. Her only concern is for the safety of the child. Guy tells her that the baby died, but Rosemary doesn't believe. "You're lying! It didn't die, you took it!" Farrow screams, struggles against her bonds and gnashes her teeth in rage. Rosemary is no longer the sick pregnant woman, but the mother cat whose cub has been stolen from her den. Nothing matters except recovering the child.

Kitchen knife in hand, she sneaks into the Castavets' apartment and discovers her baby. It rests in a bassinet draped in black velvet, an inverted cross hanging where a Sesame Street mobile would ordinarily dangle. She walks over and looks inside, then recoils in horror. Farrow covers her mouth with her hand and swallows a scream. She looks around furtively, in shock and repulsion.

"What have you done to it? What have you done to its eyes?" She howls in confusion and anguish.

"He has his father's eyes," Roman replies calmly. Then he sweet-talks Rosemary. "Why don't you help us out, Rosemary? You don't have to join if you don't want to, just be a mother to your baby."

Rosemary doesn't answer. But when her son begins to cry, she can't resist walking over to the bassinet to try and soothe him. She reaches into the crib and adjusts the baby. She begins to slowly rock the bassinet. The child stops crying. She warms. Suddenly, Farrow's face relaxes and the beginning of a smile finds its way to her lips. Her change of expression is a small one, but it says everything. Rosemary does not look relieved, or even happy, exactly. She looks content. Farrow informs us, ever so gently, that Rosemary has found her place. She will mother her son, simply because she must. The child is the spawn of Satan, but is of her flesh as well. She belongs to it as much as it belongs to her.

The film closes with this final image, one of the most haunting closing shots in any genre film, the horror equivalent of Charlie Chaplin's immortal happy-sad grin at the conclusion of *Modern Times*.

In addition to serving as the focal point of nearly every scene, Farrow (without credit) also sang the eerie lullaby that serves as the film's signature theme. Released as a single, "Lullaby from *Rosemary's Baby*" climbed to Number 111 on the Billboard pop charts. It's difficult to imagine what else the actress could have done to ensure the film's success, short of traveling to theaters and selling popcorn.

Her Herculean efforts helped make *Rosemary's Baby* a smash with both critics and audiences. The film's success cleared the path for a succession of demon-child

Rosemary Woodhouse (Mia Farrow) grabs a knife with the intention of recovering her child by any means necessary.

movies that followed, including *It's Alive* (1973), *The Exorcist* (1974, itself a widely influential film), *The Omen* (1976) and its sequels, and *Audrey Rose* (1977), to name only a few. It also spawned a poorly conceived made-for-TV sequel, *Look What Happened to Rosemary's Baby* (1976), starring Patty Duke Astin.

Farrow dabbled on the fringes of the horror genre in a couple of misfires. *Secret Ceremony* (1968), which co-starred Robert Mitchum and Elizabeth Taylor, proved to be a big-budget bomb. *See No Evil* (1971) fared little better. Her only other full-blooded chiller, *Full Circle* (a.k.a. *The Haunting of Julia*, 1977), was another dud. She appeared memorably opposite Robert Redford in *The Great Gatsby* (1974) and began a lengthy association with director Woody Allen that included the acclaimed pictures *The Purple Rose of Cairo* (1985) and *Hannah and Her Sisters* (1986). Farrow earned considerable Oscar "buzz" for *Rosemary's Baby* but failed to receive a nomination in a very competitive year. The nominees for Best Actress were Katharine Hepburn and Barbra Streisand (who were declared co-winners), Patricia Neal, Vanessa Redgrave and Joanne Woodward. Ruth Gordon won the Oscar for Best Actress in a Supporting Role for her turn as Minnie. Given that Farrow's performance is even more impressive — and far more important to the success of the film — than Gordon's, one could argue that Farrow at least deserved that elusive nomination.

But perhaps the highest tribute to Farrow's work in *Rosemary's Baby* is Rosemary Woodhouse herself. By the time the movie is over, Rosemary seems like far more than a fictional character. In my introduction to this book, one of my definitions of a "great performance" was "one where the actor is so convincing and realistic that his or her character seems to take on a life of its own, possessing a fully realized personality separate from that of its creator." Now I can confess that those words were written with this performance in mind.

Rosemary stands as one of the best-realized, most three-dimensional portraits in horror movie history.

Ellen Burstyn and Linda Blair in *The Exorcist* (1973)—Although best-remembered for its depictions of graphic blasphemy, at its core *The Exorcist* remains something much simpler and more compelling: It is the story of a mother and her daughter. The film scared audiences senseless, and retains much of its ability to frighten because we watch the story unfold through the eyes of a caring mother horrified by what her little girl has become. We believe that Chris MacNeil loves her daughter Regan, and fears for the child's life, even her soul.

Playing mother and daughter, Ellen Burstyn and Linda Blair form the two poles of the axis around which this landmark movie revolves.

Burstyn came to *The Exorcist* as a hot commodity, having scored an Oscar nomination for her previous film, director Peter Bogdanovich's *The Last Picture Show* (1971). A former model and showgirl, Burstyn (born Edna Mae Gilhooley) had worked on Broadway and in television, and studied acting with Lee Strasberg at the prestigious Actor's Studio in New York. Blair, a child model with a couple of minor film appearances to her credit, was chosen from among hundreds who auditioned for the role.

Neither of them could have anticipated the fanatical extremes to which director William Friedkin pushed his cast during this film's grueling 15-month shoot. Friedkin insisted on realism and would do almost anything to elicit a genuine reaction — even firing a pistol on the set or slapping an actor across the face immediately prior to a take. Both Blair and Burstyn suffered back injuries in separate incidents during the production, and in both cases Friedkin used the footage showing the actresses' expressions of actual pain.

Other factors conspired to bring layers of realism to the actors' performances. For one, many among the cast and crew shared a pervasive feeling of unease because of the subject matter. "It deals with very heavy forces and I was a little worried about what that would mean, working with those," said Burstyn in the BBC documentary *The Fear of God: The Making of the Exorcist*. Also, Burstyn was one of many who worried about how working on the film would affect 12-year-old Blair, who was called upon to say and act out many vile and disturbing things. Blair herself, from all reports, was nonplussed by the experience, but Burstyn and others remained genuinely concerned.

As a result of all this, it becomes difficult to separate in *The Exorcist* what is good acting from what is true emotion. Of course, some might argue that no such distinction exists. Ultimately what matters is what appears on the screen, and in this instance what appears on the screen is simply stunning.

The Exorcist opens with lengthy movements that introduce the two priests who will eventually attempt to free Regan from the grip of demonic possession. But the story doesn't begin in earnest until Burstyn and Blair appear.

When the audience meets Chris MacNeil, she is lying in bed on her stomach. With her right hand she scribbles notes in the margins of a script. (In a further blurring of art and life, Burstyn's character is a well-known actress.) With her left hand she holds a cigarette, which she places to her lips and withdraws without lighting, a recurring nervous gesture. She hears a sound from Regan's room, rises, puts on her robe and walks gingerly to investigate. When she enters her daughter's room, she shivers and crosses her arms against the cold. She checks on Regan, who is sleeping soundly, then shuts an open window and returns to stroke the head of the sleeping girl. "Sure do love you," she whispers, as she bows to kiss Regan's head.

Regan is a happy, apple-cheeked youngster who yearns for a pony and steals a cookie from the kitchen. Chris, the playfully indulgent mother, chases Regan out of the kitchen and wrestles with her over the pilfered snack. Early scenes like these do nothing to advance the story *per se*, but do everything to establish the affection between mother and daughter that forms the film's emotional core. Chris and Regan love each other. In these few moments, in the way they address each other and through simple but telling gestures, Burstyn and Blair make this palpably clear.

Consider, for instance, a brief scene in which Chris tucks Regan into bed. Chris collects a movie magazine (with herself on the cover) from her daughter and cleans a stray eyelash from the girl's face. The way Burstyn removes this eyelash lends the scene a genuine sense of casual, motherly affection. It's one of many bits of "hand" business that Burstyn integrates into her performance. Her hands always seem to be in frame, usually near her face, for one reason or another. She uses her expressive fingers to subtly underscore her line readings.

More character-embellishing scenes follow, including a key sequence in which Chris struggles to reach Regan's estranged father overseas by telephone, with great weeping and gnashing of teeth (not to mention profanity). Pacing with a telephone in her hands, irate, near tears, Burstyn's voice grows shrill with frustration: "Don't tell me to be calm, Goddammit, I've been on this fucking phone for 20 minutes!" It's Regan's birthday. Chris understands that not hearing from her father will hurt Regan, and it pains Chris to think of Regan being in pain. This we gather more from Burstyn's anguished tone and body language than from the dialogue itself.

As this scene continues, the camera reveals Blair, standing in her bedroom doorway, secretly listening to her exasperated mother's profane tirade. While Chris continues her battle with the operator, Blair sighs, rolls her eyes and goes to bed, suggesting that Regan is more resigned to her father's neglect than Chris understands. Although audiences buzzed about Blair's notorious sequences later in the film, her finest and most important work occurs during these early moments.

Throughout these early scenes, clues are dropped that Regan may be in contact with some malevolent supernatural force. Chris doesn't begin to realize this until Regan interrupts a dinner party her mother is hosting. A blank-faced Blair wanders into the crowded living room and tells one of the guests, who is preparing for a plane

Chris MacNeill (Ellen Burstyn) pleads with Father Damien Karras (Jason Miller) to perform an exorcism on her daughter, in *The Exorcist* (1974).

trip, "You're going to die up there." She then urinates on the carpet. Blair's deadpan delivery and robotic demeanor are strikingly different from her earlier scenes.

For her part, Burstyn seems more confused than anything else, which is precisely appropriate to her character and the scenario. After the urination incident, Chris rushes to her daughter and asks, "Honey, what's the matter?" She apologizes to her guests and whisks the girl upstairs for a bath. Chris lovingly bathes her daughter, but Regan only stares like a zombie. Still in her party dress (with its sleeves rolled up), Chris sponges water onto Regan's back and asks her tenderly, "Regan, why did you say that?" Burstyn's tone of voice is warm and comforting, but she still sounds perplexed. After an awkward silence, Regan asks, "Mother, what's wrong with me?" Chris reassures her, "It's just like the doctor said. It's nerves, that's all. You just take your pills and you'll be fine, really. Okay?" Burstyn sounds confident, suggesting that Chris actually believes this.

As Regan's "condition" worsens, Chris' faith in medicine and psychology weakens and finally breaks. The first shock arrives when Chris enters Regan's room to discover the girl's bed shaking and rising off the floor. At this sight, Burstyn's eyes grow as round as saucers, her jaw drops and she takes a step backward. Chris recovers her courage and throws herself on the bed to protect her screaming daughter.

Cut to a hallway at a doctor's office. Burstyn listens eagerly, chewing on her thumbnail, but clearly doesn't buy the physician's diagnosis (that Regan's problems are the result of a rare chemical imbalance caused by a lesion in the brain). Burstyn's voice shakes as she describes the movement of the bed, which, Chris argues, could not have been caused by Regan's convulsions. On the verge of tears, her head heavy with worry, she nonetheless grants permission for a series of tests.

This opens the door to a series of nightmarish-looking, futile medical procedures as horrific as anything in the film. Chris watches her daughter wince in pain as medical technicians stick a needle in the girl's neck. Burstyn winces and curls her fingers as they tape down Regan's neck and lock her head in place. Blair flinches, cowers and sobs inconsolably. The two actresses are never on screen together during this sequence. Their scenes could have been shot weeks apart. Yet Burstyn seems completely connected to Blair. We get the impression Chris would rather endure the pain herself than watch her daughter go through this. And the physical separation between the two characters only amplifies their agony.

Things slide further downhill once the medical team begins to search for a psychological cause for Regan's problems. During her interview with a psychiatrist, the possessed Regan knocks the doctor to the floor and taunts him by raising her skirt and chanting, "Fuck me, fuck me!" Then she begins slapping herself across the face. Chris watches all this from across the room, looking shocked, then horrified, then something worse. Burstyn's face turns red. Tears streak her cheeks. She throws her head back and howls, "Nooooo!" The word becomes a kind of primal scream, an inarticulate cry of raw anguish.

Further examinations, including one with a hypnotized Regan, prove even more disastrous. Afterward, a panel of psychiatrists and specialists blames Regan's condition on a "guilt complex." Chris can't swallow this lame explanation either. "Eighty-eight doctors and all you can tell me with all of your bullshit is...." She can't even finish the sentence. Burstyn buries her face in her hands. She seems utterly defeated, without hope. Then one of the doctors suggests pursuing an exorcism.

Hidden behind glasses, gloves, an overcoat and a scarf, dragging nervously on a cigarette, Chris meets Father Damien Karras (Jason Miller). Burstyn fumbles with small talk and pussyfoots around the subject for a short while, then asks, with an air of poorly affected casualness, "How do you go about getting an exorcism?" At first Karras is reluctant to help, but Chris wins him over with an impassioned plea. Burstyn's heartrending delivery makes this one of the finest monologues ever featured in a horror film.

Karras is seated at a table in Chris' basement. Chris stands in front of him. Her tone is insistent but calm. It's a kind of forced calm, as if all her fear and resentment was being held in by baling wire and chewing gum, and might come spilling out at any second. "Show me Regan's double — same face, same voice, everything — and I'd know it wasn't Regan," she says, bending at the waist and putting her hands on the table so she can look Karras in the eye. "I'd know in my gut and I'm telling you that thing upstairs isn't my daughter." Her iron-willed certainty is more convincing and, perhaps unexpectedly, more touching than a teary-eyed gush of emotion.

Burstyn's brilliance proves the old adage that "all acting is reacting." For most of the rest of the film, Chris doesn't initiate events; she struggles to process them. The movie drags us through shock after shock, most of which are registered through

"Your mother darns socks in jail!" (Or something like that.) Regan MacNeill (Linda Blair), in the grip of possession, taunts Father Merrin (Max von Sydow) in *The Exorcist* (1974). (Photograph courtesy Bryan Senn.)

Burstyn's performance. Without ever losing hold of her character, she becomes a walking reflection of the audience's intended reaction—distressed about Regan's safety, yet revolted and terrified by the unfolding events.

On the other hand, the film's famously shocking latter scenes—projectile vomiting, head-spinning and other weirdness—reduce Blair to, essentially, an animated prop. She has little to do except stay strapped to the bed and glare spitefully at Fathers Karras and Merrin (Max von Sydow). Heavy makeup obscures her features almost entirely. Mercedes McCambridge dubbed all of Blair's demonic dialogue. For some of the most graphic sequences, a diminutive adult double, and sometimes a dummy, substituted for Blair. Despite this, Blair's portrayal emerged as the most talked-about of all the performances in the picture. In the American Film Institute's "100 Movies, 100 Heroes and Villains" poll in 2003, Regan MacNeil was voted the ninth greatest villain of all time (somewhat misleadingly, since Regan herself wasn't the villain, but rather the demon within her).

Although *The Exorcist* proved to be a critically divisive film (many observers were turned off by its graphic sequences and profanity), it earned a whopping ten

Academy Award nominations, including Best Actress in a Leading Role (Burstyn), Best Actress in a Supporting Role (Blair), Best Actor in a Supporting Role (Miller), Best Director and Best Picture. The Golden Globes voted Blair Best Supporting Actress and named the film Best Drama. The picture proved an even greater success with audiences, who made it the top-grossing horror movie of all time. In many cities, fans lined up around the block, even in rain and snow, a scene that recalled the first runs of *Frankenstein* in 1931 and *Psycho* in 1960. Although its record gross was eventually eclipsed by horror blockbusters such as *The Silence of the Lambs* (1991), *Scream* (1996) and *The Sixth Sense* (1999), if you adjust for inflation and factor in re-releases, *The Exorcist* remains one of the greatest box office champions in the history of the genre.

The Exorcist, itself the progeny of *Rosemary's Baby*, would spawn a whole generation of horror films. In the mid-to-late 1970s, screens were inundated with movies about demonic possession or some type of confrontations with Satan himself: *The Devil's Rain* (1975), *The Sentinel, To the Devil... A Daughter, Burnt Offerings* (all 1976), *Devil Dog: The Hound of Hell* (1978, featuring a possessed pooch) among many others, not to mention Mario Bava's *House of Exorcism* (1976, a.k.a. *Lisa and the Devil*) and numerous other European derivations.

It also sired a pair of disappointing sequels. The first, *Exorcist II: The Heretic*, continued the tale of Regan MacNeil, again played by Blair. Other than Blair, however, none of the key personnel from the original film returned, and *The Heretic* went down as one of the more infamous flops in Hollywood history. Author William Peter Blatty adapted and directed *Exorcist III: Legion*, based on his own follow-up novel, but it fared little better. A prequel, *Exorcist IV: The Beginning*, was in production as of this writing.

The careers of Burstyn and Blair went in opposite directions following *The Exorcist*.

Burstyn, already twice Oscar-nominated, finally won the Academy Award for her moving lead performance in director Martin Scorsese's *Alice Doesn't Live Here Anymore* (1974). She also won the British Academy Award as Best Actress for *Alice*. That same year, Burstyn won a Tony for her performance in the Broadway production of *Same Time, Next Year*. She reprised her role in the film adaptation of this play and received a fourth Academy Award nomination. In the 1980s she appeared in several television movies and received two Emmy nominations. She became the first female president of Actor's Equity in 1982, a post she held for three years. In 2000 she received the National Board of Review's Career Achievement Award and was named co-president of the Actor's Studio. She continues to work on stage and in movies but, so far, has not made another horror film.

Blair, on the other hand, has appeared in very little other than low-budget horror films and other exploitation fare. Like so many stars whose initial success came in horror movies, she found herself typecast. In addition to *The Heretic*, she starred in *Hell Night* and *Roller Boogie* (both 1979), *Chained Heat* (1983), *Grotesque* (1988), *Witchery* (1988), *The Chilling* (1989), *House 5* (1990) and the straight-to-video spoof *Blair Bitch Project* (1999), among others. She continues to act. She also sometimes appears at horror film conventions and has her own clothing line. Blair received death threats during *The Exorcist*'s initial release. As a young adult, she was arrested on drug charges and suffered other personal problems, but Blair has never blamed her difficulties on playing Regan MacNeil.

During its 2000 theatrical reissue, *The Exorcist* was promoted as "The Scariest Movie of All Time." It may not live up to that billing, but it remains a powerful picture. And much of its power radiates from the superb performance of Burstyn and the touching presence of Blair.

Sissy Spacek in *Carrie* (1976)

—Sissy Spacek's audition for the title role in *Carrie* must rank among the gutsiest in the long, colorful history of Hollywood casting.

For starters, Spacek was supposed to audition for a different part altogether. Director Brian DePalma wanted her to read for the role of Carrie's tormentor, Chris Hargenson, eventually portrayed by Nancy Allen. Spacek had other ideas. The night before, she reread Stephen King's source novel cover to cover. In the morning, "I rubbed Vaseline in my hair and put on an old sailor suit my mother made for me in the seventh grade," Spacek reports in the documentary "Acting Carrie," included on the *Carrie* DVD. "I was really into it." The moment she walked in the room, DePalma realized he had found his Carrie.

Spacek's unorthodox audition set the tone for her entire performance — audacious, offbeat and unforgettable.

Like Ellen Burstyn, Spacek studied acting under Lee Strasberg at the Actor's Studio in New York. She also modeled, sang, appeared on stage and television, and earned a few thankless supporting parts in low-budget feature films. *Carrie* was her first leading role, and she devoted herself to it whole-heartedly. During the production, Spacek kept herself apart from the rest of the cast. She filled her dressing room with religious books and played "heavy classical music"— things of interest to Carrie, not to Sissy.

Yet despite these Method devices, Spacek's performance is something of a throwback. Although not without subtlety, it remains highly stylized — closer to Vincent Price than Constantin Stanislavsky. It took courage for Spacek to step outside of her Actor's Studio box, but the move paid off handsomely. Her daring work perfectly suits DePalma's approach, which is equally stylized. He integrates slow motion photography, bizarre tilted camera angles, split-screens and other visual artifices, including an impressionistic, Hitchcockian lighting scheme. The film's other performers also paint in broad strokes, especially Piper Laurie as Carrie's mother, Margaret. A quiet, naturalistic portrayal would have been drowned out amid this cacophony.

Within the first minute of the film, Spacek establishes her character as a loner and a misfit, and introduces a lexicon of physical shorthand that she uses throughout the film to illustrate Carrie's anxiety and self-loathing. The camera dollies in on a group of high school girls playing volleyball. Chatter informs us that it's game point. The opposing team hits the ball in Carrie's direction. Spacek flails awkwardly at the passing ball, which she misses, losing the game for her team. The girls head for the showers. She stands there, mute, while her classmates walk by and insult her (one even raps her on the head with a baseball cap). Spacek stares at the ground, looking ashamed. Her long, straight hair hangs in her face, obscuring her features. When the insults begin, her hands reflexively cover her ears.

The volleyball scene leads directly into the famous sequence in which Carrie, while showering, gets her first period. When the blood appears, Spacek looks baffled, terrified. She rushes, panicked, from the shower, naked, blood on her fingers. "Help me, help me!" she screams in terror (her first dialogue in the film). But her classmates only taunt the traumatized girl and pelt her with tampons and maxi pads. Carrie retreats to the shower, where she cowers in a corner, shell-shocked. Spacek's heartrending work makes this scene uncomfortable to watch, no matter how familiar with it viewers may be.

Life is, if anything, worse for Carrie at home than at school. She's the daughter of a crazed religious zealot (Laurie) who never told her about "the birds and the bees." When Carrie, sobbing, asks, "Why didn't you tell me, Mama?," her mother ignores her, then smacks her in the face with a religious pamphlet and forces her to repeat lines like, "Eve was weak." Throughout the film, Margaret White expresses no empathy for her daughter whatsoever. Instead, she tries to dominate Carrie through her warped religious beliefs. She tells Carrie that the "curse of blood" is upon her for her sins. Then, while her daughter kicks and shrieks, she drags Carrie across the room by her hair and locks her in a small, dark closet. At first, Spacek screams and kicks. Then she calms herself, lights a candle on a tiny altar in the closet and begins to recite the Lord's Prayer, her eyes wide and desperate. Hours later, finally freed from the closet, Carrie thanks her mother and kisses her.

Spacek's approach is considerably more restrained than Laurie's scenery-gnawing antics, but it remains exaggerated, especially in the way she utilizes her East Texas accent. At times—when she delivers lines like "Why didn't you tell me, Mama?"—she sounds as if she's doing a Sissy Spacek impression instead of simply being Sissy Spacek. Yet, again, this suits the piece. There's no logical reason why Carrie would have such an accent in the first place. None of the other characters in the film do, not even Carrie's mother. The accent works because it presents another barrier between Carrie and her classmates, something else that makes her different and awkward.

Through her accent, an array of physical gestures and her hesitant, half-mumbled delivery, Spacek creates an aura of acute discomfort and loneliness so convincing it becomes virtually impenetrable. To fully appreciate how effective her performance is, consider that as a teenager Spacek was voted Homecoming Queen at Quitman (Texas) High School—a biographical tidbit that seems irreconcilable with Carrie White.

Carrie is walking through the library with an armful of books, a pencil in her teeth, when beau hunk Tommy Ross (William Katt) surprisingly approaches her. Spacek quickly spits out the pencil and clutches the books against her bosom, like a shield. Tommy asks her to the prom. She looks him straight in the face (for the first time), incredulous. Then she dips her head slightly, so that her hair falls over her face, turns and bolts from the library without answering.

Kindly phys ed teacher Miss Collins (Betty Buckley) discovers Carrie hiding in a dark corner under a stairwell. Spacek is sitting alone with her knees together, a pile of books on her lap and her hands folded over the top of the books. She's looking down, her face again hidden behind her hair. "What's wrong?" Miss Collins asks. "I got invited to the prom," Spacek replies, ruefully. "They're just trying to trick me again, I know."

The teacher forces her to look at herself in a nearby mirror. She pulls the hair back from Carrie's face and lifts her chin. "Now that's a pretty girl," Miss Collins says. A shy smile finds its way to Spacek's face. She begins to warm to the sight of her own reflection, to see herself for the first time through the eyes of someone other than her mother.

Earlier, we've seen Carrie check out library books about ESP and telekinesis. Her growing understanding of her psychic abilities symbolizes her coming of age, of her grasping her "powers" as a woman. At last feeling strong enough to stand up to her mother, she agrees to attend the prom with Tommy.

Carrie informs her mother of this momentous decision over dinner, on a dark and stormy night in a candlelit room with a painting of the Last Supper hanging in the background. She and her mother are seated at opposing ends of a long table, so Carrie has to speak more loudly, more forcefully, than usual to be heard. "All the kids think I'm funny. I don't want to be funny, I want to be normal," Spacek says, her voice shaking. "I want to try to be a whole person before…." But, before Carrie can complete her thought, Laurie throws a cup of coffee in her daughter's face. As always, she remains completely oblivious to her daughter's feelings or perspective.

This time, however, when Margaret commands Carrie to "Go to your closet," Spacek replies with a quiet but firm, "No." Crying, covering her ears with her hands again, she pleads, "Everyone isn't bad, Mama. Everything isn't a sin." When her mother tries to walk away, Carrie uses her power to slam shut all the windows in the house. Then she looks at Laurie, her face wet with tears, her voice full of screwed-up courage, and declares, "I'm goin', Mama, and things are gonna change around here."

Carrie's prom night arrives. When she tells a female classmate, "I'm nervous," the girl offers to let her sit with their group. At last, it seems, she is being accepted. Although she remains somewhat skittish—she would rather sit at a table with her date and sip punch than mix with the other students—Carrie is gaining a new confidence. This Spacek informs us through subtle changes in her posture and mannerisms. Instead of her usual shapeless dresses and sweaters, Carrie wears a clingy pink dress that reveals her form. Her hair is combed back, out of her face, so her eyes are visible, and she looks at her classmates straight on, without averting her eyes. She makes no hand motions toward her ears. She sits straighter and in general seems much more at ease. Basking in the glow of a compliment by Miss Collins, and in the attention of her handsome date, she smiles, her first true, relaxed smile of the film, and even laughs. "It's like being on Mars," she tells Miss Collins.

She and Tommy dance. While they dance, he kisses her and she melts into his arms. Her bliss climaxes when she is named Prom Queen. Spacek's face radiates something like rapture—pure joy. Her eyes are moist and she beams an incredulous smile.

Then her conniving classmates drop a bucket of pig blood on her head. Spacek's jaw drops, her eyes pop wide in shock and horror as blood covers her hair and ruins

Bloody good show: Carrie White (Sissy Spacek), doused in pig blood, goes into "some kind of a Zen trance" in *Carrie* (1976).

her dress. She hunches over, assuming the familiar posture of the misfit. Her hands reflexively cover her ears. She begins to visually regress, retreating to her former posture and gestures. She's horrified and humiliated, feeling betrayed beyond comprehension. Then something else begins to happen. Spacek's expression suddenly freezes. Her face takes on a kind of granite-like quality. She looks around the room slowly, almost robotically, but staring with burning, laser-like intensity. "If looks could kill," as they say.

"Sissy, once she got that blood on, she went into some kind of Zen trance that's difficult for me to recreate or understand how she did it," DePalma says in "Acting Carrie." "She just did this thing that was so terrifying."

After wiping out nearly the entire high school in her fiery wrath, she retreats to her house and into the arms of her mother. On the way home she walks with her arms out stiff at her sides, her fingers slanted at odd angles, like a latter day Frankenstein Monster or perhaps Conrad Veidt's somnambulist from *The Cabinet of Dr. Caligari*. She bathes and then seeks her mother's arms. "Mama, Mama, they laughed at me," Spacek sobs. "Hold me, Mama, hold me." But Margaret literally stabs her daughter in the back. Spacek's look of shock and anguish, as she reels from this mortal wound, physical and emotional, provides not only the most affecting moment in the film, but one of the most moving moments in any horror movie.

For her stunning work in *Carrie*, Spacek earned an Academy Award nomination. "I remember people saying, 'Oh, you won't get a nomination.... The Academy would never nominate a role from a horror film.' So we were all surprised," Spacek says in "Acting Carrie." She lost to Faye Dunaway in *Network*, but her reputation was established. Spacek went on to win an Oscar for her portrayal of country music legend Loretta Lynn in *Coal Miner's Daughter* (1980) and earn another nomination, this time for Supporting Actress, for her portrayal of the ditzy sister in *Crimes of the Heart* (1986). Despite the fact that she is not "Hollywood beautiful," and therefore more difficult to cast, Spacek has worked regularly in quality films and often received good notices. Her other post–*Carrie* pictures include *3 Women* (1977), *Missing* (1982), *JFK* (1991), *Affliction* (1997) and *In the Bedroom* (2001).

So far, she has made no more appearances in the horror genre, although footage from the original film was used in *The Rage: Carrie 2* (1999). Despite its title, this lukewarm sequel focused on one of Carrie's classmates, not Carrie herself. *Carrie* also spawned a short-lived Broadway musical and, in 2002, a forgettable made-for-TV remake. Even though its direct descendants have washed out, the influence of *Carrie* has been lasting and widespread.

Producer Herman Cohen struck gold with a string of teen-centric horrors in the late 1950s, spearheaded by *I Was a Teenage Werewolf* (1957). A raft of imitators soon followed, but by the early 1960s this wave of youth-oriented horrors had crested. For the better part of 15 years, teenagers virtually disappeared from horror movies. The success of *Carrie* paved the way for movies like *Halloween* (1978) and *Friday the 13th* (1980), which also featured teenaged protagonists. In fact, throughout the 1980s and early '90s, teenagers threatened to overrun the genre: The many *Halloween* and *Friday the 13th* sequels, the *Nightmare on Elm Street* series, *Prom Night*, and later the *Scream* trilogy and *I Saw What You Did Last Summer* films, among many others, were all teen-themed.

Yet, few of her successors could rekindle the flame that illuminated Carrie White. Thanks to Spacek's courageous and emotionally searing portrayal, Carrie endures as a symbol of the joys and agonies of life as a teenager—forever trapped in transformation from girl to woman, like a butterfly crushed while leaving its cocoon.

Jamie Lee Curtis in *Halloween* (1978)

—After her first day of shooting on *Halloween*, Jamie Lee Curtis was worried.

"I remember going home and thinking I was going to be fired," Curtis reports in the DVD documentary "Halloween Unmasked." "I just thought I sucked."

Her anxiety was, to say the least, unfounded.

Curtis could not foresee all the rewards that would be reaped, in due time, from her performance: For herself, a long and accomplished acting career; for scary movies, a popular resurgence; for fellow actresses, a new type of heroine who broke the "scream queen" mold; and for genre fans, one of the most beloved and enduring characters in modern horror cinema. Not bad for a young actress who, that first day, simply wanted to keep her job.

Curtis, the daughter of Tony Curtis and Janet Leigh, began acting in school plays while studying law. Rather than pursue a legal career, she signed a contract with Universal Pictures and made guest appearances on television series, including *Columbo*, *Charlie's Angels* and *The Love Boat*, eventually earning a recurring role on the *Operation Petticoat* series (which was based on one of her father's movies). She was still virtually unknown, and relatively inexperienced, when she auditioned for *Halloween*.

"We saw a lot of girls for the Laurie Strode character," producer Debra Hill says in "Halloween Unmasked." Curtis "didn't come with all the acting chops that most of the girls were portraying at the time, she was just real and fresh and she so wanted the role." Hill's choice of adjectives ("real and fresh") perfectly describes Curtis' performance. Her approach is remarkably unaffected and convincing. It is, in many respects, the antithesis of Sissy Spacek's brilliant but stylized portrayal of *Carrie*, another horror film teenager whose memory lingered in the public mind as *Halloween* began shooting. If acting were special effects, Spacek's performance would be the equivalent of old-fashioned stop-motion animation — obviously fake but so beautiful that audiences love it anyway. Even the most advanced modern FX technology can't produce anything half as believable as Curtis' Laurie Strode.

In addition to this astounding verisimilitude, her performance contains a kind of inner strength and resilience that's central to her character's appeal. What sets Curtis apart from nearly all the "scream queens" that preceded her — or, for that matter, followed her — is that she never sees Laurie Strode as a victim. In "Halloween Unmasked," Curtis calls Laurie "by far, up until *True Lies*, the best part I ever had." She describes her character as someone who is "intelligent, forthright, [and] fought back against adversity." These attributes are, of course, displayed during Laurie's climactic confrontation with the maniacal Michael Myers. But Curtis first demonstrates these qualities through her subtle handling of low-key moments early in the film. She appears 11 minutes into the narrative, dressed in a turtleneck sweater, a skirt, tights and sensible shoes, with a bag slung over one shoulder and carrying an armload of books. Laurie looks like a studious, socially timid young woman, and Curtis quietly embellishes this image. She walks to school with friends, but lets the other girls do most of the talking. Curtis listens attentively, always appearing engaged, never simply waiting to speak her lines.

Laurie stops to comfort young Tommy (Brian Andrews), whom she sometimes baby-sits, because the boy has been taunted by his classmates. The kindness and humor Curtis brings to this brief scene open a wellspring of goodwill that help bond Laurie with the audience throughout the remainder of the film.

The most revealing of these early scenes takes place at school. Again, it's a mostly silent sequence. Curtis sits at her desk, her arms and legs crossed and a pen resting against her lips — looking bored with the lesson. She glances out the window and spots something out of place — a station wagon with a correctional department seal on the door (stolen by Michael during his escape from a mental institution), parked across from the school. She looks harder at the car, narrowing her eyes, gears obviously turning in her head. Suddenly, the teacher asks Laurie a question. Caught off-guard, Laurie politely asks, "Ma'am?" Curtis quickly checks her notes, her eyes darting toward a pad of paper, then provides a detailed answer. In a subtle but succinct manner, this scene informs viewers not just that Laurie is smart and respectful of her elders, but that she's observant, can think on her feet and reacts quickly. These are the abilities that enable her to survive her battle with Michael.

Despite all these winning qualities, however, Laurie remains a vulnerable, imperfect (and therefore realistic) character. Contrary to the myth created by revisionist critics, Laurie isn't a squeaky-clean, virginal "good girl." Riding in a car with her friend Annie (Nancy Loomis), Laurie takes a few tokes from a joint. And never is it made entirely clear that Laurie is a virgin. She confesses to having a crush on one of her classmates. Curtis' deft handling of this dialogue suggests that Laurie is very much interested in sex, but too acutely shy to act on her feelings.

She's not fearless, either. After catching several brief glimpses of Michael in the background, or out of the corner of her eye, she becomes spooked. Lying in bed, trying to gather her nerves, Curtis whispers, almost pleading with herself, "Calm down, this is ridiculous." Of course, you could argue that this actually represents another strength. Laurie may be frightened, but at least she's aware that something is wrong. The rest of the town hasn't a clue.

Laurie Strode emerges as a fully realized, three-dimensional personality, as opposed to the typical shrieking cardboard cut-out, as seen in subsequent slasher flicks. And the entire film coils itself around her performance. She serves as the perfect foil for Michael Myers (Nick Castle). He remains, as the film's crew referred to him, "the Shape," a not only faceless but utterly unknowable bogeyman, a terrifying silhouette. Director John Carpenter builds tension patiently but incessantly, everything leading to the final showdown between the polar opposites of Laurie and Michael. This confrontation doesn't occur until 76 minutes into the 92-minute film, but seems to consume a larger percentage of the movie's running time (at least in the audience's memory) due to its emotional impact. The intensity of that impact arises from viewers' identification with Laurie.

Once she and Michael finally meet face-to-face (or face-to-mask), Curtis' performance takes on a new dimension in its sheer physicality. She's asked to run, jump, fall, limp, crawl and, of course, fight — the kind of stuff usually reserved for the Arnold Schwarzeneggers and Sylvester Stallones of the world. All this she executes flawlessly, using her movements as outward expressions of Laurie's emotions.

The battle is joined when Laurie decides to check in on a friend of hers, who is baby-sitting nearby. She discovers the bodies of four of her classmates, as well as a displaced tombstone, in an upstairs bedroom. Curtis shrieks and recoils in horror, backs out of the room and begins to sob. Michael, sneaking up on Laurie from behind, swipes at her with a large kitchen knife. He delivers only a glancing blow, but causes her to fall backwards over a stair rail. (A stunt double takes this fall.) Traumatized, terrified and injured, Laurie limps to the front door, finds it locked, then moves to the laundry room, bashes out the glass door and hobbles over to the neighbors' house, with Michael in pursuit. "Oh God, help me please!" Curtis screams. The neighbors ignore her, perhaps thinking it's a Halloween prank.

Curtis meets the physical demands of this sequence without losing her mental focus; she remains fully engaged throughout. As in that early classroom scene, she says little but shows much. Not only does she look scared — really scared — but she makes it clear that Laurie is wracking her brain to decide what to do next. She does the smart things — running away, crying out for help. When those fail, she's forced to undertake more aggressive measures. Her situation is complicated further by the fact that she was baby-sitting Tommy and a young girl, and must protect them — as well as herself — from Michael. She rushes back to Tommy's house. She tries to use the phone, but Michael has cut the line. He lumbers into the room, brandishing that giant knife. "Please stop, please!" Curtis pleads desperately. When he continues to advance, she stabs him in the neck with a knitting needle.

Under the impression that she has dispatched the villain, Laurie gathers up the children, intending to walk them to a working phone. Tommy asks what happened to "the boogie man." "I killed him," Curtis says. She sounds as if she's just realizing this herself, her voice tinged with both disbelief and sadness. Laurie never thought she could kill anyone.

As it turns out, of course, she hasn't. Michael springs out at them, having shaken off his neck injury, and a whole new round of cat-and-mouse begins between the killer and the baby-sitter.

Just when it seems we have seen everything Curtis can possibly offer, she cranks the intensity of her performance up an extra notch. She grits her teeth and her eyes flash back and forth — thinking, always thinking. She rushes into a bedroom closet and ties shut the doors. This won't keep Michael out for long, and she knows it. Cowering on the floor of the closet, she grabs a clothes hanger and begins to untwist it (she will use it to jab Michael in the eye). As she untwists the wire, a scream spills out of her, almost involuntarily. There's no particular, immediate cause for this scream, it simply wells up from inside her and cannot be contained. It's a tiny but chilling bit of business, chilling because it seems so real, so "in the moment." *Halloween* is loaded with such spine-tingling, in-the-moment moments, which is why it remains scary even on repeated viewings, when audiences know what's coming.

Laurie Strode blazed the trail for other tough-but-vulnerable horror and sci-fi heroines that followed, including Sigourney Weaver's Ellen Ripley, Neve Campbell's Sidney Prescott and Jodie Foster's Clarice Starling. At first, however, her watershed performance did little to improve Curtis' own career. She was unable to find work for seven months following *Halloween*. Finally, Carpenter hired Curtis for a supporting role in his *Halloween* follow-up, *The Fog* (1979). Three more low-budget chillers followed: *Prom Night* (1980), *Halloween II* and *Terror Train* (both 1981).

Curtis earned good reviews for her performance as doomed model Dorothy Stratten in the 1981 television movie *The Death of a Centerfold*. She broke through to mainstream audiences with an endearing supporting performance in the Eddie Murphy–Dan Aykroyd hit *Trading Places* (1983), which revealed Curtis' flair for comedy. That gift served her well in many subsequent comedies, especially *A Fish Called Wanda* (1988). From 1989 to 1992, she co-starred in the television sitcom *Anything but Love*. With her unique combination of dramatic acumen, comedic timing and physical toughness, Curtis seemed tailor-made for her role in director James Cameron's action-comedy *True Lies* (1994). More recently, she established a second career for herself as an author of children's books. She continues to headline major films, such as the thriller *Virus* (1998) and Disney's 2003 update of *Freaky Friday*.

"I can trace my whole career back to *Halloween*," Curtis says in the documentary "Unmasking the Horror," included on the *Halloween H20: Twenty Years Later* DVD. Sometimes out of necessity, other times out of affection, Curtis returned to the character of Laurie Strode three times.

The first and least of these came in Carpenter's ill-conceived *Halloween II*, which picks up precisely where the first film left off. Strode remains injured, drugged and unconscious for most of the film, as Michael murders the staff at the hospital where she was taken to treat her wounds suffered in the first movie. Once Laurie wakes up, Curtis can do little more than recreate the physicality of her battle with Michael from the original film. She does this well, but we've seen it all before.

Four more sequels, none of which featured Laurie or Curtis, followed. Curtis

Laurie Strode (Jamie Lee Curtis) discovers the bodies of three of her friends in *Halloween* (1978). Curtis' performance was a cut above.

herself supplied the idea for *Halloween H20* (1998), which marked her return to the franchise. Twenty years after the events of the first two films, Laurie continues to struggle with the emotional fallout of that terrifying night. She faked her own death to throw Michael off her trail, and now serves as the dean of an exclusive private academy. She's divorced, has a drinking problem and seems alienated from her teenaged son. When Michael finds her, at first she runs. But then she decides to stop running and face her personal demon once and for all. Grabbing a fire ax, she calls Michael out by name, and becomes the aggressor. Curtis' work is magnificent throughout, helping make *H20* not only the best of the Halloween sequels, but one of the most satisfying follow-ups in genre history.

The next entry, *Halloween Resurrection* (2002), featured Curtis in a brief pre-credit sequence that undercuts the basic premise of *H20*. Nevertheless, she contributes a credible, affecting performance.

Along with *Psycho* (which, coincidentally, starred Curtis' mom), *Halloween* stands among the most influential of all modern horror films. Like *Psycho*, it sparked a resurgence of interest in the genre and spawned countless clones. Throughout the 1980s and early 1990s, the terms "horror film" and "slasher movie" became virtually synonymous. For more than a decade, a procession of silent, usually masked or disfigured killers stalked endless numbers of young women.

But only rarely did any of *Halloween*'s imitators approach the sophistication and emotional impact of the original. Quickly, the slasher movement devolved into a succession of mindless gore fests, typified by the rigidly formulaic *Friday the 13th* films, whose hockey-masked villain, Jason Vorhees, eventually rivaled Michael Myers in popularity. What the makers of these second rate knock-offs failed to realize, however, was that *Halloween* triumphed not because of Michael Myers, but because of the combination of Michael Myers and Laurie Strode.

Michael proved easy to copy, but Laurie was impossible to duplicate.

Kathy Bates in *Misery* (1990)

— "I'm not a movie star type," Annie Wilkes says at one point in *Misery*, in what must have been an ironic moment for Kathy Bates.

Bates became available for *Misery* when she was passed over for the Hollywood adaptation of her Broadway triumph, *Frankie and Johnny in the Clair de Lune*. Even though the female lead in the hit play had been written especially for the plain-looking, chunky-framed Bates, studio executives chose to cast a movie star type — sex kitten Michelle Pfeiffer. This probably wasn't the first time Bates lost a role to a prettier, thinner actress, but it must have been the bitterest loss.

Through *Misery*, she would find sweet retribution.

Bates, a native of Memphis, Tennessee, earned a BFA in acting from Southern Methodist University in 1969 and promptly began her theatrical career. For the next two decades she worked primarily on stage, but also served a stint on the soap opera *All My Children*, made a few other television appearances and played supporting parts in the films *Come Back to the Five and Dime, Jimmy Dean, Jimmy Dean* (1982) and *Arthur 2: On the Rocks* (1988). Although she was a marquee name on Broadway, most moviegoers met Kathy Bates as Annie Wilkes. She made an unforgettable first impression.

Misery is a superbly crafted chiller and a near-masterpiece of sustained suspense, but it's also, essentially, a character study. Although a few ancillary figures putter around its fringes, the narrative focuses almost exclusively on Annie and author Paul Sheldon (James Caan), and Sheldon spends most of the film simply reacting to Annie. She provides the beginning point, center and ending point for the entire story. Not since *Rosemary's Baby* had a hit horror film relied so heavily on a single female character, or on its lead actress. As a result, Annie Wilkes remains one of the most complex and fascinating of all movie psychos.

Bates once aptly described Annie as a "personality stew." *Misery* hides as much of Annie's past as it reveals. Viewers must piece together the back-story from bits of information — newspaper clippings in a scrapbook, stray lines of dialogue — and from Bates' mesmerizing performance. She's asked to appear funny, scary, sympathetic and menacing, often all at the same time. Bates somehow pulls this off, and in the process she accomplishes something even more impressive: She leaves viewers convinced that there is far more to Annie than meets the eye, that she holds unfathomable depths of yearning, heartache and rage. In this aspect, her characterization recalls Orson Welles' performance in *Citizen Kane* and Peter O'Toole's portrayal of *Lawrence of Arabia*, two other explorations of complicated and ultimately unknowable protagonists. Because Bates convinces audiences that they are seeing only the tip of the iceberg,

Writer Paul Sheldon (James Caan) and his "Number One Fan," Annie Wilkes (Kathy Bates), in *Misery* (1990). Bates helps make Wilkes one of the most complex of all movie psychos.

the inconsistencies in Annie's behavior and the murkiness of her motivations seem authentic, even inevitable, rather than distracting.

Bates' physique lends an additional layer of believability. The role requires a woman who is somewhat imposing, physically. We must believe that she can heave Caan on to her shoulder and lug him, in a fireman's carry, back to her house through knee-deep snow. Although Bates doesn't perform this stunt herself, audiences never question Annie's ability to do this. (Try that one, Michelle Pfeiffer!)

As the opening credits roll, Sheldon, a reformed author of romance novels, puts the finishing touches on a new, literary novel he hopes will establish him as a serious writer. He tosses the manuscript into a leather satchel, drives out in his 1965 Mustang, loses control of his car in a snowstorm and skids off the road. Annie rescues him — prying open his door with a crowbar, pulling him out of the vehicle and carrying him home. Sheldon has been badly injured in the crash, suffering multiple compound fractures in both legs.

At first, the author can hardly believe his good fortune, not only at his rescue, but also at the fact that his rescuer is a trained nurse and his self-proclaimed "Number One fan." Bates buzzes around his bedside and hovers over him like an attentive mother, spoon-feeding him and shaving him. Sheldon first realizes something is amiss when Annie admits that on the night of his accident, "In a way I was following you."

She explains that while he was writing in seclusion at a nearby lodge, she sat outside his cabin, looking at the light in his window and wondering "what was going on in the room of the world's greatest writer." She sighs dreamily, like a schoolgirl with a crush. But her childish adoration and motherly pampering hide the reality of the situation: Sheldon is trapped, and she has no intention of setting him free.

Annie babbles at length about how much she loves Sheldon's romance novels, which star a character named Misery Chastain. (The film's title is a pun within a pun, since romance novels are known in the trade as "miseries.") "Forgive me for prattling away and making you feel all oogy," she says, uttering the first of many infantile euphemisms Annie employs. Bates' deft delivery leverages the tension created between the silliness of Annie's euphemisms and the scariness of the thoughts they disguise.

Annie is prone to fits of displaced anger and sudden, terrifying mood swings. The first of these erupts while Annie spoon-feeds Sheldon tomato soup and complains to him about the use of profanity in his literary manuscript. Her tone of voice quickly hardens, beginning as a sort of gentle, maternal chastisement and escalating into a gravelly howl of moral outrage. She stands, her body literally shaking with rage, and spills the soup onto the bed. "Look there, look what you made me do!" She yells, snarling, furious. Then, in a flash, the tension drains from her face, replaced by a look of mild chagrin. She apologizes immediately, her tone of voice once again feathery. "I love you, Paul," she says softly. Then, realizing she has overstepped, adds: "Your mind, your creativity, that's all I meant."

Nevertheless, Annie clearly fixates romantically on the author. "Oh, Paul, what a poet you are!" she declares, moon-faced, in a later scene, using the kind of inane romantic platitudes found in her beloved romance novels. Annie is a jumble of romantic confusion and sexual frustration. Although she adores the idea of romance — lying in bed, eating Cheetos and watching *Love Connection* — Annie appears incapable of loving real people. Her offhand racism ("What's the ceiling that dago painted?") provides further evidence of this. Her true affections seem reserved for fictional characters (and her pet sow). She doesn't even love the real Sheldon. She loves her image of him, created by his celebrity, and she turns on him when the real man fails to match her expectations.

This happens when Annie finishes reading Sheldon's latest bodice-ripper, which is published while he is in her care. In an attempt to end his romance novel career, Sheldon has killed off the protagonist of his series, Annie's beloved Misery Chastain. Rather than a fit of howling rage, Bates responds with an icy indictment, which in context seems far scarier: "I thought you were good, Paul, but you're not good. You're just another lying old dirty birdy."

She forces him to burn his literary manuscript and write a new romance novel, "Misery's Return." To this end, she buys him a typewriter, paper, a chair and card table at which to write. When Sheldon asks her to return the paper and buy another type, Annie erupts again.

"Anything else I can get you while I'm in town?" Bates asks in a clipped tone, the anger just beginning to seep in. "Any other crucial requirements that need satisfying?" Her voice now drips with sarcasm. "I go out of my way for you. I do everything to make you happy." Her delivery quickens, her tone becomes even shriller, and her shoulders tighten. "I feed you, I clean you, I dress you and what thanks do I get? 'Oh, you bought the wrong paper, Annie. I can't write on this paper, Annie.' Well, I'll get you your stupid paper but you'd just better show me a little more appreciation around here, Mr. Man!" She berates him mercilessly. By the end of this breathless monologue, Bates is screaming at the top of her lungs, her eyes bulging.

While his tormentor is out, Sheldon escapes from his room and discovers Annie's scrapbook. The clippings suggest that she is not merely a crazed fan but also a serial killer who murdered her own father, a college classmate and even a series of infants during her career as a maternity nurse. This leads to the film's most notorious scene, in which Annie "hobbles" Sheldon — breaking both of his ankles with a sledgehammer — as punishment for leaving his room. At the conclusion of this gruesome procedure, while Sheldon writhes in pain, moaning in agony and gasping for breath, Annie says, "God I love you." The dreamy look in Bates' eye and a note of arousal in her voice suggests one of several possible motivations for her killings and other cruelty: It's a source of sexual gratification, perhaps her only such source.

In another of the film's most compelling sequences, Bates looks and behaves strikingly different. She appears tired, haggard, her hair disheveled. Instead of gazing lovingly (or glaring spitefully) at Sheldon, she looks away from him. "I know you don't love me, don't say you do." Her expression is nearly blank and her voice is an eerie monotone. "You'll never know the fear of losing someone like you, if you're somebody like me." Despite all we know about Annie, and as much as we fear her, audiences can't help feeling at least somewhat sympathetic toward her in this scene. Then she pulls a revolver out of the pocket of her housecoat. "I have this gun. Sometimes I think about using it. I better go now. I might put bullets in it." Bates' voice is a shaky whisper, suggesting that she's barely in control of herself. In this marvelous sequence, Bates strikes a Karloffian balance between menace and pathos.

For her superb work in *Misery*, Bates corralled a herd of glowing reviews and other honors, including the Golden Globe for Best Actress in a Drama and an Academy Award. The next year, as the reigning Best Actress Oscar champion, Bates presented Anthony Hopkins his Academy Award for *The Silence of the Lambs* (1991) — the only time in history that such an exchange has occurred between two horror film performers. Following *Misery*, Bates landed memorable roles in *At Play in the Fields of the Lord*, *Fried Green Tomatoes* (both 1991) and *Used People* (1992), cementing her position as, if not "a movie star type," then a respected leading actress, a label she would probably prefer. She earned more rave reviews for her supporting role as the "Unsinkable" Molly Brown in *Titanic* (1997) and as Jack Nicholson's love interest (of sorts) in *About Schmidt* (2002). She also served as a member of the Academy of Motion Picture Arts and Sciences Board of Governors.

Director Rob Reiner and Bates tried to recapture the *Misery* magic by reuniting for another Stephen King adaptation, *Dolores Claiborne* (1995), but the results were disappointing. She made an unbilled cameo in the television miniseries *The Stand* (1994). Her other genre credits include an appearance in the 1996 remake *Diabolique* and the eminently forgettable *My Best Friend Is a Vampire* (1988). But with her masterful portrayal in *Misery*, Bates doesn't need any further genre credits to earn the undying gratitude of horror fans.

In 2003, when the American Film Institute released its "100 Heroes and Villains" poll, Annie Wilkes appeared on the list at Number 17 among the Top 50 movie villains of all time, which placed her in the company of Hannibal Lecter (Number 1), Norman Bates (Number 2), Bela Lugosi's Dracula (Number 33) and Bette Davis' "Baby" Jane Hudson (Number 44), among others. It was a fitting tribute to Bates' brilliance, just in case that little golden statuette wasn't enough.

Oh, and one more thing: While *Misery* played to packed houses and garnered Bates an Oscar, Pfeiffer's *Frankie and Johnny* sank at the box office and was quickly forgotten.

Jodie Foster in *The Silence of the Lambs* (1992)—Horror cinema is a realm of monsters and victims. The monsters come in all varieties, from the supernatural (Bela Lugosi's Dracula) to the all-too-human (Bette Davis' "Baby" Jane Hudson). Sometimes the line between monster and victim blurs (as with Anthony Perkins' Norman Bates), and characters elicit as much pathos as fear. Most horror films feature survivors—near-victims whose actions border on the heroic (like Jamie Lee Curtis' resourceful Laurie Strode). But true heroes—characters fully aware of the monster's powers, yet who willingly put themselves in harm's way—remain a rarity in the genre. Peter Cushing's Prof. Van Helsing is one of the rare examples. So is Jodie Foster's Clarice Starling, from *The Silence of the Lambs*.

In fact, Foster's portrayal is exceptional even among the exceptions. As Clarice, Foster forges a unique, new icon—the female horror hero. This means not simply that she is a hero and that she is a woman, but that the abilities she uses to vanquish the monster are stereotypically feminine. Unlike "macho" heroines such as Sigourney Weaver's Ellen Ripley from the *Alien* films or Linda Hamilton's Sarah Connor from the *Terminator* pictures, Clarice doesn't triumph because of her physical strength and endurance. Rather, she succeeds because she is sensitive and observant. As Foster herself puts it, in an audio commentary included on the Criterion Collection DVD of *Silence of the Lambs*, "Clarice is a real female hero, not a bad imitation of a male hero."

Foster began her acting career in a Coppertone suntan lotion commercial at age three. This led to a multi-picture deal with Walt Disney Studios, where she made films such as *Freaky Friday* (1977). She also supplied the voice of Pugsly for the "Addams Family" cartoon television series. When she was just 14, she earned her first Oscar nomination for her stunning performance as a teenage prostitute in director Martin Scorsese's *Taxi Driver* (1976). She continued her career part-time, as she finished first in her class at an exclusive academy in France and graduated *magna cum laude* from Yale in 1985. Although she had no formal acting training, Foster won two Academy Awards before her thirtieth birthday. The first of these came for her wrenching portrayal of a rape victim in *The Accused* (1988). The second would be for *Lambs*.

Following *The Accused*, Foster had her pick of plum roles, but she lobbied director Jonathan Demme to play Clarice. Her enthusiasm won him over, even though she wasn't his first choice. Foster's extraordinary commitment to the character translates into a sensational performance, one of the subtlest and most touching in the history of the genre. She remains emotionally invested throughout, as she develops and embellishes a series of keynotes that resonate throughout her portrayal.

The first of these is the West Virginia accent Foster adopts for Clarice. It may or may not be authentic, but it's distinctive and sounds natural. Without ever slipping out of this accent, she subtly alters it during key scenes to underscore Clarice's emotions.

Another hallmark of Foster's performance is the aching vulnerability at its core. Clarice isn't some ice-cold, wisecracking James Bond, she's a real person who frightens relatively easily. "She's very afraid of being the victim of anything," Foster says. Throughout the film, Clarice seems to be marshalling her strength, summoning the courage to move forward despite her obvious—and reasonable—trepidation.

She grows bolder as the story progresses, but Foster never loses sight of the idea that Clarice is only a trainee, and is somewhat awestruck to find herself in the middle of an ultra–high-profile case. Clarice remains slightly timid, especially around authority figures. Foster speaks in hushed, clipped tones, especially in conversation with her superior, Jack Crawford (Scott Glenn).

Finally, Foster sells the audience on the idea that Clarice possesses, in her words, a "probing, microscopic eye." Clarice's senses are very finely attuned. She notices significant details that other detectives may have overlooked. In the end, her acute senses save her life and enable her to vanquish the serial killer, Buffalo Bill (Ted Levine).

In the film's opening sequence, Clarice, training on an obstacle course, is called in for a meeting with Crawford, head of the FBI's Behavioral Sciences unit. She rushes over, still in her perspiration-drenched sweats, and waits for Crawford in his office. Her eyes are drawn to a bulletin board full of newspaper clippings, crime scene photos and other items related to the Buffalo Bill case. As she silently surveys this morbid display, a series of emotions flashes across Foster's face: revulsion, fascination and ultimately exhilaration. This, too, becomes a recurring motif in her portrayal: Making visible Clarice's often contradictory emotions, especially the friction between her anxiety and her ambition.

Speaking with Crawford, and later with Dr. Chilton (Anthony Heald), Foster seems shy and slightly awkward. She speaks softly and at low volume, barely above a whisper at times. She also tends to look down at her shoes and avoid eye contact. She politely addresses colleagues as "sir" or "ma'am."

Chilton runs the asylum that houses captured serial killer Hannibal Lecter (Anthony Hopkins). When Clarice arrives to interview Lecter, Chilton flirts with her. Foster gulps, looks down, fidgets uncomfortably and forces a half-grin. Chilton persists, and eventually Clarice can't take any more. "I graduated from UVA, sir. It is not a charm school," Foster retorts, her voice rippling with half-suppressed indignation. She speaks more loudly, more sharply and with a slightly heavier accent. Clarice, we learn, is trying to lose her accent. In times of stress, when Clarice is less focused on her diction, Foster lays on the accent a bit thicker.

During her first interview with Lecter, Clarice teeters on the edge of overwhelming terror. As she walks down the long, dark corridor to Lecter's cell, she endures the taunts of the other inmates and struggles to hold her emotions in check. It's tempting to wonder how, if at all, Foster's approach to this scene may have been informed by her unfortunate connection with real-life psycho John Hinkley, Jr. Hinkley, who was infatuated with Foster, attempted to assassinate President Ronald Reagan in much the same way that Travis Bickle (Robert DeNiro) attempts to assassinate a presidential candidate in *Taxi Driver*. At a minimum, Foster understood the dangers of making oneself known to a homicidal lunatic.

When Lecter asks Clarice to step closer to his cell so he can inspect her identification, Foster purses her lips and stares straight ahead, as if she's trying to look straight through Lecter, instead of directly at him. Then she sits in a folding chair. She acknowledges, as Lecter has discerned from her ID, that she is a trainee, but tries to spin the admission to ingratiate herself to her reluctant interviewee.

"Yes, I am a student. I'm here to learn from you," says Foster, looking pained, laboring to stay in control of the interview. Suddenly Lecter demonstrates his powers of observation by naming Clarice's brands of skin cream and perfume. Foster looks left and right, shifts in her seat and tries to redirect the discussion by asking about Lecter's sketches. Despite Lecter's taunts, she remains courteous, forthright and direct. Then Lecter assaults her with a withering series of speculations about her upbringing. ("You know what you look like to me, with your good bag and your cheap shoes? You look like a rube.") Foster's eyes water as Lecter's rant continues, and another parade of conflicting emotions plays across her face. Hopkins comments on this moment in the same audio commentary: "You see about five different thoughts going through her face as she tries to sort of maintain her dignity, yet she's on the point of tears because he's so destroyed her. I think that's a great piece of acting."

Choking back tears, Foster keeps her head high, sets her jaw and fires back. No longer looking away, Foster levels a smoldering stare directly at Lecter. Humiliation has only made Clarice more determined than ever to complete her task. "You see a lot, Doctor," she says, her voice crackling with pain and anger. "But are you strong enough to point that high-powered perception at yourself?"

Clarice grows more confident with Lecter in subsequent interviews. During the next one, having come in from the rain, she sits cross-legged on the floor, with a towel over her head. Then Lecter offers to assist with the Buffalo Bill case. "I'll help you catch him, Clarice," he coos. Foster drops the towel, stands and gazes at Lecter, her curiosity piqued. In this moment, Clarice's ambition overtakes her fear.

Another key sequence occurs soon afterward, when she accompanies Crawford and assists with the autopsy of Buffalo Bill's latest victim, back in her home state of West Virginia. Clarice, obviously, is ill at ease, surrounded by a dozen or more strapping, good-old-boy local lawmen, all eating donuts and drinking coffee over a body bag containing the victim. Yet she summons up the courage to usher the locals out so they can proceed with the autopsy. Again, under stress, her accent grows more pronounced: "Uh, 'scuse me. 'Scuse me, gentlemen. Officers and gentlemen, listen here now. There's things we need to do for her."

When the bag is unzipped and the body revealed, Foster again looks on with mixed emotions: horror, excitement, compassion and ambition. What lies ahead is gruesome, heartbreaking work, but it's what she has committed herself to and trained for. She brings her keen powers of observation to bear on the body and ascertains that the victim was from an urban area (based on the style of her nail polish), and spots a moth carapace lodged in the victim's throat. "She starts out as one woman and after this [autopsy] scene she's somebody totally different," Foster says in the DVD commentary. "This is where the hero accepts the tasks. From then on, she's totally obsessed with finding the killer of this woman."

Her determination to catch Buffalo Bill becomes apparent during Clarice's next interview with Lecter. He toys with her, hinting indirectly without divulging anything very helpful. His demeanor stays loose and leisurely, while she becomes a coiled spring. "You're so close to the way you're going to catch him, do you know that?" Hopkins says, languidly. "No—tell me why," Foster replies quickly, her words sharp, frustrated. Her entire body is tense. She's literally on the edge of her seat.

Lecter trades information for details about Clarice's childhood and personal life. Some read a sexual or romantic component into these exchanges, but Foster, Hopkins and Demme deny this was their intent, and there's little evidence of it in the film. When, during her final interview with Lecter, he jokes, "People will say we're in love," Clarice recoils. Foster breathes in, takes a step back and looks sickened.

She is more intent than ever in this last session, bordering on panicky in her exasperated pleas for Lecter to reveal Buffalo Bill's identity. "Doctor, we don't have any more time for this now!" she complains. But Lecter insists they continue their "quid pro quo" arrangement, so Clarice relates the story of how, as a young girl, she was sent away from her uncle's farm after trying in vain to save a lamb from the slaughter. Clarice becomes so engrossed in the story that she forgets about Buffalo Bill, at least for a few minutes. As she tells her tale, the camera dollies in. Foster's eyes glisten and grow moist. She delivers her lines breathlessly and her voice softens into a near-whisper. "I thought if I could save just one, but he was so heavy... so heavy...." She falls silent and looks away. With the Buffalo Bill case, Clarice is trying to save a different sort of lamb, a young woman abducted by the killer, who keeps his victims alive for a short time before killing them.

Originally, Demme planned a surrealistic flashback sequence, involving crane shots and other elaborate camera movements, to dramatize this story, with Foster heard only in voiceover. But after viewing the rushes, he scrapped the idea. "The greatest shots in the world visualizing what she's talking about couldn't begin to match the power of her telling of it," Demme says in the audio commentary. "How could you cut away from that face?"

Silence of the Lambs concludes with the inevitable showdown between Clarice and Buffalo Bill. All the threads of Foster's performance weave together to make this an unforgettable climax.

Clarice's mental radar clicks on when Bill makes a rude remark about a murder victim: "Was she a great big, fat person?"

"She was a big girl, sir," Foster replies, and shoots him a look of sufferance, edged with suspicion. Bill invites her into his home, where she spots a telltale moth resting on a spool of thread. A look of cold realization grips her, and she quietly unsnaps the holster of her sidearm. She tries to maintain her cool, but can only contain herself for a few more seconds. She draws her revolver and shouts, "Freeze!"

Foster pronounces the word as if it contained two syllables, her accent suddenly its thickest of the entire film. When she commands him to "spread your legs," it sounds more like "sprayed yer laigs." Clarice is no longer even remotely concerned with looking or sounding proper—she only cares about rescuing the young victim and apprehending the killer.

Bill flees into his house-of-horrors basement and Clarice follows. Foster sets her jaw and grits her teeth, sweating and grunting as she searches for the killer. Bill, wearing a pair of night vision goggles, traps her in a pitch-dark room, but Clarice's sensory powers rescue her. She hears the click of Bill cocking his pistol, spins and fires.

For her gripping performance, Foster earned glowing reviews and a nearly clean sweep of all the Best Actress awards doled out in 1992, including her second Oscar. Editor Phil Hardy's *Horror Film Encyclopedia* reflects the general consensus: "Foster carries the picture as Agent Clarice Starling, an unusually detailed protagonist who is presented as a complex individual without seeming to trail soap-opera traumas."

In all, *Silence of the Lambs* raked in five Academy Awards, including Best Picture, Best Director, Best Actor (Hopkins) and Best Adapted Screenplay. It was also a blockbuster hit, spawning two sequels and an ongoing series of imitations—chillers like *Seven* and the aptly titled *Copycat* (both 1995), which walk the border between the police procedural and the horror film. However, few of its successors have employed horrific elements as expertly as *Lambs* or created monsters as memorable as Hannibal Lecter and Buffalo Bill. And none have introduced a hero the equal of Clarice Starling.

Foster made her directorial debut with an episode of the television horror anthology *Tales from the Darkside* in 1984. Following *Lambs*, she starred in the science fiction epic *Contact* (1997) and in David Fincher's claustrophobic thriller *Panic Room* (2002). For the most part, however, she has stuck with non-genre productions, such as *Nell* (1994), which earned her a fourth Oscar nomination.

In the wake of *Lambs*' Oscar sweep, Foster said she would be willing to play Clarice again in a sequel. However, it took nearly a decade for author Thomas Harris to write the novel, and Foster balked after reading the story Harris had concocted. She was displeased with the way Clarice was portrayed, and backed out of the film adaptation *Hannibal* (2001). Julianne Moore assumed the role, but Foster proved irreplaceable. In fairness to Moore, however, it's unlikely that even Foster herself could have duplicated the magic of *Silence of the Lambs*. For most actors, such a perfect alignment of player and part comes just once in a lifetime—if it arrives at all.

Within horror cinema, characters like Clarice Starling come along about as frequently.

Other Leading Ladies—While researching and writing this section of this book, it became apparent that examining the contributions women have made to the horror genre, and how their performances reflected the changing roles of women over the course of the 20th century, would make for a compelling book in and of

Opposite: Good as gold: A beaming Jodie Foster poses with her well-earned Oscar for ***The Silence of the Lambs*** (1992).

itself. I could provide only a bird's eye-level overview of the subject here, which forced me to make some agonizing choices about which performances to review in depth. Many of the following "other" portrayals are landmarks themselves:

Any discussion of horror's "leading ladies" must pay tribute to the original "scream queen," **Fay Wray**. She began her career in silent films and worked regularly, in all sorts of pictures until 1958. She returned to the screen to co-star with Henry Fonda in the television movie *Gideon's Trumpet* in 1980, 57 years after her first screen appearance. Yet she remains best known for shrieking her way through a series of Golden Age chillers: *Doctor X, The Most Dangerous Game* (both 1932), *The Vampire Bat, Mystery of the Wax Museum, King Kong* (all 1933), *Black Moon* and *The Clairvoyant* (both 1934). She routinely brought more to these projects than her wafer-thin roles merited.

Although immortalized for playing "beauty" to Kong's "beast" in Merian C. Cooper's landmark fantasy, Wray's finest genre work came in the lesser known Cooper film *The Most Dangerous Game*. She plays Eve Trowbridge, the female captive of crazed sportsman Count Zaroff (Leslie Banks), who hunts human castaways on his remote island home. Wray's performance divides cleanly into two equally impressive parts. During the story's first half, she deftly handles tricky dialogue scenes, such as one in which she tries to act nonchalant in front of Zaroff, while simultaneously warning new arrival Bob Rainsford (Joel McCrea) that he's in danger. In the second half, with Eve and Taylor on the run from Zaroff, Wray's expressive physicality takes center stage. Not until Jamie Lee Curtis in *Halloween*, some 56 years later, would an actress perform action sequences so memorably in a horror film.

Miriam Hopkins made the most of her lone genre appearance as Ivy, the star-crossed barmaid from director Rouben Mamoulian's *Dr. Jekyll and Mr. Hyde* (1931). Her scenes with co-star Fredric March rank among the most erotic (when March is Jekyll) and harrowing (when March is Hyde) of the era. Despite limited screen time, Hopkins creates a believable, multi-faceted (good-hearted, sexy, vulnerable) character. Even the great Ingrid Bergman, who played the role of Ivy in the 1941 remake, couldn't match Hopkins' exquisite performance.

Frances Drake delivered one of the most resonant supporting performances of horror's Golden Age as the object of Peter Lorre's obsessive affection in *Mad Love* (1935). Drake tackles a number of emotionally pitched sequences, all of which she plays expertly, using her large, expressive eyes to great effect. In one of the film's most memorable sequences, she attempts to fool her deranged admirer by posing as a wax likeness of herself. Standing perfectly still, trying not even to breathe, she radiates tension. Drake also co-starred with Boris Karloff and Bela Lugosi in *The Invisible Ray* (1936).

Some would argue that any list of this type should include **Elsa Lanchester**'s iconic role in *Bride of Frankenstein* (1935). Lanchester was a fine actress, but *Bride* does not rank among her best work. Makeup genius Jack Pierce deserves most of the credit for the enduring image of the Bride. Lanchester appears as this character for a scant few minutes, hisses and gets blown to smithereens. This is not the stuff of a great performance.

Margaret Hamilton rates a mention for her timeless portrayal of the Wicked

King and Queen: "Scream Queen" Fay Wray is pictured here with her most famous co-star, from *King Kong* (1933).

Witch of the West in *The Wizard of Oz* (1939). This may not be a horror film, but Hamilton's is definitely a horror performance, and a scary one at that. Hamilton may have given more children nightmares than any other actress! Her performance provides the textbook illustration of fairy tale-style evil.

Russian-born **Maria Ouspenskaya**, who studied acting under Constantin Stanislavsky, won critical acclaim during her Continental stage career and on Broadway. She founded the School of Dramatic Art in New York and became one of the first Method disciples in Hollywood. Ouspenskaya received an Academy Award nomination, as Best Actress in a Supporting Role, for *Dodsworth* in 1936. Yet, for all these accomplishments, she remains best known for her evocative performance as Maleva, the kind-hearted gypsy woman who befriends Larry Talbot (Lon Chaney, Jr.) in *The Wolf Man* (1941) and *Frankenstein Meets the Wolf Man* (1943). Maleva remains one of the most vividly drawn supporting characters in horror cinema, and a fitting tribute to Ouspenskaya's formidable talent. The actress also appeared in the Universal mystery-chiller *The Mystery of Marie Roget* (1942) and RKO's *Tarzan and the Amazons* (1945).

If Fay Wray was the queen of horror films in the 1930s, then **Evelyn Ankers** inherited her crown in the 1940s. The Chilean-born Ankers appeared in more horror

Ilona Carr (Evelyn Ankers) tries to worm her way back into the affections of professor Norman Reed (Lon Chaney, Jr.) in *Weird Woman* (1944). This is Ankers' most atypical, yet finest, performance.

and borderline horror films than any other actress of the decade, often starring opposite Lon Chaney, Jr. (whom she detested personally). Her filmography includes *Hold That Ghost*, *The Wolf Man* (both 1941), *Sherlock Holmes and the Voice of Terror*, *The Ghost of Frankenstein*, *The Great Impersonation* (all 1942), *Captive Wild Woman*, *Son of Dracula*, *The Mad Ghoul* (all 1943), *Weird Woman*, *Jungle Woman*, *The Invisible Man's Revenge*, *The Pearl of Death* (all 1944), *The Frozen Ghost* (1945) and *Tarzan's Magic Fountain* (1949). Ankers always performed capably, usually cast as the "good girl" menaced by the monster. She plays this role to near-perfection in *The Wolf Man*, as the sweetheart of the doomed Larry Talbot (Chaney).

Ankers displayed unexpected range as Ilona Carr, the jealous ex-lover of sociologist Norman Reed (Chaney again), in *Weird Woman*. Ilona is a would-be homewrecker who, unable to pry Norman away from his new wife (Anne Gwynne), conspires to set the professor's colleagues and students against him. Ankers' silkysmooth handling of this material suggests that, given half a chance, she might have become the feminine counterpart of the world's greatest cad, George Sanders. Ankers finds herself out of her depth in the film's final scenes, which require her to undergo a nervous breakdown, but her work in *Weird Woman* remains the most unusual and satisfying of her career.

Louise Allbritton's vivid villainy enlivens the underrated *Son of Dracula* (1943). Allbritton affects a cold, diamond-hard demeanor, playing a conniving Southern Belle who willingly gives herself to Dracula in order to gain eternal life. She later tries to seduce her fiancé into killing Dracula and joining her as one of the undead. Allbritton acts circles around a badly miscast Lon Chaney, Jr., and walks away with one of the most striking performances of the decade. Sadly, this was the only genre appearance for Allbritton, whose too-short big-screen career spanned 22 films, from 1942 to 1949.

Esteemed British actress **Anna Lee** claimed the co-starring role in producer Val Lewton's chiller *Bedlam* (1946), opposite Boris Karloff. She plays a sharp-tongued critic of Master Sims, administrator of the notorious St. Mary's of Bethlehem (Bedlam) asylum. Her assured, straight-faced performance lends credibility to this hoary melodrama about a headstrong woman wrongly committed to Sim's not-so-tender care. Lee appeared alongside Karloff once before, in the British mad medico movie *The Man Who Lived Again* (a.k.a. *The Man Who Changed His Mind*, 1936). Later, she played a memorable supporting role in *What Ever Happened to Baby Jane?* (1962), as the Hudson sisters' neighbor, and appeared in the *Baby Jane*–like *Picture Mommy Dead* (1966). Her prolific screen career stretched from 1932 to 1994 and also included films such as *How Green Was My Valley* (1941), *Fort Apache* (1948) and *The Sound of Music* (1965).

Gloria Talbott's startling performance in *I Married a Monster from Outer Space* (1958) goes a long way toward making this overlooked film far more gripping and resonant than its asinine title suggests. Talbott enjoys a rare female leading role in a science fiction chiller from this era, painting a touching portrait of a confused, frightened woman who realizes her husband has literally become a monster. Only *I Married a Monster*'s shaky status as a horror film (most would classify it as sci-fi) precludes this portrayal from detailed discussion. Talbott's fine work here seems to have been an anomaly. She was terrible in the title role of *Daughter of Dr. Jekyll* (1957) and forgettable in *The Cyclops* (1957) and *The Leech Woman* (1960).

Coleen Gray, however, sank her teeth into the meaty title role of *The Leech Woman* (1960). Her Jekyll-and-Hyde part calls for her to play a bitter, fiftyish lush who transforms herself into a beautiful, sexually predatory young woman — by killing young men. She excels in both facets of this characterization, despite the handicap of some unconvincing age makeup. Gray made other memorable film appearances as Victor Mature's devoted wife in *Kiss of Death* (1947) and as a femme fatale in Stanley Kubrick's *The Killing* (1956). Her other genre credits include *The Vampire* (1957) and *The Phantom Planet* (1961).

Although *Psycho* (1960) remains Anthony Perkins' film, at least from an acting perspective, director Alfred Hitchcock's carefully constructed cinematic funhouse would have crumbled if audiences didn't sympathize with Marion Crane. **Janet Leigh**'s vivid, Oscar-nominated performance draws viewers into the narrative and sets them up for the shocks that follow. Leigh excelled in a number of roles, but this remains her finest work. Because of *Psycho*, the actress became readily associated with horror films, but she didn't return to the genre until much later in her career, for *The Fog* (1980) and *Halloween H20: Twenty Years Later* (1998), both of which featured her daughter, Jamie Lee Curtis.

The gifted **Julie Harris** worked primarily on the stage, but made occasional appearances in film and television, including a single, unforgettable horror movie, *The Haunting* (1963). Harris plays Eleanor Lance, a timid, bookish young woman who joins a group of researchers investigating psychic phenomena at a notorious haunted house. Eleanor becomes the focal point for all the ghostly goings-on in the house, and the lens through which the audience sees the story. Utilizing voiceover narration, the film takes the viewer inside Eleanor's mind itself, as she begins to crack under the pressure of numerous unexplainable events. Harris exploits this showy role brilliantly. Everything about *The Haunting* is first-rate, but Harris' performance stands as one of this watershed film's primary strengths.

Daliah Lavi delivered one of the greatest performances that most people have never seen in director Mario Bava's kinky chiller *The Whip and the Body*. Butchered by censors all over the world in 1963, it had its initial American release in a truncated version sporting the incomprehensible title *What!* The film languished, overlooked and under-appreciated, for decades until it was finally restored to director Mario Bava's original vision (and title) for U.S. DVD release. Lavi portrays Nevenka, a young heiress entangled in a sadomasochistic relationship with her brother-in-law, Kurt (Christopher Lee). After Kurt is killed, Nevenka believes his ghost has returned to torment (and arouse) her. Lavi's confident, touching and uninhibited performance makes Nevenka perhaps the most emotionally complex character ever to grace a European horror film.

When British actress **Barbara Shelley** made her film debut in Terence Fisher's 1953 mystery *Mantrap*, neither she nor her director could have suspected they would eventually become readily associated with monster movies. Yet Fisher emerged as England's foremost director of screen chillers, and Shelley, beginning with *Cat Girl* (1957), appeared in more genre films than any other actress during the next ten years: *Blood of the Vampire* (1958), *Village of the Damned* (1960), *Shadow of the Cat* (1961), *The Gorgon* (1964), *Dracula, Prince of Darkness* and *Rasputin, the Mad Monk* (both 1966) and *Quatermass and the Pit* (1967), adding a touch of class to even the most meager of these productions. She later returned to the genre for *Ghost Story* (1974) and the television movie *Dark Angel* (1987).

Shelley's best performances came in near-horror movies, rather than full-blooded chillers — the historical melodrama *Rasputin* and the science fiction yarns *Village of the Damned* and *Quatermass and the Pit*. She's particularly effective in the *Quatermass* picture. A five million-year-old Martian space capsule is unearthed during a London subway expansion. The spacecraft, it turns out, is a living entity, and Shelley becomes the conduit for extraterrestrial psychic energy emitted by the craft. The actress' levelheaded, naturalistic performance lends emotional credibility to this risible scenario.

Fellow Brit **Hazel Court** rivaled Shelley in popularity during this era. Shelley may have been the more skilled actress, but Court had more sex appeal. Court's early performances are a bit awkward, but she improved markedly throughout her career and contributed memorable portrayals to several early '60s chillers, none more striking than her turn in *The Masque of the Read Death* (1964). Court plays Juliana, a courtesan who has fallen out of favor with the jaded Prince Prospero (Vincent Price). Desperate to recapture his interest, she throws herself into his satanic rituals and even brands herself, all to no avail. Price achieves thespian perfection as Prospero, but Court's performance proves surprisingly moving. Her filmography also includes *Ghost Ship* (1952), *Devil Girl from Mars* (1954), *The Curse of Frankenstein* (1957), *The Man Who Could Cheat Death* (1959), *Dr. Blood's Coffin* (1961), *The Premature Burial* (1962), *The Raven* (1963) and an uncredited cameo appearance in *Omen III: The Final Conflict* (1981).

Sigourney Weaver and **Glenn Close** both deserve a tip of the cap for their Oscar nominations for *Aliens* (1986) and *Fatal Attraction* (1987), two films that skirt the periphery of the horror genre. Both performances are impeccable.

And, finally, apologies to all the actresses whose fine work just missed appearing in this section. I would love to go on, but I've run out of book.

Appendix: Horror Cinema and the Academy Awards

They lurked in haunted houses, stalked through foggy forests and reigned in Carpathian castles. And, for decades, they have haunted the imaginations of movie fans around the world. But one place always remained safe from the great horror stars—the Academy Awards presentation.

Legendary performers such as Boris Karloff, Bela Lugosi, Vincent Price and Peter Cushing share zero Academy Awards. This is hardly surprising since, usually, actors who appear in horror films can expect nothing better than kind reviews as their highest reward even for a brilliant portrayal. There are notable exceptions, of course, and the tide may be turning. In both 1999 (Haley Joel Osment in *The Sixth Sense*) and 2000 (Willem Dafoe in *Shadow of the Vampire*), actors appearing in horror films were nominated for Best Actor in a Supporting Role. Nevertheless, for most of cinema history, horror films have not garnered the critical respect afforded other movies. Apparently they carry less critical cache than other genre pictures like Westerns or musicals.

A quick scan of the Academy Award record book returns some surprising results, in terms of what performances gained Oscar recognition, and which did not.

Oscar-nominated Horror Performances

What follows is a chronological list of horror and borderline-horror films that featured performances honored by the Academy of Motion Picture Arts and Sciences. For the sake of consistency with the remainder of this book, I have excluded performances from fantasy and science fiction films.

For some reason, the Academy has more readily honored performances by women in horror films. Of the 32 Oscar nominees to emerge from horror and borderline-horror films, 23 have been women (that's nearly 72 percent). Five of the seven Oscar winners from this group were women.

1931: Fredric March. Won for Best Actor in a Leading Role for *Dr. Jekyll and Mr. Hyde.*—One of the watershed performances in horror cinema history, and a worthy Oscar champion (although perhaps not as worthy as Boris Karloff's Frankenstein Monster, which failed to earn a nomination). March's accomplishment was diminished slightly when the Academy elected to give a second Oscar in the same category to Wallace Beery, nominated for his work in the boxing drama *The Champ*. Beery had finished just one vote behind March in the balloting.

1937: Robert Montgomery. Nominated for Best Actor in a Leading Role for *Night Must Fall*. Plays a likable young man who may or may not be a murderer, carrying the head of a decapitated victim in a hatbox. Best known as a light comic actor, Montgomery showed unexpected range in this borderline-horror gem.

1937: Dame May Whitty. Nominated for Best Actress in a Supporting Role for *Night Must Fall.*—Whitty, always an impressive performer, here plays the crusty old woman who hires Montgomery as her live-in handyman.

1937: Roland Young. Nominated for Best Actor in a Supporting Role for *Topper*. Young plays the title role in this comedy, about an ordinary guy whose life is turned upside-down by a pair of friendly ghosts.

1941: Walter Huston. Nominated for Best Actor in a Leading Role for *All That Money Can Buy*, a.k.a. *The Devil and Daniel Webster*. Huston plays "Scratch" in this adaptation of this classic yarn about a farmer who sells his soul to the Devil, but wins it back in a very unusual "court."

1944: Charles Boyer. Nominated for Best Actor in a Leading Role for *Gaslight*. In this borderline-horror suspense film, Boyer plays the duplicitous husband of a wealthy widow. He intends to drive her insane in order to gain control of her estate.

1944: Ingrid Bergman. Won Best Actress in a Leading Role for *Gaslight*. She earned the Oscar for her tumultuous performance as Boyer's bedeviled wife.

1944: Angela Lansbury. Nominated for Best Actress in a Supporting Role for *Gaslight*. Lansbury provides a memorable performance as Nancy, Bergman's confidant.

1945: Angela Lansbury. Nominated for Best Actress in a Supporting Role for *The Picture of Dorian Gray*. As Sibyl, Lansbury gives another remarkable performance in this superb adaptation of the classic Oscar Wilde story. The rest of the ensemble cast also excels.

1946: Ethel Barrymore. Nominated for Best Actress in a Supporting Role for *The Spiral Staircase*. Barrymore is very good in this taut little thriller from director Robert Siodmak. But her portrayal pales next to Dorothy McGuire's harrowing lead performance as a mute woman being stalked by a killer.

1956: Nancy Kelly. Nominated for Best Actress in a Leading Role for *The Bad Seed*. Kelly was nominated for her performance as the mother of a psychotic young girl in this borderline-horror drama. Unfortunately, all the performances in this film seem campy and badly dated today, especially Kelly's.

1956: Patty McCormack. Nominated for Best Actress in a Supporting Role for *The Bad Seed*. She plays Nancy Kelly's homicidal daughter. Her performance hasn't aged well, either.

1956: Eileen Heckart. Nominated for Best Actress in a Supporting Role for *The Bad Seed*. Yet another overrated performance from this film. She's not as bad as Kelly or McCormack, however.

1960: Janet Leigh. Nominated for Best Actress in a Supporting Role for *Psycho*. Honored for her ageless portrayal of the doomed Marion Crane in Alfred Hitchcock's landmark chiller.

1962: Bette Davis. Nominated for Best Actress in a Leading Role for *What Ever Happened to Baby Jane?* Davis' courageous, mesmerizing performance as an aging former child star earned her a well-deserved Oscar nomination (the last of her eight — she won two).

1962: Victor Buono. Nominated for Best Actor in a Supporting Role for *What Ever Happened to Baby Jane?* Buono plays the oily, unctuous accompanist Jane hires for her planned return to the stage. He is simply marvelous in the role.

1962: Angela Lansbury. Nominated for Best Actress in a Supporting Role for *The Manchurian Candidate*. Lansbury contributes a chilling, career-best performance as the mother of a brainwashed assassin in John Frankenheimer's classic paranoid thriller. This film borders both the science fiction and horror genres.

1964: Agnes Moorehead. Nominated for Best Actress in a Supporting Role for *Hush ... Hush, Sweet Charlotte*. Moorehead, always a brilliant actress, plays Bette Davis' long-suffering servant in this *Baby Jane* clone.

1968: Ruth Gordon. Won Best Actress in a Supporting Role for *Rosemary's Baby*. Gordon, another reliable veteran actress, plays Mia Farrow's apparently kindly neighbor, who's secretly plotting to mate Farrow with Satan himself.

1973: Ellen Burstyn. Nominated for Best Actress in a Leading Role for *The Exorcist*. Burstyn offers one of the most haunting performances in horror cinema history, playing the mother of a young girl possessed by the Devil.

1973: Linda Blair. Nominated for Best Actress in a Supporting Role for *The Exorcist*. Blair matches Burstyn note-for-note as Regan, Burstyn's possessed daughter.

1973: Jason Miller. Nominated for Best Actor in a Supporting Role for *The Exorcist*. Miller also excels as Father Karras, the young priest who battles to free Regan from Satan's grasp.

1976: Sissy Spacek. Nominated for Best Actress in a Leading Role for *Carrie*. Spacek was nominated for her evocative portrayal in the title role of this chiller about an awkward teenage girl with telekinetic abilities.

1976: Piper Laurie. Nominated for Best Actress in a Supporting Role for *Carrie*. She played Spacek's abusive, repressed mother.

1986: Sigourney Weaver. Nominated for Best Actress in a Leading Role for *Aliens*. Weaver, who was impressive in the first *Alien* film (1979) tops herself in her second turn as Ripley, the tough-nosed but kind-hearted survivor-heroine. Generally, I have excluded science fiction films from this list, but *Aliens* includes enough horror elements to push it to the borders of horror.

1987: Glenn Close. Nominated for Best Actress in a Leading Role for *Fatal Attraction*. Close gives a bone-chilling performance as the Michael Douglas' obsessed, homicidal ex-lover in this borderline-horror thriller.

1987: Anne Archer. Nominated for Best Actress in a Supporting Role for *Fatal Attraction*. She plays the faithful wife of the philandering Douglas.

1990: Kathy Bates. Won Best Actress in a Leading Role for *Misery*. Bates plays author James Caan's "Number One Fan" in this twisted chiller. She holds Caan hostage, tortures him and forces him to write a romance novel. Truly terrifying.

1990: Whoopi Goldberg. Won Best Actress in a Supporting Role for *Ghost*. Earned the Oscar for her primarily comic portrayal of a phony medium who suddenly becomes the conduit for a real ghost, who's trying to solve the mystery of his own murder.

1991: Anthony Hopkins. Won Best Actor in a Leading Role for *The Silence of the Lambs*. "I ate his liver with some fava beans and a nice Chianti."

1991: Jodie Foster. Won Best Actress in a Leading Role for *The Silence of the Lambs*. Foster is the glue that holds this superb chiller together.

1999: Haley Joel Osment. Nominated for Best Actor in a Supporting Role for *The Sixth Sense*. Osment provides the emotional center for this masterful horror film. Arguably, he deserved a nomination in the Leading Role category.

2000: Willem Dafoe. Nominated for Best Actor in a Supporting Role for *Shadow of the Vampire*. Dafoe plays Max Schreck, the actor who played Count Orlok in F.W. Murnau's classic *Nosferatu*. The film's conceit is that Schreck was a real vampire. Dafoe does an amazing Schreck imitation, but fails to build a fully developed character.

In addition, two men have earned nominations for portraying horror film personalities. In 1994, Martin Landau won Best Actor in a Supporting Role for *Ed Wood*. Landau earned the Oscar for his colorful, unforgettable portrayal of horror icon Bela Lugosi. In 1997, Ian McKellan was nominated for Best Actor in a Leading Role for *Gods and Monsters*. McKellan deserved to win, but did not, for his moving performance as legendary horror director James Whale. Later, McKellan was nominated in the Supporting Actor category for his role as the wizard Gandalf *in The Lord of the Rings: The Fellowship of the Rings* (2001).

Noteworthy Performances That Did Not Receive Oscar Nominations

This list could be quite lengthy, but here are a few of the more striking omissions by the Academy, followed by the Academy's choices for the same year.

Bela Lugosi as *Dracula* (1931)—Eligible for the 1930-31 Academy Awards. Lionel Barrymore won the Oscar for *A Free Soul*. The Academy's other nominees were Richard Dix for *Cimarron*, Adolphe Menjou for *The Front Page*, Fredric March for *The Royal Family of Broadway* and Jackie Cooper for *Skippy*.

Boris Karloff in *Frankenstein* (1931)—Eligible for the 1931-32 Academy Awards. Fredric March and Wallace Beery were co-winners, for *Dr. Jekyll and Mr. Hyde* and *The Champ*, respectively. The Academy's other nominee was Alfred Lunt in *The Guardsman*.

Claude Rains in *The Invisible Man* and Charles Laughton in *Island of Lost Souls* (both 1933)—Charles Laughton won the Oscar for *The Private Life of Henry VIII*. The Academy's other nominees were Leslie Howard for *Berkeley Square* and Paul Muni for *I Am a Fugitive from a Chain Gang*.

Peter Lorre in *Mad Love* (1935)—Victor McLaglen won the Oscar for *The Informer*. The Academy's other nominees were Paul Muni for *Black Fury* and Clark Gable, Charles Laughton and Franchot Tone for *Mutiny on the Bounty*.

Lon Chaney, Jr., as *The Wolf Man* (1941)—Gary Cooper won the Oscar for *Sergeant York*. The Academy's other nominees were Orson Welles for *Citizen Kane*, Walter Huston for *All That Money Can Buy*, Robert Montgomery for *Here Comes Mr. Jordan* and Cary Grant for *Penny Serenade*.

Peter Cushing in *Horror of Dracula* (1958)—Another Brit, David Niven, won the Oscar for *Separate Tables*. The Academy's other nominees were Paul Newman for *Cat on a Hot Tin Roof*, Tony Curtis for *The Defiant Ones*, Sidney Poitier for *The Defiant Ones* and Spencer Tracy for *The Old Man and the Sea*.

Anthony Perkins in *Psycho* (1960)—Burt Lancaster won the Oscar for *Elmer Gantry*. The Academy's other nominees were Jack Lemmon in *The Apartment*, Laurence Olivier in *The Entertainer*, Spencer Tracy in *Inherit the Wind* and Trevor Howard in *Sons and Lovers*.

Vincent Price in *The Masque of the Red Death* (1964)—Rex Harrison won the Oscar for *My Fair Lady*. The Academy's other nominees were Anthony Quinn for *Zorba the Greek*, Richard Burton and Peter O'Toole for *Becket* and Peter Sellers for *Dr. Strangelove*.

Mia Farrow in *Rosemary's Baby*, Duane Jones in *Night of the Living Dead*, Boris Karloff in *Targets*, Christopher Lee in *The Devil's Bride* and Vincent Price in *The Conqueror Worm* (all 1968)—Cliff Robertson won the Oscar for *Charly* in the

Best Actor in a Leading Role category. The Academy's other nominees for that award were Alan Bates in *The Fixer*, Alan Arkin *in The Heart is a Lonely Hunter*, Peter O'Toole for *The Lion in Winter* and Ron Moody for *Oliver!* Barbra Streisand (for *Funny Girl*) and Katharine Hepburn (for *The Lion in Winter*) were co-winners in the Best Actress in a Leading Role category. The Academy's other nominees for that award were Vanessa Redgrave for *Isadora*, Joanne Woodward for *Rachel, Rachel* and Patricia Neal for *The Subject Was Roses*.

Jamie Lee Curtis in *Halloween* (1978) — Jane Fonda won the Oscar for *Coming Home*. The Academy's other nominees were Ingrid Bergman in *Autumn Sonata*, Geraldine Page in *Interiors*, Ellen Burstyn in *Same Time, Next Year* and Jill Clayburgh in *An Unmarried Woman*.

Horror Performers Who Have Been Nominated for Academy Awards

Genre fans may be surprised to learn that some actors and actresses recognizable from horror films earned Oscar nominations for non-horror roles. This list includes some of the more notable of these performers:

Lionel Barrymore — Star of two Tod Browning chillers (*Mark of the Vampire* and *The Devil-Doll*) was named Best Actor in a Leading Role for his performance in *A Free Soul* (1931).

Joan Crawford — Won the Oscar for Best Actress in a Leading Role for the noir classic *Mildred Pierce* (1945) and earned other nominations for *Humoresque* (1946) and *Sudden Fear* (1952). She began her career in silent films, including the Tod Browning-Lon Chaney classic *The Unknown* (1927), co-starred in the influential *What Ever Happened to Baby Jane?* (1962) and ended her career in a string of decreasingly impressive horror and science fiction films, including director William Castle's campy *Strait-Jacket*.

Emil Jannings — The man who played Mephisto in F.W. Murnau's *Faust* won the first-ever Oscar for Best Actor in a Leading Role for his performances in *Way of the Flesh* (1927) and *The Last Command* (1928).

Elsa Lanchester — The Bride of Frankenstein herself was nominated as Best Actress in a Supporting Role for her work in *Come to the Stable* (1949).

Charles Laughton — Won the Oscar for Best Actor in a Leading Role for *The Private Life of Henry VIII* (1933) and earned nominations for *Mutiny on the Bounty* (1935) and *Witness for the Prosecution* (1957). Genre fans remember Laughton from films such as *The Old Dark House* (1932), *Island of Lost Souls* (1933) and *The Hunchback of Notre Dame* (1939). He was married to Elsa Lanchester.

J. Carrol Naish—Familiar to horror fans primarily for his portrayal of Daniel, the lovesick hunchback in *House of Frankenstein*. He was nominated for Best Actor in a Supporting Role for *A Medal for Benny* (1945).

Maria Ouspenskaya—Best remembered as Maleva, the old gypsy woman from *The Wolf Man*, Ouspenskaya was nominated as Best Actress in a Supporting Role for *Dodsworth* (1936). Ouspenskaya also taught acting, and was one of the first to bring the Stanislavsky "Method" to Hollywood.

Anthony Perkins—Before he played Norman Bates in *Psycho*, Perkins was nominated for Best Actor in a Supporting Role for *Friendly Persuasion* (1956), a Civil War drama starring Gary Cooper. Perkins played a troubled teenager, as he often did at this point in his career.

Claude Rains—One of Hollywood's most distinguished actors, Rains earned four Academy Award nominations for Best Actor in a Supporting Role: *Mr. Smith Goes to Washington* (1939, as a corrupt senator), *Casablanca* (1942, as the morally suspect chief of police), *Mr. Skeffington* (1944, as the selfless husband of Bette Davis) and *Notorious* (as a lovestruck Nazi spy). He earned the unflagging devotion of genre fans for his performances in *The Invisible Man* (1933), *The Wolf Man* (1941) and *Phantom of the Opera* (1943), among other films.

Basil Rathbone—Was twice nominated as Best Actor in a Supporting Role (for *Romeo and Juliet* in 1936 and *If I Were King* in 1938), but never won an Oscar. His list of horror credits is long and distinguished.

Gale Sondergaard—One of the screen's all-time great villainesses got her due from the Academy in 1936, when she won the Oscar for Best Actress in a Supporting Role, based on her devilishly delightful performance in *Anthony Adverse* as Olivia De Havilland's nemesis.

Erich von Stroheim—"The Man You Love to Hate" earned a nomination as Best Actor in a Supporting Role for his stern yet evocative portrayal of Norma Desmond's husband-turned-butler in *Sunset Blvd.* (1950).

Bibliography

Books

Beck, Calvin Thomas. *Heroes of the Horrors*. New York: Collier Books, 1975.
Bogdanovich, Peter. *Who the Devil Made It*. New York: Alfred A. Knopf, 1997.
Bona, Damien, and Mason Wiley. *Inside Oscar: 10th Anniversary Edition, The Unofficial History of the Academy Awards*. New York: Ballantine Books, 1996.
Brunas, John, Michael Brunas, and Tom Weaver. *Universal Horrors: The Studio's Classic Films, 1931–1946*. Jefferson NC: McFarland, 1990.
Cohen, Daniel. *Science Fiction's Greatest Monsters*. New York: Archway, 1980.
Corman, Roger, and Jim Jerome. *How I Made a Hundred Movies in Hollywood and Never Lost a Dime*. New York: Da Capo, 1990.
Coughlin, James T., Gregory William Mank and Dwight D. Frye. *Dwight Frye's Last Laugh*. Baltimore, MD: Midnight Marquee Press, 1997.
Curtis, James. *James Whale: A New World of Gods and Monsters*. London: Faber and Faber, 1998.
Dewey, Donald. *James Stewart, A Biography*. Atlanta GA: Turner Publishing, 1996.
Edelson, Edward. *Great Monsters of the Movies*. New York: Archway, 1973.
_____. *Great Science Fiction from the Movies*. New York: Archway, 1975.
Everson, William K. *The Bad Guys: A Pictorial History of the Movie Villain*. New York: Bonanza Books, 1964.
_____. *Classics of the Horror Film: From the Days of the Silent Film to The Exorcist*. New York: Citadel Press, 1974.
_____. *More Classics of the Horror Film: Fifty Years of Great Chillers*. Secaucus NJ: Citadel Press, 1986.
Gottlieb, Sidney (ed.). *Hitchcock on Hitchcock*. Berkeley CA: University of California Press, 1995.
Hardy, Phil (ed.). *Horror: The Aurum Film Encyclopedia*. London: Aurum Press, 1985.
_____ (ed.). *The Overlook Film Encyclopedia Science Fiction*. Woodstock NY: Overlook, 1984.
Hogan, David J. *Dark Romance: Sexuality in the Horror Film*. Jefferson NC: McFarland, 1986.
Jensen, Paul M. *Boris Karloff and His Films*. South Brunswick/New York: A.S. Barnes, 1974.
_____. *The Men Who Made the Monsters*. New York: Twayne Publishers, 1996.
Johnson, Tom, and Deborah Del Vecchio. *Hammer Films: An Exhaustive Filmography*. Jefferson, NC: McFarland, 1996.
Kohl, Leonard J. *Sinister Serials of Boris Karloff, Bela Lugosi and Lon Chaney, Jr*. Baltimore MD: Midnight Marquee Press, 2000.
Lee, Christopher. *Christopher Lee: Tall, Dark and Gruesome*. Baltimore MD: Midnight Marquee Press, 1977, 1997, 1999.
Leigh, Janet and Christopher Nickens. *Psycho: The Classic Thriller*. New York: Harmony Books, 1995.

Lindsay, Cynthia. *Dear Boris: The Life of William Henry Pratt a.k.a. Boris Karloff*. New York: Proscenium Press, 1975.

McCarty, John. *The Fearmakers: The Screen's Directorial Masters of Suspense and Terror*. New York: St. Martin's Press, 1994.

_____. *Movie Psychos and Madmen: Film Psychopaths from Jekyll and Hyde to Hannibal Lecter*. New York: Citadel Press, 1993.

Madison, Bob (ed.). *Dracula: The First Hundred Years*. Baltimore MD: Midnight Marquee Press, 1997.

Mank, Gregory William. *Hollywood Cauldron: Thirteen Horror Films from the Genre's Golden Age*. Jefferson NC: McFarland, 1994.

_____. *Hollywood's Maddest Doctors: Lionel Atwill, Colin Clive, George Zucco*. Baltimore MD: Midnight Marquee Press, 1998.

_____. *Karloff and Lugosi: The Story of a Haunting Collaboration*. Jefferson NC: McFarland, 1990.

_____. *Women in Horror Films, 1930s*. Jefferson NC: McFarland, 1999.

_____. *Women in Horror Films, 1940s*. Jefferson NC: McFarland, 1999.

Miller, David. *The Peter Cushing Companion*. London: Reynolds & Hearn, 2000.

Miller, Mark A. *Christopher Lee and Peter Cushing and Horror Cinema: A Filmography of Their 22 Collaborations*. Jefferson NC: McFarland, 1995.

Moss, Robert F. *Karloff and Company: The Horror Film*. New York: Pyramid Communications, 1974.

Naschy, Paul; Hodges, Mike (trans.). *Memoirs of a Wolfman*. Baltimore MD: Midnight Marquee Press, 1997/2000.

Pitts, Michael R. *Horror Film Stars*. Jefferson NC: McFarland, 2002.

Price, Michael H. and George E. Turner. *Forgotten Horrors*. Baltimore MD: Midnight Marquee Press, 1999.

_____ and _____. *Forgotten Horrors 2: Beyond the Horror Ban*. Baltimore MD: Midnight Marquee Press, 2001.

_____ and _____. *Human Monsters: The Bizarre Psychology of Movie Villains*. Northampton MA: Kitchen Sink Press, 1995.

Price, Victoria. *Vincent Price: A Daughter's Biography*. New York: St. Martin's Press, 1999.

Rhodes, Gary D. *Lugosi: His Life in Films, On Stage and in the Hearts of Horror Fans*. Jefferson NC: McFarland, 1999.

_____ (ed.). *Horror at the Drive-In*. Jefferson NC: McFarland, 2003.

Rigby, Jonathan. *English Gothic: A Century of Horror Cinema*. London: Reynolds & Hearn, 2000.

Riley, Philip J. (ed.). *Abbott and Costello Meet Frankenstein: Universal Filmscript Series Classic Comedy Films, Volume 1*. Absecon NJ: MagicImage Filmbooks, 1990.

_____ (ed.). *The Bride of Frankenstein: Universal Filmscript Series Classic Horror Films, Volume 2*. Absecon NJ: MagicImage Filmbooks, 1989.

_____ (ed.). *Dracula: Universal Filmscript Series Classic Horror Films, Volume 13*. Absecon NJ: MagicImage Filmbooks, 1990.

_____ (ed.). *Frankenstein: Universal Filmscript Series Classic Horror Films, Volume 1*. Absecon NJ: MagicImage Filmbooks, 1989.

_____ (ed.). *Frankenstein Meets the Wolf Man: Universal Filmscript Series Classic Horror Films, Volume 5*. Absecon NJ: MagicImage Filmbooks, 1990.

_____ (ed.). *The Ghost of Frankenstein: Universal Filmscript Series Classic Horror Films, Volume 4*. Absecon NJ: MagicImage Filmbooks, 1990.

_____ (ed.). *House of Dracula: Universal Filmscript Series Classic Horror Films, Volume 16*. Absecon NJ: MagicImage Filmbooks, 1993.

_____ (ed.). *House of Frankenstein: Universal Filmscript Series Classic Horror Films, Volume 6*. Absecon NJ: MagicImage Filmbooks, 1991.

_____ (ed.). *The Mummy: Universal Filmscript Series Classic Horror Films, Volume 7*. Absecon NJ: MagicImage Filmbooks, 1989.

_____ (ed.). *Son of Frankenstein: Universal Filmscript Series Classic Horror Films, Volume 3.* Absecon NJ: MagicImage Filmbooks, 1990.
_____ (ed.). *The Wolf Man: Universal Filmscript Series Classic Horror Films, Volume 12.* Absecon NJ: MagicImage Filmbooks, 1993.
Russo, John. *The Complete "Night of the Living Dead."* Pittsburgh PA: Imagine, 1985.
Savada, Elias, and David J. Skal. *Dark Carnival: The Secret World of Tod Browning, Hollywood's Master of the Macabre.* New York: Anchor Books, 1995.
Senn, Bryan. *Drums of Terror: Voodoo in the Cinema.* Baltimore MD: Midnight Marquee Press, 1998.
_____. *Golden Horrors: An Illustrated Critical Filmography, 1931–1939.* Jefferson NC: McFarland, 1996.
Silver, Alain, and James Ursini (ed.). *Horror Film Reader.* New York: Proscenium, 2000.
Skal, David J. *Hollywood Gothic: The Tangled Web of Dracula from Novel to Stage to Screen.* New York: W.W. Norton & Company, 1990.
_____. *The Monster Show: A Cultural History of Horror.* New York: W.W. Norton & Company, 1993.
_____. *Screams of Reason: Mad Science and Modern Culture.* New York: W.W. Norton & Company, 1998.
_____. *V Is for Vampire: The A–Z Guide to Everything Undead.* New York: Plume Books, 1996.
Spoto, Donald. *The Art of Alfred Hitchcock: Fifty Years of His Motion Pictures.* New York: Anchor Books, 1976, 1992.
_____. *The Dark Side of Genius: The Life of Alfred Hitchcock.* New York: De Capo Press, 1983, 1999.
Stanley, John. *Creature Features: The Science Fiction, Fantasy and Horror Movie Guide.* New York: Berkeley Boulevard, 1997, 2000.
Svehla, Gary J., and Susan Svehla (eds.). *Bela Lugosi.* Baltimore MD: Midnight Marquee Press, 1995.
_____, and _____ (eds.). *Boris Karloff.* Baltimore MD: Midnight Marquee Press, 1996.
_____, and _____ (eds.). *Cinematic Hauntings.* Baltimore MD: Midnight Marquee Press, 1996.
_____, and _____ (eds.). *Guilty Pleasures of the Horror Film.* Baltimore MD: Midnight Marquee Press, 1996.
_____, and _____ (eds.). *Lon Chaney, Jr.* Baltimore MD: Midnight Marquee Press, 1997.
_____, and _____ (eds.). *Peter Lorre.* Baltimore MD: Midnight Marquee Press, 1999.
_____, and _____ (eds.). *Vincent Price.* Baltimore MD: Midnight Marquee Press, 1998.
Truffaut, Francois. *Hitchcock Truffaut.* New York: Touchstone, 1984.
Weaver, Tom. *It Came from Weaver Five: Interviews with Moviemakers in the SF and Horror Traditions.* Jefferson NC: McFarland, 1996.
_____. *John Carradine: The Films.* Jefferson NC: McFarland, 1999.
_____. *Monsters, Mutants and Heavenly Creatures: Confessions of 14 Classic Sci-Fi Horrormeisters.* Baltimore MD: Midnight Marquee Press, 1996.
_____. *Poverty Row Horrors!: Monogram, PRC and Republic Horror Films of the Forties.* Jefferson NC: McFarland, 1993.
_____. *Return of the B Science Fiction and Horror Heroes.* Jefferson NC: McFarland, 1988, 1991.
Weldon, Michael J. *The Psychotronic Video Guide.* New York: St. Martin's Griffin, 1996.
Winecoff, Charles. *Split Image: The Life of Anthony Hopkins.* New York: Dutton, 1996.
Wright, Gene. *Horrorshows: The A–Z of Horror in Film, Television, Radio and Theater.* New York: Facts on File Publications, 1986.

Periodicals

Castle of Frankenstein
Chiller Theatre
Cinefantastique
Cinemacabre
Cult Movies
Entertainment Weekly

Famous Monsters of Filmland
Fangoria
Film Threat
Filmfax
Films of the Golden Age
The Hollywood Reporter
Little Shoppe of Horrors
Mad About Movies
Midnight Marquee
Monsters from the Vault
Monsterscene
Movie Club
The New Republic
The New York Times
Photoplay
Premiere
Scarlet Street
The Spectator
TV Guide
Variety
Video Watchdog
Videooze

Electronic Media

All Movie Guide www.allmovie.com
DVD Drive-In www.dvddrive-in.com
Horror-Wood webzine www.horror-wood.com
The Internet Movie Database www.imdb.com
Mondo Digital www.mondo-digital.com

DVD and VHS Supplemental Materials from the Following Home Video Releases

Abbott & Costello Meet Frankenstein (Universal Home Video)
Alien (20th Century–Fox Home Video)
Aliens (20th Century–Fox Home Video)
An American Werewolf in London (Universal Home Video)
Black Sabbath (Image Entertainment)
Black Sunday (Image Entertainment)
Blood and Black Lace (VCI Home Video)
Bluebeard (Allday Entertainment)
Bride of Frankenstein (Universal Home Video)
Carnival of Souls (The Criterion Collection)
Carrie (MGM Home Entertainment)
The Comedy of Terrors/The Raven (MGM Home Entertainment)
The Creature from the Black Lagoon (Universal Home Video)
The Diabolical Dr. Z (Mondo Macabro)
Dr. Jekyll versus the Werewolf (Mondo Macabro)
Dracula (Universal Home Video)
Dracula, Prince of Darkness (Anchor Bay Entertainment)
The Exorcist (Warner Home Video)
Faust (Kino International)
The Flesh and the Fiends (Image Entertainment)
Frankenstein (Universal Home Video)
Frankenstein Created Woman (Anchor Bay Entertainment)
Halloween (Anchor Bay Entertainment)
Halloween II (Universal Home Video)
Halloween H20: 20 Years Later (Dimension Home Video)
Halloween Resurrection (Dimension Home Video)
The Haunted Palace/Tower of London (MGM Home Entertainment)
The Haunting (Warner Home Video)

The Invisible Man (Universal Home Video)
The Masque of the Red Death/The Premature Burial (MGM Home Entertainment)
Misery (MGM Home Entertainment)
The Most Dangerous Game (The Criterion Collection)
The Mummy (Universal Home Video)
The Mummy's Shroud (Anchor Bay Entertainment)
Night of the Living Dead (Elite Entertainment)
The Old Dark House (Image Entertainment)
Peeping Tom (The Criterion Collection)
Phantom of the Opera (Universal Home Video)
Quatermass and the Pit (Anchor Bay Entertainment)
Rasputin, the Mad Monk (Anchor Bay Entertainment)
The Reptile (Anchor Bay Entertainment)
Scream (Dimension Home Video)
Scream 2 (Dimension Home Video)
Scream 3 (Dimension Home Video)
The Silence of the Lambs (The Criterion Collection)
The Sixth Sense (Hollywood Pictures Home Video)
The Sorcerers (Metrodome Distribution Ltd.)
Star Wars Episode II: Attack of the Clones (20th Century–Fox Home Video)
Suspiria (Anchor Bay Entertainment)
Targets (Paramount Home Entertainment)
The Tingler (Columbia/Tri-Star Home Video)
The Tomb of Ligeia/An Evening of Edgar Allan Poe (MGM Home Entertainment)
The Vampire (Mondo Macabro)
Werewolf Shadow (Anchor Bay Entertainment)
What Ever Happened to Baby Jane? (Warner Home Video)
The Whip and the Body (VCI Home Video)
Witchfinder General (Metrodome Distribution Ltd.)
The Wolf Man (Universal Home Video)
Young Frankenstein (20th Century–Fox Home Video)

Index

Abbott, Bud 50
Abbott & Costello Meet Dr. Jekyll and Mr. Hyde 52
Abbott & Costello Meet Frankenstein 41, 50–52, 86, 89, 132
Abbott & Costello Meet the Killer, Boris Karloff 52
The Abominable Dr. Phibes 9, 100–103
The Abominable Snowman 118
About Schmidt 221
The Accused 222
Acquanetta 75
The Addams Family (cartoon) 222,
The Adventures of Robin Hood 128, 151
The Adventures of Sherlock Holmes 79, 83
Affliction 213
The African Queen 141
Agar, John 130
Agutter, Jenny 180
AI: Artificial Intelligence 176
Aldrich, Robert 194, 198
Alias Nick Beal 131
Alice Doesn't Live Here Anymore 208
Alien 238
Aliens 233, 237
All About Eve 194
All My Children (TV) 218
All That Money Can Buy 190, 236, 239
Allbritton, Louise 231
Allen, Nancy 209
Allen, Woody 202
Allgood, Sara 152
The Alligator People 84
An American Werewolf in London 180
Ames, Leon 43

Amplas, John 179
Andrews, Brian 214
Andrews, Julie 148
Angel Street (play) 91
Ankers, Evelyn 81, 87, 183, 229–231
Anthony Adverse 239
Anything but Love (TV) 216
The Apartment 239
The Ape Man 53
Archer, Anne 238
Arkin, Alan 240
Arlen, Richard 146
Arnold, Tracy 165
Arrighi, Nike 126
Arsenic and Old Lace (play) 15
Arthur 2: On the Rocks 218
Asher, Jane 95, 96
Astaire, Fred 13
Astin, Patty Duke 202
At Play in the Fields of the Lord 221
The Attic 132
Atwill, Lionel 54–61, 66, 89, 92
Aubert, Lenore 50
Audrey Rose 202
Autumn Sonata 240
The Awful Dr. Orloff 136
Aykroyd, Dan 216

Bacall, Lauren 148
The Bad Seed 236–237
Baker, Robert 112
Baker, Tom 99
Balderston, John L. 68, 184
Balsam, Robert 156
Banks, Leslie 142, 176–177, 228
Barrymore, Ethel 236
Barrymore, John 9, 142
Barrymore, Lionel 141, 239, 240

Bates, Alan 240
Bates, Kathy ii, iv, 218–222, 238
Bates, Ralph 136
Batman (1989) 133
Batman (TV) 194
Bava, Mario 3, 127, 134, 136, 232
The Beast of Yucca Flats 130
The Beast with Five Fingers 72, 130
Beck, Helen 105
Becket 239
Bedlam 35, 231
Beery, Wallace 236, 239
Bellamy, Madge 44
Bellamy, Ralph 201
Bennett, Constance 91
Bergman, Ingrid 151, 228, 236, 239
Berkeley Square 239
Berman, Monty 112
Bernard, James 121
The Best Years of Our Lives 142
La Bete Humain 190
Bey, Turhan 81
Beyond the Forest 194
Billy the Kid versus Dracula 78
The Birds 160
Bjornstrand, Gunnar 178
The Black Camel 65
The Black Castle 86
The Black Cat (1934) 21–24, 46–48, 74
Black Friday 178
Black Fury 239
Black Moon 228
The Black Room 24–27
Black Sabbath 36
The Black Sleep 130
Black Sunday 134, 135

The Black Swan 83, 152
The Black Zoo 134
Blackmer, Sidney 199
Blair, Linda 203–209, 237
Blair Bitch Project 208
A Blind Bargain 13
Bloch, Robert 156
Blood and Black Lace 136
Blood of the Vampire 232
Blue Eyes of the Broken Doll see *House of Psychotic Women*
Bluebeard 74–77
Bodeen, DeWitt 190
The Body Snatcher 29–32
Boehm, Carl 179
Bogart, Humphrey 128, 141
Bogdanovich, Peter 32, 33, 34, 203
The Boogie Man Will Get You 72
Boyer, Charles 236
The Boys from Brazil 134
Bradstreet, Charles 50
Brahm, John 152
The Brainiac 132
Bram Stoker's Dracula 64, 137
Branagh, Kenneth 141
Bride of Frankenstein 18, 66, 74, 129, 177, 228
Bride of the Monster 53, 130
Brides of Dracula 123
The Brood 134
Brooks, Mel 180
Browning, Tod 2, 39, 41, 189, 240
Bruce, David 81
Bruce, Lenny 39
Bruce, Nigel 83
The Brute Man 130, 133
Buckley, Betty 210
Buono, Victor 196, 237
Buried Alive 133, 146
Burke, Kathleen 55
Burnt Offerings 134, 198, 208
Burstyn, Ellen 203–209, 237
Burton, Richard 239
Burton, Tim 37, 38, 53, 92, 133
Byron, Arthur 19
Byron, Kathleen 117

Caan, James 218, 219, 238
The Cabinet of Dr. Caligari 3, 7, 9, 128, 212
Calling Dr. Death 130
Cameron, James 216
Campbell, Neve 183, 216
Cape Fear 178
Captain Blood 54, 61, 128

Captains Courageous 78
Captive Wild Woman 75, 78, 230
Carlson, Veronica 118
Carradine, John 41, 73–78, 79, 83, 104, 120, 121, 133, 137, 215
Carreras, Michael 105, 102
Carrey, Jim 37
Carrie 209–213, 214, 237
Carter, Ann 193
Casablanca 128, 151, 241
Cassavetes, John 199
Castle, Nick 215
Castle, William 92, 240
Castle of Blood 134
Castle of the Monsters 132
The Cat and the Canary (1939) 83
Cat Girl 232
Cat on a Hot Tin Roof 239
Cat People (1942) 189–193
The Cauldron of Blood 32
Chained Heat 208
The Champ 236, 239
Champagne for Caesar 91, 103
Chaney, John 8
Chaney, Lon 7–13, 18, 84, 89, 100, 104, 150, 169, 176, 240
Chaney, Lon, Jr. 8, 18, 38, 41, 49, 50, 52, 84–90, 100, 120, 128, 183, 185, 229, 230, 231, 239
Chaplin, Charles 71, 201
Charlie's Angels (TV) 213
Charly 239
Chase, Chevy 148
The Chilling 208
A Chump at Oxford 105
Churchill, Marguerite 27, 28, 188
The Cider House Rules 176
Cimarron 239
Citizen Kane 218, 239
The Clairvoyant 151, 228
Clarke, Mae 183
Clarke, Robert 130
Clayburgh, Jill 240
Clive, Colin 15, 65, 68, 79, 129, 177, 184
Clive, E. E. 150
Close, Glenn 233, 237
Coal Miner's Daughter 212
Cohen, Herman 213
Collette, Toni 174
Collinson, Madeline 117
Collinson, Mary 117
Columbo (TV) 213
Come Back to the Five and

Dime, Jimmy Dean, Jimmy Dean 218
Come to the Stable 240
The Comedy of Terrors 72, 73, 94
Coming Home 240
The Conqueror Worm 97–100, 239
Contact 227
Conway, Tom 192
Cook, Elisha, Jr. 65
Cooper, Gary 239, 241
Cooper, Jackie 239
Cooper, Merian C. 228
Copycat 227
Corman, Roger 33, 92, 131, 134
Corridors of Blood 35, 127
Cortez, Ricardo 27
Costello, Lou 50, 51
Cotten, Joseph 101
Count Dracula 123
The Count of Cagliostro 128
Count Yorga, Vampire 136
Court, Hazel 232–233
Craven, Wes 3, 137
Crawford, Joan 194–195, 240
The Creeping Flesh 119
Cregar, Laird 152–156, 157
Creighton, Cleva 8
The Crime of Dr. Crespi 66, 128
Crimes of the Heart 212
The Criminal Code 33, 35
The Crimson Altar 32
The Curse of Frankenstein 15, 109, 127, 233
The Curse of the Cat People 193
Curse of the Crimson Altar 134
The Curse of the Crying Woman 132
Curse of the Demon 179
The Curse of the Werewolf 134
Curtis, Jamie Lee 213–218, 222, 228, 232
Curtis, Tony 213, 239
Curtiz, Michael 27, 92
Cushing, Peter 1, 3, 13, 104–119, 120, 121, 127, 132, 133, 134, 136, 141, 184, 189, 222, 235, 239
The Cyclops 231

Dafoe, Willem 179, 235, 238
The Damned 134
Danger—Love at Work 189
Daniell, Henry 29
Dark Angel 232
Dark Eyes of London see *The Human Monster*

The Dark Secret of Harvest Home 198
Darkman 9
Daughter of Dr. Jekyll 231
Davis, Bette 183, 193–198, 222, 237
Dead and Buried 137
Dead Men Walk 65, 83
Dead Ringer 198
Dear Dead Delilah 198
The Death of a Centerfold (TV) 216
Death of a Salesman 142
Death Takes a Holiday 142
Deathmaster 136
The Defiant Ones 239
DeHavilland, Olivia 241
Demented Death Farm Massacre 78
DeMille, Katherine 25, 26
Demme, Jonathan 169–170, 222, 225
The Demons 136
DeNiro, Robert 4, 142, 179, 224
DePalma, Brian 209
The Desert Fox 84
Devan, Carrie 76
The Devil and Daniel Webster see *All That Money Can Buy*
The Devil Bat 53
The Devil Commands 35
Devil Dog: Hound of Hell 208
Devil-Doll 240
Devil Girl from Mars 233
The Devil in the Cheese (play) 62
The Devil Is a Woman 61
The Devil Rides Out see *The Devil's Bride*
The Devils 134
The Devil's Bride 124–127, 239
The Devil's Rain 208
The Diabolical Dr. Z 136
Diabolique (1996) 221
Diary of a Madman 95
Dieterle, William 83, 190
Diffring, Anton 124
Dix, Richard 239
Dr. Blood's Coffin 233
Dr. Heckle and Mr. Hype 134
Dr. Jekyll and Mr. Hyde (1920) 9, 128
Dr. Jekyll and Mr. Hyde (1931) 7, 141–145, 228, 236, 239
Dr. Jekyll and Sister Hyde 136
Dr. Phibes Rises Again 136
Dr. Renault's Secret 130
Dr. Strangelove, or How I Learned to Stop Worrying and Love the Bomb 58, 239
Dr. Terror's House of Horrors 134
Doctor X 145, 228
Dodsworth 229, 240
Dolores Claiborne 221
Douglas, Michael 238
Dracula (1931) 2, 7, 15, 38, 39–41, 42, 61, 63–65, 128, 133, 184, 189, 239
Dracula (1977) 64
Dracula (1979) 64, 133
Dracula (Spanish version) 64
Dracula (TV) 64
Dracula and Son 123
Dracula, Prince of Darkness 123, 232
Dracula vs. Frankenstein 130–136
Dracula's Daughter 41, 53, 184–189
Drake, Frances 69, 228
Dreyfuss, Richard 180
Dunaway, Faye 212
Dunne, Griffin 180
Dwyer, Hillary 97

Ed Wood 38, 238
Edward Scissorhands 92
Eerie Tales 128
Elmer Gantry 239
Englund, Robert 102, 136–137
The Entertainer 239
Escape from New York 133
The Exorcist 202, 203–209, 237
Exorcist II: The Heretic 208
Exorcist III 208
Exorcist IV: The Beginning 208

The Face at the Window 129
The Face Behind the Mask 72, 73
Fantastic Voyage 133
Farrow, John 198
Farrow, Mia 198–203, 239
Fatal Attraction 233, 237
Faust (1926) 176, 240
Fear in the Night 136
Fear Strikes Out 159
Feldman, Marty 180
La Femme en Bleu 193
The Fiendish Ghouls see *Mania*
Fincher, David 227
Fingers at the Window 129
Fire, Richard 167
A Fish Called Wanda 216

Fisher, Terrence 120, 232
The Fixer 240
Fleming, Ian 119
The Flesh and the Fiends see *Mania*
The Flesh Eaters 130
Fletcher, Bramwell 19
The Fly (1958) 92
The Flying Serpent 83
The Fog 216, 232
Fonda, Henry 32, 228
Fonda, Jane 240
Foolish Wives 128
Ford, John 78
Forrest Gump 173
Fort, Garrett 184
Fort Apache 231
Foster, Jodie 170, 216, 222–227, 238
The Four Musketeers 134
Fox, Sidney 43
Francis, Arlene 42
Franco, Jesus 136
Frankenheimer, John 237
Frankenstein (1931) 3, 7, 14, 15–19, 35, 38, 53, 61, 65, 74, 128, 129, 133, 145, 183, 208, 236, 239
Frankenstein Island 75
Frankenstein Meets the Wolf Man 24, 48, 89, 229
Frankenstein Must Be Destroyed 118
Frankenstein 1970 14, 18
Frankham, David 94
Frankie and Johnny 222
Frankie and Johnny in the Clair de Lune (play) 218
Franz, Arthur 130
Frazer, Robert 44, 45
Freaky Friday (1977) 222
Freaky Friday (2003) 216
Freddie vs. Jason 137
A Free Soul 141, 239, 240
Freund, Karl 68
Friday the 13th 213, 218
Fried Green Tomatoes 221
Friedkin, William 203
Friendly Persuasion 159, 241
Frogs 132
From Beyond the Grave 133
From Hell 152
The Front Page 239
The Frozen Ghost 130, 230
Frye, Dwight 16, 39, 61–66, 133, 150
Full Circle 202
Fuller, Sam 14
Fulton, John P. 151
Funny Girl 240

Gabin, Jean 190
Gable, Clark 239
Galaxy of Terror 137
Ganja & Hess 161
Garland, Judy 84
Gaslight 236
Gaunt, Valerie 121, 122
Gemini Twins see *Twins of Evil*
German Robles 132
Ghost 238
The Ghost 134
The Ghost of Frankenstein 49, 60, 85, 230
Ghost Ship (1952) 233
Ghost Story 232
The Ghoul (1933) 21, 177
Gideon's Trumpet (TV) 228
Gladiator 134
Glenn, Scott 223
Gods and Monsters 238
Goldberg, Whoopi 238
Der Golem (1920) 7
Gor 134
Gordon, Ruth 199, 202, 237
The Gorgon 124, 232
Gough, Michael 107, 123, 128, 133–134
Grand Ilusion 128
Grant, Cary 239
Grapes of Wrath 74, 78
Gray, Charles 125
Gray, Coleen 231
The Great Gabbo 128
The Great Gatsby 202
The Great Impersonation 230
Greene, Leon 124
Greenstreet, Sidney 68
Grey, Nan 187
Grier, Rosey 132
The Grinch 37
Grodin, Charles 200
Grotesque 208
The Guardsman 239
Gwenn, Edmund 27, 28
Gwynn, Michael 111
Gwynne, Anne 230

Haigh, Peter 99
Hall, Thurston 25
Halloween 3, 133, 213–218, 228
Halloween II 216
Halloween H20: Twenty Years Later 216–217, 232
Halloween Resurrection 217
Halperin, Victor 45
Hamilton, Linda 222
Hamilton, Margaret 228–229
Hamlet 105

The Hands of Orlac 128
Hannah and Her Sisters 202
Hannibal 172, 227
Hardman, Karl 162
Hardwicke, Sir Cedric 180
Hardy, Oliver 105
Harrigan William 151
Harris, Julie 232
Harris, Marilyn 16
Harrison, Rex 239
Harron, John 44
Harvey, Paul 27
Hastings, Hazel 8
Hatfield, Hurd 180
Hatton, Rondo 130, 131, 133
The Haunted Palace 95
The Haunted Strangler 35
The Haunting 180, 232
The Haunting of Julia see *Full Circle*
Hawks, Howard 35
Haxan see *Witchcraft Through the Ages*
Heald, Anthony 223
The Heart Is a Lonely Hunter 240
Heaven Can Wait (1943) 152
Heckart, Eileen 237
Hell Night 208
Helm, Fay 88
Henry, Portrait of a Serial Killer 164–169
Henson, Jim 39
Hepburn, Katharine 32, 194, 202, 239
Herbert, Holmes 142
Here Comes Mr. Jordan 239
Herzog, Werner 176
High Noon 89
Hill, Debra 213
Hinds, Anthony 120
History Is Made at Night 129
Hitchcock, Alfred 67, 151, 156, 159, 160, 231, 236
Hitler's Madman 78
Hobart, Rose 142
Hobbes, Halliwell 142
Hogarth, Tony 64
Hohl, Arthur 147
Hold That Ghost 230
Holden, Gloria 184–189
Hope, Bob 83
Hopkins, Anthony ii, iv, 137, 141, 144, 169–172, 221, 222, 225, 238
Hopkins, Miriam 228
The Horrible Dr. Hitchcock 134
Horror Hospital 134
The Horror of Dracula 64, 106–109, 120–124, 134, 239

The Horror of Frankenstein 136
Horror Rises from the Tomb 136
The Hound of the Baskervilles (1959) 118, 127
House 5 208
The House in Nightmare Park 132
House of Dracula 41, 60, 78, 89, 121
House of Exorcism 208
House of Frankenstein 18, 41, 60, 78, 83, 89, 121, 129, 241
House of Horrors 130
House of Psychotic Women 136
The House of the Seven Gables 91, 103
House of Usher (1960) 95
House of Usher (1988) 133, 134
House of Wax 9, 92, 102–103
House on Haunted Hill 92, 104
How Green Was My Valley 231
How the Grinch Stole Christmas (TV) 36
Howard, Leslie 239
Howard, Trevor 239
Hsueh, Nancy 33
Hull, Warren 27
The Human Monster 37, 52
Humoresque 240
The Hunchback of Notre Dame (1923) 9, 12
The Hunchback of Notre Dame (1939) 83, 145, 180, 240
The Hunchback of the Morgue 136
Hush ... Hush, Sweet Charlotte 198, 237
Huston, Walter 236, 239

I Am a Fugitive from a Chain Gang 239
I Married a Monster from Outer Space 231
I Married a Witch 142
I Saw What You Did 213
I Wake Up Screaming 152
I Was a Teenage Werewolf 213
I'll Never Forget What's-His-Name 134
In the Bedroom 213
The Informer 239
Inherit the Wind 239
Inside the Actors Studio (TV) 169
Interiors 240
Invisible Agent 72
The Invisible Ghost 53

The Invisible Man 145, 148–152, 239, 240
The Invisible Man Returns 91
The Invisible Man's Revenge 78, 230
The Invisible Ray 35, 228
Isadora 240
Island of Lost Souls 48, 52, 145–148, 239, 240
Island of the Doomed 136
It's Alive 202

Jackson, Peter 127
Jameson, Joyce 94
Jane Eyre 129
Jannings, Emil 176, 240
Jaws 180
Jesse James 74
Jezebel 194
JFK 213
Johann, Zita 19
Johnson, Noble 43
Johnson, Tor 130
Jones, Chuck 36
Jones, Duane 160–164, 239
Journey's End (play) 79, 129
The Jungle Captive 130
Jungle Woman 130, 230

Karloff, Boris 1, 2, 3, 7, 9, 13–37, 38, 46–48, 52, 58, 65, 86, 89, 100, 103, 104, 127, 128, 129, 137, 141, 145, 169, 184, 189, 228, 231, 235, 236, 239
Katt, William 210
Kelly, Gene 84
Kelly, Nancy 236
Kerry, Norman 11
Killer Bats see *The Devil Bat*
The Killers 148
The Killing 231
King, George 129
King, Stephen 209, 221
King Kong 43, 228, 229
Kiss of Death 231
Konga 134
Kosleck, Martin 130
Kruger, Otto 187
Kubrick, Stanley 231

Laemmle, Carl 12, 194
Lancaster, Burt 148, 239
Lanchester, Elsa 228, 240
Landau, Martin 38, 238
Landis, John 180
Landis, Monty 32
Lang, Fritz 66–68
Lansbury, Angela 180, 236, 237

The Last Command 240
The Last Picture Show 203
Laughton, Charles 84, 145–148, 180, 239, 240
Laura 91, 103
Laurel, Stan 105
Laurie, Piper 209, 237
Laverick, June 113, 114
Lavi, Daliah 127, 232
Lawrence of Arabia 218
Leachman, Cloris 180
Lee, Anna 231
Lee, Christopher 3, 7, 15, 16, 104, 106, 119–127, 132, 133, 136, 137, 183, 232, 239
The Leech Woman 231
Leigh, Janet 158, 159, 213, 231–232, 237
Lemmon, Jack 239
Leni, Paul 128
Levine, Ted 172, 223
Lewton, Val 29, 32, 75, 189, 193
The Life of Emile Zola 184
The Lion in Winter 240
Lisa and the Devil see *House of Exorcism*
Little, Dwight 137
The Living Head 132
Lodge, John 56
The Lodger (1944) 152–156
The Lodger (play) 54
London After Midnight 9, 13
The Long Hair of Death 134
Look Homeward, Angel (play) 159
Look What Happened to Rosemary's Baby (TV) 202
Loomis, Nancy 214
The Lord of the Rings: The Fellowship of the Ring 127, 238
The Lord of the Rings: The Two Towers 127
Loring, Teala 77
Lorre, Peter 18, 66–73, 79, 94, 104, 129, 228, 239
The Lost Patrol 27
The Lost Weekend 131
The Love Boat (TV) 213
Love from a Stranger 129
Lubitsch, Ernst 152
Lucas, George 127
Lugosi, Bela 1, 2, 3, 7, 13, 21, 24, 31, 37–54, 58, 66, 83, 84, 86, 89, 100, 104, 121, 128, 137, 141, 142, 144, 145, 147, 156, 178, 184, 189, 222, 228, 235, 238, 239
Lunt, Alfred 239
Lust for a Vampire 136

M 66–68
MacGinnis, Niall 179
Macnee, Patrick 119
The Mad Doctor 129, 130
The Mad Doctor of Market Street 61
The Mad Ghoul 80–83, 230
Mad Love 68–71, 129, 228, 239
The Mad Magician 104
The Mad Monster 83
Madame Bovary 83
Madame Sin 198
Mademoiselle Fifi 193
Madhouse 136
Malden, Karl 141
The Maltese Falcon (1931) 65
The Maltese Falcon (1941) 65, 68, 73
The Man and the Monster 132
The Man in the Iron Mask 105
The Man in the White Suit 133
Man Made Monster 54, 61, 85, 89
The Man Who Changed His Mind see *The Man Who Lived Again*
The Man Who Cheated Life 128
The Man Who Could Cheat Death 124, 233
The Man Who Knew Too Much 67
The Man Who Laughs 128
The Man Who Lived Again 231
The Man Who Reclaimed His Head 90, 151
The Man with the Golden Gun 127
The Manchurian Candidate 237
Mania 112–115, 133
Maniac 134
Manners, David 21, 46
A Man's Man (play) 62
Mantrap 232
March, Fredric 141, 228, 236, 239
The Mark of the Vampire 41, 52, 141, 240
Mars, Kenneth 58
Marsh, Carol 107
Marsh, Marian 25, 143
Martin 179
Mary Poppins 148
Mary Shelley's Frankenstein 141
The Mask of Dimitrios 73

The Mask of Fu Manchu 35, 36, 145
Mason, James 84
The Masque of the Red Death 95–97, 233, 239
Master of the World 95
Matheson, Richard 64, 92
Matthews, Francis 110
Mature, Victor 231
McCambridge, Mercedes 207
McCarty, Patti 76
McCormack, Patty 237
McCrea, Joel 84, 177, 228
McDonald, Philip 29
McGuire, Dorothy 236
McKellan, Ian 238
McLaglen, Victor 239
McNaughton, John 164, 167
A Medal for Benny 129, 241
Menjou, Adolphe 239
Mildred Pierce 240
Milestone, Lewis 85
Milland, Ray 131–132
Miller, Jason 205, 206, 208, 237
Mima (play) 62
The Miracle Man 8–9
Miracles for Sale 189
Misery 218–222, 238
Missing 213
Mr. Skeffington 241
Mr. Smith Goes to Washington 241
Mitchell, Cameron 136
Mitchell, Thomas 180
Mitchum, Robert 4, 178, 202
Mix, Tom 104
Modern Times 201
Mohr, Hal 28
The Monster 13
The Monster Maker 130
Montgomery, Robert 177–178, 236, 239
Moody, Ron 240
Moonbase 3 (TV) 136
Moore, Eva 177
Moore, Julianne 227
Moorehead, Agnes 198, 237
The Most Dangerous Game 142, 176–177, 228
Mother Riley Meets the Vampire 38
Mower, Patrick 124
The Mummy (1932) 19–21
The Mummy (1959) 118
The Mummy's Curse 86, 130
The Mummy's Ghost 78, 86
The Mummy's Hand 79, 80, 83
The Mummy's Shroud 133

The Mummy's Tomb 86
Muni, Paul 239
Murder Motel 136
Murders in the Rue Morgue (1932) 41–43
Murders in the Zoo 55–58
Murnau, F. W. 176, 179, 238, 240
Murphy, Eddie 216
Musuraca, Nicholas 193
Mutiny on the Bounty 145, 239, 240
My Best Friend Is a Vampire 221
My Fair Lady 239
My Favorite Blonde 83
Myers, Henry 84
The Mystery of Edwin Drood 151
The Mystery of Marie Roget 229
The Mystery of the Mary Celeste see *The Phantom Ship*
Mystery of the Wax Museum 9, 54, 61, 92, 102, 228

Nagel, Anne 61
Naish, J. Carrol 90, 128, 129, 241
The Nanny 198
Naschy, Paul 134–135
Naughton, David 180
Neal, Patricia 202, 240
Neill, Roy William 24
Nell 227
Network 212
Newman, Paul 239
Night Must Fall 177–178, 236
Night of the Blood Monster 136
Night of the Ghouls 130
The Night of the Hunter 4, 145, 178
Night of the Living Dead 3, 160–164, 239
The Nightmare Before Christmas 37
Nightmare Café (TV) 137
Nightmare Castle 134
Nightmare in Wax 136
A Nightmare on Elm Street 136, 137
A Nightmare on Elm Street III: Dream Warriors 137
976-EVIL 137
1984 (TV) 105, 133
Niven, David 239
Norman, Maidie 196
North, Virginia 101

North West Mounted Police 85
Nosferatu (1922) 7, 9, 176, 179, 238
Nosferatu (1979) 176
Notorious 151
Now, Voyager 194

Oberon, Merle 152
O'Brien, Edmund 180
O'Connor, Una 150
O'Dea, Judith 161
Of Mice and Men (1939) 85, 89
Of Mice and Men (play) 85
Ogilvy, Ian 98
O'Hara, Maureen 180
O'Kelly, Tim 33
The Old Dark House (1932) 35, 145, 177, 240
The Old Man and the Sea 239
Oliver! 134, 240
Olivier, Laurence 105, 239
The Omen 202
Omen III: The Final Conflict 233
On Golden Pond 32
One Million B.C. 85
Operation Petticoat (TV) 213
Ophuls, Max 193
O'Quinn, Terry 179
Osment, Haley Joel 172–176, 235, 238
O'Sullivan, Maureen 198
O'Toole, Peter 218, 239, 240
Ouspenskaya, Maria 229, 240
Out of Africa 134
Outside the Law 13

Pack, Charles Lloyd 110
Page, Geraldine 198, 240
Paget, Debra 94
Panic in Year Zero! 131
Panic Room 227
Paranoiac 134
Parker, Jean 75, 76
The Pearl of Death 130, 230
Peck, Gregory 84
Peeping Tom 179
Penny Serenade 239
Perkins, Anthony 141, 142, 144, 156–160, 169, 189, 222, 231, 239, 241
Peter Pan (play) 15
Peyton Place (TV) 198
Pfeiffer, Michelle 218, 219, 221
The Phantom of the Opera (1925) 3, 9–12, 150
The Phantom of the Opera (1943) 151, 240
The Phantom of the Opera (1962) 134

The Phantom of the Opera (1988) 137
Phantom of the Rue Morgue 141
The Phantom Planet 231
The Phantom Ship 52
Philbin, Mary 9, 10
Phillips, Robin 118
Pichel, Irving 185
Picture Mommy Dead 231
The Picture of Dorian Gray 180, 236
Pierce, Jack 15, 19, 21, 48, 82, 88, 228
Pierce, Maggie 92, 93
The Pit and the Pendulum (1961) 95, 134
The Pit and the Pendulum (1990) 134
Plan 9 from Outer Space 130
Pleasence, Donald 113, 133
Poitier, Sidney 239
Polanski, Roman 126, 198
Power, Tyrone 84
The Premature Burial 131–132, 233
Preminger, Otto 91, 189
Price, Vincent 1, 3, 13, 68, 90–104, 117, 134, 136, 148, 184, 209, 235, 239
The Prisoner of Shark Island 74, 78
The Private Life of Henry VIII 145, 239, 240
Prom Night 213, 216
Psycho (1960) 142, 156–160, 208, 217, 231–232, 237, 239
Psycho II 160
Psycho III 160
Psycho IV: The Beginning 160
The Purple Rose of Cairo 202

Quarry, Robert 136
Quatermass and the Pit 232
Quinn, Anthony 239

Rachel, Rachel 240
The Rage: Carrie 2 213
Rains, Claude 86, 90, 148–152, 239, 241
Randolph, Jane 50, 192
Rasputin 128
Rasputin, the Mad Monk 127, 232
Rathbone, Basil 48, 58, 83, 94, 118, 128–129, 241
The Raven (1935) 52
The Raven (1963) 36, 72, 73, 94, 103, 233
Red Dragon 172

Redford, Robert 202
Redgrave, Vanessa 202, 240
Reed, Carol 134
Reed, Oliver 134
Reeves, Michael 97, 99
Reiner, Rob 221
Renoir, Jean 128, 129, 190
The Reptile 133
The Return of Dr. X 141
Return from Witch Mountain 198
The Return of Chandu 184
Return of Count Yorga 136
The Return of the Vampire 41
The Revenge of Frankenstein 109–112
Revolt of the Zombies 45
Reynolds, Debbie 198
Richard III 133
Ridges, Stanley 178
Ripper, Michael 64, 133
Robertson, Cliff 239
Robinson, Edward G. 92
Roller Boogie 208
Romeo and Juliet (1936) 239
Romero, Cesar 194
Romero, George 3, 137, 160, 164, 179
La Ronde 193
Rooker, Michael 164–169
Rose, George 113
Rosemary's Baby 126, 198–203, 208, 218, 237, 239
Route 66 (TV) 18
The Royal Family of Broadway 142, 239
Rubio, Pablo Alvarez 64
Ruggles, Charlie 55
Russell, Robert 97
Russell, Rosalind 178
Russo, John 160
Ryan, Robert 79

Sahara 129
Salazar, Abel 132
Same Time, Next Year 208, 240
Sanders, George 56, 180, 230
Sangster, Jimmy 64, 121
Santo 132
Santo and the Blue Demon vs. Dracula and the Wolf Man 133
Santo in the Treasure of Dracula 132–133
Santo in the Wax Museum 132
Santo vs. Frankenstein's Daughter 133
Santo vs. the Martians 132
Santo vs. the Vampire Women 132

Sawyer, Joseph 27
Scarface 35
Scars of Dracula 3, 123
Scheider, Roy 180
Schreck, Max 9, 176, 179, 238
Schwarzenegger, Arnold 215
Scorsese, Martin 208, 222
Scott, Randolph 57
Scott, Zachary 129
Scream 183, 208
Scream, Pretty Peggy 198
Secret Ceremony 202
See No Evil 202
Sellers, Peter 58, 239
The Sentinel 208
Separate Tables 239
Sergeant York 239
Service De Luxe 91
Seven 227
The Seventh Seal 178–179
Shadow of the Cat 232
Shadow of the Vampire 176, 179, 235, 238
Shatter 118
Shaw, Robert 180
Shelley, Barbara 183, 232
Shepherd, Jack 64
Sherlock Holmes and the Secret Weapon 61
Sherlock Holmes and the Voice of Terror 230
She-Wolf of London 130
The Shootist 32
The Shuttered Room 134
Shyamalan, M. Night 3, 173
The Silence of the Lambs 137, 169–172, 208, 221, 222–227, 238
Silent Night, Bloody Night 78
Simon, Simone 189–193
Sinatra, Frank 198
Siodmak, Robert 236
Sitting Pretty (play) 62
The Sixth Sense 172–176, 208, 235, 238
Skippy 239
Slaughter, Tod 129
Smith, Kent 190
Son of Dracula 41, 80, 85, 86, 230, 231
Son of Frankenstein 18, 48–50, 58–61, 85, 128, 189, 193
Sondergaard, Gale 241
Sons and Lovers 239
Sorel, Sonia 75
The Sound of Music 231
The Southerner 129
Spacek, Sissy 209–213, 214, 237
Spasms 134

Speilberg, Steven 176
Spider Baby 89
The Spider Woman Strikes Back 130, 131
The Spiral Staircase 236
Stagecoach 74, 78
Stallone, Sylvester 215
The Stand (TV) 221
Stanwyck, Barbara 14
A Star Is Born 142
Star Wars 119
Star Wars Episode II: Attack of the Clones 127
Steele, Barbara 134, 135
Stefano, Joseph 156–157
The Stepfather 179
Stevens, George 105
Stossel, Ludwig 77
Strait-Jacket 198, 240
Strange Confession 90, 129
Strange, Glenn 50, 83
Strange, Robert 27
The Strange Door 145
Stranger on the Third Floor 72–73
Strawn, Arthur 24
A Streetcar Named Desire 141
Streisand, Barbra 202, 239
Stribling, Melissa 122
Stuart, Gloria 151
The Student of Prague see *The Man Who Cheated Life*
The Subject Was Roses 240
Sudden Fear 240
Sugar Hill 136
Summerville, Slim 194
Sunset Blvd. 128, 241
Superman: The Movie 169
Supernatural 45
Swanson, Gloria 128
Sweeny Todd: The Demon Barber of Fleet Street 129

Talbott, Gloria 231
Tales from the Crypt 118–119
Tales from the Darkside (TV) 227
Tales of Terror 72, 73, 92–95, 103, 128
Tally, Ted 171
Tamblyn, Russ 180
Targets 32–35, 239
Tarzan and the Amazons 229
Tarzan and the Mermaids 83
Tarzan's Magic Fountain 230
Taste the Blood of Dracula 136
Taxi Driver 4, 142, 179, 222, 224
Taylor, Elizabeth 202
Tea and Sympathy (play) 159

Tell It to the Marines 13
The Terror 33
Terror in the Wax Museum 132
Terror Train 216
The Texas Chainsaw Massacre (1974) 3
Theater of Blood 90
Thesiger, Ernest 177, 178
They Drive by Night (1938) 177
The Thing with Two Heads 132
This Gun for Hire 152
Thomas, Damien 116
Thompson, Marshall 130
The Three Musketeers 91, 134
3 Women 213
Thriller (TV) 15
THX–1138 133
The Tingler 92
Titanic (1997) 221
To Have and Have Not 148
To the Devil ... A Daughter 208
Tobey, Kenneth 130
Tomb of Ligeia 92, 95, 103–104
Tone, Franchot 239
The Toolbox Murders 136
Topper 236
Tourneur, Jacques 189, 193
Tourneur, Maurice 189
Tower of London (1939) 91, 103
Towles, Tom 165
Tracy, Spencer 239
Trading Spaces 216
The Trial 160
True Lies 214, 216
20,000 Leagues Under the Sea 72
Twins of Dracula see *Twins of Evil*
Twins of Evil 115–117
The Two Faces of Dr. Jekyll 134

Ulmer, Edgar G. 46, 74, 75
The Uncanny 132
Uncle Was a Vampire 123
The Unearthly 130
The Unholy Three (1925) 9
The Unholy Three (1930) 9
The Uninvited 131
The Unknown 9, 12–13, 240
An Unmarried Woman 240
Used People 221
Usher, Guy 53

The Vampire (1957, America) 231
The Vampire (1957, Mexico) 132
The Vampire Bat 61, 66, 145, 228
The Vampire's Coffin 132
Van Eyssen, John 106, 121
Van Sloan, Edward 16, 19, 187
Veidt, Conrad 9, 128, 212
Venom 134
Verdugo, Elena 129
Vernon, Howard 136
Victoria Regina (play) 91
Vigil in the Night 105
Village of the Damned (1960) 232
A Virgin Among the Living Dead 136
Virus 216
Le Voleur 189
von Stroheim, Erich 66, 128, 241
von Sydow, Max 207
Voodoo Island 14
Voodoo Man 53, 74
Voyage to the Bottom of the Sea 72

Wade, Russell 30
Waits, Tom 64
The Walking Dead 27–29
Walsh, Dermot 113
Warbeck, David 116
The Watcher in the Woods 198
Waxworks 128
Way of the Flesh 240
Wayne, John 13, 32
Weaver, Sigourney 216, 222, 233, 238
Weine, Robert 128
Weird Woman 230–231
Weissmuller, Johnny 83, 198
Welles, Orson 7, 91, 160, 218, 239
Wells, Jacqueline 21, 46
Werewolf vs. the Vampire Women 136
West of Shanghai 35
West of Zanzibar 9
Westmore, Wally 142
Weston, David 96
Whale, James 2, 15, 16, 79, 105, 109, 127, 129, 148, 177, 238
What! 127, 232
What Ever Happened to Baby Jane? 193–198, 231, 237, 240
Whatever Happened to Aunt Alice? 198

Index

What's the Matter with Helen? 198
While Paris Sleeps 9
The Whip and the Body see *What!*
Whitty, Dame Mae 178, 236
Wicked Stepmother 198
The Wicker Man 127
Wilder, Billy 128
Wilder, Gene 180
Willis, Bruce 173, 175
Wilson 66
Winters, Shelley 198
Witchcraft Through the Ages 7
Witchery 208

Witchfinder General see *The Conqueror Worm*
The Witch's Mirror 132
Witness for the Prosecution 145, 240
The Wizard of Oz 229
The Wolf Man 52, 85, 86–89, 151, 229, 230, 239, 241
Wood, Edward D., Jr. 52, 130
Woodward, Joanne 202, 240
Woolfson, P. J. 68
The World of the Vampires 132
Wray, Fay 66, 84, 177, 183, 228, 229
Wynn, Hugh 69

X — The Man with the X-Ray Eyes 132

You Only Live Twice 133
You'll Find Out 72
Young, Roland 236
Young Frankenstein 58, 180

Zanuck, Darryl F. 189
Zorba the Greek 239
Zucco, George 80–83, 180

www.ingramcontent.com/pod-product-compliance
Ingram Content Group UK Ltd.
Pitfield, Milton Keynes, MK11 3LW, UK
UKHW050537150426
5217IPUK00026B/1973